Analyzing Human Behavior in Cyberspace

Zheng Yan
University at Albany (SUNY), USA

A volume in the Advances in Human
and Social Aspects of Technology
(AHSAT) Book Series

Published in the United States of America by
IGI Global
Information Science Reference (an imprint of IGI Global)
701 E. Chocolate Avenue
Hershey PA, USA 17033
Tel: 717-533-8845
Fax: 717-533-8661
E-mail: cust@igi-global.com
Web site: http://www.igi-global.com

Library of Congress Cataloging-in-Publication Data

Names: Yan, Zheng, 1958- editor.
Title: Analyzing human behavior in cyberspace / Zheng Yan, editor.
Description: Hershey, PA : Information Science Reference, 2018. | Includes
   bibliographical references.
Identifiers: LCCN 2018016417| ISBN 9781522571285 (hardcover) | ISBN
   9781522571292 (ebook)
Subjects: LCSH: Online social networks--Psychological aspects. | Electronic
   commerce. | Computer crimes. | Consumer behavior. | Computer
   users--Psychology.
Classification: LCC HM742 .A55 2018 | DDC 302.30285--dc23 LC record available at https://lccn.
loc.gov/2018016417

This book is published in the IGI Global book series Advances in Human and Social Aspects of Technology (AHSAT) (ISSN: 2328-1316; eISSN: 2328-1324)

British Cataloguing in Publication Data
A Cataloguing in Publication record for this book is available from the British Library.

All work contributed to this book is new, previously-unpublished material.
The views expressed in this book are those of the authors, but not necessarily of the publisher.

For electronic access to this publication, please contact: eresources@igi-global.com.

Advances in Human and Social Aspects of Technology (AHSAT) Book Series

ISSN:2328-1316
EISSN:2328-1324

Editor-in-Chief: Ashish Dwivedi, The University of Hull, UK

MISSION

In recent years, the societal impact of technology has been noted as we become increasingly more connected and are presented with more digital tools and devices. With the popularity of digital devices such as cell phones and tablets, it is crucial to consider the implications of our digital dependence and the presence of technology in our everyday lives.

The **Advances in Human and Social Aspects of Technology (AHSAT) Book Series** seeks to explore the ways in which society and human beings have been affected by technology and how the technological revolution has changed the way we conduct our lives as well as our behavior. The AHSAT book series aims to publish the most cutting-edge research on human behavior and interaction with technology and the ways in which the digital age is changing society.

COVERAGE

- Technoself
- Technology Adoption
- Technology and Social Change
- ICTs and social change
- Digital Identity
- Cultural Influence of ICTs
- Technology Dependence
- Philosophy of technology
- Computer-Mediated Communication
- Human-Computer Interaction

IGI Global is currently accepting manuscripts for publication within this series. To submit a proposal for a volume in this series, please contact our Acquisition Editors at Acquisitions@igi-global.com or visit: http://www.igi-global.com/publish/.

Titles in this Series

For a list of additional titles in this series, please visit:
https://www.igi-global.com/book-series/advances-human-social-aspects-technology/37145

Handbook of Research on Multicultural Perspectives on Gender and Aging
Rekha Pande (University of Hyderabad, India) and Theo van der Weide (Radboud University Nijmegen, The Netherlands)
Information Science Reference • ©2018 • 340pp • H/C (ISBN: 9781522547723) • US $195.00

Narratives and the Role of Philosophy in Cross-Disciplinary Studies Emerging Research ...
Ana-Maria Pascal (Regent's University London, UK)
Information Science Reference • ©2018 • 198pp • H/C (ISBN: 9781522555728) • US $135.00

Information Visualization Techniques in the Social Sciences and Humanities
Veslava Osinska (Nicolaus Copernicus University, Poland) and Grzegorz Osinski (College of Social and Media Culture, Poland)
Information Science Reference • ©2018 • 356pp • H/C (ISBN: 9781522549901) • US $195.00

Handbook of Research on Civic Engagement and Social Change in Contemporary Society
Susheel Chhabra (Periyar Management and Computer College, India)
Information Science Reference • ©2018 • 445pp • H/C (ISBN: 9781522541974) • US $245.00

Corporate and Global Standardization Initiatives in Contemporary Society
Kai Jakobs (RWTH Aachen University, Germany)
Information Science Reference • ©2018 • 394pp • H/C (ISBN: 9781522553205) • US $205.00

Computational Psychoanalysis and Formal Bi-Logic Frameworks
Giuseppe Iurato (Independent Researcher, Italy)
Information Science Reference • ©2018 • 332pp • H/C (ISBN: 9781522541288) • US $215.00

Psychological, Social, and Cultural Aspects of Internet Addiction
Bahadir Bozoglan (IF Weinheim Institute, Germany)
Information Science Reference • ©2018 • 390pp • H/C (ISBN: 9781522534778) • US $200.00

For an entire list of titles in this series, please visit:
https://www.igi-global.com/book-series/advances-human-social-aspects-technology/37145

701 East Chocolate Avenue, Hershey, PA 17033, USA
Tel: 717-533-8845 x100 • Fax: 717-533-8661
E-Mail: cust@igi-global.com • www.igi-global.com

Table of Contents

Section 3
Activity-Focused Cyber Behavior

Section 4
Effect-Focused Cyber Behavior

Detailed Table of Contents

Section 1
User-Focused Cyber Behavior

Chapter 1

Luka Lucić, Pratt Institute, USA
Lora E. Liharska, Teachers College, Columbia University, USA

The potential benefits of the Internet in providing stand-in educational experiences to displaced young people cannot be overstated. However, actualizing these educational potentials requires much future work in research and practice. By describing the initial theoretical and practical considerations for how these potential benefits can be translated into real-life benefits for refugee children, this chapter serves as an initial step in that direction.

Chapter 2

John Chapin, Pennsylvania State University, USA

The purpose of this chapter is to document the extent of Facebook use and cyberbullying among adolescents. It is based on a study theoretically grounded in third-person perception (TPP), the belief that media messages affect other people more than oneself. As Facebook establishes itself as the dominant social network, users expose themselves to a level of bullying not possible in the analog world. The study found that 84% of adolescents (middle school through college undergraduates) use Facebook, and that most users log on daily. While 30% of the sample reported being cyberbullied, only 12.5% quit using the site and only 18% told a parent or school official. Despite heavy use and exposure, adolescents exhibit TPP, believing others are more likely to be negatively affected by Facebook use. A range of self-protective behaviors from precautionary (deleting or blocking abusive users) to reactionary (quitting Facebook) were related to decreased degrees of TPP. Implications for prevention education are discussed.

Chapter 3

Satoko Ezoe, Shimane University, Japan
Masahiro Toda, Notre Dame Seishin University, Japan

Smartphone use has rapidly developed in recent years and become an established part of daily life in many countries. As various applications have been developed as communication tools for use with smartphones, allowing the internet to become more accessible, patterns of dependence have been routinely reported particularly among adolescents. In this chapter, the authors reviewed the previous studies about the relationships of smartphone dependence to chronotype and gender among adolescents. Chronotype refers to preference for sleep-wake timing: for example, morning types go to bed, get up, and experience peak alertness and performance earlier in the day than do evening types. It was found that the light emitted from media screen in the evening before bedtime may delay the circadian rhythm. In addition, excessive smartphone use may lead to sleep disturbances. Recent studies suggested that evening types and females may be more prone to become smartphone dependent.

Section 2
Technology-Focused Cyber Behavior

Chapter 4

Xiaoqian Liu, University of Chinese Academy of Sciences, China
Tingshao Zhu, University of Chinese Academy of Sciences, China

In this chapter, a kind of emotion recognition method based on gait using a customized smart bracelet with a built-in acceleration sensor was introduced in detail. The results showed that the classification accuracies of angry-neutral, happy-neutral, angry-happy, and angry-happy-neutral using the acceleration data of wrist are 91.3%, 88.5%, 88.5%, and 81.2%, respectively. Besides, the wearable devices and motion-sensing technology application in psychology research have been further discussed, and non-contact emotion identification and mental health monitoring based on offline behaviors were reviewed summarily.

Chapter 5

Nan Zhao, University of Chinese Academy of Sciences, China
Tingshao Zhu, University of Chinese Academy of Sciences, China

As today's online social network (OSN) has become a part of our daily life, the huge amount of OSN behavior data could be a new data source to detect and understand individual differences, especially on mental aspects. Based on the findings revealing the relationships between personality and online behavior records, the authors tried to extract relevant features from both OSN usage behaviors and OSN textual posts, and trained models by machine learning methods to predict the OSN user's personality. The results showed fairly good predictive accuracy in Chinese OSN. The authors also reviewed the same kind of studies in more pervasive OSNs, focusing on what behavior data are used in predicting psychological profiles and how to use them effectively. It is foreseeable that more types of OSN data could be utilized in recognizing more psychological indices, and the predictive accuracy would be further improved. Meanwhile, the model-predicted psychological profiles are becoming an option of measurements in psychological studies, when the classical methods are not applicable.

Chapter 6

Ayse Kok Arslan, Oxford Alumni Silicon Valley Network, USA

Based on the results of the evaluation of an embedded engineering learning on social cloud model, the author suggests whether an "Imagineering" approach to learning is and complies with design principles leading to creative products. It can also provide an evidence for whether the SC supports co-learning environments which contributes to the efficiency of the process. Not only training institutions, but also knowledge enterprises should have a ready infrastructure for network systems to access the cloud technology. This chapter discusses the options of a design model on social cloud.

Chapter 7

Yujia Peng, University of California – Los Angeles, USA

As a new way of implementing human-computer interface, brain-computer interfaces (BCI) dramatically changed the user experiences and have broad applications in cyber behavior research. This chapter aims to provide an overall picture of the BCI science and its role in cyberpsychology. The chapter starts with an introduction of the concept, components, and the history and development of BCI. It is then followed by an overview of neuroimaging technologies and signals commonly used in BCI. Then, different applications of BCI on both the clinical population and the general population are summarized in connection with cyberpsychology. Specifically, applications include communication, rehabilitation, entertainments, learning, marketing, and authentication. The chapter concludes with the future directions of BCI.

Section 3
Activity-Focused Cyber Behavior

Chapter 8

David Messer, Arizona State University, USA
Caroline E. Shanholtz, University of Arizona, USA
Abhik Chowdhury, Arizona State University, USA

The internet holds considerable potential to improve the world's health. Noncommunicable, or so-called lifestyle, diseases are responsible for more than three-fifths of all deaths worldwide. With over half of the world's population now online, public health officials and entrepreneurs have developed a growing array of digitally mediated interventions to encourage healthy lifestyle choices. In this chapter, the authors discuss online and digitally mediated interventions, provide examples of their use, and summarize recommendations for future research and development. Particular attention is paid to online education, social media support groups, adaptive and gamified interventions, and emerging technologies such as ambient and wearable sensors and artificial intelligence.

Chapter 9

Chandra Sekhar Patro, Gayatri Vidya Parishad College of Engineering, India

The emergence and rapid escalation of e-retailing has triggered many changes in daily life of the shoppers as well as the marketers. E-retailing is playing a major role in the Indian economy and is expected to change the current scenario of shopping from physical stores to e-stores. Similarly, changes in consumers' attitudes along with the availability of cheaper and reliable technology have led to a significant growth in online sales around the world. The chapter aims to examine the shoppers' attitudes towards e-shopping and also to find the critical reasons for not shopping through online. The results reveal that the shoppers are still hesitating to purchase online. The most important reasons for not shopping online are preferring to buy by touching and feeling, online security and privacy, and customer service quality. The factors influencing to buy online are being able to get detailed product information, product delivery, convenience, product quality, and competitive prices. These results also have some practical implications for managers and strategists of e-stores.

Chapter 10

Children and adolescents are actively engaged in a digital world in which blogs, social networking sites, watching videos, and instant messaging are a typical part of their daily lives. Their immersion in the digital world has occurred for as long as they remember, with many not knowing a world without our modern technological advances. Although the digital age has brought us many conveniences in our daily lives, there is a darker side to children's and adolescents' involvement with these technologies, such as cyberbullying. This chapter draws on research from around the world, utilizing a variety of research designs, to describe the nature, extent, causes, and consequences associated with children's and adolescents' involvement in cyberbullying. Concluding the chapter is a solutions and recommendations section in which it is argued that cyberbullying is a global concern, affecting all aspects of society, requiring a whole-community approach.

Chapter 11

The major purpose of this chapter is to understand average user's decision-making process in cybersecurity by reviewing and integrating several major theoretical frameworks discussed and applied in decision making processes in cybersecurity. The average users are the ones who do not realize or understand when or how to perform security-critical decisions, the ones who are unmotivated to comply with company and school cybersecurity policies and procedures due to inconvenience, and the ones who do not have sufficient knowledge in cybersecurity to make sound security decisions. It is important to discuss and understand the role of such users and their behaviors based on systematic analysis so that we can identify potential factors causing "poor" security decisions and find ways to reduce the likelihood of being victims of cyber-attacks. The ultimate goal is to provide insights and make recommendations on how to foster individual's cyber acumen and cultivate a more effective decision-making process.

Section 4
Effect-Focused Cyber Behavior

Chapter 12

The impact of both intentional and unintentional exposure to internet pornography on adolescents has been debated in the literature for decades. However, the differences in the operational definitions of pornography and exposure, not to mention the differences in methodology and sampling, make it difficult to synthesize findings and identify patterns across studies. In addition, the majority of the research has employed a rather broad measure of "exposure to general pornography" by adolescents in order to understand the impact of early exposure to pornography; however, internet pornography includes a wide range of sexually explicit materials, not just adult pornography. Thus, the goal of this chapter is to explore the relationship between nondeviant pornography use and deviant pornography use (e.g., child pornography) by discussing the Seigfried-Spellar study which examined the role of individual differences and age of onset in deviant pornography use.

Chapter 13

This chapter started by introducing a recent research study that disclosed adolescent victim experiences across seven major types of cyberbullying, significant gender and age differences, and reasons for not reporting incidents of cyberbullying to adults. The chapter then related the research findings to major areas in the literature on the nature and forms of cyberbullying in contrast to traditional forms of bullying, its prevalence among school-aged youths, the effects of gender and age on adolescent victim experiences of cyberbullying, and the factors that contribute to adolescent attitude toward reporting cyberbullying incidents to adults. The chapter suggested that future research should further explore issues such as how various types of cyberbullying affect adolescent mental wellbeing, how age and gender affect school-aged youth victim experiences of various forms of cyberbullying, and how professionals and other adults may help adolescents counter cyberbullying.

Chapter 14

    Maria José D. Martins, Polytechnic Institute of Portalegre, Portugal &
        University of Lisbon, Portugal
    Ana Margarida Veiga Simão, University of Lisbon, Portugal
    Ana Paula Caetano, University of Lisbon, Portugal
    Isabel Freire, University of Lisbon, Portugal
    Armanda Matos, University of Coimbra, Portugal
    Cristina C. Vieira, University of Lisbon, Portugal
    Teresa Pessoa, University of Lisbon, Portugal
    João Amado, University of Lisbon, Portugal

This chapter review some of the principal personal and situational factors established through recent international research that contribute to explain the phenomenon of cyber-victimization and cyber-aggression among adolescents, as well as its relations with socio-demographic variables (age, sex, grade level). Personal factors, like emotions, motives, normative beliefs, and moral disengagement were discussed jointly with situational factors, as the role of peers, friends, school and family environments, in addition to the possible interactions of these variables on cyber-bullying. The chapter ends with a discussion of future directions about the research on this phenomenon, namely in what concern educational programs that can use digital technology to help adolescents, schools and families to deal with cyber-bullying.

Preface

INTRODUCTION

After completing the three-volume book *Encyclopedia of Cyber Behavior* in 2005, I am honored to work with a group of international scholars on an edited book, *Analyzing Human Behavior in Cyberspace*, in 2017. Now I am pleased to write the preface, focusing on three closely related but conceptually different topics that originate from the book title: human behavior, human behavior in cyberspace, and analyzing human behavior in cyberspace.

HUMAN BEHAVIOR

Nature is one of the highest-quality academic journal. It defines human behavior as "the way humans act and interact. It is based on and influenced by several factors, such as genetic make-up, culture and individual values and attitudes" (see https://www.nature.com/subjects/human-behaviour). This definition is relatively straightforward and capture two defining feature of human behavior: (1) it has to do with humans rather than animals and (2) it has to do with how humans act and interact. *Encyclopædia Britannica* is one of the most authoritative reference encyclopedias. Three eminent scholars, Marc Bornstein, Richard M. Lerner, and Jerome Kagan, defined human behavior as "the potential and expressed capacity for physical, mental, and social activity during the phases of human life" (see https://www.britannica.com/topic/human-behavior). This definition is relatively sophisticated and focuses on three important features of human behavior: (1) it includes both potential and expressed capacity rather than just manifested one, (2) it covers multiple aspects of human activities, mainly physical, mental, and social ones; and (3) it emphasizes on the relationship between human behavior and life-span human development, which is understandable given these three scholars are developmental scientists. These definitions reveal the initial complexity of human behavior.

There exist a wide variety of types of human behavior, such as health behavior, organization behavior, entrepreneurial behavior, violent behavior, economic behavior, sexual behavior, consumer behavior, social behavior, motor behavior, aggressive behavior, addictive behavior, creative behavior, machine behavior, and cyber behavior. Many of these types of human behavior are actually names or part of names of academic journals, an important indication of strong research interests, accumulated knowledge base, and broad social impacts of these important types of human behavior. These types of human behavior show further the complexity of human behavior.

Researchers have been studying human behavior for centuries. The field of studying human behavior is typically called behavioral sciences. Behavioral science essentially is an interdisciplinary field that examines human behavior across various disciplines, including psychology, sociology, biology, medicine, law, business, education, criminology, neuroscience, psychiatry, economics, and anthropology. Besides these well-established disciplines, new disciplines such as behavioral economics, social neuroscience, and dynamic network systems have been emerging strongly with major breakthroughs in understanding human behavior. Here are three examples on behavioral economics. In 1978, political scientist Herbert Simon received the Nobel Prize in Economics for his work on for his pioneering research into the decision-making process within economic organizations using his theory of bounded rationality. In 2002, psychologist Daniel Kahneman was awarded the Nobel Memorial Prize in Economic Sciences (shared with experimental economist Vernon Smith) for his work on cognitive basis for a series of common human errors based on his cognitive models of decision-making under risk and uncertainty. In 2017, economist Richard Thaler was the recipient of the Nobel Memorial Prize in Economics for his pioneering work in incorporating psychologically realistic assumptions into analyses of economic decision-making by showing human traits of limited rationality, social preferences, and lack of self-control systematically affect individual decisions as well as market outcomes. These important human behavior studies demonstrate the complexity and importance of human behavior.

HUMAN BEHAVIOR IN CYBERSPACE

As one specific type of human behavior, human behavior in cyberspace is often simply called cyber behavior. While cyber behavior can be defined in various different ways, the simplest and broadest definition could be that cyber behavior is human behavior in cyber space. Based on this definition, cyber behavior is simply a hybrid of two entities: cyber space and human behavior. Based on this definition, any physical, social, or mental activities that humans engage in connecting to and interacting with the Internet could be broadly considered cyber behavior, as long as it directly concerns human beings and it is objectively observed in cyber space.

There exists a wide variety of types of cyber behavior, such as e-learning, e-voting, e-shopping, e-pornography, and e-therapy. These various types of cyber behavior have been repeatedly observed in a wide variety of sectors of cyber space, such as cyber education, cyber government, cyber commerce, cyber law, and cyber medicine. There also exist a wide variety of aspects of cyber behavior, including cognitive (e.g., cyber reasoning and cyber decision making), social (e.g., cyber security and cyber social capital), emotional (e.g., cyber attitude and cyber beliefs), and physical (e.g., Internet addiction and computer vision syndrome). In addition, a wide variety of contributing factors (e.g., gender and personality), resulting effects (e.g., the disinhibition effect and the time replacement effect), underlying processes (e.g., the dual process mechanism and the cognitive workload process) that are related to cyber behavior have been widely reported.

In a sense, human behavior can be roughly divided into two types that exist separately but are seamlessly interrelated: real-world behavior that is mainly observed in the real world, and cyber behavior that is observed mainly in cyber space. Real-world behavior has been observed continuously since the first day of human history. In contrast, cyber behavior emerged only a few decades ago after the Internet was invented and widely used. Despite the relatively young age of cyber behavior, it seems that nobody would now question the independent existence of cyber behavior in modern society. In fact, many researchers would agree that cyber behavior is a new and unique human phenomenon that is ubiquitous, complex, dynamic, and important. With the still rapid development of Internet technologies and the even much wider use of the Internet in society, many new types of cyber behavior will emerge in the decades to come.

The study of cyber behavior is essentially a multi-sector multi-disciplinary field of research. In the past 30 years, extensive scientific knowledge has rapidly accumulated to reveal various types of cyber behaviors in a wide variety of sectors of cyber space. It has become an emerged field of research and currently is at the stage of rapid growth. The publication of the *Encyclopedia of Cyber Behavior* in 2005 is strong evidence of the current status of development of the field as an emerged one.

To further earlier efforts in synthesizing and disseminating knowledge in the field of cyber behavior, the *Encyclopedia of Cyber Behavior* was published collects more than 100 chapters by more than 200 scholars across the world, with a total of 650,000 words, to cover the breadth and depth of all substantial knowledge concerning cyber behavior. Given the multi-component, multi-sector, and multi-discipline nature of cyber behavior, the encyclopedia uses a diamond-shaped hierarchical structure to organize and present its content. Specifically, there are 10 sections in the encyclopedia, with approximately 10 chapters within each section. It starts with one section on various general overarching issues of cyber behavior. It then uses three sections together to cover three key components of cyber behavior (i.e., cyber technologies, cyber populations, and cyber interactions) and then continues with five section on five major sectors of cyber space (i.e., cyber law, cyber business, cyber health, cyber government, and cyber education). It ends with one section on diversity of cyber behavior across different countries. Various disciplines (e.g., behavioral sciences, history of science, technology, sociology, psychology, communications, politics, law, criminology, business, health, and education) are mapped out onto different sections of chapters to reflect the multi-disciplinary nature of the field. While works included in an encyclopedia vary in the breadth of content and the depth of presentation depending on the target audience, an encyclopedia generally is a strong indication of existence of substantial important knowledge that has been accumulated over time in a general or specific subject domain. The *Encyclopedia of Cyber Behavior* synthesizes the existing knowledge of cyber behavior in a wide variety of disciplines into one single platform, indicating cyber behavior research has changed from an emerging field into an emerged field, and in the future will certainly become an established field.

Specifically, during the 30 years, this field of research on cyber behavior has developed its fundamental knowledge base, formed a critical mass of researchers, and began to generate broad social impacts.

Regarding the fundamental knowledge base, extensive research has documented that human behaviors in cyber space (1) involve a wide variety of specific Internet software applications, including email, websites, text messaging, chat rooms, social network sites, smart phones, twitter, and games; (2) includes different types of cyber behavior, such as emailing, web browsing, instant messaging, texting, e-publishing, e-navigating, e-searching, e-gaming, e-learning, e-shopping, e-dating, e-therapy, e-reading, e-communicating, e-dating, online file sharing, and cyber bullying; (3) is subject to various factors that influence cyber behavior, including personality, age, technology literacy, education, social and economic status, attitude, culture, social structure, technology infrastructure, or legal systems; and (4) has various positive and negative consequences on physical, cognitive, social, and emotional aspects of Internet users, both online in the cyber world and offline in the real world.

At present, there are at 30 journals that exclusively or frequently publish studies on cyber behavior with an annual publication of approximately 1,000 articles. These scientific publication outlets include well-estalished ones, such as *Computers in Human Behavior, Cyber Psychology & Behavior* (now *Cyberpsychology, Behavior, and Social Networking), Social Science Computer Review, Journal of Educational Computing Research, Journal of Medical Internet Research, Journal of the American Society for Information Science and Technology, International Journal of Human-Computer Studies, Journal of Computer-Mediated Communication,*

Journal of Social Issues, American Behavioral Scientist, and *Journal of Applied Developmental Psychology.* Some recently launched journals that have already made an impact include *Policy and Internet, International Journal of Cyber Criminology, International Journal of CyberBehavior, Psychology and Learning, International Journal of Internet Science, Journal of Online Behavior, New Media & Society,* and *Telematics and Informatics.*

Regarding the critical mass of researchers, in the past 30 years, hundreds of researchers in various fields of study across the world have contributed to the science of human behaviors in cyber space. Highly productive research groups across the world led by prominent leading experts include: PEW Research Center's Internet & American Life Project Led by Lee Rainie at PEW, the *HomeNet* group led by Robert Kraut and Sara Kiesler at Carnegie Melon, Berkman Center for Internet & Society led by Charles Nesson and other co-directors at Harvard, NetLab led by Barry Wellman at Toronto, The Crimes against Children Research Center led by David Finkelhor at University of New Hampshire, The Center for Mobile Communication Studies led by James Katz at Rutgers, The multimedia learning research group led by Richard Mayer at UCSB, The Oxford Internet Institute led by William Dutton and Helen Margetts at Oxford, The Children's Digital Multimedia Center led by Patricia Greenfield and Kaveri Subrahmanyam at UCLA, The Center for research on Children, Adolescents and the Media led by Patti Valkenburg at the University of Amsterdam, EU Kids Online led by Sonia Livingstone at London School of Economics and Political Science, The World Internet Project led by Jeffrey Cole at USC, The research group of HomeNetToo led by Linda Jackson at Michigan State, just to name a few.

Regarding the intellectual and social impacts, the science of cyber behavior has produced profound and broad intellectual and social impacts and implications for various areas such as psychological effects, digital divides between ethnic and social groups, e-learning, Internet safety, Internet crimes, e-health, e-government, e-commerce, and Internet research methodology. Besides Turtle's significant works discussed above, good examples include: (1) the series of research reports produced and disseminated by PEW Research Center's Internet & American Life Project. This series is so influential across the world that it has now become an intellectual "compass" pointing the future trends of the social impact of the Internet. (2) The most cited journal article regarding cyber behavior by Kraut, Patterson, Lundmark, Kiesler, Mukophadhyay, & Scherlis entitled *Internet paradox: A social technology that reduces social involvement and psychological well-being?.* Since their seminal article was published in 1998, at one time point, nearly 50% of the journal articles regarding cyber behavior was devoted to the issue of impacts of Internet on psychological wellbeing.

ANALYZING HUMAN BEHAVIOR IN CYBERSPACE

As shown in Figure 1, despite the extremely wide variety of cyber behavior, any cyber behavior primarily concerns four basic elements: cyber users, cyber technologies, cyber activities, and cyber effects. In other words, in cyberspace, diverse users (e.g., ordinary users and people with special needs) interact with different technologies (e.g., text messenger and online games) in order to perform various activities (e.g., e-learning and e-shopping) and generate complex effects (e.g., positive and negative effects on cognition and emotion). Based on the four elements, cyber behavior could be categorized into four general types: (1) user-based cyber behavior, (2) technology-based cyber behavior, (3) activity-based cyber behavior, and (4) effect-based cyber behavior. Extensive research has been conducted to study each of the four types of cyber behavior, accumulating scientific knowledge about cyber behavior and revealing the extreme complexity of cyber behavior. In this book, this four-element conceptual model is used to analyze four types of cyber behavior in four major sections, (1) user-focused cyber behavior, (2) technology-focused cyber behavior, (3) activity-focused cyber behavior, and (4) effect-focused cyber behavior.

ORGANIZATION OF THE BOOK

The first section of the book includes the first three chapters and primarily concerns user-focused cyber behavior. Chapter 1 written by Lucic and Liharska focuses on a very special group of cyber users, young refugees undergoing migration. Their work shows that refugee children and adolescents can use Internet and mobile device to receive various types of humanitarian aids for their survival. More importantly, they can use these technologies to have specially designed formal education online for fostering their language, cognitive, and social development along the migratory journey and in refugee camps.

Figure 1. The four basic elements of cyber behavior

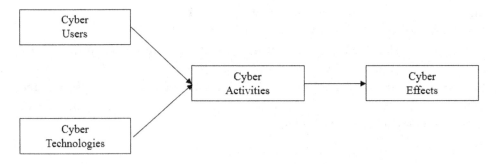

Chapter 2 contributed by John Chapin focuses on American adolescents. He applied *third-person perception*, one of important concepts in media research, to adolescents' cyberbullying behavior in Facebook. His work shows that among adolescents those were being bullied in Facebook, only half of them used self-protective behavior and believed that others rather than themselves are more likely to be negatively affected by Facebook use.

Chapter 3 in this section by Satoko Ezoe and Masahiro Toda focuses on Japanese adolescents. They used a concept called chronotype to describe how different types of adolescents in terms of their sleep-wake preferences (e.g., the morning type or the evening type) will receive different impacts of mobile phone use on their sleeping patterns.

The second section of the book consists of four chapter and mainly concerns technology-focused cyber behavior. Chapter 4 by Xiaoqian Liu and Tingshao Zhu focuses on how to use smart wrist bracelets and mobile sensors to recognize people's real-time emotions (e.g., angry, happy, and neutral) with a high level of accuracy rate. Their work in pioneering a smart mobile technology and a computational method will make important contributions to cyber behavior research, especially to cyber emotion research.

Chapter 5 written by Nan Zhao and Tingshao Zhu also focuses on how to use computational methods to analyze the big data of of individual social network behavior and predict personality and other psychological profiles. This process involves extracting useful features from the original social network records, training the computational models, calculating the personality scores, and predict psychological features.

Chapter 6 by Ayse Kok Arslan presents a new model that uses embedded engineering learning on social cloud in the broad context of emerging technologies, including augmented reality, mobility, social media, cloud computing, big data, and embedded systems. He described how to use this model for new creative e-learning activities.

Chapter 7 presented by Yujia Peng provides an updated review on the current knowledge about brain-computer interfaces and its profound implications to cyber behavior research. Here, brain-computer interfaces, a technology increasingly used in the field of human-computer interaction, can have significant potentials to lead to our new understanding of e-communication, e-rehabilitation, e-entertainments, e-learning, e-marketing, and e-authentication for both humans with and without special needs.

The third section of the book includes four chapters and essentially concerns activity-focused cyber behavior. Chapter 8 contributed by David Messer and his research team focuses on e-interventions, promoting various activity-oriented cyber behavior for healthy lifestyles. It includes online education, social media support groups, adaptive and gamified interventions.

Chapter 9 by Chandra Sekhar Patro summarizes the research on what factors influence Indian customers' attitudes and behaviors of e-shopping. It was found that the factors enhancing online shopping are detailed product information, product delivery, shopping convenience, product quality, and competitive prices. They also found that the factor discouraging online shopping are preference of touching products, online security and privacy, and customer service quality.

Chapter 10 contributed by Michelle Wright summarizes prevalence, characteristics, and consequences, and coping strategies of cyberbullying among children and adolescents in elementary, middle, and high schools across various countries. The content of this chapter is particularly comprehensive, covering cross-sectional, longitudinal, qualitative, and quantitative findings from psychology, education, media studies, communication, social work, sociology, and computer science.

Chapter 11 presented by Michelle Liu proposes a theoretical model of cybersecurity decision making process. In this model, different key elements of regular persons' decision making process are specified, contributing the current knowledge of activity-focused cyber behavior in general and cybersecurity behavior in particular.

The last section of the book has three chapters and concerns effect-focused cyber behavior. Chapter 12 written by Kathryn Seigfried-Spellar deals with cyber pornography, one of the most studied effect-focused cyber behavior in the field. Instead of a general discussion of cyber pornography, Kathryn Seigfried-Spellar has reviewed a wide variety of specific topics, including nondeviant pornography use (adult-only pornography) vs. deviant pornography use (e.g., child pornography), intentional exposure vs. unintentional exposure, and consumers vs. non-consumers of Internet pornography.

Chapter 13 by Minghui Gao focuses on current status adolescents' victim experiences of cyberbullying. He specified seven types of cyberbullying, flaming, denigration, online harassment, cyberstalking, outing, masquerade, and exclusion. Furthermore, along with real-life cases, he further summarized harmful impacts of cyberbullying on adolescent victims' mental health, social well-being, school experience, life quality, and future careers.

Chapter 14 by Maria José D. Martins and her research team, like the previous chapter by Minghui Gao, also examines negative effects of cyberbullying. However, their focus is on personal factors (e.g., age, gender, emotion, and personality) and situational factors (e.g., peers; family; and school) of the two sides of cyberbullying, cyber-victimization and cyber-aggression.

CONCLUSION

In conclusion, while completing this book project, I would like to end the preface with special acknowledgement to individuals who have made significant contributions to a successful completion of the book.

I would like first to thank Dr. Robert Atkinson for his wise counsels and thoughtful supports during our tenure of co-editing the *International Journal of Cyber Behavior, Psychology, & Learning* since 2012.

I would like to thank all IGI Global staff members involved in the project for their support, patience, and guidance. It has been a great pleasure and a personal honor for me to work with each of them.

I really thank all the reviewers for their time and work reviewing all the proposals and chapters in a timely and thoughtful manner.

Finally, this has been a humble and rewarding experience for me to edit the book with nearly 50 authors around the world. Without each and every of them, this project would have simply been impossible to complete. For them, I am really grateful. I hope that we will continue working together to describe, explain, and predict observed or emerging cyber behavior.

Zheng Yan
University at Albany (SUNY), USA
Albany/Boston, April 4th, 2018

Section 1
User–Focused Cyber Behavior

Chapter 1

"They Are Thirsty for Internet More Than Water":
Learning and Cognitive Development Among Young Refugees Undergoing Migration

Luka Lucić
Pratt Institute, USA

Lora E. Liharska
Teachers College, Columbia University, USA

ABSTRACT

The potential benefits of the Internet in providing stand-in educational experiences to displaced young people cannot be overstated. However, actualizing these educational potentials requires much future work in research and practice. By describing the initial theoretical and practical considerations for how these potential benefits can be translated into real-life benefits for refugee children, this chapter serves as an initial step in that direction.

INTRODUCTION: THE NEED FOR CONNECTIVITY

Be a good neighbor, open your network! This is the slogan of Projekat Otvorena Mreža (Project Open Net). Based in Osijek – a town situated at the trijunction of the Croatian, Hungarian and Serbian borders – Project Open Net is an open source inspired volunteer organization that started by encouraging residents to safely

DOI: 10.4018/978-1-5225-7128-5.ch001

open their wireless networks to others in need of free Internet access. The project began in 2009 with the local aim of facilitating community progress and mutual cooperation among the residents of Osijek (Kelava, 2013). However, beginning in 2015, as thousands of refugees from Syria, Iraq, Afghanistan, and beyond embarked upon a mass migration toward Western Europe, the project's mission abruptly transformed and gathered a transnational character. Many refugees chose to travel via the Balkan route, which spans Greece, Bulgaria, and Macedonia in the south, and Serbia, Hungary, and Croatia in the north. As it happens, one of the main points of transit along the Balkan route is the town of Osijek, home to Project Open Net.

According to a report by European Border and Coast Guard Agency, Frontex Risk Analysis Unit (2017) more than 700 thousand displaced people took the Balkan route in 2015. The countries of the Western Balkans– historically more accustomed to sending economic and political migrants abroad than receiving them (Sardon, 2001) – are rarely the final intended destinations for refugees forced out of their homes by the conflicts in the Middle East and Levant. Instead, the countries of the Western Balkans are the transit points along a migratory journey for those refugees seeking the economic and political stability of Western Europe. And since a refugee journey from the Middle East to Germany, Sweden, or Denmark can last many months, refugees often spend considerable amounts of time passing through Athens, Thessaloniki, Skopje, and Belgrade, or staying in refugee camps such as those in Šid, Slavonski Brod, and Tovarnik – a town located in close proximity to Osijek.

Prolonged stops along the journey allow aid workers across the Western Balkans to get to know refugees and assemble a profile of their most imminent needs. Aside from basic existential necessities such as food, water, clothing, and shelter, reports from the field increasingly highlight an especially poignant need: *the need for connectivity*. More specifically, access to the Internet, usually via refugees' smartphones, has been identified not only as essential for the purpose of interpersonal interaction and connection, but also as critically important for organizing the migratory journey (GSMA, 2017). Aid agencies have seized upon this need quickly. A report by the United Nations High Commissioner for Refugees (UNHCR) notes that connectivity has the potential to transform the way aid agencies respond to the protection needs of displaced peoples, by creating "a powerful multiplier effect, boosting the well being of refugees and of the communities that host them" (UNHCR, 2016).

Volunteer groups and non-governmental organizations (NGOs) – such as Project Open Net and Refugee Aid Miksalište (located near Belgrade's bus and train stations) – have also quickly recognized the need for connectivity. To meet it, these organizations often feature big green "Free WiFi" signs posted on their office doors. However, volunteers of Project Open Net have gone even further. To expand their reach, they created mobile WiFi kits by hacking a home router, connecting the router to a battery and packing everything into backpacks with antennas sticking out (Schroeder, 2015). Equipped this way, the volunteers disperse into crowds of refugees on the move, with signs on their backs that read: "Free WiFi – Internet without borders for Europe without borders" (Figure 1). In September 2015, a report from the volunteers working as walking WiFi hubs along the Balkan Route explained: "refugees are thirsty for the Internet more than water. Loads of people stopped us and asked to connect online – thankful that they can get in touch with their friends and family."

Despite efforts like these, free or affordable Internet access during the migratory journey is not the norm. Even though almost 90% of refugees headed to Western Europe are continuously traveling in areas covered by 3G networks (GSMA, 2017), economic and political factors make connecting to the Internet difficult and cost-prohibitive for many. For example, in their reluctance to make "the Jungle" – a now

Figure 1. A volunteer of Project Open Net serving as Walking WiFi along the Balkan Route. Equipped with mobile WiFi kits volunteers disperse into crowds of refugees on the move to provide free Internet to those in need.

infamous refugee camp near Calais – seem permanent, French authorities halted the operations of Phone Credit for Refugees and Displaced People, an organization that provides vital phone credit and Internet connection to migrants (Gillespie et al., 2016). Similarly, refugees staying at a camp near the French city of Dunkirk must often walk for miles to find free WiFi (The Economist, 2017). According to the UNHCR (2016), refugees can easily spend a third of their disposable income on staying connected. For example, refugees in France must present legal identification in order to obtain a SIM card that allows them to access the Internet. To bypass this requirement, some resort to the black market, buying more expensive SIM cards brought over from Britain.

Dynamic Affordances of Cyberspace

Access to the Internet and the affordances of cyberspace through smartphones is critically important throughout the refugee journey (GSMA, 2017). Findings from cognitive science argue that perceiving and engaging with *affordances* – broadly defined as opportunities for action that the environment provides (Gibson, 1977), is a result of people's past knowledge, activities and experiences (Jordan et al., 1998; Lakoff, 1987). In other words, the ways in which individuals make use of the affordances available to them do not typically change unless their life circumstances change considerably (Lucić, 2016c). However, the possibilities for interaction, thought, and action offered by cyberspace go beyond a refugee's pattern of Internet use prior to migration. For displaced people in the process of migration, the affordances of cyberspace serve essential practical uses and meet a number of vital socio-relational needs.

One such affordance of cyberspace provided by smartphones is access to memory capacity (e.g., cloud storage such as Google Drive). Refugees utilize cloud storage for uploading and saving materials such as documents, photos, and audio and video testimonies of the physical, social, and political conditions that required them to leave their home countries. Once refugees reach their final destinations, these materials are often used as evidence to substantiate and underpin requests for asylum. As refugees often travel for hundreds or thousands of miles, another vital affordance provided by smartphones is road navigation through offline GPS. Furthermore, smartphone-enabled connectivity makes it possible for refugees to seek help during migration and to obtain information on newer, more effective, or easier migratory routes. In some cases, such affordances can mean the difference between life and death, as with migrants attempting to cross the Mediterranean on rubber boats, who use phones to call the Italian coastguard and report accidents (Heller, Pezzani & Situ Studio, 2012).

The innovative potential of digital affordances can also be employed by organizations and individuals toward aspirational ends. In Greece, for example, appointments for registration of temporary stay in migrant camps are granted over Skype to minimize queues (Greek Council for Refugees, 2016). Crisis Info Hub, a database powered by the International Rescue Committee (IRC), provides migrants en route to Western Europe with basic, country-specific information on asylum registration processes, legal aid, medical care, and accommodation. Furthermore, access to the Internet can expand the opportunities for refugees to improve lives of other refugees. For example, Gherbtna - which translates to "loneliness in exile" - is an Android-based platform that helps Syrians arriving in Turkey to navigate Turkish services like health and education. Designed by Mojahed Akil, a 26-year-old Syrian refugee computer programmer, Gherbtna had 50,000 downloads as of September 2017 (Lepeska, 2016).

Children and youth comprise the demographic for which the affordances of cyberspace hold the greatest potential benefit. According to official UNHCR (2016) estimates, young people make up approximately 51% of all refugees. Among the 1.3 million people who sought asylum in Europe in 2015, nearly 100,000 were young refugees traveling alone (Connor, 2016). Most unaccompanied young people entering Europe are migrants from Afghanistan and Syria, often sent by parents unable to afford the price of the journey for the entire family (Collins, 2017). Given the length and difficulty of the refugee journey, and the expectation that youth migration to Europe will increase dramatically over the next 30 years (Connor, 2016; Hanson & McIntosh, 2016), the potential benefits of connectivity in the field of education cannot be overstated.

Connectivity Enables Education and Learning

Education - a basic right according to Article 22 of the 1951 U.N. Refugee Convention - is a process of developing the powers of reasoning and judgment, and of general intellectual and emotional preparation for the future. Even for well-educated adults, extensive migration that lasts many months can be a bewildering experience that's difficult to make sense of. For young people, this process can be even more challenging. Young refugees often lack access to the resources and tools provided by formal education that can help them understand the reasons for their migration, make sense of their current socio-political situations, and give meaning to their futures. In fact, of the approximately one million Syrian young people currently residing in Turkey, 40% have no access to formal education; neither do 60% of the approximately 540,000 Syrian children currently in Lebanon (3RP, Regional Refugee & Resilience Plan, 2017).

The interactive affordances of cyberspace can at least partially make up for the educational deficit among displaced young people. Access to the Internet can provide young migrants with opportunities to take part in structured online learning. Through online learning, child migrants can remotely engage with a primary education curriculum, and students at secondary and university levels can resume their disrupted educations, or at least mitigate a larger disruption. Also, and perhaps more importantly, the affordances of the Internet can provide young refugees with access to vast sources of information and resources across technologically mediated transnational landscapes. Viewed in this way, the affordances of cyberspace can provide young refugees with opportunities to make sense of and draw meaning out of their situated everyday experiences during the process of migration.

Developmental research aims to understand how children and adolescents live in a complex virtual universe, even as they carry on their lives in the physical world (Yan & Greenfield, 2006). In emphasizing the potential benefits of the affordances of cyberspace, it is important to recognize the potential dangers of technological determinism. Just because Internet-based technologies can lead to improvements in learning does not mean that simply providing access to these technologies will confer educational benefits. Analyses of the effectiveness of technology in traditional classrooms report a positive, though modest, technologically mediated improvement in learning outcomes, thus making it difficult to generalize the overall impact of technology on learning (Cheung & Slavin, 2013). In order to be effective, educational practices enabled by the affordances of connectivity must be culturally situated and developmentally relevant (Lave & Wenger, 1991; Pea, 2002, 2004). Specifically, as we argue in this work, educational practices employed via cyberspace should provide young refugees with the opportunities, tools, and resources to engage with and reflect upon the rich transnational experiences engendered by their journey.

The central aim of this chapter is to provide practical recommendations for educators to employ the affordances of cyberspace as tools for learning and development. To do so, this chapter will focus on reviewing empirical research that examines the role of language in cognitive development among migrants. First, we will show that when employed across diverse cultural landscapes, active use of language can lead to stable, long-term changes in *socio-cognitive complexity* – the capacity to construe people, objects, and ideas in culturally appropriate multidimensional ways (Benet-Martinez, Lee & Leu, 2006; Daiute & Lucić, 2011). Following the review of literature, we will focus on delineating narrative-based teaching strategies that can enable practitioners to scaffold the cognitive orientations of young refugees through structured engagement with their everyday activities within the diverse cultural frameworks they encounter along their journeys.

Theoretically, the educational practices described in this work are grounded in Vygotsky's (1983) and Bruner's (1960) *spiral curriculum* pedagogy, which views learning as a process of iterative conceptual development mediated via context-embedded activities. According to this view, learning is a process that takes place within a socio-cultural framework, not within an individual mind. Within this framework, we emphasize the role of language (actively employed) and narrative in shaping the experiences of young refugees on the road and giving meaning to their everyday activities. In other words, we view the everyday activities of refugees along a migratory journey – such as moving through unknown countries, encountering foreign geographical and social landscapes, and managing culturally diverse social norms and unknown languages – as holding latent developmental potentials that can be engaged and activated through the structured use of educational practices. By outlining educational practices specifically designed to encourage an analytical perspective towards the process of migration, we seek to introduce more formal, narrative-based curricular components that can empower this population and provide them with a sense of being grounded in an increasingly transnational world.

By focusing on interpersonal communication, participation in communities of mind, reflection on personal experience, and socialization of everyday practices, this work treats the active use of language as a tool for structuring thought and organizing consciousness (Vygotsky, 1978; Wittgenstein, 1952). The recommendations described here are predicated upon the idea that narrative-based activities can engage with and build upon the (sometimes latent) knowledge acquired by young refugees through everyday activities along the migratory journey. In other words, the mere act of storytelling employs narrative to explore an individual's thoughts and feelings about experiences that have shaped, or are shaping, their life in profound ways. Given that narrative is the principal way in which humans form representations, consider (alternative) futures, and organize and understand time and action, the act of storytelling also draws on paradigmatic, temporal, and projective categories as tools for organizing, understanding, and making meaning of experiences narrated (Nelson, 1985; Abbott, 2002). In fact, research confirms that structuring narrative activities for educational purposes can affect the development of socio-cognitive functions (Daiute & Reddy, 1993; Nelson, 1985; Wood, Brunner & Ross, 1976). Coupling insights gained from the pedagogical uses of narrative with the affordances of cyberspace can have a multiplier effect and expand the reach and impact of educational activities.

Language Is a Tool That Scaffolds Cognitive Complexity

A series of studies conducted by the first author (Lucić, 2013, 2016a, 2016b) employ the methodology of narrative analysis to highlight the role of language as a tool for scaffolding the development of psychological functions among migrants toward multicultural cognitive orientations. Specifically, the studies reviewed here sought to answer the questions: 1) What are the different ways that migrant youth use language to make sense of technologically mediated interpersonal interactions and to resolve conflicts across bicultural and monocultural interpersonal landscapes? 2) How do the approaches to sense-making and conflict resolution across technologically mediated interpersonal interactions of migrant youth differ from those of their non-migrant peers?

The answers to these questions emerge from a series of qualitative and quantitative narrative analyses examining the written language interactions of 44 young people who participated in a quasi-experimental research workshop in November 2011. Twenty-five of the participants in the study were immigrant youth coming from a range of different countries outside of the U.S., while the remaining 19 participants were U.S. born youth who functioned as a control group. The mean age for both groups was 17 years old at the time of the study. The lengths of time spent in the U.S. by the immigrant youth ranged from a few months to 16 years, with a mean of six years. At the time of the study, 12 participants were relatively new to the country (had spent less than five years in the U.S.), while 13 had been living in the country for more than six years.

During the workshop, participants were asked to, through writing, make sense of a vignette depicting a text-message-mediated interpersonal interaction embedded among monocultural and bicultural social interactions (for a complete description of the experimental procedure including the reprints of the instrument, see Lucić, 2013, 2016b). *Monocultural* social interactions are defined as those interactions in which an entire peer group shares the same cultural origin, while *bicultural* social interactions are defined as those in which individuals that form a peer group come from two different cultural backgrounds. The content of the vignette depicted an ambiguous text-messaging interaction between two fictional characters, Alex and Kai, who are in the process of planning a meeting using their smartphones. The vignette contains three normative A-B sequences, in which initiating message A receives response message B – such as Kai messaging Alex at 10:59AM: *Hey, when r u comin over? Let me know, cause I wanna plan*, and Alex responding at 12:36PM: *Like around 6 ill b there*. The vignette also contained a fourth sequence, at the start of which the normative A-B sequence is broken, and the sequential organization appears as A-A'. In other words, the vignette ends when Kai sends two text messages in close temporal succession of each other, without receiving an answer from Alex. The goal of this discursive rupture was to increase the ambiguity of a common and largely benign conflict that occurs in a text-messaging interaction by adding a formal conversational character often indicative of trouble or problem. Namely, leaving a text message unanswered or greatly diverging from the average response time is, in the etiquette of SMS discourse, often indicative of content or relationship problems (Laursen, 2005).

The design of the study sought to engage the participants in the process of conflict resolution and sense-making across both monocultural and bicultural landscapes. *Sense-making* is defined as a psychological process situated in interaction with extant social, cultural, and physical environments, which employs language actively woven into a narrative as a tool for organizing consciousness and perception (Lucić, 2016a). In order to vary the cultural origin of the interlocutors Alex and Kai and constrain the text-messaging discourse to either a monocultural or a bicultural social interaction, two writing prompts were used. In the first condition, both Kai and Alex are presented as sharing the study participant's cultural background; in the second condition, Kai shares the subject's cultural background while Alex is presented as being born and raised in the U.S. The order of the writing prompts was balanced, with half of the participants engaging first with the first condition, while the other half engaged first with the second condition. In each condition, participants were instructed to read the vignette first and then narrate their answers to following questions: 1) What were the interlocutors thinking and feeling while texting that they did not express in their messages? 2) What happened next? Did Kai and Alex resolve the conflict? How did they resolve the conflict?

Primary analysis of the data was conducted using the methodology of narrative inquiry (Daiute, 2014). According to the theory behind this methodological approach, narrative organization is thought to reflect the socio-relational and cognitive aspects of the participants' experiences, thoughts, and feelings, both as enacted and represented. Labov and Waletzky (1967) made initial steps in articulating this approach within the field of sociolinguistics. Their goal was to establish a direct connection between fundamental narrative structures and their originating socio-cultural functions. According to this viewpoint, grammar, which is implicit to a narrative, is not solely employed as a tool of logical analysis, but can also be used to offer more nuanced information about the pragmatic features of the activities referenced in a narrative (Labov, 1997). In other words, by examining the formal narrative properties (how something is said), it is possible to also study the individual's relation to context from which the narrative arose (why it was said and what socio-relational role the produced discourse is meant to play).

In line with this theoretical view, the goal of the narrative analyses employed in this work was to understand what participants are narrating by focusing on how they are narrating it. Nine key evaluative markers were used to explore how participants conceptualized the thoughts and feelings of monocultural and bicultural others (Lucić, 2013); three markers were used to explore their conflict resolution strategies (Lucić, 2016b). These markers included: 1) logical/hypothetical words, 2) causal connectors and evaluative devices indicative of internal states, such as cognition and affect, and 3) physical, communicative, and psychological strategies for conflict resolution (for a full description of the coding criteria and procedure see Lucić, 2013, 2016b).

The units of analysis for each written response were individual words, rather than clauses or sentences. For example, each time the word *'probably'* appeared in the text it was coded as a logical/hypothetical word. Similarly, when *'because'* appeared in the text, it was coded as a causal connector. If the word 'because' appeared more than once in a projective narrative, it was coded as a causal connector every time it appeared and met the criteria for inclusion.

Cognitive Complexity Develops Through Interpersonal Interaction

The results of the studies suggest that rather than experiencing a "culture clash" of being torn between multiple cultural frameworks, immigrant youth gradually build *socio-cognitive complexity* – the capacity to construe people, objects, and ideas in culturally appropriate multidimensional ways (Benet-Martinez, Lee & Leu, 2006; Daiute & Lucić, 2011). In other words, socio-cognitive complexity allows immigrants to coordinate diverse ways of interpreting interpersonal interactions across bicultural and monocultural social contexts. As opposed to their non-migrant peers, who largely employ the same cognitive style across both bicultural and monocultural social interactions, immigrant youth – especially after residing in the host country for longer than five years – learn how to shift their approach to sense-making based on the cultural belonging of their interlocutor.

More specifically, immigrant youth use logical/hypothetical words such as *if, probably, perhaps, might,* and *may,* and causal connectors such as *because, then, therefore,* and *since,* more frequently in monocultural social interactions than in bicultural ones. These findings suggest heightened cognitive awareness of the familiar monocultural social context, which in turn allows a greater flexibility and variability of the highly sophisticated cognitive functions within it. On the other hand, to make sense of bicultural social interactions, migrants rely on affective function and use words such as *want, worried,* and *overwhelmed,* and physical conflict resolution strategies (e.g., *going out for a drink, bringing flowers*). Why do migrant youth use affect to make sense of interactions across relatively less known bicultural social interactions, while at the same time reserving causation and logical function for the interactions among their own cultural group?

Answers to this question emerge when we consider the use of affect in narratives crafted by members of the host society, in this case the U.S. born youth. Namely, U.S. born youth focused on affective words (such as *happy, sad, disrespected, upset, worried*) significantly more frequently in narratives toward the monocultural group than they did in the narratives encompassing their interactions with immigrant youth. Hence, the findings of the study suggest a *discursive learning process* through which prolonged discursive interactions with non-migrant peers facilitate the development of cognitive complexity in migrant youth. In other words, through repeated social interaction with their U.S. born peers, migrant youth develop (and learn how to employ) the dialogue structure employed by their peers.

In understanding the dynamics of the discursive learning processes, Vygotsky's (1978) concept of the *Zone of Proximal Development* (ZPD) provides insights into the role of language as a tool for facilitating the development of cognitive complexity. ZPD is defined as the difference between the "actual developmental level as determined by independent problem solving" and the higher level of "potential development as determined through problem solving under adult guidance or in collaboration with more capable peers" (Vygotsky, 1978, p.86). Importantly, the ZPD can also be used to conceptualize practical recommendations (discussed at length in this chapter) for educational activities that can be implemented with refugee youth.

A way to conceptualize the findings from this series of studies is to view the migrants' narrative responses to the vignette depicting monocultural social interactions as their *actual developmental level*. From the perspective of enculturation, the developmental processes occurring within migrants' own cultural frameworks have been occurring far longer than the acculturative processes that began following their arrival to the host society. Thus, it is reasonable to assume that migrant youth would be more familiar with the cultural frameworks of their own immigrant groups (at least at the start of their migratory process) than they would be with mainstream U.S. culture. Following this line of reasoning, migrants' *potential developmental level* would be revealed by their narrative responses to the vignette representing bicultural interactions. Given that the immigrant youth engaged in the surveyed research are developing in the United States, and are thus *acculturating* to the rules, roles, and norms of U.S. society, members of this society can be seen as *more capable peers* with regards to their ways of being and interacting within U.S. society. Viewed this way, the data suggest that prolonged interactions with their U.S. born peers act as a scaffold for immigrant youth, who progressively learn how to shift interpretive frames based on the cultural background of their interlocutor.

Research on Multicultural Cognitive Development

Recent research on migrant social and cultural development has been particularly prolific in articulating the phenomenon of development across diverse cultural contexts. Central to this line of research is the idea that individuals have culturally specific meaning systems – learned associative networks of ideas, values, beliefs, and knowledge, that are shared by individuals within the same culture (Geertz, 1973; D'Andrade, 1984). These cultural meaning systems are interpretative frames that affect individuals' affect, cognition, and behavior (Hong, Chiu, & Kung, 1997; Kashima, 2000; Mendoza-Denton, Shoda, Ayduk, & Mischel, 1999). Recent empirical research

11

highlights that the social and cultural development of migrants often involves what Du Bois (1990) termed "double consciousness" – the articulation of two (or more) cultural meaning systems, often simultaneously (Hong, Morris, Chiu & Benet-Martínez, 2000; Haritatos & Benet-Martinez, 2002; Benet-Martínez, Leu, Lee, & Morris, 2002; Padilla, 2006; Lucić, 2013; Padilla, 2008; Suárez-Orozco & Suárez-Orozco, 2002). Such "double-conscious" individuals are considered multicultural and often include immigrants, refugees, sojourners (e.g., international students and expatriates), indigenous peoples, ethnic minorities, those in interethnic relationships, and mixed-ethnicity individuals (Berry, 2006a; Padilla, 2006).

Research on multicultural development confirms that migrants are often able to operate using multiple cultural codes (Suárez-Orozco, Todorova, & Qin, 2006), navigate across diverse cultures, form flexible self-identities (Mistry & Wu, 2010), and effectively manage the process of living in multiple cultural settings (Cooper, 2003). For example, research examining relational flexibility by immigrants found that Bosnian immigrants living in the U.S. focused on understanding and applying U.S. social norms across their everyday activities, while their same-age peers living in Bosnia focused critically on Bosnian societal norms (Daiute & Lucić, 2010). As a result of these dual socialization processes, migrants often develop certain meta-cognitive advantages, such as intellectual flexibility and creativity (Benet-Martínez, Lee, & Leu, 2006; Tadmor, Tetlock, & Peng, 2009), and increased ability to detect, process, and organize everyday cultural meanings (Benet-Martinez, Lee, & Leu, 2006; Dörnyei & Ushioda, 2009; Lvovich, 1997).

On an interpersonal level, migrants have different emotional experiences based on their memberships in and interactions with diverse socio-cultural groups (Ko, Lee, Yoon, Kwon, & Mather, 2010; Smith & Neumann, 2005), and are able to modify communicative and interactive practices as a result of migration (Gratier, 2003). For example, research by Gratier (2003) showed that Indian immigrant mother–infant dyads exhibited different vocal interaction patterns than those exhibited by members of the home country (Indians) *and* members of the host country (Americans). This suggests that the immigrant mothers had modified their interactive practices as a result of acculturation, and that the infant children of immigrants partake in implicit cultural communicative practices that are specific to their immigration context.

Research on Cyber Behavior of Migrants

The widespread use of smartphone-based technologies, such as cross-platform mobile messaging applications, for peer-to-peer communication constitutes a new and important dimension in the study of migrant social and cultural development. Owing largely to the time-space compression of interpersonal interaction through increasingly complex mediascapes, migration is no longer seen as a clean and more or less permanent break with the country of origin (Appadurai, 1997; Suarez-Orozco, 2000; Lucić, 2016b). Rather, migration is best understood as a multidirectional dynamic movement: a networked system facilitated to a large extent by information and communication technologies such as the Internet and smartphones (Alonso & Oiarzabal, 2010).

Not surprisingly, over the past decade, research has increasingly focused on the cyber behavior of immigrants (for a review, see Wenli & Wenting, 2012). Examining specifically the role of cyber behaviors in enriching the multiplicity and fluidity of the immigrant identity, Emily and Paul (2009) explore how immigrants utilize the Internet to create a variety of transboundary networks that foster a sense of identity in a virtual place. During the critical periods of social and material disadvantage following migration, the affordances of cyberspace can be used to develop and strengthen young immigrants' evolving identities as they engage in settling into and adjusting to a new society (Elias & Lemish, 2009). Thus, cyberspace is an important medium through which immigrant identity can be articulated, refined, and renegotiated (Ignacio, 2000).

While research focusing specifically on multicultural cognitive development among refugees is currently scarce, existing work points promisingly in the direction of the potential uses of new media affordances, including the Internet, for educational purposes. Yoon (2011) examines how media literacy education can be implemented to enhance the cultural competency of North Korean refugees. The findings suggest that deliberately designed educational curriculums can capitalize on the connection between current affairs and media literacy lessons, through media mapping exercises, critical film watching, and comparison of various news sources about current events relevant to the refugee experience. Mikal and Woodfield (2015) explore how Iraqi and Sudanese refugees living in the U.S. use the Internet to access support in their daily lives. Their findings suggest that Internet adoption and use varies widely by cultural group, and that adult refugees can be reluctant to engage in online exploration or form online support communities. Furthermore, the results highlight that children frequently serve as brokers of online knowledge for adults, by assisting parents with online activities (Mikal & Woodfield, 2015). Additionally, the authors point out that Internet use by refugee adults generally follows online pathways employed prior to migration, such as connecting with friends and relatives and finding news and information about sports teams. On the other hand, young refugees' Internet use is more malleable – while they use Facebook to connect with friends and search for news about their favorite sports teams, they also engage with websites to access information about school, and even to take courses online (Mikal & Woodfield, 2015).

However, most of the studies surveyed above, including the series of studies by the first author, examine cyber behavior independently of attempts at furthering the cognitive development of migrants through organized curriculum. The remainder of this chapter will describe a set of easy-to-implement practical recommendations that can enable educational professionals to employ the affordances of cyberspace to scaffold migrant and refugee psychological functions toward greater cognitive complexity. These recommendations for educational content and activities draw directly from the everyday activities of migrant children (traveling, living in refugee camps and among strangers in foreign lands, etc.), in order to give paradigmatic and conceptual shape to their lived experiences and allow for the development of more complex psychological functions.

Narrative Can Be Employed to Organize Internet-Based Curriculum for Global Migrants

Young people learn most effectively by actively constructing knowledge from a combination of experience, interpretation, and structured interaction (Bransford, Brown, Cocking 1999; Greeno, 1996; Roschelle, 2000). When placed in the relatively passive role of receiving information from lectures and text (the *transmission model* of learning), students often fail to develop sufficient understanding to apply what they have learned to situations outside of the classroom (Bransford & Schwartz, 2001). Fortunately, refugee children and youth traveling along the Balkan route have an abundance of experience. What they often lack are the curricular components of interpretation and structured interaction that typically characterize more formal educational approaches and help students transform experience into learning.

Cognitive research shows that learning is most effective when four fundamental characteristics are present: 1) active engagement with one's surroundings, 2) participation in groups with others, 3) frequent interaction with and feedback from teachers or peers, and 4) connection to real-world experiences and contexts (Bransford, Brown, & Cocking, 1999). Given the enormous benefits that development across diverse cultural contexts can confer, organizing educational efforts that assist young refugees in making sense of migration by actively engaging with their rich everyday experiences should be one of the key goals of educators. Three theoretical tools identified by Daiute (2013) as inherent affordances of the virtual world – *vast sources of information, interactivity,* and *multimodality* – are well suited to such pedagogical interventions. These tools have the potential to engage the four above-mentioned fundamental characteristics essential for learning and enable educators to scaffold activities that support young refugees in the process of transnational development.

Learning and the acquisition of skills associated with greater cognitive complexity can be fruitfully conceived as a hierarchical process during which component cultural skills are combined through appropriate orchestration into "higher multicultural skills" for the purpose of mastering new, more complex tasks (Bruner, 1973). Therefore, the recommendations that follow are designed iteratively, so that students can revisit topics of cultural, interpersonal, and spatial diversity several times, from multiple perspectives, in order to progressively acquire higher-order cognitive functions. This iterative component is important because the development of higher-order multicultural skills reflects a unique cultural form of adaptation that involves both an overlay on, and a reorganization of, more basic monocultural functions (Glick, 2004).

Analyzing and Comparing News Reports

One of the inherent affordances of cyberspace is that it provides the individual with quick access to *vast sources of information*. Given the ever-increasing amount of information available on the Internet, young people across the world need to develop skills for accessing, filtering, understanding, and synthesizing information. Introducing young refugees on the move to this affordance can be accomplished by constructing assignments that ask them to identify, analyze and compare two or more news reports centered on one notable event that bears direct relevance to their lives.

After identifying and reading two or more articles about a relevant topic, five further pedagogical steps could be taken to help students transform their experiences into learning. These steps consist of asking students to 1) identify divergent or contrary information across two or more news reports, 2) construct a timeline of events presented in reports, 3) engage in critical analysis of sources, 4) assume the perspectives of various individuals referenced in articles through group discussion, and 5) actively employ language to expand, correct, or even re-write one or more articles, in blog form, based on personal experiences with the topic. From a pedagogical standpoint, engaging students with this type of activities has the potential to activate a multitude of processes identified by narrative theory as being directly tied to cognitive development. These processes include making sense of temporal and causal relations among people and events, engaging in and coordinating the perspectives of different actors and their spatial and temporal relations, and imagining possible alternative futures (Nelson, 1985, 1996).

Engaging young refugees in the process of locating online news reports on a relevant topic can advance their skills for accessing information on the Internet. Students can then be asked to read the articles closely and identify divergent or contrary information by comparing the articles to one another as well as to their own knowledge regarding the topic. For example, in 2015, a Hungarian government initiative to build a razor-wire border fence to stop the flow of refugees from Serbia and Croatia into Hungary was the subject of much controversy. News coverage of the event varied widely in its assessment of the initiative's impact. Depending on the political, national, or ideological orientation of the news source, the decision to build the fence was either justified as giving refugees the opportunity to enter through official checkpoints and claim asylum in accordance with international and European law or criticized vigorously as being unhumanitarian. A January 2016 article in the journal *Nature* even argued that the fence endangers wildlife by blocking the migration of brown bears, wolves, lynxes and red deer across the border, thus jeopardizing the connectivity of species populations through habitat fragmentation (Linnell, 2016).

Asking students to construct timelines of the events discussed in news articles can facilitate the development of temporal and causal thinking. By comparing and contrasting two or more timelines presented in news reports on the same topic, students can notice the similarities and discrepancies between them. Such observations can motivate young refugees to attempt to make sense of the temporal relations among events within a story. On a more conceptual level, employing this type of educational activities can lead students to further insights about the relationship between a temporal structure employed in a narrative and the narrative meaning that the structure itself creates.

Engaging young refugees in critical analysis of sources is a further pedagogical step that can be taken. This involves instructing students to create lists of the sources cited in each article, and the views attributed to each of these sources. As sources are typically explicitly named within news reports, and their views or opinions are usually quoted, this task should be rather straightforward for older students. Younger students completing the task can be paired with more advanced peers (as discussed below). In fact, research shows that engaging in dyadic interaction with peers enhances the quality of reasoning about a topic (Kuhn, Shaw & Felton, 1997). Through this activity, students can learn that personal accounts of the same event can vary widely in, among other things, the ways in which narrative is used to support an argument. This, in turn, can advance students' argumentation skills, if a focus is placed on analysis of argument substantiation. Moreover, through this process students can learn to distinguish between primary and secondary sources of information, and between investigative journalism and ideological opinion pieces (which typically do not rely on sources). This is especially relevant in the context of today's polarized media environment, in which the distinction between real and fake news is increasingly called into question.

Through writing and discussion with peers, educators can enable the development of perspective-taking by asking young refugees to assume the various perspectives of individuals quoted or mentioned in articles. Guiding questions similar to those used in the series of studies conducted by the first author – such as *What did* [person quoted in the text] *think or feel but did not express?* – can be used to stimulate this process. Engaging children in discussions with older children or more capable peers of the same age can activate the ZPD discussed earlier in this work. Through reflection and problem solving in collaboration with more capable peers, students can gradually ascend to the level of potential development.

Given that migration and exile can often be quite lonely experiences for young people (Collins, 2017), collaborative learning experiences can be of paramount importance to psychological well-being. Research confirms that social interactions can often drive children's reasons for learning (Roschelle et al., 2001). Because a child's social identity is enhanced by participation in a community or by membership in a group, engaging children in collective and collaborative group reflections can be more motivational that relying solely on individual work. Moreover, collaborative work in learning communities with other refugees can confer psychosocial benefits and help young refugees establish a sense of belonging.

Finally, by using the affordances of cyberspace – such as free blogging platforms like Wordpress.com – young refugees can be tasked with actively employing language to expand, correct, or even re-write one or more articles based on personal experiences with the topic. Research shows that when children write narratives combining subject matter with personal experience, they use narrative as a mode of learning (Daiute & Griffin, 1993). In their written narratives, students can reflect upon current events in the same way that they interpret their personal experiences, and perhaps learn to fuse the two approaches.

Mapping Migration

In an educational unit on *mapping migration*, educators can harness the powers of *interactivity* and *multimodality* by employing applications such as Google Maps and Wikipedia to develop young refugees' abilities to conceptualize their spatial locations and coordinate the perspectives of different actors or audiences. By asking refugee students to visually contrast the starting points of their migration with their current locations, they can begin acquiring basic yet essential geographical and conceptual knowledge. Acquisition of this type of knowledge can be expanded by instructing young refugees to organize their journeys as narratives through blog posts with prompts such as: *Describe your experiences of the towns, cities, and countries you journeyed over to get to where you are today.* By listing, relating, and comparing these locations, a number of conceptual categories tied to *class inclusion* can be disembedded directly from a young person's lived experience. Class inclusion is part of a hierarchical integration process through which a student gains an understanding of a singular concept – such as the town of Osijek – being part of a subset included within a larger class –the country of Croatia – within a yet larger class – Eastern Europe. Additionally, mapping migration exercises can engage relational understating by asking young refugees to relationally describe the positions of the countries, cities, and towns that they are moving through (e.g., "Bulgaria is north of Greece and east of Serbia").

Depending on students' ages, a plethora of additional activities within this mapping unit can be utilized to emphasize specific relational or quantitative concepts, such as *number* (for younger children), and *length, height, quantity*, and *distance* (for older children or youth). These activities involve engaging students with data (obtained from free and reliable websites such as Wikipedia) on the distances between places along the route, the population sizes of countries, cities, and towns, the lengths of roads, and the heights of hills and mountains. They can be especially beneficial to younger children who are in the process of acquiring capacities for self-regulation. Once basic concepts (distance, height, length) have been mastered, additional higher-order *self-regulatory* concepts can develop. For example, children who have acquired the concept of number are well on their way to mastering the concept of time, which on the intrapersonal level becomes self-regulatory. Having an understanding of time allows children to structure their own activities according to units of time, and thus perform daily activities more efficiently, or engage in entirely new activities that require temporal ordering and processing.

Travel Story

Following from the mapping unit, a further educational unit employing the tool of *multimodality* can center on creating a *travel story* via easily accessible smartphone applications such as Instagram. Multimodality involves creating assignments that require the synthesis of moving and still images, words, and sounds. Such activities can be flexibly employed in the field to provide a context in which young refugees can combine narrative-based reflective and creative capacities while critically engaging with their geographical locations along the migratory journey. Through juxtaposition and contraposition, a multimodal tool such as the Instagram story can create a different system of signification, thus transcending the collective contribution of its constituent parts (still and moving images, sound, and narration) and affording students the opportunity to create new knowledge by building on their everyday activities.

Fostering cyber-based educational activities through which refugee children can construct digital narratives, and use them to interact and collaborate with refugee peers, friends back home, and even same age peers in their destination countries, can advance the development of multicultural cognitive orientations. Practitioners of this approach note that digital stories have wide appeal among children, youth, and adults "because they typically privilege a personal voice and allow participants to draw on popular culture and local knowledge" (Hull & Nelson, 2005, p. 231). Educators can construct assignments that facilitate the development of multimodal personal narratives by first engaging students in the activities of data gathering, storyboarding, and crafting voiceover text. Such tasks provide students with the means to merge personal motivations, frustrations, dreams, and desires, with active sources of knowledge. On a cognitive level, such assignments can engage young refugees in the processes of logically and explicitly connecting two or more separate themes (or subthemes) by ordering or subordinating one theme to the other(s). Additionally, this type of assignments can engage the processes of perspective taking; if students are encouraged to imagine different audiences that may hear and see their stories, they can learn to look at their own lives through the eyes of others.

CONCLUSION

Unlike at any other point in human history, refugees fleeing from war-torn and economically devastated regions during the 21st century have the potential to take advantage of the affordances provided by the Internet. Current global trends suggest that the number of refugees will continue to rise. Therefore, it can be assumed that the demand for connectivity among this population will also continue to grow, and the affordances of the Internet will become central to the delivery of all forms of humanitarian aid, including education. As an entire generation of displaced young people is growing up on the road, often with no access to formal education, harnessing the potential of these affordances to facilitate cognitive development in refugee children is critically important. In outlining the educational practices presented in this chapter, we sought to introduce more formal, narrative-based curricular components of interpretation and structured interaction into the already experientially rich activities of young refugees on the move. These components are often seen as necessary preconditions to helping students transform experience into learning.

Grounded in the theory of narrative development, empirical work on the use of language in the process of cognitive development suggests specific practical curriculum recommendations. The purpose of these recommendations is to enable educational professionals to use the Internet in ways that allow young refugees to reflect upon their situated experiences along the migratory journey. The curriculum recommendations provided in this chapter are specifically tailored to the unique circumstances of refugee children and youth. They build on the everyday activities of young migrants on the road in ways that allow them to engage with their rich transnational experiences. Considered as learning activities, each recommendation has the capacity to expand imagination, knowledge, thought, and action across diverse cultural landscapes. While the primary goal of these recommendations is to facilitate increasing cognitive and relational complexity among young migrants, a related goal is to enable them to view their experiences as unique and valuable.

Given the growing demand for connectivity, and the educational potentials connectivity can offer, more research and evidence-based practices are needed in this field. Even though the recommendations outlined in this work build upon years of research examining the pedagogical uses of narrative in traditional classroom settings, empirical evidence for employing such practices with refugee youth in the process of migration does not yet exist. One important avenue for future work is identifying ways in which the practical challenges of implementation of educational programs in such circumstances can be overcome. An obvious practical challenge is language diversity among refugee youth, aid workers, and educators. This problem could potentially be solved through the use of emerging digital neural-translation platforms such as Google Translate, but the exact utility of such systems to the processes of educational implementation needs to be studied. Perhaps the most difficult challenge is that trained and skilled educators are rarely present along the migratory journey and in refugee camps. Therefore, in addition to relying on peer-to-peer interaction as a proven method of learning, future work must identify the best methods for training aid workers and parents (if they are present) to organize educational processes and serve as interpersonal resources.

Media coverage of the refugee crisis in Europe has shown that mobile technology is a lifeline for refugees navigating their journeys and resettling in European countries. However, the top ten refugee-hosting countries in the world are not in Europe. In fact, in areas of the globe beyond Europe, where long-term and persistent refugee crises are common, providing connectivity to refugees is significantly more challenging. For example, in 2014, the aid organization CARE Jordan began using online courses developed by Edraak—a large-scale online learning system supported by the Queen Rania Foundation—in the Jordanian Azraq refugee camp (GSMA, 2017). However, following the dramatic increase in the number of Syrian refugees arriving to the camp in 2015, scaling-up of the program proved difficult to manage. One of the primary reasons was financial sustainability – Edraak is a not-for-profit organization and its robust learning system requires complex infrastructure and trained staff. In recognition of the financial hurdles of delivering organized educational experiences to refugees, we sought to develop curriculum recommendations that rely solely on the already existent affordances of cyberspace and are thus practically free to implement.

The potential benefits of the Internet in providing stand-in educational experiences to displaced young people cannot be overstated. However, actualizing these educational potentials requires much future work in research and practice. By describing the initial theoretical and practical considerations for how these potential benefits can be translated into real-life benefits for refugee children, this chapter serves as a first step in that direction.

ACKNOWLEDGMENT

This work is dedicated to the memory of Professor Joseph A. Glick of The Graduate Center, CUNY. May he rest in peace. An earlier version of this chapter was presented in June 2016 at the Questioning Aesthetics Symposium - *Migratory People, Migratory Images* hosted by NYU-Berlin.

REFERENCES

Abbott, H. (2002). *The Cambridge introduction to narrative*. Cambridge, UK: Cambridge University Press.

Alonso, A., & Oiarzabal, P. J. (2010). *Diasporas in the new media age: Identity, politics and community*. University of Nevada Press.

Appadurai, A. (1997). Fieldwork in the Era of Globalization. *Anthropology and Humanism, 22*(1), 1. doi:10.1525/ahu.1997.22.1.115

Benet-Martínez, V., & Haritatos, J. (2005). Bicultural identity integration (BII): Components and psychological antecedents. *Journal of Personality, 73*(4), 1015–1050. doi:10.1111/j.1467-6494.2005.00337.x PMID:15958143

Benet-Martínez, V., Lee, F., & Leu, J. (2006). Biculturalism and cognitive complexity: Expertise in cultural representations. *Journal of Cross-Cultural Psychology, 37*(4), 386–407. doi:10.1177/0022022106288476

Benet-Martínez, V., Leu, J., Lee, F., & Morris, M. (2002). Negotiating biculturalism: Cultural frame-switching in biculturals with oppositional vs. compatible cultural identities. *Journal of Cross-Cultural Psychology, 33*(5), 492–516. doi:10.1177/0022022102033005005

Benet-Martínez, V., Leu, J., Lee, F., & Morris, M. (2002). Negotiating biculturalism: Cultural frame-switching in biculturals with oppositional vs. compatible cultural identities. *Journal of Cross-Cultural Psychology, 33*(5), 492–516. doi:10.1177/0022022102033005005

Bogost, I. (2011). *How to Do Things with Videogames (Electronic Mediations)*. University of Minnesota Press. doi:10.5749/minnesota/9780816676460.001.0001

Bransford, J. D., Brown, A. L., & Cocking, R. R. (Eds.). (1999). *How people learn: Brain, mind, experience and school*. Washington, DC: National Academy Press.

Bruner, J. S. (1960). *The Process of education*. Cambridge, MA: Harvard University Press.

Bruner, J. S. (1973). *The relevance of education*. New York: Norton.

Cheung, A. C. K., & Slavin, R. E. (2013). The effectiveness of educational technology applications for enhancing mathematics achievement in K–12 classrooms: A meta-analysis. *Educational Research Review, 9*, 88–113. doi:10.1016/j.edurev.2013.01.001

Collins, L. (2017, February 27). Europe's Child-Refugee Crisis. *The New Yorker*.

Connor, P. (2016, August 2). *Number of Refugees to Europe Surges to Record 1.3 Million in 2015*. Pew Research Center.

Cooper, C. R. (2003). Bridging multiple worlds: Immigrant youth identity and pathways to college. *International Society for the Study of Behavioral Development Newsletter, 38*, 1–4.

D'Andrade, R. G. (1984). Cultural meaning systems. In R. A. Shweder & R. A. LeVine (Eds.), *Cultural theory: Essays on mind, self, and emotion* (pp. 88–119). Cambridge, UK: Cambridge University Press.

Daiute, C. (2013). Educational uses of the digital world for human development. *Learning Landscapes, 6*(2), 63–83.

Daiute, C. (2014). *Narrative inquiry: A dynamic approach*. Thousand Oaks, CA: Sage.

Daiute, C., & Griffin, T. M. (1993). The social construction of narrative. In C. Daiute (Ed.), *The development of literacy through social interaction*. San Francisco, CA: Jossey Bass.

Daiute, C., & Lucić, L. (2010). Situated cultural development among youth separated by war. *International Journal of Intercultural Relations, 34*(6), 615–628. doi:10.1016/j.ijintrel.2010.07.006

Daiute, C., & Lucić, L. (2011). *The Skill of Relational Complexity for Global Children and Youth in the United States*. Unpublished NSF Grant Proposal.

Dörnyei, Z., & Ushioda, E. (2009). *Motivation, language identity and the L2 self* (Vol. 36). Multilingual Matters Ltd.

Elias, N., & Zeltser-Shorer, M. (2006). Immigrants of the world unite? A virtual community of Russian-speaking immigrants on the Web. *Journal of International Communication, 12*(2), 70–90. doi:10.1080/13216597.2006.9752014

Emily, S., & Paul, A. (2009). Creating and inhabiting virtual places: Indian immigrants in cyberspace. *National Identities, 11*(2), 127–147. doi:10.1080/14608940902891161

Frontex Risk Analysis Unit. (2017). *The Western Balkans Annual Risk Analysis 2017.* European Border and Coast Guard Agency. Accessed 11/11/17 from http://frontex.europa.eu/assets/Publications/Risk_Analysis/WB_ARA_2017.pdf

Geertz, C. (1973). *The interpretation of cultures.* New York: Basic Books.

Gibson, J. J. (1977). The Theory of Affordances. In R. Shaw & J. Bransford (Eds.), *Perceiving, Acting, and Knowing: Toward an Ecological Psychology* (pp. 67–82). Hillsdale, NJ: Lawrence Erlbaum.

Gillespie, M., Ampofo, L., Cheesman, M., Faith, B., Iliadou, E., Issa, A., Osseiran, S., & Skleparis, D. (2016). *Mapping Refugee Media Journeys: Smartphones and Social Media Networks.* Project Report. The Open University / France Médias Monde.

GSMA. (2017). *The Importance of Mobile for Refugees: A Landscape of New Services and Approaches.* Accessed 11/11/17 from https://www.gsma.com/mobilefordevelopment/wp-content/uploads/2017/02/The-Importance-of-mobile-for-refugees_a-landscape-of-new-services-and-approaches.pdf

Haritatos, J., & Benet-Martínez, V. (2002). Bicultural identities: The interface of cultural, personality, and socio- cognitive processes. *Journal of Research in Personality, 36*(6), 598–606. doi:10.1016/S0092-6566(02)00510-X

Heller, P. (2012). *Forensic Oceanography Report on the "Left-To-Die Boat."* Situ Studio.

Hong, Y. Y., Chiu, C. Y., & Kung, T. (1997). Bringing culture out in front: Effects of cultural meaning system activation on social cognition. In K. Leung, Y. Kashima, U. Kim, & S. Yamaguchi (Eds.), *Progress in Asian social psychology* (Vol. 1, pp. 135–146). Singapore: Wiley.

Hong, Y. Y., Morris, M., Chiu, C. Y., & Benet-Martínez, V. (2000). Multicultural minds: A dynamic constructivist approach to culture and cognition. *The American Psychologist, 55*(7), 709–720. doi:10.1037/0003-066X.55.7.709 PMID:10916861

Ignacio, N. (2000). "Ain't I a Filipino (woman)": An analysis of authorship and authority through the construction of "Filipina" on the net. *The Sociological Quarterly, 41*(4), 551–572. doi:10.1111/j.1533-8525.2000.tb00073.x

Jordan, T., Raubal, M., Gartrell, B., & Egenhofer, M. (1998). An affordance-based model of place in GIS. *Eight International Symposium on Spatial Data Handling,* 98–109.

Kashima, Y. (2000). Conceptions of culture and person for psychology. *Journal of Cross-Cultural Psychology*, *31*(1), 14–32. doi:10.1177/0022022100031001003

Kelava, M. (2013, October 23). *Budi dobar susjed, podjeli internet vezu! H-alter*. Retrieved November 2, 2017, from http://h-alter.org/vijesti/budi-dobar-susjed-podijeli-internet-vezu

Ko, S.-G., Lee, T.-H., Yoon, H.-Y., Kwon, J.-H., & Mather, M. (2010). How does context affect assessments of facial emotion? The role of culture and age. *Psychology and Aging*.

Labov, W. (1997). Narrative analysis: Oral versions of personal experience. *Journal of Narrative and Life History*, *1997*, 7.

Labov, W., & Waletzky, J. (1967). Narrative analysis: Oral versions of personal experience. In J. Helm (Ed.), *Essays on the verbal and visual arts* (pp. 12–44). Seattle, WA: University of Washington Press.

Lakoff, G. (1987). *Women, Fire, and Dangerous Things*. Chicago, IL: University of Chicago Press. doi:10.7208/chicago/9780226471013.001.0001

Laursen, D. (2005). Please reply! The replying norm in adolescent SMS communication. In R. Harper, L. Palen, & A. Taylor (Eds.), *The Inside Text: Social, Cultural and Design Perspectives on SMS* (pp. 53–73). Dordrecht, The Netherlands: Springer. doi:10.1007/1-4020-3060-6_4

Lave, J., & Wenger, E. (1991). *Situated Learning: Legitimate peripheral participation*. New York: Cambridge University Press. doi:10.1017/CBO9780511815355

Lepeska, D. (2016). Refugees and the Technology of Exile. *The Wilson Quarterly*. Accessed 11/11/17 from https://wilsonquarterly.com/quarterly/looking-back-moving-forward/refugees-and-the-technology-of-exile/

Linnell, J. (2016, January 13) Border controls: Refugee fences fragment wildlife. *Nature*.

Lucić, L. (2013). Use of evaluative devices by youth for sense-making of culturally diverse interactions. *International Journal of Intercultural Relations*, *37*(4), 434–449. doi:10.1016/j.ijintrel.2013.04.003

Lucić, L. (2016a). Changing landscapes, changing narratives: Socio-cultural approach for teaching global migrants. *Pedagogy, Culture & Society*, *24*(2), 221–237. doi:10.1080/14681366.2016.1149504

Lucić, L. (2016b). Narrative approaches to conflict resolution across technologically mediated landscapes. *International Journal of Cyber Behavior, Psychology and Learning, 6*(1), 42–59. doi:10.4018/IJCBPL.2016010103

Lucić, L. (2016c). Developmental affordances of war-torn landscapes: Growing up in Sarajevo under siege. *Human Development, 59*(2-3), 81–106. doi:10.1159/000448228

Lucić, L. (2017, April). *"Not everyone wants to go to Western Europe": Exploring the decision of Syrian Refugees to permanently settle in Turkey.* Presented at: Mapping the Discursive Landscape, Center for the Humanities, The Graduate Center of The City University of New York.

Lvovich, N. (1997). *The multilingual self: An inquiry into language learning.* Hillsdale, NJ: Lawrence Erlbaum.

Mendoza-Denton, R., Shoda, Y., Ayduk, O., & Mischel, W. (1999). Applying cognitive-affective processing system theory to cultural differences in social behavior. In *Merging past, present, and future in cross-cultural psychology: Selected proceedings from the 14th International Congress of the International Association for Cross-Cultural Psychology* (pp. 205–217). Lisse, Netherlands: Swets & Zeitlinger.

Mikal, J. P., & Woodfield, B. (2015). Refugees, post-migration stress, and internet use: A Qualitative analysis of intercultural adjustment and internet use among Iraqi and Sudanese refugees to the United States. *Qualitative Health Research, 25*(10), 1319–1333. doi:10.1177/1049732315601089 PMID:26290542

Mistry, J., & Wu, J. (2010). Navigating cultural worlds and negotiating identities: A conceptual model. *Human Development, 53*(1), 5–25. doi:10.1159/000268136

Nelson, K. (1985). *Making sense: The acquisition of shared meaning.* New York: Academic Press.

Nelson, K. (1996). *Language in cognitive development: The emergence of the mediated mind.* Cambridge University Press. doi:10.1017/CBO9781139174619

Padilla, A. (2006). Bicultural social development. *Hispanic Journal of Behavioral Sciences, 28*(4), 467–497. doi:10.1177/0739986306294255

Pea, R. D. (2002). Learning science through collaborative visualization over the Internet. In N. Ringertz (Ed.), *Nobel Symposium: Virtual museums and public understanding of science and culture.* Stockholm, Sweden: Nobel Academy Press.

Pea, R. D. (2004). The social and technological dimensions of "scaffolding" and related theoretical concepts for learning, education and human activity. *Journal of the Learning Sciences, 13*(3), 423–451. doi:10.120715327809jls1303_6

Roschelle, J., Pea, R., Hoadley, C., Gordin, D., & Means, B. (2001). Changing how and what children learn in school with collaborative cognitive technologies. The Future of Children, 10(2), 76-101.

Sardon, J. P. (2001). Demographic Change in the Balkans since the End of the 1980s. *Population. English Selection, 13*(2), 49–70.

Schroeder, S. (2015). Refugees in Croatia can't get to the Internet, so the Internet comes to them. *Mashable.* September 15. Accessed 10/17/17 from http://mashable. com/2015/09/21/mobile-free-internet-refugees/#eM04iz5nHgqL

Schwartz, D. L. (1999). Rethinking transfer: A simple proposal with interesting implications. In *Review of research in education, 24*. Washington, DC: American Educational Research Association.

Sivin-Kachala, J., & Bialo, E. R. (1999). *1999 research report on the effectiveness of technology in schools* (6th ed.). Washington, DC: Software and Information Industry Association.

Suárez-Orozco, C., Todorova, I., & Qin, B. D. (2006). The well-being of immigrant adolescents: A longitudinal perspective on risk and protective factors. In The crisis in youth mental health. Academic Press.

Suarez-Orozco, M. M. (2000). Everything you ever wanted to know about assimilation but were afraid to ask. *Daedalus, 129*(4), 1–30.

Tadmor, C. T., Tetlock, P. E., & Peng, K. (2009). Acculturation strategies and integrative complexity: The cognitive implications of biculturalism. *Journal of Cross-Cultural Psychology, 40*(1), 105–139. doi:10.1177/0022022108326279

The Economist. (2017, February 11). Migrants with mobiles: Phones are now indispensable for refugees. *The Economist.*

UN High Commissioner for Refugees (UNHCR). (2011). *The 1951 Convention Relating to the Status of Refugees and its 1967 Protocol.* Available at: http://www. refworld.org/docid/4ec4a7f02.html [accessed 15 May 2018]

UNHCR. (2016). *Connecting Refugees: How internet and mobile connectivity can improve refugee well-being and transform humanitarian action.* Accessed 11/11/17 from http://www.unhcr.org/5770d43c4.pdf

UNHCR. (2016). *Global Trends: Forced Displacement in 2016.* United Nation High Commissioner for Refugees. Accessed 11/11/17 from http://www.unhcr.org/ globaltrends2016/

Vygotsky, L. S. (1978). *Mind in society*. Harvard University Press.

Wenli, C., & Wenting, X. (2012). *Cyber Behavior of Immigrants. The Encyclopedia of Cyber Behavior*. IGI Global.

Wittgenstein, L. (1953). *Philosophical Investigations*. Oxford, UK: Blackwell Publishing.

Wood, D. J., Bruner, J. S., & Ross, G. (1976). The role of tutoring in problem solving. *Journal of Child Psychiatry and Psychology*, *17*(2), 89–100. doi:10.1111/j.1469-7610.1976.tb00381.x PMID:932126

Yan, Z., & Greenfield, P. (Eds.). (2006). Children, adolescents, and the Internet (Special Section). *Developmental Psychology*, *42*, 391–458. PMID:16756431

Chapter 2
Adolescents, Third-Person Perception, and Facebook

John Chapin
Pennsylvania State University, USA

ABSTRACT

The purpose of this chapter is to document the extent of Facebook use and cyberbullying among adolescents. It is based on a study theoretically grounded in third-person perception (TPP), the belief that media messages affect other people more than oneself. As Facebook establishes itself as the dominant social network, users expose themselves to a level of bullying not possible in the analog world. The study found that 84% of adolescents (middle school through college undergraduates) use Facebook, and that most users log on daily. While 30% of the sample reported being cyberbullied, only 12.5% quit using the site and only 18% told a parent or school official. Despite heavy use and exposure, adolescents exhibit TPP, believing others are more likely to be negatively affected by Facebook use. A range of self-protective behaviors from precautionary (deleting or blocking abusive users) to reactionary (quitting Facebook) were related to decreased degrees of TPP. Implications for prevention education are discussed.

INTRODUCTION

Consider the numbers:

- 800 million: Number of active Facebook users (Lyons, 2012).
- 49: Percentage of Americans using Facebook (Lyons, 2012).
- >50: Percentage of American teens who have been cyber-bullied (Bullying Statistics, 2012).

DOI: 10.4018/978-1-5225-7128-5.ch002

- 10 to 15: Percentage of bullied teens who tell their parents (Bullying Statistics, 2012).
- 4,400: Number of teen suicides in the U.S. each year (CDC, 2012).

The National Crime Prevention Council (2012) defines cyber bullying as "the process of using the Internet, cell phones or other devices to send or post text or images intended to hurt or embarrass another person." This may include sending nasty messages or threats to a person's email account or cell phone, spreading rumors online or through texts, posting hurtful or threatening messages on social networking sites or web pages, stealing a person's account information to break into their account and send damaging messages, pretending to be someone else online to hurt another person, taking unflattering pictures of a person and spreading them through cell phones or the Internet, sexting or circulating sexually suggestive pictures or messages about a person.

The use of Facebook and other social media can be especially problematic, because once something is shared, it replicates and may never disappear, resurfacing at later times. Cyber bullying can be damaging to adolescents and teens. It can lead to depression, anxiety and suicide (Bullying Statistics, 2012).

The purpose of the study is to document the extent of Facebook use and cyber bullying among a sample of adolescents. The study is theoretically grounded in third-person perception, the belief that media messages affect other people more than oneself. Exploring third-person perception, Facebook use and cyber bullying may shed light on the extent of the problem and may also explain why adolescents do not report cyber bullying and do not take self-protective measures online.

THE STUDY

Procedures and Participants

Participants were recruited through school-based programs about bullying offered by Crisis Center North, a Pennsylvania women's center. Multiple school districts and universities participated. The sample (N = 1,488) was 51% male, with an average age of 15 (range = 12 (middle school) to 24 (college undergraduate)). These age ranges were selected because they coincide with reported cases of cyber bullying and dating/relationship violence.

Results

Participants believed they were less likely than others to be affected by Facebook use. This is classic Third-person perception (TPP). As predicted, participants who believed they are less influenced than others by Facebook use also believed they are less likely than others to become the victim of cyber bullying. This misperception is called optimistic bias.

Most of the participants (84%) said they use Facebook. When controlling for non-users, the average adolescent logs on daily. Enjoyment of Facebook ranged from zero (uncommon among users) to "LOVE it." Use and enjoyment emerged as the strongest predictor of TPP.

TPP increased as perceived social norms reject cyber bullying as normal. Responses to the statement, "my friends think cyber bullying is funny," ranged from strongly agree (4%) to strongly disagree (55.6%). Over half of the adolescents (64%) disagreed or strongly disagreed with this statement, indicating the subjective norm for cyber bullying is perceived to be more supportive of victims than bullies. Age emerged as a weak predictor, with TPP increasing with age. There were no differences attributable to gender or race.

Table 1 shows the percentage of adolescents who have taken steps to prevent harm on social media. Deleting friends or blocking peers was the most common action taken (50.8%). Nearly one-third of the sample (30%) said they have been electronically bullied, so an additional 20% of the sample has taken this action as a precautionary measure. The remaining behaviors are each below the 30% (affected) range, suggesting 12% to 25% of adolescents who experience cyber bullying take no action. Participants scored an average of 70% on a knowledge pre-test. Responses to individual items ranged from 89% correctly responding that deleted posts and photos from Facebook can be recovered, to 59% incorrectly responding that drug and alcohol abuse are reasonable explanations for bullying and violence.

Table 1. Percentage of adolescents who have taken self-protective behaviors

Behavior	% Taken
Deleted "friends" or blocked someone from Facebook	50.8%
Told a parent or school official about a cyber bullying incident	18.0%
Saved comments or posts to document the abuse.	17.5%
Quit using Facebook or another social networking site	12.5%
Changed cell phone number	5.7%

Discussion

As Facebook establishes itself as the dominant social network, approaching 1 billion users world-wide, adolescents expose themselves to a level of bullying not previously possible in the analog world. Facebook has a minimum age requirement of 13, but 12-year-olds in the current sample reported daily use. Adolescents over share personal information and photos on their own and have no control over what peers share on their behalf. The national statistics on teen suicide speak for themselves.

The current study found that 84% of adolescents (middle school through college undergraduates) use Facebook, and that most users log on daily. While 30% of the sample reported being cyber bullied, only 12.5% quit using the site, and only 18% told a parent or school official about the abuse. Informal discussions within the school-based sessions suggest the 30% figure may be under reported. Students routinely talked about behaviors that meet the legal definition of stalking as "normal," saying things like, "If I didn't want people to know where I am all the time, I wouldn't post it," and "That's what Facebook is for." Between the GPS tracking capabilities embedded in posted photos and literally posting locations in status updates and in applications like Foursquare and Runkeeper, escalating from cyber stalking to in-person stalking would be easy.

A possible explanation for bullied adolescents' failure to report harassment is a form of third-person perception; they believe the impact on themselves is minimal when compared to their peers. Despite heavy use and exposure, adolescents exhibit third-person perception (TPP), believing others are more likely to be affected by Facebook use. A range of self-protective behaviors from precautionary (deleting or blocking abusive users) to reactionary (quitting Facebook) were related to decreased degrees of TPP. TPP was also related to optimistic bias; adolescents who believe others are more influenced by Facebook also believe others are more likely to become the victims of cyber bullying. This information is useful to schools, parents and anti-bullying programs, suggesting a media literacy approach to prevention education may decrease TPP and increase self-protective behaviors.

The remaining predictors of TPP flesh out a better understanding of the interplay between TPP and cyber bullying. The strongest predictor of TPP was liking of and use of Facebook. TPP only decreased with experience. The more adolescents use Facebook, without experiencing cyber bullying first-hand, the more they enjoy the experience, believe they will not be adversely affected and larger the perceived gap between themselves and others. Beliefs about peers' perceptions of cyber bullying (subjective norm) widen the perceived self/other gap. Facebook can provide a positive experience for adolescents, a place to establish an identity and maintain relationships with peers. Unfortunately, it also establishes a platform for name calling, harassment and abuse. Adolescents need to be aware of the dangers, so they can take appropriate precautions and be aware of resources, if they do become victimized electronically. Partnerships between school systems and women's centers may offer a viable solution.

BACKGROUND/LITERATURE REVIEW

Outline

The study described in this chapter draws together a number of related literatures. After grounding the work in adolescents and social media, a number of studies in communications and health psychology are explored. Authors in these two disciplines don't often draw equally from the other. This is unfortunate, as the following review of the literatures shows they are clearly related and the preceding study documents the relationship. The second section introduces the reader to third-person perception (TPP), a communications theory about perceived influence of the media. The next section introduces optimistic bias, a health psychology theory that explains why people believe they are invulnerable to harm. Each of these are misperceptions that result in behaviors: People act on their perceptions, not on reality. The last section reviews the literature on subjective norms: How adolescents' perceive the attitudes of their peers impacts their own perceptions of social media and ultimately their uses and abuses of social media platforms.

Adolescents and Social Media

A report issued by the American Academy of Pediatrics (2011) outlined the benefits and risks of social media use by children and adolescents. On the positive side, staying connected with friends and family, exchanging ideas, and sharing pictures. Adolescent social media users find opportunities for community engagement, creative outlets, and expanded social circles. According to the report, the risks fall into these categories: peer-to-peer (bullying), inappropriate content, lack of understanding of privacy, and outside influences (social and corporate). The report also refers to "Facebook Depression," which emerges when adolescents spend too much time on social media and start exhibiting classic signs of depression.

A number of social media apps were designed specifically for finding sexual contacts or the "hook-up culture." Apps like Grindr and Tinder allow users to find potential sexual partners locally, using the GPS in their smart phones. The popular app Snapchat began as a means to quickly share explicit photos for a set period of time, without the receiver saving a copy of the image. Use of the app has evolved, with some users sharing benign photos and videos and others using it for more explicit purposes. Facebook also began as a hookup app limited to college students. As other users (including parents) were permitted to use the app, the social media giant evolved, becoming many things to over one billion users worldwide.

A recent study (Stevens, Dunaev, Malven, Bleakley & Hull, 2016) outlined how adolescents use social media in their sexual lives. Adolescents seek out sexual content (sexually explicit material, information about sexual health, sexual norms). Social media platforms provide an opportunity for sex-related communication and expression; According to the study, 25%-33% of adolescent social media users post or distribute provocative images, seeking feedback on their appearance or connection with other users. Finally, social media provide adolescents with tools for seeking out romantic or sexual partners, which may result in risky behaviors.

The National Academies of Sciences, Engineering, and Medicine issued a review of a decade of research on bullying (Flannery et al., 2016). According to the report, bullying and cyberbullying prevalence rates reported vary from 17.9 to 30.9% of school-aged children for the bullying behavior at school and from 6.9 to 14.8% for cyberbullying. Much of the variance can be attributed to sexual orientation, disability, and obesity. Physical consequences can be immediate (injury) or long-term (headaches, sleep disturbances). Psychological consequences include low self-esteem, depression, anxiety, self-harming, and suicide. There is some evidence to suggest links between being bullied in adolescence and perpetration of violence in adulthood.

Third-Person Perception and Social Media

Third-person perception (TPP) is the belief that negative media message influence others more than oneself. The phenomenon has been well-documented over a variety of contexts, which recently include news coverage of election polls (Kim, 2016), deceptive advertising (Xie, 2016), and the impact of religious cartoons (Webster, Li, Zhu, Luchsinger, Wan & Tatge, 2016). A third-person effect emerges when the misperception causes a behavior or attitude change. The most common third-person effect reported in the literature is support for censorship (Chung & Moon, 2016; Webster et al., 2016).

A growing literature is documenting TPP regarding social media (Antonopoulous, Veglis, Gardikiotis, Kotsakis & Kalliris, 2015; Wei & Lo, 2013). Facebook users believe they are less likely than other users to suffer negative consequences to their personal relationships and privacy (Paradise & Sullivan, 2012). Adolescents believe others are more harmed by sexting, and, in turn, support restrictions for others.

TPP and Optimistic Bias

Of the many theoretical frameworks thought to contribute to third-person perception, optimistic bias is the most promising. Optimistic bias is the belief that "bad things happen to other people" (Weinstein, 1980). More than 100 studies have documented optimistic bias in a range of health issues, including cancer (Jansen, Applebaum, Klein, Weinstein, Cook, Fogel & Sulmasy, 2011), natural disasters (Trumbo, Lueck, Marlatt & Peek, 2011), and sexually transmitted diseases (Wolfers, de Zwart & Kok, 2011). The first to link the two literatures (Chapin, 2000) found that adolescents exhibiting optimistic bias regarding risky sexual behaviors also exhibited TPP regarding the influence of safer sex (HIV) advertisements. Adolescents who exhibited first-person perception, believing they were more influenced by the TV spots than were their peers, reduced their optimistic bias to a more realistic risk perception. A number of later studies have linked the literatures in a number of contexts, including bird flu (Wei, Lo & Lu, 2007), computer knowledge (Li, 2008), and domestic violence (Chapin, 2011).

The Behavioral Component

Optimistic bias and third-person perception are both misperceptions about risk. Misperceptions are interesting in their own right, but they become more important, because people act on their misperceptions. Both literatures include a behavioral component (Behaviors and attitude changes brought about by the misperceptions). In a recent optimistic bias study of adolescents in the Netherlands, participants exhibited optimistic bias regarding sexually transmitted diseases (STDs): Adolescents believed they were less likely than their peers to contract an STD (Wolfers, de Zwart & Kok, 2011). It is well documented that people who exhibit optimistic bias are less likely to take precautions. In this case, adolescents who believed they were less likely to contract a STD were also less likely than peers to get tested. Recent studies have also linked optimistic bias with failure to use sun screen (Roberts, Gibbons, Gerrard & Alert, 2011), failure to vaccinate children (Bond & Nolan, 2011), and diminished mental health (O'Mara, McNulty & Karney, 2011).

People exhibiting TPP are also predicted to act on their perceptions, but what is described in the literature as a behavioral component is more often measured as an attitude or support for restriction. A study of video games found heavy gamers exhibited higher degrees of TPP (Schmierbach et al., 2011). TPP was related to less support for censorship of violent video games. Recent studies have also linked TPP with support for censorship (Lim & Golan, 2011), willingness to restrict product placement in film (Shin & Kim, 2011) and increased information seeking (Wei, Lo & Lu, 2011). The study of TPP and Facebook use among college students (Paradise

& Sullivan, 2012) failed to document a relationship between TPP and support for enhanced regulation of the social networking site.

Subjective Norms

Subjective norm is our perception that most people (friends, family, etc.) take a particular position on a particular topic (Fishbein & Ajzen, 1975). Consider the example of college students and gambling. College students are at an age that is highly impressionable, experimental and conducive to risk-taking. Not surprisingly, college students are three times as likely as adults to gamble. The advent of Internet gambling brings the high stakes of Las Vegas to dorm rooms across America. Students' parents likely view gambling as economically irresponsible, so personal attitudes and subjective norms are at odds. A study of 345 mid-western college students (Thrasher, Andrew & Mahony, 2007) found that both positive attitudes about gambling and perceived positive subjective norms predicted increased gambling among college students. The researchers suggest that gambling-themed campus events (casino nights, poker clubs) help create positive subjective norms that may differ from students' family perspectives, and thus may increase gambling among students.

While it has yet to be applied to violent crime, one study (Woolley & Eining, 2006) examined the applicability of subjective norms to one of the most common non-violent crimes among college students: Software piracy. Students routinely download music (mp3 files) illegally; the same principles apply to sharing software. For instance, the Microsoft Office Suite costs hundreds of dollars. "Free" versions are available online and sharing or copying CDs is commonplace. The study focused on accounting students and the expensive software packages required for coursework. The study split subjective norm into two categories: peer and authority (A business professor may not approve of piracy, but peers may be routinely engaging in the behavior). Both categories predicted piracy among accounting students. Compared to previous studies, Woolley and Eining found that students today are more aware of copyright restrictions, but also have greater access to computers, making piracy easier than ever. The study also found that students were more likely to pirate software than adults. The belief that software developers charge too much for their product and the belief that "everybody does it" support continued infractions. There have been no previous TPP studies using subjective norms as a predictor.

FUTURE RESEARCH DIRECTIONS

Understanding how children and adolescents use social media and their misperceptions about potential harms is an important first step. Addressing the problem is the next step. This information is useful to schools, parents and anti-bullying programs, suggesting a media literacy approach to prevention education may decrease optimistic bias and TPP, thereby increasing self-protective behaviors. It's important that children and adolescents have realistic perceptions of their vulnerability online, ways they can protect themselves, and the available resources once a harm has taken place. This study resulted from a collaboration between a university (Penn State) and a local women's center (Crisis Center North). Each brought specific areas of expertise resulting in free services to area schools. At the end of the school year, the partners meet to review the results and improve the curriculum specific to the needs of the schools. This model is easily replicated in other communities.

REFERENCES

American Academy of Pediatrics. (2011). *Clinical report: The impact of social media on children, adolescents, and families.* Retrieved from www.pediatrics.org/cgi/doi/10.1542/peds.2011-0054

Antonopoulous, N., Veglis, A., Gardikiotis, A., Kotsakis, R., & Kalliris, G. (2015). Web third-person effect in structural aspects of the information on media websites. *Computers in Human Behavior, 44*, 48–58. doi:10.1016/j.chb.2014.11.022

Bond, L., & Nolan, T. (2011). Making sense of perceptions of risk of diseases and vaccinations: A qualitative study combining models of health beliefs, decision-making and risk perception. *BMC Public Health, 11*(1), 1471–2458. doi:10.1186/1471-2458-11-943 PMID:22182354

Bullying Statistics. (2012). *Cyberbullying statistics.* Retrieved from http://www.bullyingstatistics.org/content/cyber-bullying-statistics.html

Centers for Disease Control and Prevention. (2012). *Youth suicide.* Retrieved from http://www.cdc.gov/violenceprevention/pub/youth_suicide.html

Chapin, J. (2000). Third-person perception and optimistic bias among urban minority at-risk youth. *Communication Research, 27*(1), 51–81. doi:10.1177/009365000027001003

Chapin, J. (2011). Optimistic bias about intimate partner violence among medical personnel. *Family Medicine, 43*(6), 429–432. PMID:21656399

Chung, S., & Moon, S. (2016). Is the third-person effect real? A critical examination of the rationales, testing methods, and previous findings of the third-person effect on censorship attitudes. *Human Communication Research*, *42*(2), 312–337. doi:10.1111/hcre.12078

Fishbein, M., & Ajzen, I. (1975). *Belief, attitude, intention and behavior: An introduction to theory and research*. Reading, MA: Addison-Wesley.

Flannery, D., Todres, J., Bradshaw, C., Amar, A., Graham, S., Hatzenbuehler, M., ... Rivara, F. (2016). Bullying prevention: A summary of the report of the National Academies of Sciences, Engineering, and Medicine. *Prevention Science*, *17*(8), 1044–1053. doi:10.100711121-016-0722-8 PMID:27722816

Jansen, L., Applebaum, P., Klein, W., Weinstein, N., Cook, J., & Sulmasy, D. (2011). Unrealistic optimism in early-phase oncology trials. *Ethics and Human Research*, *33*(1), 1–8. PMID:21314034

Kim, H. (2016). The role of emotions and culture in the third-person effect process of news coverage of election poll results. *Communication Research*, *43*(1), 109–130. doi:10.1177/0093650214558252

Li, X. (2008). Third-person effect, optimistic bias, and sufficiency resource in Internet use. *Journal of Communication*, *58*(3), 568–587. doi:10.1111/j.1460-2466.2008.00400.x

Lyons, G. (2012). *Facebook to hit a billion users in the summer. Analytics and Insights*. Retrieved from http://connect.icrossing.co.uk/facebook-hit-billion-users-summer_7709

National Crime Prevention Council. (2012). *Cyber bullying law and legal definition*. Retrieved from http://definitions.uslegal.com/c/cyber-bullying/

O'Mara, E., McNulty, J., & Karney, B. (2011). Positively biased appraisals in everyday life: When do they benefit mental health and when do they harm it? *Journal of Personality and Social Psychology*, *101*(3), 415–432. doi:10.1037/a0023332 PMID:21500926

Paradise, A., & Sullivan, M. (2012). (In)visible threats? The third-person effect in perceptions of the influence of Facebook. *Cyberpsychology, Behavior, and Social Networking*, *15*(1), 55–60. doi:10.1089/cyber.2011.0054 PMID:21988734

Roberts, M., Gibbons, F., Gerrard, M., & Alert, M. (2011). Optimism and adolescent perception of skin cancer risk. *Health Psychology*, *30*(6), 810–813. doi:10.1037/a0024380 PMID:21688914

Stevens, R., Dunaev, J., Malven, E., Bleakley, A., & Hull, S. (2016). Social media in the sexual lives of African American and Latino youth: Challenges and opportunities in the digital neighborhood. *Media and Communication, 4*(3), 60–70. doi:10.17645/mac.v4i3.524

Thrasher, R., Andrew, D., & Mahoney, D. (2007). The efficacy of the Theory of Reasoned Action to explain gambling behavior in college students. *College Students Affairs Journal, 27*(1), 57–75. PMID:20803059

Trumbo, C., Luek, M., Marlatt, H., & Peek, L. (2011). The effect of proximity to Hurricanes Katrina and Rita on subsequent hurricane outlook and optimistic bias. *Risk Analysis, 31*(12), 1907–1918. doi:10.1111/j.1539-6924.2011.01633.x PMID:21605150

Webster, L., Li, J., Zhu, Y., Luchsinger, A., Wan, A., & Tatge, M. (2016). Third-person effect, religiosity and support for censorship of satirical religious cartoons. *Journal of Media and Religion, 15*(4), 186–195. doi:10.1080/15348423.2016.12 48183

Wei, R., & Lo, V. (2007). The third-person effects of political attack ads in the 2004 U.S. presidential election. *Media Psychology, 9*(2), 367–388. doi:10.1080/15213260701291338

Wei, R., & Lo, V. (2013). Examining sexting's effects among adolescent mobile phone users. *International Journal of Mobile Communications, 11*(2), 176–193. doi:10.1504/IJMC.2013.052640

Weinstein, N. (1980). Unrealistic optimism about future life events. *Journal of Personality and Social Psychology, 39*(5), 806–460. doi:10.1037/0022-3514.39.5.806

Wolfers, M., de Zwart, O., & Kok, G. (2011). Adolescents in the Netherlands underestimate risk for sexually transmitted infections and deny the need for sexually transmitted infection testing. *AIDS Patient Care and STDs, 25*(5), 311–319. doi:10.1089/apc.2010.0186 PMID:21542726

Woolley, D., & Eining, M. (2006). Software piracy among accounting students: A longitudinal comparison of changes and sensitivity. *Journal of Information Systems, 20*(1), 49–63. doi:10.2308/jis.2006.20.1.49

Xie, G. (2016). Deceptive advertising and third-person perception: The interplay of generalized and specific suspicion. *Journal of Marketing Communications, 22*(5), 494–512. doi:10.1080/13527266.2014.918051

Chapter 3
Relationships of Smartphone Dependence With Chronotype and Gender in Adolescence

Satoko Ezoe
Shimane University, Japan

Masahiro Toda
Notre Dame Seishin University, Japan

ABSTRACT

Smartphone use has rapidly developed in recent years and become an established part of daily life in many countries. As various applications have been developed as communication tools for use with smartphones, allowing the internet to become more accessible, patterns of dependence have been routinely reported particularly among adolescents. In this chapter, the authors reviewed the previous studies about the relationships of smartphone dependence to chronotype and gender among adolescents. Chronotype refers to preference for sleep-wake timing: for example, morning types go to bed, get up, and experience peak alertness and performance earlier in the day than do evening types. It was found that the light emitted from media screen in the evening before bedtime may delay the circadian rhythm. In addition, excessive smartphone use may lead to sleep disturbances. Recent studies suggested that evening types and females may be more prone to become smartphone dependent.

DOI: 10.4018/978-1-5225-7128-5.ch003

INTRODUCTION

Smartphone Usage as a Problem

Smartphone use has rapidly developed in recent years and become an established part of daily life in many countries. According to the Ministry of Internal Affairs and Communications of Japan, the household penetration rate of mobile phone use was 95.8% at the end of 2015, with smartphones comprising 72.0% of those devices (Ministry of Internal Affairs and Communications of Japan, 2016). Although mobile phones have several positive aspects, such as the ability to communicate by email, play video games, and utilize a variety of applications (Lepp, Barkley & Karpinski, 2014), various social issues have arisen in association with overuse, including changes in interpersonal relationships, interference with school or work, physical health-related problems such as damage to fingers and forearms (Ming, Pietikainen & Hanninen, 2006), and injuries to the vertebrae of the neck and spine, sleep disturbance (Cain & Gradisar, 2010; Demirci, Akgönül & A, Akpinar, 2015), excessive use, and even dependence (addiction). As various applications such as those associated with social networking service (SNS) have been developed as communication tools for use with smartphones, allowing the Internet to become more accessible, patterns of dependence have been routinely reported (Kwon, Kim, Cho & Yang, 2013).

Because of mobility and Internet capabilities, a smartphone can induce characteristics of dependence in users, including overuse, tolerance, problems with withdrawal, difficulty with performing study or work, and a cyber-life orientation. Smartphone dependence especially among adolescents has recently become a very important problem. Previous studies conducted in South Korea of university students have indicated associations of smartphone dependence with mental health, campus life, personal relations, self-control, and life stress (Choi, Lee & Ha, 2012; Kim & Lee, 2012). Adolescents may be at higher risk for exhibiting problems seen with the use of smartphones as compared to adults, because younger individuals typically use smartphones as their primary tool to access the Internet (Kwon et al., 2013; Kim et al., 2012).

Chronotype and Its Relationship to Electronic Media Usage

Chronotype, or circadian preference, is related to the endogenous circadian clock that synchronizes humans to a 24-hour day (Adan et al., 2012). Individual circadian preferences can be used to classify individuals into three groups, as "morning type", "neither morning or evening (intermediate) type", and "evening type", though they are also seen as a continuum (Natale & Cicogna, 2002). Morning types wake up early in the morning, feel exhausted in the early evening hours, and quickly fall asleep, then usually wake up fresh in the early morning, while evening types go to sleep late at night and wake up late the next day, often with a worse feeling in the morning (Adan et al., 2012; Randler et al., 2016). There are several variables that have an impact on the chronotype of an individual. Endogenous factors include age, gender, genetic factors, and biological variables, while exogenous factors include cultural, social, and environmental influences (Adan et al., 2012; Randler et al., 2016). Previous studies have indicated that as communication technology has become widespread, media screens, such as those associated with television, video games, computers, and mobile phones, contribute to insufficient or poor-quality sleep in university students (Carney et al., 2006; Suen, Ellis Hon & Tam, 2008). Similarly, it has been shown that light emitted from a media screen in the evening before bedtime may alter circadian rhythm (Crowley, Tarokh & Carskadon, 2014). Furthermore, excessive mobile phone usage may lead to sleep disturbances (Van den Bulck, 2003; Vollmer, Michel & Randler, 2012; Kauderer & Randler, 2013; Cain & Gradisar, 2010; Demirci, Akgönül & Akpinar, 2015). It has also been suggested that evening types, especially during adolescence, may be prone to daytime sleepiness and poor school achievement (Giannotti, Cortesi, Sebastiani & Ottaviano, 2002). Furthermore, other studies have reported that depressive symptoms are associated with the evening type (Drennan, Klauber, Kripke & Goyette, 1991; Hirata et al., 2007). Thus, chronotype may contribute to an association between mobile phone dependency and depression. To further elucidate the health-effect implications of excessive mobile phone use, we considered that an evaluation that included chronotype would be important.

Study of Chronotype and Smartphone Use Among Japanese Medical Students

In our study (Toda, Nishio, Ezoe & Takeshita, 2015), we examined associations between smartphone use/dependence and chronotype, and also gender differences in regard to those associations. We administered a set of self-reporting questionnaires to 182 medical university students (122 males, 60 females) in Japan to evaluate smartphone use and chronotype. Smartphone dependence was examined using the Mobile Phone Dependence Questionnaire (Toda, Monden, Kubo & Morimoto, 2004, 2006), a self-rating questionnaire consisting of 20 items. Each response was scored on a Likert scale (0, 1, 2, 3) and the scores were then summed to provide a quantitative consolidated smartphone dependence score ranging from 0 to 60. Higher scores indicated greater dependence. In addition, we also investigated the amount of time used for voice phone, e-mail, web browsing, and the following online services on smartphones; games, Facebook, Twitter, and LINE. Chronotype was assessed using the Horne and Östberg Morningness-Eveningness Questionnaire (MEQ) (Horne & Östberg,1976), a self-rating questionnaire consisting of 19 items, with a total score ranging from 16 to 86. Higher scores indicated greater morningness. Respondents were categorized into morning and evening types, according to the MEQ scores.

The results of our study included the following. (1) There was a significant negative correlation between MEQ and MPDQ scores (r = -0.16, p < 0.05), indicating that respondents classified as evening type scored higher for smartphone dependence. In addition, a significant negative correlation was found between MEQ scores and daily duration of web browsing on smartphones (ρ= -0.18, p < 0.05). This tendency was more pronounced in females, as no such correlation was apparent in the male respondents. Males had significantly lower MEQ scores than females (t = -2.20, p < 0.05) (Table 1). (2) There was also a statistically significant relationship between use of online game services and chronotype, as evening types spent more time playing games (Z = -2.24, p < 0.05) (Table 2). Particularly with females, more evening types were online game users (χ^2 (1) = 6.42, p < 0.05) (Table 5). (3) Female evening types spent more time using Twitter (Z = -2.59, p < 0.01), while no such relationship was apparent for male respondents (Table 3).

Table 1. Scores for each questionnaire and daily duration of mobile-phone service use (Toda, Nishio, Ezoe & Takeshita, 2015)

	All subjects (n=182)		Males (n=122)		Females (n=60)	
	Values	**Correlation with MEQ**	**Values**	**Correlation with MEQ**	**Values**	**Correlation with MEQ**
MEQ[a]	471.(8.0)		46.1(6.9)		49.2 (9.7)[#]	
MPDQ[a]	29.8 (8.1)	-0.16*	29.8(8.4)	-0.07	29.8 (7.5)	-0.33*
Time of mobile-phone service usage (min)[b]						
Voice phone	5.0 (0-10.0)	-0.07	5.0 (0-10.0)	-0.08	7.5 (0-20.0)	-0.20
E-mail	30.0 (5.0-60.0)	-0.002	30.0 (5.0-60.0)	0.06	30.0 (6.3-60.0)	-0.11
Web browsing	60.0 (45.0-120.0)	-0.18*	60.0 (60.0-120.0)	-0.06	60.0 (30.0-180.0)	-0.39**

MEQ: Horne and Östberg Morningness-Eveningness Questionnaire
MPDQ: Mobile Phone Dependence Questionnaire
[a]Values are expressed as the mean (SD) and correlations as Pearson's r, * p < 0.05.
[b]Values are expressed as the median (interquartile range) and correlations as Spearman's ρ, * p < 0.05, ** p < 0.01.
Significantly different from males, [#] p < 0.05 (Student's t test).

Table 2. Comparison of time of usage for each online service between morning and evening types (Toda, Nishio, Ezoe & Takeshita, 2015)

	All subjects			
	Morning type		Evening type	
	Values	n	Values	n
Games	45.0 (30.0-67.5)	6	80.0 (60.0-120.0)*	26
Facebook	10.0 (5.0-30.0)	9	10.0 (10.0-30.0)	22
LINE	30.0 (30.0-60.0)	15	60.0 (30.0-75.0)	38
Twitter	10.0 (5.0-30.0)	9	30.0 (12.5-60.0)	17

Values are expressed as the median (interquartile range).
*Significantly different from "morning type", $p < 0.05$ (Mann-Whitney's U test).

Table 3. Comparison of time of usage for each online service between morning and evening types (Toda, Nishio, Ezoe & Takeshita, 2015)

	Males				Females			
	Morning type		Evening type		Morning type		Evening type	
	Values	n	Values	n	Values	n	Values	n
Game	60.0 (30.0-90.0)	3	75.0 (60.0-120.0)	16	30.0 (30.0-60.0)	3	95.0 (52.5-180.0)	10
Facebook	12.5 (10.0-15.0)	2	10.0 (8.8-30.0)	14	10.0 (5.0-30.0)	7	12.5 (10.0-30.0)	8
LINE	30.0 (5.0-45.0)	5	60.0 (30.0-60.0)	26	30.0 (30.0-90.0)	10	60.0 (37.5-165.0)	12
Twitter	47.5 (5.0-90.0)	2	30.0 (6.3-60.0)	12	10.0 (5.0-30.0)	7	60.0 (30.0-100.0)**	5

Values are expressed as the median (interquartile range).
**Significantly different from "morning type", $p < 0.01$ (Mann-Whitney's U test).

Table 4. Comparison of morning and evening types using listed online services (Toda, Nishio, Ezoe & Takeshita, 2015)

	All subjects		
	Morning type (n=15)	Evening type (n=40)	χ^2
Games	40.0	65.0	2.80
Facebook	60.0	55.0	0.11
LINE	100	95.0	0.78
Twitter	60.0	42.5	1.34

Table 5. Comparison of morning and evening types using listed online services (Toda, Nishio, Ezoe & Takeshita, 2015)

	Males			Females		
	Morning type (n=5)	**Evening type (n=28)**	χ^2	**Morning type (n=10)**	**Evening type (n=12)**	χ^2
Games	60.0	57.1	0.01	30.0	83.3	6.42*
Facebook	40.0	50.0	0.17	70.0	66.7	0.03
LINE	100	92.9	0.38	100	100	NC
Twitter	40.0	42.9	0.01	70.0	41.7	1.77

*p < 0.05
NC: not calculable

Our findings suggest that chronotype and smartphone use might be associated, particularly in females. In addition, we found a longer daily duration of web browsing, especially Twitter, by evening type females. Gender differences may also appear in the degree of intimacy of personal relationships, as females tend to have more intimate relationships with their peers, with online communication methods providing another means of maintaining those relationships (Barth & Kinder, 1988; Boneva, Kraut & Frohlich, 2001). Unlike most other online communication applications, Twitter does not require a specific sender/receiver, thus the duration of use tends to be extended. Prolonged use may have been more common in the present evening types.

Meanwhile, more evening type females as compared to morning type females participated in online games. It has been reported that playing computer games at night may decrease sleepiness and increase sleep latency (Higuchi, Motohashi, Liu & Maeda, 2005). Incidentally, even though we found that evening types spent more time playing online games, when stratified by gender, no such difference was apparent for either males or females. This may have been because of the small sample size, particularly of morning type, in our study.

For males, we found no statistically significant relationship between chronotype and either smartphone use or dependence. Nevertheless, MEQ scores were significantly lower in males, which is consistent with a previous study that found more eveningness in males as compared to females (Adan & Natale, 2002). In the present study, more males than females affirmatively answered: "To access the Internet, I use a personal computer/tablet terminal more than a smartphone" (33.9% vs. 15.0%, χ^2 (1) = 7.15, p < 0.01). Therefore, chronotype may be more associated in males with use of or dependence on personal computer/tablet terminals other than smartphones. This speculation is supported by previous studies that reported that males access the Internet with a personal computer for a longer duration before sleep and play video games more often in the bedroom as compared to females (Brunborg et al., 2011; Suganuma et al., 2007).

In summary, we found associations between chronotype and smartphone use/ dependence, as well as gender differences in regard to those associations. However, our research has several limitations. First, all of the subjects were medical students and the sample size was too small to be representative of the general population. Second, because of its cross-sectional design, we were not able to clarify causal direction. It is possible that individuals who use digital media at night already have a delayed sleep pattern and are unable to sleep at their designated bedtime (Cain & Gradisar, 2010). That is, excessive use of smartphones may be an epiphenomenon of sleeplessness. We hope to address these methodological problems in future studies.

Aim of This Chapter

In this chapter, we reviewed findings of previous studies regarding relationships of smartphone use/dependence with chronotype as well as gender differences in these associations among adolescents.

RELATIONSHIPS OF SMARTPHONE DEPENDENCE WITH CHRONOTYPE AND GENDER IN ADOLESCENCE

Bedroom Media Presence and Sleep

As mentioned above, Crowley, Tarokh, and Carskadon (2014) found that light emitted from media screens in the evening before bedtime may delay circadian rhythm. Cain and Gradisar (2010) reviewed findings related to bedroom media presence and sleep. Also, the National Sleep Foundation of the United States reported that adolescents who had four or more media devices in their bedrooms got significantly less sleep on both school nights and non-school nights than adolescents who had three media devices or less (National Sleep Foundation, 2006). Those adolescents with four or more devices were also more likely to fall asleep at school or while doing homework at least a few times per week, or felt tired or sleepy during the day. Adolescents with more media devices in their bedroom are also more likely to be evening types than those with fewer media devices in their bedroom. According to Cain and Gradisar (2010), bedroom media presence may have an indirect effect on sleep. Consistent with that speculation, adolescents aged 12-18 years who reported getting more than 8 hours of sleep per night have been found to engage in fewer technology-related activities after 9 pm as compared with adolescents who reported getting 6-8 hours of sleep and those who reported getting 3-5 hours of sleep (Calamaro, Mason & Ratcliffe, 2009).

Individual media items present in adolescent bedrooms have also been associated with sleep disturbance. It has been reported that exposure to mobile phone emissions at night may have an effect on melatonin onset time (Zeiter et al., 2000; Wood, Loughran & Stough, 2006), while mobile phone use has been also been shown to be associated with sleep problems (Loughran et al., 2005; Munezawa et al., 2011). In a study performed in Belgium, adolescents who reported being woken up at least occasionally by text messages were significantly more tired than those never woken by such messages (Van den Bulck, 2003). In addition, simply having a mobile phone in the bedroom has been related to delayed bedtime on weekend days and a discrepancy of more than 1 hour between weekdays and weekend bedtimes (Oka, Suzuki & Inoue, 2008).

Relationships of Smartphone Dependence With Chronotype and Gender in Adolescents

There have been few studies presented regarding the relationship between mobile phone use and chronotype. Harada et al. (2002) reported that Japanese adolescents aged 13-15 who used their mobile phone daily were more often the evening type and had later wake-up times. More recent studies indicated that eveningness preference might be related to Internet addiction or problematic Internet use (Lin & Gau, 2013; Randler, Horzum & Vollmer, 2013), as well as computer game addiction (Vollmer et al., 2014). Furthermore, Nimrod's findings (2015) indicate that morning-type individuals are more inclined toward using traditional media, whereas evening types reported significantly higher preference for use of new media platforms.

To the best of our knowledge, in addition to our investigation (Toda, Nishio, Ezoe & Taleshita, 2015), only one other study has analyzed the relationship of smartphone dependence (addiction) with chronotype and gender in adolescents. That study was conducted by Randler et al. (2016) and following are details of their findings.

In that study, relationships among smartphone addiction, age, gender, sleep, and chronotype were examined in German adolescents. Based on findings of previous studies conducted in regard to Internet and computer game addiction, they hypothesized that evening-oriented adolescents would score higher for smartphone addiction and addiction proneness. Furthermore, they investigated which of the variables, morningness-eveningness or habitual sleep duration, was a better statistical predictor to add incremental validity. They carried out two studies of different populations, focusing on two different measures of smartphone addiction, the Smartphone Addiction Proneness Scale (SAPS) and Smartphone Addiction Scale (SAS).

"Study 1" was conducted with 342 younger adolescents (176 boys, 165 girls, 1 not indicated). Findings from the SAPS, Composite Scale of Morningness (CSM), and habitual sleep-wake variables were collected at three different secondary schools in southwest Germany in 2015. "Study 2" was conducted with 208 older adolescents (146 girls, 62 boys), in which findings from the SAS, CSM, and habitual sleep-wake variables were collected at seven different schools with older students mainly in southwest Germany in 2015. The SAPS was developed by Kim et al. (2014) and translated into German by independent researchers using a parallel translation method. The SAS was originally developed by Kwon, Lee et al. (2013) and revised to a short version (SAS-SV) containing 10 items for adolescents (Kwon, Kim, Cho & Yang, 2013). The SAS-SV was also translated into German by independent researchers using a parallel translation method. The CSM was developed by Smith, Reily, and Midkiff (1989), and adapted to German by Randler (2008). That scale consists of 13 Likert items, with a total possible score ranging from 13 to 55 and higher scores reflecting high morningness. It has been used in many different countries, and showed good psychometric properties and convergent validity (Di Milia, Adan, Natale & Randler, 2013; Horzum et al., 2015). Furthermore, Randler et al. (2016) asked for bed times and rise times for both weekdays and weekends. From the obtained data, they calculated sleep length for weekdays and weekends, as well as the midpoint of sleep, which is another marker for the circadian phase. The midpoint of sleep is the clock time (midtime) between falling asleep and waking (Roenneberg et al., 2004).

The results of the study of Randler et al. (2016) included the following. (1) There were significant moderate and negative correlations of SAPS and SAS scores with CSM scores, indicating that a proclivity toward eveningness is related to smartphone dependence, while the midpoint of sleep was significantly positively related to SAPS and SAS scores, with adolescents who go to bed and sleep later more prone to smartphone dependence (Table 6). Sleep duration on weekdays was significantly negatively correlated with SAPS and SAS scores, indicating that individuals with short sleep times have greater smartphone dependence. However, weekend sleep duration was unrelated to that dependence (Table 6). (2) Multiple regression analysis (Table 7) revealed a significantly negative correlation between CSM score and SAPS score. The βvalue showed that CSM score was the most important predictor variable for SAPS score, from which gender effects emerged. Female adolescents showed a significantly higher level of smartphone proneness than male adolescents (Table 7). Similarly, multiple regression analysis (Table 8) revealed a significantly negative relationship between CSM score and SAS score. However, gender had the strongest influence. Female adolescents had a significantly higher value for the SAS than male adolescents (Table 8). Also, sleep duration on weekdays was a significant predictor of SAPS score (Table 7) but not SAS score (Table 8). (3) In Study 1, one-way analysis of covariance (ANCOVA) and Bonferroni adjustment for multiple

Table 6. Correlations among CSM score, sleep duration, midpoint of sleep, and SAPS and SAS scores with control for age and gender

	Study 1 (SAPS)	Study 2 (SAS)
CSM score	-0.347**	-0.349**
SDR, weekday	-0.192**	-0.294**
SDR, weekend	0.032	-0.041
MS, weekday	0.137*	0.265**
MS, weekend	0.219**	0.329**

SAPS: Smartphone Addiction Proneness Scale
SAS: Smartphone Addiction Scale
CSM: Composite Scale of Morningness
SDR: sleep duration
MS: midpoint of sleep
*Correlation was significant at 0.05 level.
**Correlation was significant at 0.01 level.
(Randler et al., 2016)

Table 7. Multiple regression analysis of relationships of SAPS score with independent variables in Study 1

	β	t	p
Gender	0.118*	2.188	0.029
Age	0.051	0.791	0.429
SDR, weekday	-0.171*	-2.042	0.042
SDR, weekend	0.025	0.436	0.663
MS, weekday	-0.086	-1.030	0.304
MS, weekend	-0.038	-0.482	0.630
CSM score	-0.349**	-4.967	≤0.001

SAPS: Smartphone Addiction Proneness Scale
SDR: sleep duration
MS: midpoint of sleep
CSM: Composite Scale of Morningness
*Correlation significant at 0.05 level.
**Correlation significant at 0.01 level.
(Randler et al., 2016)

post-hoc comparison tests indicated that evening type adolescents had significantly higher SAPS scores than both intermediate type and morning type adolescents. Similarly in Study 2, evening type adolescents had significantly higher SAS scores than both intermediate and morning types, and also intermediate type adolescents had significantly higher scores than the morning type. (4) Female adolescents had

Table 8. Multiple regression analysis of relationships of SAS score with independent variables in Study 2

	β	t	p
Gender	0.237**	3.645	≤0.001
Age	-0.113	-1.689	0.093
SDR, weekday	-0.101	-1.297	0.196
SDR, weekend	-0.029	-0.442	0.659
MS, weekday	0.055	0.657	0.512
MS, weekend	0.098	1.044	0.298
CSM score	-0.217*	-2.451	0.015

SAS: Smartphone Addiction Scale
SDR: sleep duration
MS: midpoint of sleep
CSM: Composite Scale of Morningness
*Correlation significant at 0.05 level.
**Correlation significant at 0.01 level.
(Randler et al., 2016)

significantly higher SAPS scores than male adolescents, with similar findings noted for SAS scores.

Randler et al. (2016) emphasized that the most remarkable and unique result of their study was that chronotype (morningness-eveningness) is an important predictor for smartphone addiction, even when taking sleep duration into account. Moreover, CSM score was the best predictor of smartphone addiction proneness in Study 1, while gender was the best predictor followed by CSM score in Study 2.

Based upon previously reported results, they discussed regarding the relationships among usage of light-emitting electronic devices including mobile phones and eveningness, as well as later bedtimes. Lemola et al. (2014) found that high mobile phone usage was related to later bedtimes and Roenneberg (2004) suggested that the prevalence for use of electronic devices, such as computers, tablets, and mobile phones, late at night is shifting individuals to a later chronotype. Similarly, Vollmer et al. (2012) found that evening types have longer screen times, and Kauderer and Randler (2013) found that evening type adolescents generally spend more time in front of a computer. Furthermore, Demirci, Akgönül, and Akpinur (2015) noted a significantly positive correlation between sleep disturbance and smartphone overuse. Together, these studies support findings showing that the light emitted by video screens (blue light) shifts individuals to eveningness.

In addition, Randler et al. (2016) found that female adolescents were more likely to be addicted to smartphones than male adolescents. Similar results have been presented in other studies (Billieux, Van der Linden & Rochat, 2008; Walsh, White, Cox & Young, 2011; Augner & Hacker, 2012; Lee, Chang, Lin & Cheng, 2014; Mok et al., 2014; Şar, Ayas & Horzum, 2015). However, some reported that males showed a higher level of problematic mobile phone usage as compared with females (Morahan-Martin & Schmacher, 2000; Takao, Takahashi, & Kitamura, 2009; Öztunç, 2013), while another report noted that no clear gender difference was found in regard to problematic mobile phone usage (Demirci et al., 2014). Thus, the findings of studies about the relationship between gender and smartphone dependence are contradictory.

FUTURE RESEARCH DIRECTIONS

Previous studies regarding the relationships of smartphone dependence with chronotype and gender have several limitations. First, the study subjects were limited and the sample size was too small to be representative of the general population. It is necessary to investigate a variety of adolescents in different countries and cultures. Second, valid and reliable scales are needed to measure smartphone dependence according usage in different cultures.

For our study (Ezoe, Iida, Inoue & Toda, 2016), we developed a Japanese version of the Smartphone Dependence Scale (J-SDS) based on findings of previous studies and used exploratory factor analysis with university students as subjects to establish a 5-facor structure: 1) craving and withdrawal, 2) overuse and tolerance, 3) virtual life orientation, 4) disturbance of concentration in class, and 5) physical symptoms. Of those, "craving and withdrawal" includes feelings of anxiety, impatience, and pain when without a smartphone, and constantly having one's smartphone in mind even when not using it, while "overuse and tolerance" refers to long and uncontrollable periods of use of one's smartphone, trying to control one's smartphone use but failing to do so, and spending an increasing amount of time using a smartphone to achieve the same level of satisfaction as previously experienced. Furthermore, the factor "virtual life orientation" includes feelings that communication with one's smartphone is more enjoyable and intimate than relationships with real-life friends or family, "disturbance of concentration in class" refers to having a difficult time concentrating in class due to smartphone use, and "physical symptoms" include headache, stiff shoulders, and pain in the wrists or at the back of the neck due to excessive smartphone use. These 5 are partially consistent with previously reported findings regarding factors related to Internet addiction, which include unpleasant feelings when off-line (withdrawal), excessive time spent on Internet-related activities (overuse and virtual life orientation), increased tolerance to the effects of time spent on Internet-related activities, and denial of associated problematic behaviors (Young, 1998). Therefore, we consider that the J-SDS has construct validity.

The values for Cronbach's alpha coefficient for the 5 factors extracted were found to be 0.87, 0.87, 0.76, 0.77, 0.69, respectively, and that for total J-SDS was 0.92. Although the value for the factor "physical symptoms" was not so high, that for total J-SDS showed good internal consistency.

In our study (Ezoe, Iida, Inoue & Toda, 2016), hours of smartphone use during weekdays as well as holidays showed a significantly positive relationship to J-SDS score. Furthermore, the score was significantly increased when the hours of smartphone use from 10 pm to 4 am and when in bed were increased. These results indicate the concurrent validity of the J-SDS.

As mentioned above, it has been reported that exposure to mobile phone emissions at night may have an effect on melatonin-onset time (Wood, Loughran & Stough, 2006), while mobile phone use has also been shown to be associated with sleep problems (Loughran et al., 2005; Munezawa et al., 2011). Munezawa et al. (2011) reported that the use of mobile phones for calling and sending text messages after turning off the lights at night was associated with sleep disturbance in Japanese adolescents (Munezawa et al., 2011). They concluded that since many adolescents frequently use a mobile phone late at night despite possible adverse effects on sleep, this lifestyle habit should be carefully considered when formulating preventive strategies against sleep disturbance in that age group. Along that line, we think that the J-SDS score can serve as a useful index of the adverse effects of smartphone use on sleep, because our results were found to be significantly associated with hours of smartphone use late at night and while in bed.

The third limitation of previous studies regarding the relationship of smartphone dependency to chronotype was that they used findings from self-reported questionnaires to determine chronotype and sleep-wake cycles. To overcome this in future investigations, objective physiological measures such as actigraphy should be utilized. We assessed chronotype and sleep-wake cycles in Japanese university students using Actiwatch Spectrum Plus (Philips Respironics Inc., 2015), as well as self-reported questionnaires including the MEQ, demographic variables, and sleep-wake cycles. Furthermore, we administered the J-SDS and Beck Depression Inventory second edition (BDI-II) (Beck, Steer, & Brown, 1996) to the same subjects. By analyzing the obtained data, we plan to clarify the relationships of smartphone dependence with chronotype, gender, and depression.

The fourth limitation of previous studies is the cross-sectional design employed, thus causal relationships were not clarified. A prospective cohort study is needed to determine whether smartphone dependence has an effect on chronotype, or inversely whether chronotype has an effect on smartphone dependence.

Circadian rhythms are regulated by an internal molecular clock and driven by negative feedback loops of clock genes that cycle across an approximate 24-hour period (Reppert & Weaver, 2002; Lowrey & Takahashi, 2004; Ko & Takahashi, 2006). Variations in timing of individual circadian rhythms are the result of endogenous factors (gene mutations and/or variations in gene regulation) (Koskenvuo et al., 2007), external environmental stimuli (Seo et al., 2000; Akashi et al., 2010), or both (Ferrante et al., 2015). Smartphone dependence/use may also be an important environmental stimulus. In a future study, relationships between clock genes and smartphone use should be evaluated to understand the complex effects of interactions between environment and genes on human behavior.

CONFLICTS OF INTEREST

The authors have no conflicts of interest to declare.

ACKNOWLEDGMENT

We thank Professor Tatsuya Takeshita, Wakayama Medical University, for the valuable comments. We also extend our appreciation to Professor Tadayuki Iida, Prefectural University of Hiroshima, and Professor Ken Inoue, Kochi University, for their collaboration. This study was supported by a JSPS KAKEN Grant-in-Aid for Scientific Research (C) (No. 15K01682).

REFERENCES

Adan, A., Archer, S. N., Hidalgo, M. P., Di Milia, L., Natale, V., & Randler, C. (2012). Circadian typology: A comprehensive review. *Chronobiology International*, *29*(9), 1153–1175. doi:10.3109/07420528.2012.719971 PMID:23004349

Adan, A., & Natale, V. (2002). Gender differences in morningness-eveningness preference. *Chronobiology International*, *19*(4), 709–720. doi:10.1081/CBI-120005390 PMID:12182498

Akashi, M., Soma, H., Yamamoto, T., Tsugitomi, A., Yamashita, S., Yamamoto, T., ... Node, K. (2010). Noninvasive method for assessing the human circadian clock using hair follicle cells. *Proceedings of the National Academy of Sciences of the United States of America*, *107*(35), 15643–15648. doi:10.1073/pnas.1003878107 PMID:20798039

Augner, C., & Hacker, G. W. (2012). Associations between problematic mobile phone use and psychological parameters in young adults. *International Journal of Public Health*, *57*(2), 437–441. doi:10.100700038-011-0234-z PMID:21290162

Barth, R. J., & Kinder, B. N. (1988). A theoretical analysis of sex differences in same-sex friendships. *Sex Roles*, *19*(5–6), 349–363. doi:10.1007/BF00289842

Beck, A. T., Steer, R. T., & Brown, G. K. (1996). *Manual for the Beck Depression Inventory-II*. San Antonio, TX: Psychological Corporation.

Billieux, J., Van der Linden, M., & Rochat, L. (2008). The role of impulsivity in actual and problematic use of mobile phone. *Applied Cognitive Psychology*, *22*(9), 1195–1210. doi:10.1002/acp.1429

Boneva, B., Kraut, R., & Frohlich, D. (2001). Using e-mail for personal relationships: The difference gender makes. *The American Behavioral Scientist*, *45*(3), 530–549. doi:10.1177/00027640121957204

Brunborg, G. S., Mentzoni, R. A., Molde, H., Myrseth, H., Skouverøe, K. J., Bjorvatn, B., & Pallesen, S. (2011). The relationship between media use in the bedroom, sleep habits and symptoms of insomnia. *Journal of Sleep Research*, *20*(4), 569–575. doi:10.1111/j.1365-2869.2011.00913.x PMID:21324013

Cain, N., & Gradisar, M. (2010). Electronic media use and sleep in school-aged children and adolescents: A review. *Sleep Medicine*, *11*(8), 735–742. doi:10.1016/j.sleep.2010.02.006 PMID:20673649

Calamaro, C. J., Mason, T. B. A., & Ratcliffe, S. J. (2009). Adolescents living the 24/7 lifestyle; effects of caffeine and technology on sleep duration and daytime functioning. [National Sleep Foundation]. *Pediatrics*, *123*(6), e1005–e1010. doi:10.1542/peds.2008-3641 PMID:19482732

Carney, C. E., Edinger, J. D., Meyer, B., Lindman, L., & Istre, T. (2006). Daily activities and sleep quality in college students. *Chronobiology International*, *23*(3), 623–637. doi:10.1080/07420520600650695 PMID:16753946

Choi, H. S., Lee, H. K., & Ha, J. (2012). The influence of smartphone addiction on mental health, campus life and personal relations—Focusing on K university students. *Journal of Korean Data & Information Science Society*, *235*(5), 1005–1015. doi:10.7465/jkdi.2012.23.5.1005

Crowley, S. J., Tarokh, L., & Carskadon, M. A. (2014). Sleep during adolescence. In S. H. Sheldon & ... (Eds.), *Principles and practice of pediatric sleep medicine* (2nd ed.; pp. 45–52). London: Elsevier.

Demirci, K., Akgönül, M., & Akpinar, A. (2015). Relationships of smartphone use severity with sleep quality, depression, and anxiety in university students. *Journal of Behavioral Addictions*, *4*(2), 85–92. doi:10.1556/2006.4.2015.010 PMID:26132913

Demirci, K., Orhan, H., Demirdas, A., Akpinar, A., & Sert, H. (2014). Validity and reliability of the Turkish Version of the Smartphone Addiction Scale in a younger population. *Bulletin of Clinical Psychopharmacology*, *24*(3), 226–234. doi:10.5455/bcp.20140710040824

Di Milia, L., Adan, A., Natale, V., & Randler, C. (2013). Reviewing the psychometric properties of contemporary circadian typology measures. *Chronobiology International*, *30*(10), 1261–1271. doi:10.3109/07420528.2013.817415 PMID:24001393

Drennan, M. D., Klauber, M. R., Kripke, D. F., & Goyette, L. M. (1991). The effects of depression and age on the Horne-Ostberg morningness-eveningness score. *Journal of Affective Disorders*, *23*(2), 93–98. doi:10.1016/0165-0327(91)90096-B PMID:1753041

Ezoe, S., Iida, T., Inoue, K., & Toda, M. (2016). Development of Japanese version of Smartphone Dependence Scale. *Open Journal of Preventive Medicine*, *6*(07), 179–185. doi:10.4236/ojpm.2016.67017

Ferrante, A., & Gellerman, D. (2015). Diurnal preference predicts phase differences in expression of human peripheral circadian clock genes. *Journal of Circadian Rhythms*, *13*(4), 1–7. PMID:27103930

Giannotti, F., Cortesi, F., Sebastiani, T., & Ottaviano, S. (2002). Circadian preference, sleep and daytime behaviour in adolescence. *Journal of Sleep Research*, *11*(3), 191–199. doi:10.1046/j.1365-2869.2002.00302.x PMID:12220314

Harada, T., Morikuni, M., & ... . (2002). Usage of mobile phone in the evening or at night makes Japanese students evening-typed and night sleep uncomfortable. *Sleep and Hypnosis*, *4*, 149–153.

Higuchi, S., Motohashi, Y., Liu, Y., & Maeda, A. (2005). Effects of playing a computer game using a bright display on presleep physiological variables, sleep latency, slow wave sleep and REM sleep. *Journal of Sleep Research*, *14*(3), 267–273. doi:10.1111/j.1365-2869.2005.00463.x PMID:16120101

Hirata, F. C., Lima, M. C., de Bruin, V. M., Nóbrega, P. R., Wenceslau, G. P., & de Bruin, P. F. (2007). Depression in medical school: The influence of morningness-eveningness. *Chronobiology International*, *24*(5), 939–946. doi:10.1080/07420520701657730 PMID:17994347

Horne, J. A., & Östberg, O. (1976). A self-assessment questionnaire to determine morningness–eveningness in human circadian rhythms. *International Journal of Chronobiology*, *4*(2), 97–110. PMID:1027738

Horzum, M. B., Randler, C., Masal, E., Beşoluk, Ş., Önder, İ., & Vollmer, C. (2015). Morningness-eveningness and the environment hypothesis – A cross-cultural comparison of Turkish and German adolescents. *Chronobiology International*, *32*(6), 814–821. doi:10.3109/07420528.2015.1041598 PMID:26061589

Kauderer, S., & Randler, C. (2013). Differences in time use among chronotypes in adolescents. *Biological Rhythm Research*, *44*(4), 601–608. doi:10.1080/09291016 .2012.721687

Kim, D. I., & Lee, Y. H. (2012). New patterns in media addiction: Is smartphone a substitute or a complement to the Internet? *Korean Journal of Youth Counseling*, *201*, 71–88.

Kim, D. I., Lee, Y. H., Lee, J., Nam, J. E. K., & Chung, Y. (2014). Development of Korean smartphone addiction proneness scale for youth. *PLoS One*, *9*(5), e97920. doi:10.1371/journal.pone.0097920 PMID:24848006

Kim, N. S., & Lee, K. E. (2012). Effects of self-control and life stress on smartphone addiction of university students. *Journal of the Korean Society of Health Informatics and Statistics*, *372*, 72–83.

Ko, C., & Takahashi, J. S. (2006). Molecular components of the mammalian circadian clock. *Human Molecular Genetics*, *15*(suppl_2), 271–277. doi:10.1093/ hmg/ddl207 PMID:16987893

Koskenvuo, M., Hublin, C., Partinen, M., Heikkilä, K., & Kaprio, J. (2007). Heritability if diurnal type: A nation-wide study of 8753 adult twin pairs. *Journal of Sleep Research*, *16*(2), 156–162. doi:10.1111/j.1365-2869.2007.00580.x PMID:17542945

Kwon, M., Kim, D. J., Cho, H., & Yang, S. (2013). The Smartphone Addiction Scale: Development and validation of a short version for adolescents. *PLoS One*, *8*(12), e83558. doi:10.1371/journal.pone.0083558 PMID:24391787

Kwon, M., Lee, J. Y., Won, W.-Y., Park, J.-W., Min, J.-A., Hahn, C., ... Kim, D.-J. (2013). Development and validation of a smartphone addiction scale (SAS). *PLoS One*, *8*(2), e56936. doi:10.1371/journal.pone.0056936 PMID:23468893

Lee, Y. K., Chang, C. T., Lin, Y., & Cheng, Z. H. (2014). The dark side of smartphone usage: Psychological traits, compulsive behavior and technostress. *Computers in Human Behavior*, *31*, 373–383. doi:10.1016/j.chb.2013.10.047

Lemola, S., Perkinson-Gloor, N., Brand, S., Dewald-Kaufmann, J. F., & Grob, A. (2014). Adolescents' electronic media use at night, sleep disturbance, and depressive symptoms in the smartphone age. *Journal of Youth and Adolescence, 44*(2), 405–418. doi:10.100710964-014-0176-x PMID:25204836

Lepp, A., Barkley, L. E., & Karpinski, A. C. (2014). The relationship between cell phone use, academic performance, anxiety, and satisfaction with life in college students. *Computers in Human Behavior, 31*, 343–350. doi:10.1016/j.chb.2013.10.049

Lin, Y. H., & Gau, S. S. F. (2013). Association between morningness-eveningness and the severity of compulseive Internet use: The moderating role of gender and parenting style. *Sleep Medicine, 14*(12), 1398–1404. doi:10.1016/j.sleep.2013.06.015 PMID:24157101

Loughran, S. P., Wood, A. W., Barton, J. M., Croft, R. J., Thompson, B., & Stough, C. (2005). The effects of electromagnetic fields emitted by mobile phones on human sleep. *Neuroreport, 16*(17), 1973–1976. doi:10.1097/01.wnr.0000186593.79705.3c PMID:16272890

Lowrey, P., & Takahashi, J. S. (2004). Mammalian circadian biology: Elucidating genome-wide levels of temporal organization. *Annual Review of Genomics and Human Genetics, 5*(1), 407–441. doi:10.1146/annurev.genom.5.061903.175925 PMID:15485355

Ming, Z., Pietikainen, S., & Hannien, O. (2006). Excessive texting in pathophysiology of first carpometacarpal joint arthritis. *Pathophysiology, 13*(4), 269–270. doi:10.1016/j.pathophys.2006.09.001 PMID:17049823

Ministry of Internal Affairs and Communications. (2016). *Communications usage trend survey*. Retrieved from http://www.soumu.go.jp/johotsusintokei/whitepaper/ja/h28/html/nc252110.html

Mok, J. Y., & Choi, S. W. (2014). Latent class analysis on internet and smartphone addiction in college students. *Neuropsychiatric Disease and Treatment, 10*, 817–828. PMID:24899806

Morahan-Martin, J., & Schumacher, P. (2000). Incidence and correlates of pathological Internet use among college students. *Computers in Human Behavior, 16*(1), 13–29. doi:10.1016/S0747-5632(99)00049-7

Munezawa, T., Kaneita, Y., Osaki, Y., Kanda, H., Minowa, M., Suzuki, K., ... Ohida, T. (2011). The association between use of mobile phones after lights out and sleep disturbances among Japanese adolescents: A nationwide cross-sectional survey. *Sleep, 34*(8), 1013–1020. doi:10.5665/SLEEP.1152 PMID:21804663

Natale, V., & Cicogna, P. (2002). Morningness-eveningness dimension: Is it really a continuum? *Personality and Individual Differences, 32*(5), 809–816. doi:10.1016/S0191-8869(01)00085-X

National Sleep Foundation. (2006). *2006 Sleep in America Poll*. Washington, DC: National Sleep Foundation.

Nimrod, G. (2015). Early birds and night owls: Difference in media preferences, usages, and environments. *International Journal of Communication, 9*, 21.

Oka, Y., Suzuki, S., & Inoue, Y. (2008). Bedtime activities, sleep environment, and sleep/wake patterns of Japanese elementary school children. *Behavioral Sleep Medicine, 6*(4), 220–233. doi:10.1080/15402000802371338 PMID:18853306

Öztunç, M. (2013). Analysis of problematic mobile phone use, feelings of shyness and loneliness in accordance with several variables. *Procedia: Social and Behavioral Sciences, 106*, 456–466. doi:10.1016/j.sbspro.2013.12.051

Randler, C. (2008). Psychometric properties of the German version of the Composite Scale of Morningness. *Biological Rhythm Research, 39*(2), 151–161. doi:10.1080/09291010701424796

Randler, C., Horzum, M. B., & Vollmer, C. (2013). Internet addiction and its relationship to chronotype and personality in a Turkish University student sample. *Social Science Computer Review, 32*(4), 484–495. doi:10.1177/0894439313511055

Randler, C., & Wolfgang, L. (2016). Smartphone addiction proneness in relation to sleep and morningness-eveningness in German adolescents. *Journal of Behavioral Addictions 5* (3), 465-473. *Journal of Biological Rhythms, 19*(3), 193–195.

Reppert, S. M., & Weaver, D. R. (2002). Coordination of circadian timing in mammals. *Nature, 418*(6901), 935–941. doi:10.1038/nature00965 PMID:12198538

Roenneberg, T. (2004). *The decline in human seasonality*. Academic Press.

Roenneberg, T., Kuehnle, T., Pramstaller, P. P., Ricken, J., Havel, M., Guth, A., & Merrow, M. (2004). A marker for the end of adolescence. *Current Biology, 14*(24), R1038–R1039. doi:10.1016/j.cub.2004.11.039 PMID:15620633

Şar, A. H., Ayas, T., & Horzum, M. B. (2015). Developing the smart phone addiction scale and its validity and reliability study. *Online Journal of Technology Addiction & Cyberbullying, 2*(3), 1–17.

Seo, Y. J., Matsumoto, K., Park, Y., Shinkoda, H., & Noh, T. (2000). The relationship between sleep and shift system, age, and chronotype in shift workers. *Biological Rhythm Research, 31*(5), 559–579. doi:10.1076/brhm.31.5.559.5655

Smith, C. S., Reily, C., & Midkiff, K. (1989). Evaluation of three circadian rhythm questionnaires with suggestions for an improved measure of morningness. *The Journal of Applied Psychology, 74*(5), 728–738. doi:10.1037/0021-9010.74.5.728 PMID:2793773

Suen, L. K., Ellis Hon, K. L., & Tam, W. W. (2008). Association between sleep behavior and sleep-related factors among university students in Hong Kong. *Chronobiology International, 25*(5), 760–775. doi:10.1080/07420520802397186 PMID:18780202

Suganuma, N., Kikuchi, T., Yanagi, K., Yamamura, S., Morishima, H., Adachi, H., & Takeda, M. (2007). Using electronic media before sleep can curtail sleep time and result in self-perceived insufficient sleep. *Sleep and Biological Rhythms, 5*(3), 204–214. doi:10.1111/j.1479-8425.2007.00276.x

Takao, M., Takahashi, S., & Kitamura, M. (2009). Addictive personality and problematic mobile phone use. *Cyberpsychology & Behavior, 12*(5), 501–507. doi:10.1089/cpb.2009.0022 PMID:19817562

Toda, M., Monden, K., Kubo, K., & Morimoto, K. (2004). Cellular phone dependence tendency of female university students. *Japanese Journal of Hygiene, 59*(4), 383–386. doi:10.1265/jjh.59.383 PMID:15626025

Toda, M., Monden, K., Kubo, K., & Morimoto, K. (2006). Mobile phone dependence and health-related lifestyle of university students. *Social Behavior and Personality, 34*(10), 1277–1284. doi:10.2224bp.2006.34.10.1277

Toda, M., Nishio, N., Ezoe, S., & Takeshita, T. (2015). Chronotype and smartphone use among Japanese medical students. *International Journal of Cyber Behavior, Psychology and Learning, 5*(2), 75–80. doi:10.4018/IJCBPL.2015040106

Van den Bulck, J. (2003). Text messaging as a cause of sleep interruption in adolescents, evidence from a cross-sectional study. *Journal of Sleep Research, 12*(3), 263. doi:10.1046/j.1365-2869.2003.00362.x PMID:12941066

Vollmer, C., Michel, U., & Randler, C. (2012). Outdoor light at night (LAN) is correlated with eveningness in adolescents. *Chronobiology International, 29*(4), 502–508. doi:10.3109/07420528.2011.635232 PMID:22214237

Vollmer, C., Randler, C., Horzum, M. B., & Ayas, T. (2014). Computer game addiction in adolescents and its relationship to chronotype and personality. *SAGE Open, 4*(1), 1–9. doi:10.1177/2158244013518054

Walsh, S. P., White, K. M., Cox, S., & Young, R. M. (2011). Keeping in constant touch: The predictors of young Australians' mobile phone involvement. *Computers in Human Behavior, 27*(1), 333–342. doi:10.1016/j.chb.2010.08.011

Wood, A. W., Loughran, S. P., & Stough, C. (2006). Does evening exposure to mobile phone radiation affect subsequent metatonin production? *International Journal of Radiation Biology, 82*(2), 69–76. doi:10.1080/09553000600599775 PMID:16546905

Young, K. S. (1998). *Caught in the Net.* New York: John Wiley & Sons.

Zeiter, J. M., & Dijk, D.-J. (2000). Sensitivity of the Human Circadian Pacemaker to Nocturnal Light: Melatonin Phase Resetting and Suppression. *The Journal of Physiology, 526*(3), 695–702. doi:10.1111/j.1469-7793.2000.00695.x PMID:10922269

Section 2
Technology–Focused Cyber Behavior

Chapter 4
Automatical Emotion Recognition Based on Daily Gait

Xiaoqian Liu
University of Chinese Academy of Sciences, China

Tingshao Zhu
University of Chinese Academy of Sciences, China

ABSTRACT

In this chapter, a kind of emotion recognition method based on gait using a customized smart bracelet with a built-in acceleration sensor was introduced in detail. The results showed that the classification accuracies of angry-neutral, happy-neutral, angry-happy, and angry-happy-neutral using the acceleration data of wrist are 91.3%, 88.5%, 88.5%, and 81.2%, respectively. Besides, the wearable devices and motion-sensing technology application in psychology research have been further discussed, and non-contact emotion identification and mental health monitoring based on offline behaviors were reviewed summarily.

INTRODUCTION

Brief Review of the Literature About the Relevance Between Emotion and Offline Behaviors

Emotion expression plays an important role in human communication, especially for Chinese, who saying the same words with different emotions may indicate different or even opposite meanings. Therefore, emotion recognition is a necessary

DOI: 10.4018/978-1-5225-7128-5.ch004

and valuable research for human-computer interaction applications. For example, if a service robot could automatically and accurately perceive and respond to the user's emotion (such as anger, happiness or sadness), it could correspondingly provide services with high-quality.

It was James, the father of American psychology, who gave the earliest definition of emotion. In his article published in 1884, he stated that emotion is a feeling of physical changes, which leads to emotional perception. Any emotion is associated with certain physical changes, including facial expression, muscle tension and visceral activities (James, 1884). Lazarus considered emotion is the combination of physiological disturbance, affection and action tendencies that do not need to show (Smith, 1990).

As early as the 19th century, Darwin suggested that different emotions correspond to certain gestures; for example, when a person is in anger, the body would be trembling and the chest swelling. Gunes et al. (2015) pointed out that emotion analysis based on physical expression (bodily expression) is of great significance, firstly, providing a long-distance emotion identification method, secondly, providing a vague emotion identification method. Wallbot (1998) found that the relationship between postures and arousal degree is more closely than that between postures and specific emotions; that is to say, a particular emotion does not necessarily correspond to a particular gesture, but is associated with emotional arousal level. The research by De Meijer showed that different types of emotion could be recognized based on the number, type, and intensity of gestures (Meijer, 1989). Crane and Gross (2007) indicated that emotions are associated with physical movements; they have identified velocity, cadence, head orientation and the motion range of shoulder and elbow as significant physical parameters which are affected by emotions. Several emotion recognition approaches have been proposed and to some degree progressed. According to the characteristics used in emotion recognition, those approaches could be classified as facial expressions-based, linguistics-based, physiological parameters-based, gestures-based and body motions-based (Peter & Beale, 2008).

Walking is one of the most common behaviors in people's daily life, and many psychological studies supported that emotions can be expressed in gait and recognized by human observers (Montepare et al., 1999; Janssen et al., 2008; Karg et al., 2010). Montepare et al. (1987) pointed out that the trait and diversity of walking style have different effects on emotions. Besides, sadness and anger are easier to be identified than neutral or happy emotions by human observers. In addition, Michalak et al. (2009) supported that sadness and depression could be reflected in walking.

In recent years, machine learning approaches have been applied in assistant therapeutic equipment for patients with gait disorders, gait-based identity recognition, and human motion identification (Kale et al., 2004; Man et al.., 2006). Prior to training model, dimension reduction is often considered. Principal Component Analysis

(PCA), Kernel Principal Component Analysis (KPCA), and Linear discriminant analysis (LDA) are all effective dimension reduction methods. Michelle and Robert employed PCA and Fourier Transformation to realize data reduction, and classified emotions into four utilizing Naive Bayes, 1-Nearest Neighbor and SVM, respectively. The best classification accuracy is 72% when using Naive Bayes (Karg et al., 2009). Janssen et al. (2008) figured out the emotion recognition method from walking based on artificial Neural Nets.

Outline of the Proposed Method

In this part, we will introduce a kind of emotion recognition method based on gait using a customized smart bracelet with a built-in acceleration sensor. The acceleration data for emotion recognition is obtained by a customized smart bracelet with a built-in acceleration sensor worn in people's wrist and ankle when person is walking. Our proposed method could recognize three different kinds of human emotions: happiness, anger and neutral state, with outstanding performance. The procedure consists of data collection, data preprocessing, and feature extraction and classification.

Data Collection

In order to obtain the acceleration data of ankle and wrist in walking when people is neutral, angry or happy, we used a customized smart bracelet with a built-in acceleration sensor, which can collect the acceleration data along x, y and z axis at five times per second. The collected data are recorded in memory in the form which could be read by the corresponding software.

We designed two experiments to collect the acceleration data under different emotions. The first experiment is to collect the acceleration data of ankle and wrist when a person is walking in neutral and angry state, respectively, and the second when the person is neutral and happy, respectively.

Together 123 healthy participants (59 males) were recruited. Each experiment is a two-phrase procedure. Take the first experiment as example. The processes are introduced in detail as following. In the first phrase, the participants were required to walk back and forth in the special rectangle (1-meter wide and 5-meter long) in two minutes, and the instructor recorded the start and end time of the walk on a Tablet. In the second phrase, the participants were required to watch a short emotional film clip, which could make the participants angry. After watching the clip, the participants were asked to walk back and forth in the special rectangle for about two minutes, and the instructor recorded the start and end time of the walk. In the second experiment, the two-phrase procedure is the same to the first experiment except that, in the second phrase, the participants would watch a different short emotional film clip, which could make the participants happy. The interval of the two experiments is at least four hours in order to avoid the situation that the film clip in the first experiment would affect the participants' emotion state in the second experiment.

Data Preprocessing

The acceleration data collected by the customized smart bracelet may include noise and blur because of vibration when the participants were walking. To improve the recognition rate, we deployed Moving Average Filter for each axis of acceleration data of both ankle and wrist to eliminate the noise and blur, and make the acceleration data smoother. Moving Average Filter is a well-known low-pass filter for discrete time signals, which is defined by:

$$\text{Output}\left[\text{i}\right] = \frac{1}{\omega}\sum_{j=0}^{\omega-1} Input\left[i+j\right]$$

The Input represents the original three-axis acceleration data collected by the smart bracelet with a built-in acceleration sensor, and the Output represents the export of Moving Average Filter. The parameter ω is the window size of the Moving Average Filter, which is the key to preprocess the original acceleration data. In this paper, we set $\omega \in \{3,5\}$.

Five records could be recorded per second by the customized smart bracelet and each record consists of the acceleration data in x, y and z axis. For one minutes, 300 records would be obtained. Considering the 300 records is huge and it is difficult for feature extraction in computing, we used a sliding window to divide the data into several slices with uniform size. In this paper, the size of the sliding window is set at 128, and the coverage ratio is 50%.

Feature Extraction and Classification

To figure out the hidden characteristics and universality of the obtained acceleration data and improve the classification accuracy, relevant features are extracted in the temporal domain, frequency domain and temporal-frequency domain, respectively, from the acceleration data.

Temporal-Domain Feature

For each axis, we calculated the skewness, kurtosis and standard deviation of the data. Besides, the correlation coefficient is calculated between every two axes. So there are four features extracted for each axis in the temporal domain totally.

Frequency-Domain Feature

Frequency domain feature is extracted by transforming the acceleration data from the temporal domain to the frequency domain. For each axis, we calculated the mean value and standard deviation of Power Spectral Density (PSD), respectively, as the frequency-domain features.

Temporal-Frequency Feature

As the features extracted in the temporal domain and frequency domain may be not comprehensive, accumulating studies are trying to combine both of the temporal domain and frequency domain information to extract temporal-frequency features, which could represent the characteristics of the temporal domain and frequency domain synchronously. Fast Fourier Transform (FFT) is an algorithm which could convert the signal from its original domain (often temporal or spatial) to another form of representation in the frequency domain. We conducted FFT for the temporal-domain features and selected the top 32 amplitude coefficients of FFT as the time-frequency features.

Feature Selection

For each axis, we extracted 38 features respectively from the temporal domain, frequency domain and temporal-frequency domain. Thus, we obtained $38 * 3$ features totally. Considering the curse of dimensionality and redundancy of data, efficient dimension reduction is required before the application of different classifiers. We deployed Principle Component Analysis (PCA) to realize feature selection.

Classification

We built classifiers using Support Vector Machine (SVM) for emotion recognition and the classification accuracy of all the above classifiers were calculated using standard 10-fold cross-validation.

Description of the Results

The performance of each classifier is evaluated according to the classification accuracy Q (which could also be called emotion recognition rate in this paper), which is defined by:

$$Q = \frac{The\,number\,of\,samples\,which\,are\,classified\,correctly}{The\,total\,number\,of\,samples}$$

And the emotion recognition results are shown in Table 1.

Brief Discussion

The results show that the accuracy of the emotion classification model is influenced by the value of ω. Under the same conditions, for each classifier, the classification result is better when using the acceleration data of wrist than that of ankle. The classification accuracies of angry-neutral, happy-neutral, angry-happy and angry-happy-neutral using the acceleration data of wrist are 91.3%, 88.5%, 88.5% and 81.2%, respectively. The results revealed that emotions would influence the style of gait.

REVIEW OF MAJOR AREAS

Offline Behaviors Data Acquisition Methods Based on Wearable Devices and Motion-Sensing Technology

Offline behaviors can be represented by the acceleration data of the key joints of the body, which could be recorded through contact or non-contact equipments.

Table 1. The emotion recognition results with SVM

ω	Acceleration data	Q			
		Angry-Neutral	Happy-Neutral	Happy-Angry	Happy-Neutral-Angry
$\omega = 3$	Ankle	72.50%	80.9%	79.1%	68.6%
	Wrist	86.0%	88.5%	88.5%	79.6%
$\omega = 5$	Ankle	71.3%	71.7%	71.1%	62.3%
	Wrist	91.3%	78.2%	82.5%	81.2%

Note: ω, the window size of the Moving Average Filter; SVM, Support Vector Machine.

For contact equipments, some wearable devices such as smart watch, smart bracelet and smart phone could record three-dimensional (3D) acceleration data of wrist and transfer the data to a computing device (Figure 1).

For non-contact equipments, we could use Microsoft Kinect to capture 3D motion information of 25 key joints of the body. The Microsoft Kinect is a low-cost, portable, camera-based sensor system, with the official software development kit (SDK) (Gaukrodger et al., 2013; Stone et al., 2015; Clark et al., 2013). As a marker-free motion capture system, Kinect could continuously monitor 3D body movement patterns, and is a practical option to develop an inexpensive, widely available motion recognition system in human daily walks (Figure 2).

Wearable Devices and Motion-Sensing Technology Applications in Psychology and Emotion Recognition Based on Offline Behaviors

Emotion is the mental experience with high intensity and high hedonic content (pleasure/displeasure) (Cabanac, 2002), which deeply affects our daily behaviors by regulating individual's motivation (Lang, Bradley & Cuthbert, 1998), social interaction (Lopes et al., 2005) and cognitive processes (Forgas, 1995). Walking is a most common daily offline behavior, which is easily observed, and the body motion and style of walking have been found by psychologists to reflect the walker's emotional states.

Figure 1. Smart phone and smart bracelet

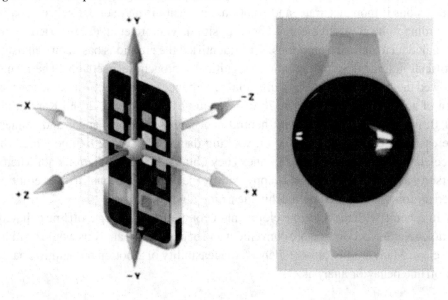

Figure 2. Stick figure and location of body joint centers recorded by Kinect

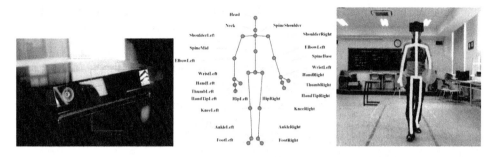

Many researchers have paid close attention to gait analysis. Frank et al. (2011) theoretically demonstrated that two purposes could be achieved through gait analysis; one is to identify different activities, and the other is to identify people. They put a mobile phone into a front pocket of pants and recorded the acceleration information by the mobile phone, followed by using SVM algorithm to distinguish different activities, such as walking, running, jumping, and jogging. Clark et al. (2012) evaluated the feasibility of using Kinect for motion analysis. They compared the performance of Kinect with that of 3D camera, and the correlation coefficient of two set results is above 0.90.

Many studies have found that emotion identification could be realized through offline behavior analysis. Ekman et al. (1967) recruited 50 college students and identified six kinds of emotions including fear, happiness, surprise, anger, disgust and contempt according to the features of body acts, body position, facial expressions and head orientation. In that study, they found that judging emotions by facial expressions is more accurate, and emotional intensity is more effectively evaluated according to head orientation and body position. Venture et al. (2014) tried to use the gait data to describe emotions. They identified the emotions based on gait using artificial judgment and automatic recognition approach, respectively. The results showed that the accuracy rate of artificial judgment can reach 90%, and the average rate of automatic recognition is 78%. Two studies (Karg et al., 2009; Karg et al., 2010) found that compared with neutral and happy emotions, anger and sadness are easier to be identified based on walking data. Cui et al. (2016) collected the acceleration data using a smart phone. They obtained the acceleration data when a person was in neutral, angry and happy state, respectively, and constructed a emotion recognition model based on machine learning algorithm.

In general, with the rapid development of computer technology, offline behavior data acquisition becomes more convenient and behavior data analysis would be more efficient. Many studies have evidenced the feasibility of emotion recognition based on offline behavior analysis.

FUTURE RESEARCH DIRECTIONS

A Follow-Up Research With Mental Health Monitoring Based on Daily Gait

Accelerometer is widely used in wearable devices because of its advantages of small size, low cost, low power consumption and high sensitivity. The behavior data collected through the acceleration sensor could be used for the movement signal analysis and motion recognition. Motion recognition can be used in many applications, such as health monitoring and exercise monitoring. In addition, motion-sensing technology is another popular means of acquiring behavior data, with the biggest advantage of non-contact motion information collection, being more suitable for daily health monitoring.

Researchers have found that there is a certain correlation between offline behaviors and mental health. In early 1921, Kraepelin pointed out that behavior changes should be taken as one of the core symptoms of mental health (Kraepelin, 1921). Compared with other offline behaviors, the pace is easy to measure and is a reliable and stable variable for the assessment of patients suffering from mental illness. Fritz and Lusardi (2009) took walking speed as an effective predictor of health.

With the help of intelligent wearable devices and non-contact somatosensory equipments, behavior data could be collected in real-time. Through establishing the association between mental health indicators and behavioral features, we could construct the automatic mental health prediction system.

Diagnosis of Depression Based on Gait Analysis

Depression is a serious mental illness with depression as the core and accompanied by multiple symptoms. The symptoms of depressed patients are diverse, and different subjects may exhibit different trait combinations or different degrees of symptoms (Schrijvers, Hulstijn & Sabbe, 2008), thus increasing the difficulty of diagnosis.

Based on the existing research findings, behavioral assessment could be used as an effective tool for screening and treatment of depressed patients. Lemke et al. (2000) compared the differences of gait between depressed patients and healthy individuals, and found that compared with healthy people, patients with depression were with significantly slower pace, shorter step and less time of feet support and cycle. Sanders et al. (2012) found that although the pace is negatively correlated with depressive symptoms, the pace has significant predictive value for depressive symptoms of male depressed patients.

The smart phones, wearable devices and somatosensory devices could obtain the daily activities information of patients with depression, and automatically calculate and analyze their depression tendency and emotional state, which can provide more diagnostic value for doctors, and also help patients understand their own mental state, playing a helpful role for the diagnosis and treatment of mental illnesses.

Non-Contact Emotion Identification and Mental Health Monitoring Based on More Offline Behaviors

Mental Health Monitoring Based on Facial Expressions

Being depressed is the core symptom of depression, and facial expressions are the most intuitive for observation. A previous study (Berenbaum, 1992) showed that the facial expression recognition is a better method to identify the mood of patients with mental diseases than questionnaires, because a questionnaire can only distinguish between patients and ordinary people but not between different diseases, and emotion recognition can present differences between different patients. Considering the types of facial expressions, patients with depression had less happy expression and lower emotional intensity (Renneberg, Heyn, Gebhard & Bachmann, 2005). Most of depressed patients have more sadness and disgust and less happiness than mild depression (Ekman & Rosenberg, 1997). The study of Peham et al. (2015) found that the real smile of depressed group was significantly reduced compared with healthy group.

Kinect can capture the motion information of as much as 1,347 key facial points (Figure 3), and give real-time feedback of the depth information of each key point in the form of (X, Y, Z) three-dimensional coordinates. We can record the changes of facial expressions by Kinect, and construct a depression tendency prediction model based on the facial motion information.

Mental Health Monitoring Based on Voices

People's discourse is greatly influenced by their emotional state. Evolution enables people to perceive the emotional state of the speaker through his/her tone. For the machine, if we can input the corresponding phonetic features related to emotions, we can identify the emotion in the speech. Many audio features should be extracted first to build the mapping between voices and emotions or mental health status. Some studies have proposed lots of audio features, which could be classified into three categories: (1) prosodic features, such as pronunciation duration, pitch, amplitude and speed; (2) spectral features, such as Mel-frequency cepstral coefficients, spectral features change parameters, and periodic parameters; (3) quality characteristics, such as channel, pronunciation accuracy, harmonic to noise ratio, and relative density.

Figure 3. Facial key point tracking based on Kinect

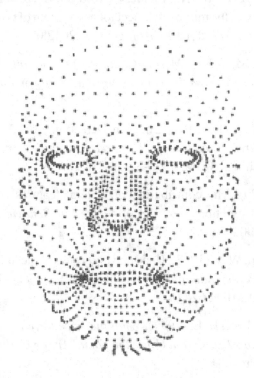

Then, some classical machine learning algorithms can be used to build the emotion classification models and mental health prediction models.

Depression recognition based on audio and facial features own some advantages in practical applications. First of all, the patient does not need to complete difficult or time-consuming tasks, and only needs to record the conversation and facial movements during his or her consultation. Secondly, the means of data recording is non-contacted, which helps to obtain the nature and true information.

REFERENCES

Berenbaum, H. (1992). Posed facial expressions of emotion in schizophrenia and depression. *Psychological Medicine*, *22*(4), 929–937. doi:10.1017/S0033291700038502 PMID:1362618

Cabanac, M. (2002). What is emotion? *Behavioural Processes*, *60*(2), 69–83. doi:10.1016/S0376-6357(02)00078-5 PMID:12426062

Clark, R. A., Pua, Y. H., Fortin, K., Ritchie, C., Webster, K. E., Denehy, L., & Bryant, A. L. (2012). Validity of the microsoft kinect for assessment of postural control. *Gait & Posture*, *36*(3), 372–377. doi:10.1016/j.gaitpost.2012.03.033 PMID:22633015

Crane, E., & Gross, M. (2007). *Motion Capture and Emotion: Affect Detection in Whole Body Movement*. In *Affective Computing and Intelligent Interaction*. Springer Berlin Heidelberg.

Cui, L., Li, S., & Zhu, T. (2016). Emotion Detection from Natural Walking. In *International Conference on Human Centered Computing* (pp.23-33). Springer International Publishing. 10.1007/978-3-319-31854-7_3

de Meijer, M. (1989). The contribution of general features of body movement to the attribution of emotions. *Journal of Nonverbal Behavior*, *13*(4), 247–268. doi:10.1007/BF00990296

Ekman, P., & Friesen, W. V. (1967). Head and body cues in the judgment of emotion: A reformulation. *Perceptual and Motor Skills*, *24*(3), 711–724. doi:10.2466/pms.1967.24.3.711 PMID:5622764

Ekman, P., & Rosenberg, E. L. (1997). *What the Face Reveals: Basic and Applied Studies of Spontaneous Expression Using the Facial Action Coding System (FACS)*. Oxford University Press.

Forgas, J. P. (1995). Mood and judgment: The affect infusion model (AIM). *Psychological Bulletin*, *117*(1), 39–66. doi:10.1037/0033-2909.117.1.39 PMID:7870863

Frank, J., Mannor, S., & Precup, D. (2011). *Activity Recognition with Mobile Phones*. In *Machine Learning and Knowledge Discovery in Databases*. Springer Berlin Heidelberg. doi:10.1007/978-3-642-23808-6_44

Fritz, S., & Lusardi, M. (2009). White paper: "walking speed: the sixth vital sign. *Journal of Geriatric Physical Therapy*, *32*(2), 46. doi:10.1519/00139143-200932020-00002 PMID:20039582

James, W. (1884). What Is an Emotion? *Mind*, *9*(34), 188–205. doi:10.1093/mind/os-IX.34.188

Janssen, D., Schöllhorn, W. I., Lubienetzki, J., Fölling, K., Kokenge, H., & Davids, K. (2008). Recognition of emotions in gait patterns by means of artificial neural nets. *Journal of Nonverbal Behavior*, *32*(2), 79–92. doi:10.100710919-007-0045-3

Kale, A., Sundaresan, A., Rajagopalan, A. N., Cuntoor, N. P., Roy-Chowdhury, A. K., & Krüger, V. (2004). Identification of humans using gait. *IEEE Transactions on Image Processing, 13*(9), 1163-1173.

Karg, M., Jenke, R., Kühnlenz, K., & Buss, M. (2009). A Two-fold PCA-Approach for Inter-Individual Recognition of Emotions in Natural Walking. In *Machine Learning and Data Mining in Pattern Recognition, International Conference, Mldm 2009, Leipzig, Germany, July 2009, Poster Proceedings* (pp. 51-61). DBLP.

Karg, M., Kühnlenz, K., & Buss, M. (2010). Recognition of affect based on gait patterns. *IEEE Transactions on Systems Man & Cybernetics Part B Cybernetics, 40*(4), 1050-61.

Kraepelin, E. (1921). Dementia praecox and paraphrenia. *The Journal of Nervous and Mental Disease, 54*(54), 384. doi:10.1097/00005053-192110000-00104

Lang, P. J., Bradley, M. M., & Cuthbert, B. N. (1998). Emotion, motivation, and anxiety: Brain mechanisms and psychophysiology. *Biological Psychiatry, 44*(12), 1248–1263. doi:10.1016/S0006-3223(98)00275-3 PMID:9861468

Lemke, M. R., Wendorff, T., Mieth, B., Buhl, K., & Linnemann, M. (2000). Spatiotemporal gait patterns during over ground locomotion in major depression compared with healthy controls. *Journal of Psychiatric Research, 34*(4–5), 277–283. doi:10.1016/S0022-3956(00)00017-0 PMID:11104839

Lopes, P. N., Salovey, P., Côté, S., Beers, M., & Petty, R. E. (2005). Emotion regulation abilities and the quality of social interaction. *Emotion (Washington, D.C.), 5*(1), 113–118. doi:10.1037/1528-3542.5.1.113 PMID:15755224

Man, J., & Bhanu, B. (2006). Individual recognition using gait energy image. *IEEE Transactions on Pattern Analysis and Machine Intelligence, 28*(2), 316–322. doi:10.1109/TPAMI.2006.38 PMID:16468626

Michalak, J., Troje, N. F., Fischer, J., Vollmar, P., Heidenreich, T., & Schulte, D. (2009). Embodiment of sadness and depression--gait patterns associated with dysphoric mood. *Psychosomatic Medicine, 71*(5), 580–587. doi:10.1097/PSY.0b013e3181a2515c PMID:19414617

Montepare, J., Koff, E., Zaitchik, D., & Albert, M. (1999). The use of body movements and gestures as cues to emotions in younger and older adults. *Journal of Nonverbal Behavior, 23*(2), 133–152. doi:10.1023/A:1021435526134

Montepare, J. M., Goldstein, S. B., & Clausen, A. (1987). The identification of emotions from gait information. *Journal of Nonverbal Behavior*, *11*(1), 33–42. doi:10.1007/BF00999605

Peham, D., Bock, A., Schiestl, C., Huber, E., Zimmermann, J., Kratzer, D., ... Benecke, C. (2015). Facial Affective Behavior in Mental Disorder. *Journal of Nonverbal Behavior*, *39*(4), 371–396. doi:10.100710919-015-0216-6

Peter, C., & Beale, R. (2008). *Affect and Emotion in Human-Computer Interaction*. Springer Berlin Heidelberg. doi:10.1007/978-3-540-85099-1

Renneberg, B., Heyn, K., Gebhard, R., & Bachmann, S. (2005). Facial expression of emotions in borderline personality disorder and depression. *Journal of Behavior Therapy and Experimental Psychiatry*, *36*(3), 183–196. doi:10.1016/j.jbtep.2005.05.002 PMID:15950175

Sanders, J. B., Bremmer, M. A., Deeg, D. J. H., & Beekman, A. T. F. (2012). Do Depressive Symptoms and Gait Speed Impairment Predict Each Other's Incidence? A 16-Year Prospective Study in the Community. *Journal of the American Geriatrics Society*, *60*(9), 1673–1680. doi:10.1111/j.1532-5415.2012.04114.x PMID:22905679

Schrijvers, D., Hulstijn, W., & Sabbe, B. G. C. (2008). Psychomotor symptoms in depression: A diagnostic, pathophysiological and therapeutic tool. *Journal of Affective Disorders*, *109*(1–2), 1–20. doi:10.1016/j.jad.2007.10.019 PMID:18082896

Smith, C. A., & Lazarus, R. S. (1990). Emotion and adaptation. In L. A. Pervin (Ed.), *Handbook of Personality: Theory and Research* (pp. 609–636). New York: Guilford. Retrieved from http://people.ict.usc.edu/~gratch/CSCI534/Readings/Smith&Lazarus90.pdf

Venture, G., Kadone, H., Zhang, T., Grèzes, J., Berthoz, A., & Hicheur, H. (2014). Recognizing emotions conveyed by human gait. *International Journal of Social Robotics*, *6*(4), 621–632. doi:10.100712369-014-0243-1

Wallbott, H. G. (1998). Bodily expression of emotion. *European Journal of Social Psychology*, *28*(6), 879–896. doi:10.1002/(SICI)1099-0992(1998110)28:6<879::AID-EJSP901>3.0.CO;2-W

Chapter 5
Psychological Profiles Prediction Using Online Social Network Behavior Data

Nan Zhao
University of Chinese Academy of Sciences, China

Tingshao Zhu
University of Chinese Academy of Sciences, China

ABSTRACT

As today's online social network (OSN) has become a part of our daily life, the huge amount of OSN behavior data could be a new data source to detect and understand individual differences, especially on mental aspects. Based on the findings revealing the relationships between personality and online behavior records, the authors tried to extract relevant features from both OSN usage behaviors and OSN textual posts, and trained models by machine learning methods to predict the OSN user's personality. The results showed fairly good predictive accuracy in Chinese OSN. The authors also reviewed the same kind of studies in more pervasive OSNs, focusing on what behavior data are used in predicting psychological profiles and how to use them effectively. It is foreseeable that more types of OSN data could be utilized in recognizing more psychological indices, and the predictive accuracy would be further improved. Meanwhile, the model-predicted psychological profiles are becoming an option of measurements in psychological studies, when the classical methods are not applicable.

DOI: 10.4018/978-1-5225-7128-5.ch005

INTRODUCTION

The Relationship Between Personality and Online Social Network (OSN) Behaviors: Why Predicting Personality Through OSN Data Is Possible

Besides the innumerable conveniences brought by the internet, the cyberspace also provides us an unprecedented window through which we are able to see the disparity among many millions of individuals. When we mention the difference among individuals, we are usually talking about personality, which is the visible consistent behavior patterns and interpersonal processes originating within the individual (Burger, 2008), as well as the internal distinct traits of cognition and emotion (Mischel, Shoda & Ayduk, 2007). To a great extent, it is the different personalities of internet users which lead to their various, individualized online behaviors.

There have been a lot of studies revealing the correlations between personalities and variety of online behaviors. Baker and Moore (2008) investigated the blogging behavior of Myspace users and reported that the intending bloggers scored higher on psychological distress, self-blame, and venting and scored lower on social integration. Kosinski et al. (2012) found psychologically meaningful relationships between personality and preferences to website and website categories. Psychologists have revealed that the personality characteristics of internet users were relevant to the overall pattern of choosing online services (Hamburger & Ben-Artzi, 2000), as well as the usage of certain functions or aspects of the internet, such as using Wikipedia (Amichai–Hamburger et al., 2008), online dating (Hall, 2010), playing online game (Charlton & Danforth, 2010), and online shopping (Huang & Yang, 2010).

Along with the enormous popularity of Online Social Networks (OSN) in recent years, such as Facebook, Twitter, Instagram and LinkedIn, many researchers put their attention on the OSN behaviors, partly because the OSN services often integrated many functions into a single platform and the use of OSN is bound with personal identity. Series of studies revealing the relationships between the users' personality and their OSN behaviors largely enhanced our knowledge about how online behavior data reflecting personality characteristics. Correa, Hinsley and De Zuniga (2010) found that the Big-Five personality scores could predict the engagement of social media. Gosling et al. (2011) found that the Big-Five personality traits were correlated with both self-reported Facebook-related behaviors and observable profile information, and OSN users extended their offline personalities into the domains of OSNs. Lee, Ahn and Kim (2014) reported that the user's personality may influence several aspects of Facebook usage, including photo uploads, status updates, and number of friends at Facebook Wall, and *Like*, *Comment*, and *Share* at Facebook News Feed. Some other researchers paid attention to the content posted on OSN, and found that the topics updated on Facebook reflected personality characters including Big-Five dimensions, self-esteem and narcissism (Marshall, Lefringhausen & Ferenczi, 2015).

The large amount of empirical evidences of the relationships between personality (and some other psychological profiles) and online behavior records clearly suggests the possibility of recognizing the user's personality through their online behavior data. However, it is not easy to make judgment on the individual's characteristics as to disclose the correlations between their personality and their behavioral indices. Schwartz et al. (2013) analyzed about 700 million words and phrases from Facebook massages, and calculated the correlations between more than 50 different LIWC (Linguistic Inquiry and Word Count, Pennebaker et al., 2015) categories and Big-Five personality. There showed many significant correlations between language use on Facebook and personality, confirming the connections between them, but the correlation coefficients were fairly low, which means that each single behavioral index (LIWC category) cannot effectively predict personality by itself. So one plausible idea seems to be integrating many personality-relevant online behavioral parameters into a predictive model, as the common practice in the big data mining.

Outline of the Methods

In this part, we will introduce our exploration on predicting the OSN user's personality based on their online behavior data. We extracted useful features from the original OSN records, and then trained and tested the models which could calculate the personality scores based on the OSN behavioral features. We chose Big-Five personality traits (Costa & McCrae, 1992) as the goal of prediction, as it is one of the most widely accepted personality structure in academia. The original OSN data we used was collected from Sina Weibo, which is the most popular public, twitter-like Chinese OSN, and had more than 300 million users till 2014.

Data Collection

We randomly sent invitation through Sina Weibo platform to active Weibo users (with more than 500 posts), inviting them to give us the permission to download their digital records on Weibo, and finish the Big Five Inventory (BFI, Gosling, Rentfrow & Swann, 2003). For the Weibo usage data (the record of using behavior), such as the information of the user's profile, the timeline and categories of updates, the user's tags, the list of followings and followers, etc., we collected them by calling APIs provided by Sina Weibo. For the text of Weibo posts, we downloaded them through web crawlers. Both these Weibo usage records and Weibo posts are public by default and everyone is able see them on the Weibo platform without authorization of the publisher. Finally, 547 active Weibo users were included in building the predictive model based on the Weibo usage data (Li et al., 2014), and 1,552 active Weibo users were included in building the predictive model based on the Weibo post data (Liu & Zhu, 2016).

Feature Extraction

From Weibo usage data, we extracted features from two aspects. The Static features refer to those changing little over time, including: (a) profiles, (b) self-expression behaviors, (c) privacy settings and (d) interpersonal behaviors. The Dynamic features refer to those obviously changing over time, such as the post updates, the @ mentions, the use of apps, etc. The Dynamic features of each Weibo user could be different during different lengths of the observation time, and we extracted these features in a series of observation period from 0 day to 120 days (for more details, see Li et al., 2014).

For Weibo post data, a simple way of feature extraction is by the language processing tool LIWC (Pennebaker et al., 2015), which could count the frequency of words of more than 80 psychologically or linguistically meaningful categories. We used a simplified Chinese version of LIWC (Zhao et al., 2016) to change the Weibo post text of each user into a matrix, representing the score of each category during each observation period (by week). To better extract effective features from Weibo post data, we then conducted unsupervised feature learning based on Stacked Autoencoders, and constructed objective and comprehensive representation of Weibo language using from the original matrix (for more details, see Liu & Zhu, 2016).

Model Training

In order recognize Weibo user's personality traits based on the Weibo usage data, we trained SVM models to distinguish the high-scoring and low-scoring individuals, and PaceRegression models to calculate trait scores of each dimension, through the method of 5-fold cross validation. With the extracted Weibo linguistic features vectors by LIWC and deep-learning processing, we used linear regression algorithm to train the model predicting the scores of personality traits, by 10-fold cross validation.

Description of the Results

To estimate the predictive models based on Weibo usage data, we used accuracy estimation to evaluate SVM models. As a classification model, the expected accuracy of a baseline model was 50%. For PaceRegression Models, we calculated the Pearson correlation coefficient between predicted scores and questionnaire scores, and relative absolute error (RAE) which presented a ratio of mean absolute error (MAE) between established model and baseline model. Results of model evaluation were shown in Figure 1, which indicated changes in values of accuracy, correlation coefficient and RAE on each personality dimension for different lengths of observation period. The green lines represented the average estimation of evaluation results of all 8 non-zero-day models.

The efficiency of the personality prediction models based on the Weibo post data was also estimated by the Pearson correlation coefficient between the predicted scores and the questionnaire scores. To compare the different ways of feature extraction and selection, we utilized five different kinds of attributes to train the personality prediction model: the attributes produced with the help of LIWC without feature selection (Attribute 1), the attributes selected from Attribute 1 by Principal Component Analysis (PCA) (Attribute2), by Stepwise (Attribute 3), and by Lasso (Attribute 4), and the feature vector obtained through Stacked Antoencoders (SAE) (Attribute SAE). Table 1 shows the correlation coefficients (r) for the linear regression model using each attribute on each trait of Big-Five personality.

Figure 1. The results of evaluating the personality prediction models based on the Weibo usage data (Li et al., 2014)

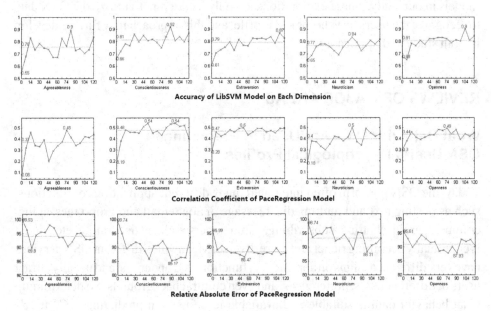

Table 1. The results of evaluating the personality prediction models based on the Weibo post data

Attributes	r_A	r_C	r_E	r_N	r_O
Attribute 1 (Original)	0.101	0.185	0.104	0.083	0.181
Attribute 2 (PCA)	0.111	0.217	0.105	0.124	0.187
Attribute 3 (Stepwise)	0.122	0.264	0.170	0.130	0.225
Attribute 4 (Lasso)	0.121	0.207	0.079	0.093	0.114
Attribute SAE	0.258	0.400	0.350	0.325	0.424

(Liu & Zhu, 2016).

Brief Discussion

The results of building and testing personality prediction models based on Weibo records show the feasibility of using OSN data, to predict the user's personality. As shown in Figure 1, the accuracies of distinguishing high-scoring and low-scoring individuals achieved around 0.8, and the calculated personality trait scores were moderately correlated with the questionnaire scores. In Table 1, the correlation coefficients between predictive results based on the Attribute SAE and the questionnaire scores were also achieved moderate level. Both usage records and textual posts could be used to extract effective features and train the predictive models in our study. These explorations are only an attempt to utilize the OSN data to recognize the user's psychological profile, and this approach may further develop in both study and application.

REVIEWS OF MAJOR AREAS

What Behavior Data Are Used in Predicting OSN User's Psychological Profiles

Today, the OSN platform often integrated many different applications or functions, such as posting text and multimedia, message dialog, email and group messaging, comment, group chatting, subscribing, gaming, personalized decorating, etc., and it is continually becoming richer and more diverse. Meanwhile, different OSN services have very different designs on appearance, function, and openness, and usually attract users of different goals, preferences, and even cultural backgrounds. So determining what behavior data is suitable and available to be used in predicting OSN user's psychological profiles could be a complex issue, and the behavior parameters used in published studies also showed the variety and complexity.

The textual expressions on OSN is an important data resource reflecting the users' psychological profiles. Schwartz et al. (2013) made use of the text of about 15.4 million tweets to predict Big-Five personality traits, and similar data resources were also utilized in some other predictive studies based on Twitter (Skowron et al., 2016; Liu et al., 2016). Liu, Wang and Jiang (2016) used the Facebook status messages to build personality prediction models, which was also included in Tandera et al.'s (2017) personality prediction system as a data resource.

The OSN usage behaviors is another important data resource which have been used in predicting the user's psychological profiles. Bachrach et al. (2012) used Facebook usage profiles such as the size and density of their friendship network, number uploaded photos, number of events attended, etc., to predict user's personality. Kosinski et al. (2013) and Youyou et al. (2015) developed predictive models of personality traits using Facebook likes. In Tandera et al.'s (2017) study of constructing a Facebook-based personality prediction system, the connections among users were also included serving personality prediction as SNA (Social Network Analysis) feature. When Baik et al. (2016) built the model to predict the Facebook user's personality traits related to consumer behavior, both usage actions such as "Like" and the friendship relationships were used as the data source.

Besides text, increasing amount of multimedia materials are posted by the OSN users today. The photos on OSN have become another important data source in building prediction models. Eftekhar, Fullwood and Morris (2014) tried to utilize both Facebook photos and photo-related activities to predict the Big-Five personality traits of users. As Liu et al. (2016) reported, based on more than 66,000 Twitter users' profile pictures, their personality could be predicted with robust accuracy. In Skowron et al.'s (2016) study of building personality prediction models with fusing social media cues from both Twitter and Instagram, the posted photos on Instagram were well utilized.

How to Use the OSN Behavior Data Effectively in Predicting Psychological Profiles

Face to the massive data reflecting the OSN user's psychological profiles, a crucial step is to convert the original data into the data set which could be directly input into the predictive model. Ideally this conversion should retain the information relevant to the target psychological index as much as possible, and reduce the irrelevant noise, which is the process of feature extraction and selection.

The techniques of natural language processing are utilized to extract effective features from the textual OSN data. The close-vocabulary tools which containing priori human-judged word category could be a simple and effective choice. For example, LIWC has been used in several published studies of model prediction as the feature extraction tool for OSN texts (e.g., Liu et al., 2016; Liu, Wang & Jiang, 2016; Tandera et al., 2017), probably because it could cover the psychologically meaningful expressions fairly well. Other tools such as SPLICE (Structured Programming for Linguistic Cue Extraction, Tandera et al., 2017) and ANEW (Affective Norms for English Words dictionary, Skowron et al., 2016) have also been conducted in processing the textual data. Moreover, Schwartz et al. (2013) proposed an open-vocabulary approach for OSN textual feature extraction, which is more data-driven and does not rely on priori designed lexicon. In some other studies, the OSN text was firstly transformed into some other parameters, such as emotion feature, and then put into predictive models (Lewenberg, Bachrach & Volkova, 2015). The algorithms of deep learning were also applied in some study (Liu & Zhu, 2016) to better extract and select features from the textual data.

Some records of the OSN usage behavior are numeric, such as the number of friends /followings/followers, the number of photos, the number of status updates, etc. (Bachrach et al., 2012; Li et al., 2014), which could be directly used as the feature vector for model predicting. Some other OSN usage has to be changed into the form that is suitable for further analysis. For example, Facebook Like is the expression of positive association between the user and variety of online and offline objects, and represents one of the most generic kinds of digital footprint. Kosinski et al. (2013) and Youyou et al. (2015) constructed a sparse user–Like matrix, whose entries were set to 1 if there existed an association between a user and a Like and 0 otherwise. Then the dimensionality of this matrix was reduced through singular-value decomposition (SVD) and the top 100 SVD components were selected as the features used by the personality prediction model. Sometimes the time-sequential information was also considered in feature extraction from the OSN usage data. Calculate the statistic variables in different time interval could be a way to include such information (Li et al., 2014). Some other study reported to use Fast Fourier Transform (FFT) to extract the time-sequential features of OSN data (Liu & Zhu, 2016).

In some case, the researchers manually coded the photos achieved from OSN platform into different categories depending on the content, and used the numeric category statistics as the feature for prediction (Eftekhar, Fullwood & Morris, 2014). In some other studies, both physical and content attributes of images were included in feature extraction. In Skowron et al.'s study (2016), the features of Instagram images included Pleasure-Arousal-Dominance (PAD) rating, brightness, saturation, hue-related and content-based features such as person's face or full body. And the features extracted by Liu et al. (2016) from Twitter images included color, image composition, image demographics, facial presentation, and Facial expressions recognized by Face++ (Zhou et al., 2013).

FUTURE RESEARCH DIRECTIONS

Continuous Improvement in Prediction: More Exploitable Data, More Psychological Indices, and Higher Accuracy

Recognizing psychological profiles such as personality could have great value in both study and practice, which is driving researchers to make use of more OSN data, predict more psychological indices and achieve higher predictive accuracy. The rapidly developing OSN products and social networking ecosystem also propose the requirement of new methods and techniques to expand the scope of exploitable data, as the functions and privacy settings are in the continuous changing. As the model prediction method, the accuracy is determined by not only the effectiveness of feature extraction, but also the capability of the algorithm for model training. The future development of machine learning algorithms would help to increase the predictive accuracy as well as the applicability of the models.

Besides personality characters, there have been some other psychological indices which were predicted by models based on OSN data. For example, Lewenberg, Bachrach and Volkova (2015) used the tweets data to predict the topics or areas the user interested in. He et al. (2014) predicted Facebook user's self-monitoring skills using their textual posts. Hao et al. (2014) and Chen et al. (2017) built models predicting the OSN user's subjective well-being based on their online expressions. The mental health status could also been reflected on the OSN and been recognized with the help of predictive model. De Choudhury et al. (2013) tried to predict the depression scores measured by CES-D of Twitter users based on both their usage behavior and their textual expressions.

One Important Step Forward: The Psychological Study Based on the Model Predicted Psychological Indices

The approach that using OSN data to predict the psychological profiles of the OSN users provides new angles in the domain of psychological studies. One view is that it would help psychology become a more predictive science, rather than near-totally focusing on explaining the causes of behavior (Yarkoni & Westfall, 2017). Another thought could be: as we are able to get knowledge of individual's characters or mental status just through their OSN data, could we use these predicted variables to serve the exploration on the causes of behavior, just as the questionnaire measurements. In other words, could the model prediction be a new method of psychometrics proving reliable and valid psychological parameters?

As shown in many cases above, in the published studies the correlations between the predicted value and the values achieved by other classical methods of measurement (usually questionnaire) were usually in the moderate level. This level is not more than the acceptable reliability of psychological scales. And the OSN as a data resource also has some inherent limitations, for example, it is impossible to cover the population who does not use certain OSN platform. Such inherent limitations of OSN may be not negligible in case of explaining the causes of behavior. However, in some conditions where the other methods are not applicable, using predictive model as the tool of measurement could be a helpful attempt. A good example is Youyou et al.'s study (2017), which tested their research hypothesis based on analyzing the model predicted personality scores. Through this method, they successfully eliminated the reference-group effect which always exists as a crucial confounding factor when using the questionnaire method. Another example is Liu et al.'s study (2018), which revealed the short-term change of mental health status of the domestic violence victims. Since the happening of a domestic violence cannot be foreseen, it used to be impossible to measure the victim's mental health status in matched time before and after the domestic violence incident. In this study, they utilized the model predicted mental health indices, and realized the before/after measurement perfectly matching the time of incident.

REFERENCES

Amichai–Hamburger, Y., Lamdan, N., Madiel, R., & Hayat, T. (2008). Personality characteristics of Wikipedia members. *Cyberpsychology & Behavior, 11*(6), 679–681. doi:10.1089/cpb.2007.0225 PMID:18954273

Bachrach, Y., Kosinski, M., Graepel, T., Kohli, P., & Stillwell, D. (2012, June). Personality and patterns of Facebook usage. In *Proceedings of the 4th Annual ACM Web Science Conference* (pp. 24-32). ACM. 10.1145/2380718.2380722

Baik, J., Lee, K., Lee, S., Kim, Y., & Choi, J. (2016). Predicting personality traits related to consumer behavior using SNS analysis. *New Review of Hypermedia and Multimedia, 22*(3), 189–206. doi:10.1080/13614568.2016.1152313

Baker, J. R., & Moore, S. M. (2008). Distress, coping, and blogging: Comparing new Myspace users by their intention to blog. *Cyberpsychology & Behavior, 11*(1), 81–85. doi:10.1089/cpb.2007.9930 PMID:18275317

Burger, J. M. (2008). *Personality* (7th ed.). Belmont: Thomson Higher Education.

Charlton, J. P., & Danforth, I. D. (2010). Validating the distinction between computer addiction and engagement: Online game playing and personality. *Behaviour & Information Technology, 29*(6), 601–613. doi:10.1080/01449290903401978

Chen, L., Gong, T., Kosinski, M., Stillwell, D., & Davidson, R. L. (2017). Building a profile of subjective well-being for social media users. *PLoS One, 12*(11), e0187278. doi:10.1371/journal.pone.0187278 PMID:29135991

Correa, T., Hinsley, A. W., & De Zuniga, H. G. (2010). Who interacts on the Web?: The intersection of users' personality and social media use. *Computers in Human Behavior, 26*(2), 247–253. doi:10.1016/j.chb.2009.09.003

Costa, P. T., & MacCrae, R. R. (1992). *Revised NEO personality inventory (NEO PI-R) and NEO five-factor inventory (NEO-FFI): Professional manual*. Psychological Assessment Resources, Incorporated.

Eftekhar, A., Fullwood, C., & Morris, N. (2014). Capturing personality from Facebook photos and photo-related activities: How much exposure do you need? *Computers in Human Behavior, 37*, 162–170. doi:10.1016/j.chb.2014.04.048

Gosling, S. D., Augustine, A. A., Vazire, S., Holtzman, N., & Gaddis, S. (2011). Manifestations of personality in online social networks: Self-reported Facebook-related behaviors and observable profile information. *Cyberpsychology, Behavior, and Social Networking, 14*(9), 483–488. doi:10.1089/cyber.2010.0087 PMID:21254929

Gosling, S. D., Rentfrow, P. J., & Swann, W. B. Jr. (2003). A very brief measure of the Big-Five personality domains. *Journal of Research in Personality, 37*(6), 504–528. doi:10.1016/S0092-6566(03)00046-1

Hall, J. A., Park, N., Song, H., & Cody, M. J. (2010). Strategic misrepresentation in online dating: The effects of gender, self-monitoring, and personality traits. *Journal of Social and Personal Relationships, 27*(1), 117–135. doi:10.1177/0265407509349633

Hamburger, Y. A., & Ben-Artzi, E. (2000). The relationship between extraversion and neuroticism and the different uses of the Internet. *Computers in Human Behavior, 16*(4), 441–449. doi:10.1016/S0747-5632(00)00017-0

Hao, B., Li, L., Gao, R., Li, A., & Zhu, T. (2014, August). Sensing subjective well-being from social media. In *International Conference on Active Media Technology* (pp. 324-335). Springer.

He, Q., Glas, C. A., Kosinski, M., Stillwell, D. J., & Veldkamp, B. P. (2014). Predicting self-monitoring skills using textual posts on Facebook. *Computers in Human Behavior, 33*, 69–78. doi:10.1016/j.chb.2013.12.026

Huang, J. H., & Yang, Y. C. (2010). The relationship between personality traits and online shopping motivations. *Social Behavior and Personality, 38*(5), 673–679. doi:10.2224bp.2010.38.5.673

Kosinski, M., Stillwell, D., & Graepel, T. (2013). Private traits and attributes are predictable from digital records of human behavior. *Proceedings of the National Academy of Sciences of the United States of America, 110*(15), 5802–5805. doi:10.1073/pnas.1218772110 PMID:23479631

Kosinski, M., Stillwell, D., Kohli, P., Bachrach, Y., & Graepel, T. (2012). Personality and website choice. *Age, 15*(51.10), 21-24.

Lee, E., Ahn, J., & Kim, Y. J. (2014). Personality traits and self-presentation at Facebook. *Personality and Individual Differences, 69*, 162–167. doi:10.1016/j.paid.2014.05.020

Lewenberg, Y., Bachrach, Y., & Volkova, S. (2015, October). Using emotions to predict user interest areas in online social networks. In *Data Science and Advanced Analytics (DSAA), 2015. 36678 2015. IEEE International Conference on* (pp. 1-10). IEEE. 10.1109/DSAA.2015.7344887

Li, L., Li, A., Hao, B., Guan, Z., & Zhu, T. (2014). Predicting active users' personality based on micro-blogging behaviors. *PLoS One, 9*(1), e84997. doi:10.1371/journal.pone.0084997 PMID:24465462

Liu, L., Preotiuc-Pietro, D., Samani, Z. R., Moghaddam, M. E., & Ungar, L. H. (2016, May). *Analyzing Personality through Social Media Profile Picture Choice* (pp. 211–220). ICWSM.

Liu, M., Xue, J., Zhao, N., Wang, X., Jiao, D., & Zhu, T. (2018, February). Using Social Media to Explore the Consequences of Domestic Violence on Mental Health. *Journal of Interpersonal Violence*. doi:10.1177/0886260518757756 PMID:29441804

Liu, X., & Zhu, T. (2016). Deep learning for constructing microblog behavior representation to identify social media user's personality. *PeerJ Computer Science, 2*, e81. doi:10.7717/peerj-cs.81

Liu, Y., Wang, J., & Jiang, Y. (2016). PT-LDA: A latent variable model to predict personality traits of social network users. *Neurocomputing, 210*, 155–163. doi:10.1016/j.neucom.2015.10.144

Marshall, T. C., Lefringhausen, K., & Ferenczi, N. (2015). The Big Five, self-esteem, and narcissism as predictors of the topics people write about in Facebook status updates. *Personality and Individual Differences, 85*, 35–40. doi:10.1016/j.paid.2015.04.039

Mischel, W., Shoda, Y., & Ayduk, O. (2007). *Introduction to personality: Toward an integrative science of the person*. John Wiley & Sons.

Pennebaker, J. W., Boyd, R. L., Jordan, K., & Blackburn, K. (2015). *The development and psychometric properties of LIWC2015*. Academic Press.

Schwartz, H. A., Eichstaedt, J. C., Kern, M. L., Dziurzynski, L., Ramones, S. M., Agrawal, M., ... Ungar, L. H. (2013). Personality, gender, and age in the language of social media: The open-vocabulary approach. *PLoS One*, *8*(9), e73791. doi:10.1371/journal.pone.0073791 PMID:24086296

Skowron, M., Tkalčič, M., Ferwerda, B., & Schedl, M. (2016, April). Fusing social media cues: personality prediction from twitter and instagram. In *Proceedings of the 25th international conference companion on world wide web* (pp. 107-108). International World Wide Web Conferences Steering Committee. 10.1145/2872518.2889368

Tandera, T., Suhartono, D., Wongso, R., & Prasetio, Y. L. (2017). Personality Prediction System from Facebook Users. *Procedia Computer Science*, *116*, 604–611. doi:10.1016/j.procs.2017.10.016

Yarkoni, T., & Westfall, J. (2017). Choosing prediction over explanation in psychology: Lessons from machine learning. *Perspectives on Psychological Science*, *12*(6), 1100–1122. doi:10.1177/1745691617693393 PMID:28841086

Youyou, W., Kosinski, M., & Stillwell, D. (2015). Computer-based personality judgments are more accurate than those made by humans. *Proceedings of the National Academy of Sciences of the United States of America*, *112*(4), 1036–1040. doi:10.1073/pnas.1418680112 PMID:25583507

Zhou, E., Fan, H., Cao, Z., Jiang, Y., & Yin, Q. (2013, December). Extensive facial landmark localization with coarse-to-fine convolutional network cascade. In *Computer Vision Workshops (ICCVW), 2013 IEEE International Conference on* (pp. 386-391). IEEE. 10.1109/ICCVW.2013.58

Chapter 6
A Design Model of Embedded Engineering Learning on Social Cloud

Ayse Kok Arslan
Oxford Alumni Silicon Valley Network, USA

ABSTRACT

Based on the results of the evaluation of an embedded engineering learning on social cloud model, the author suggests whether an "Imagineering" approach to learning is and complies with design principles leading to creative products. It can also provide an evidence for whether the SC supports co-learning environments which contributes to the efficiency of the process. Not only training institutions, but also knowledge enterprises should have a ready infrastructure for network systems to access the cloud technology. This chapter discusses the options of a design model on social cloud.

INTRODUCTION: EMBEDDED SYSTEM

Our future is driven mainly by disruptive technologies and the convergence of the technological trends. Among these technologies, augmented reality, mobility, social media, cloud computing, big data and embedded systems have shown tremendous growth. With regard to these developments, the software industry improved on an ongoing basis to fulfill a variety of needs in our daily life concerning the safe and convenient use of electronic devices (Barr & Massa, 2006; Jacobson, 2001). At the same time, given the rapid proliferation of these technologies, relevant policies need to be developed that facilitate the development of embedded systems.

DOI: 10.4018/978-1-5225-7128-5.ch006

In our times of creative economy, the professional development of the production and management workforce plays an important role for the development of creative thinking skills (Henri, 1992). Especially, when it comes to the competency development in the field of ICT (Information Communication Technologies), the development of the abilities of software team to fulfil the needs of the embedded systems industry becomes crucial more than ever. Furthermore, this issue also needs the involvement of training institutes to equip the personnel in engineering sectors with required practical skills as well as to update their curriculum with regard to the embedded systems industry.

Embedded System refers to a built-in or programmable capability device that is managed by a combination of specific computer hardware and software designed for a specific purpose. Embedded System relates to the process for designing pragmatic inventions and innovations. Among the examples of possible hosts of an embedded system, medical equipment, industrial machines, airplanes, automobiles, household appliances, vending machines, cameras and toys can be counted (Barr & Massa, 2006; Johnson & Johnson, 1994;Harris, 2000-01; Schnabel & Ham, 2014).

Let's take an example of Raspberry PI as an Embedded Device which is a hardware board. Such a system development does not only include hardware design, components selections and a firmware design, but also a development of GUI based applications along with cloud computing and remote access of devices.

In summary, any real time gadget which can be seen by naked eyes is an embedded device which includes multiple works that combine best performance and best user experience.

SOCIAL CLOUD

Social Cloud (SC) refers to the service-sharing and resource framework based on the relationships between members of a social network. This involves the online co-working process that is specific of many social-specialized electronic platforms. (Chard et al., 2012; Schnabel & Ham, 2014; Chard et al., 2010; Babaoglu & Marzolla, 2014).

Furthermore, SC is a scalable computing model as users can contribute important resources that are dynamically prepared and freely shared among various collaborators (Haas et al., 2013;Chard et al., 2010; Babaoglu & Marzolla, 2014).

The tenets of SC has been famously put into use by the Berkeley Open Infrastructure for Network Computing (BOINC), serving as the largest computing grid in the world. Another service that makes use of social cloud computing is Subutai Social which allows peer-to-peer sharing of hardware resources globally or within a small network.

SOCIAL AND COLLABORATIVE NATURE OF LEARNING

Both the collaborative and social aspects of learning are important for education in the 21st century in order to go beyond the textbook and artifacts confined within their classrooms based on the learners' need. The more learning can happen outside of the classroom the better equipped will be the individuals to appreciate various perspectives as they start to think critically about the common issues and challenges the humanity is facing today.

There is a need for education models of how ICT can effectively be integrated into meaningful learning experiences. Scholars such as Clifford, Friesen and Jardine (Chard et al., 2012) argued that "that stakeholders in education should rethink not only the forms of collaboration and communication, but also the nature of their work when it comes to integrating these new technologies" (p. 1). In a similar vein, Jonassen, Peck and Wilson (Haas et al., 2013; Haythornthwaite, 2006) asserted that ICT should be utilized as a medium to construct relevant knowledge- in the sense of a generative processing- rather than as a medium to merely deliver instruction.

The following three C's are required in order for all educators- ranging from pre-service teachers, inservice teachers to teacher educators to integrate ICT to enhance metacognitive awareness, knowledge construction as well as critical discourse: constructivism, collaboration and critical thinking.

CONSTRUCTIVISM AS CORE OF THE SOCIAL CLOUD MODEL

Before delving into the details of the Social Cloud model it is crucial to understand the pedagogical frameworks underpinning this model.

As online learning has moved from a static content environment to a collaborative, constructivist and learner-centric environment we are being reminded that that learning is essentially a social activity, in which knowledge construction occurs through communication and interactions with others." (Chard et al., 2012; Dictionarist, 2016).

The most prevalent theoretical perspectives concerning online learning are mostly related to social constructivism with a focus on collaborative discourse (Haas et al., 2013; Harris, 2000-01) and the individual development of meaning through construction and sharing of texts and other social artefacts (Haas et al., 2013; Haythornthwaite, 2006).

Before proceeding with these different constructivist theories, it may be useful to briefly mention the characteristics of constructivism. According to constructivism, learning is an active rather than passive process where new insights are developed and knowledge is based on what one already knows (Haythornthwaite, 2006; Jacobsen,

2001). As the teachers scaffold and organize information into conceptual clusters of problems, new conflicting experiences cause "perturbations in the knowledge structures" (Jacobsen, 2001, Johnson & Johnson, 1994) Constructivist strategies such as problem-solving, critical thinking, reasoning and the reflective use of knowledge can be effectively implemented via the interactive environments provided by the computers (Henri, 1992; Jacobsen, 2001]

Two of the several different constructivist-learning theories that are related to web-based learning are cognitive or critical constructivism and social constructivism. To begin with, social constructivism is a closely related set of ideas that focus on the individual development of meaning through communication and the active construction and sharing of social artefacts, including texts rather than receiving them passively from the environment (McLoughlin & Luca, 2000;Newmann & Wehlage, 1993). Through conversational language used in a social context the emerging patterns are negotiated into meaning and the construct of the "zone of proximinal development" is bridged via deeper learning (Parab et al., 2008). So, learning occurs through joint problem-solving between partners and social interaction (Kanoun, 2016).

With regard to the development of creative thinking skills and facilitation of critical discourse it is believed that these collaborations and sharing processes increase the quality of dialogue between participants as a tool to construct knowledge (Parab et al., 2008; Schnabel & Ham, 2014)and make learners get apprenticed into "communities of practice" which embody certain beliefs and behaviours (Kanoun, 2016).A dialogue within these communities of practice is an exchange of information that takes place either directly via a semiotic medium such as language and other signs, or indirectly via tools such as computer interfaces (Parab et al., 2008). Computer softwares, such as web sites, can be considered as both a tool and a language in terms of the medium. Dialogue in online learning situations can be divided into four types (SIPA, 2012):

1. **Dialogue of the content development process:** A teacher learns while creating content for students during the design process
2. **Dialogue of each student with content:** The student acts and writes in response to the content being read
3. **Dialogue of students with teacher:** This refers to the negotiation and clarification of ideas
4. **Dialogue of students with other students:** Students test their ideas and learn by teaching other students

In a similar vein, a Web presence is pursued by the teachers due to the following reasons: (Johnson & Johnson, 1994; Newmann & Wehlage,1993; SIPA, 2012).

Teachers might want to share information concerning a particular subject with their peers. They might want to write authentically and communicatively to an audience that extends beyond the walls of classrooms (SIPA, 2012).

Still another learning theory within the framework of constructivism is the cognitive or critical constructivism where knowledge is constructed through the interactions of the student with their corresponding socio-cultural environment rather than through the interactions with other people as is the case in social constructivism (SIPA, 2012; Sonawane et al.,2014; Scardamalia & Bereiter, 2003). New experiences cause the cognitive schemas to get altered in order to make sense of the new information (Slotte & Tynjälä,2005).

After this detailed literature overview on constructivism, it would be useful to have a detailed look on the Social Cloud model.

EDUCATION AND SOCIAL CLOUD

Given the transformation of various industries due to the implementation of cloud, social and mobile technologies, training institutions also start to put more emphasis on how to increase the learner engagement via means of these technologies. Given the disruptive and innovative potential of these technologies, it is no wonder that they are revolutionizing both the society and education, by disrupting old models of learning and teaching.

According to some scholars (Chard et al., 2012; Haas et al, 2013), these converged technologies can be positioned as follows: cloud as the core; mobile as its edge; and social as the connections between endpoints.

Such a positioning describes the transformational technologies within the relevant context along with the technical and services infrastructure required to deliver the ideal user experience where everyone becomes social by being connected wherever they go (mobile), and whenever they would like to access data whenever they like (cloud). (Chard et al., 2012; Dictionarist, 2016; Haas et al., 2013).

According to Gartner, cloud is a delivery model for required computing resources and related activities by supporting both the scale and speed required due to the advances of social and mobile applications. The cloud essentially provides access to capabilities that would otherwise be inaccessible. Without the existence of cloud computing, the current scale of social interactions and the level of data and functional varieties enabled by mobile access would be unimaginable (Gartner, 2017).

As the cloud enables different communities to co-exist in the same *workspace* rather than being isolated in a stand-alone environment, it also provides an ecosystem for a wide variety of both unstructured and structured data forms. Eventually, all of this data in cloud-based communities can be connected through cloud services or mobile endpoints in a streamlined manner.

By offering opportunities for virtualization and aggregation of computing resources, economies of scale can be achieved which would be unimaginable in the absence of cloud computing. Due to the fact that virtual instances can be terminated or enabled at any time, only the employed computing resources are subject to payment. Let's have a look at the main features of cloud computing which supports both the scale and the reach of social and mobile applications:

- **Broad Network Access:** This enables the availability of capabilities via the network and access via means of conventional mechanisms which encourage the use by heterogeneous thin or thick client platforms (e.g., mobile phones, laptops, and personal digital assistants (PDAs)).
- **On-Demand Self-Service:** Various computing capabilities such as server time and network storage can be managed automatically without any need for human interaction.
- **Rapid Elasticity:** This concept refers to the fact that due the elasticity of the resources they can be scaled out and released quickly so that the end users have the feeling as if the resources are unlimited and can be put into use in any quantity at any time.
- **Resource Pooling:** This concept refers to the ability of pooling dispersed computing resources to serve various learners assigning different physical and virtual resources based on individual learner demand.
- **Measured Service:** This concept refers to resource optimization by leveraging a measurement capability at relevant abstraction level based on service type (e.g., active user accounts, storage and bandwidth). Providers and consumers can monitor, control, and report on services with transparency, empowering consumers with the ability to precisely match expenses to IT demand.

Within this regard, the researcher decided to design an Embedded Engineering Learning (EEL) on Social Cloud model to enhance creative thinking and production skills of the learners. A conceptual framework of a training model was organized, and the suitability of the learning activities was examined. The procedures in this model were the ways to create devices to support the teaching and learning for the participants to use them efficiently.

AN DESIGN EXAMPLE OF EMBEDDED ENGINEERING LEARNING ON SOCIAL CLOUD

In order to describe in detail the design of an embedded engineering learning model on social cloud, first a conceptual framework will be provided. Next, various features of the research design will be described in detail.

Conceptual Framework

The conceptual framework entails the following four essential components in the learning design model as displayed in Figure 1. Let's briefly explain what these four components are:

- **Embedded Systems:** As defined at the beginning, Embedded System is a programmable or built-in capability device is which controlled by a computer or the combination of computer hardware and software re- modeled for a specific purpose.
- **Jigsaw Classroom:** This is a method of organizing classroom activity that makes students dependent on each other to succeed. It breaks classes into groups and breaks assignments into pieces that the group assembles to complete the (jigsaw) puzzle. Given the highly sophisticated level of knowledge to develop new technologies, collaboration among peers based on subject expertise is at the heart of this method.

Figure 1. The conceptual framework of an embedded engineering learning on social cloud model to enhance creative thinking and creative product

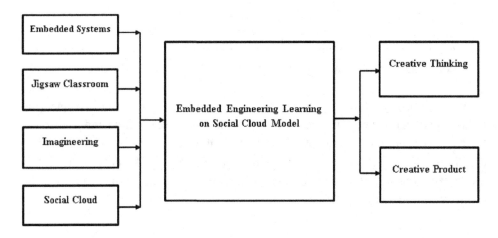

- **Imagineering:** This concept refers to the combination of imagination and engineering so that the ultimate output is not only sophisticated from a technical point of view but also highly creative and has an impact on the user's life in terms of its convenience and effectiveness.
- **Social Cloud:** This concept generalizes cloud computing to include the sharing, bartering and renting of computing resources across peers whose owners and operators are verified through social network. It expands cloud computing past the confines of formal commercial data centers operated by cloud providers to include anyone interested in participating within the cloud services sharing economy.

While these four elements are the inputs of the embedded engineering learning model on the social cloud, the final outputs are both a creative thinking mechanism and a creative product. Through a constant mutual interplay, these four components generate a mechanism for creative thinking which ultimately leads to creative products.

The Research Design

The population of the suggested research study includes subject matter experts involved in an embedded system information technology and instructional design. These experts have been chosen via means of purposive sampling of individuals with an in-depth design experience in Silicon Valley, California. The variables are as follows:

- Independent variable→ an Embedded Engineering Learning on Social Cloud Model to enhance Creative Thinking and Creative Production
- Dependent variable →the evaluation of the model's appropriateness

Research Process

This research study has the following two phases:

1. Development of EEL Model on SC which includes the following steps:
   a. Analysis and synthesis of documents and prior research related to the aspects of Embedded System, Collaborative (Jigsaw), Imagineering, and Social Cloud.
   b. Data collection and analysis based on previous research studies and available documentation.

c. Presentation of the model to advisors and experts for consideration by means of in-depth interviews.

d. Creation of the tools for evaluating the appropriateness of the model.

2. Evaluation of EEL Model on SC which includes the following steps:

a. Presentation of the developed Model to the seven experts from the fields of embedded system, information technology and instructional design.

b. Improvement of the Model based on the suggestions of the experts.

c. Presentation of the Model in the form of a diagram accompanied by a report.

d. Analysis of the results of the evaluation based on the mean and standard deviation. The evaluation form consists of a 5-point Likert scale ranging from very good, good, moderate to poor and very poor.

The Potential Design Outcomes

It is aimed to deliver two major outcomes with this study: One is the outcome of the design as described in this section; and the outcome of the evaluation to be presented in the next section.

Figure 2 displays an EEL model on SC to support creative thinking. This model consists of 7 components along with 22 procedures:

Figure 2. An embedded engineering learning on social cloud model to enhance creative thinking and creative product

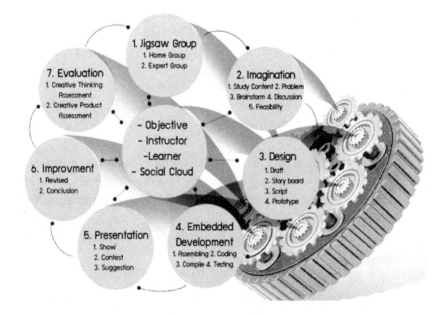

- **Component 1 – Jigsaw Group:** This component brings 3-6 individual learners into groups based on the following levels: skilled, medium, and weak. It ideally includes Main Group and Expert Group.
- **Component 2 – Imagination:** This component enables the learners to imagine by brainstorming. The following 5 steps are implemented when it comes to sharing opinions:
  - Content study especially with regard to the procedures in theoretical lessons in each subject,
  - Problem statement including a hypothesis,
  - Brainstorming (including some alternative solutions),
  - Discussion, and
  - Feasibility (analysis of the possibility and practicality of the creative solution).
- **Component 3 – Design:** This component enables the learners to support each other's design by use of their imagination. Its main steps are as follows:
  - The process of drafting,
  - The process of writing the story board,
  - The process of writing the script, and
  - The process of creating a prototype.
- **Component 4 – Embedded Development:** This component enables the learners to help each other develop their work during its modelling stage. Its main steps are as follows:
  - Assembling,
  - Coding,
  - Evaluating, and
  - Testing.
- **Component 5 – Presentation:** This component enables the learners to present their work. The lecturers may prefer to construct a competition which includes voting and provision of feedback to develop better work in the future. Its main steps are as follows:
  - Displaying the finalized model
  - Competition (let the learners compete with each other), and
  - Suggesting exemplary models (by discussing with other lecturers and learners).
- **Component 6 – Improvement:** This component enables the learners to share their opinions among each other to fix and improve upon their group work and to finalize the results by evaluating the advantages, disadvantages as well as potential issues. Its main steps are as follows:
  - Revision was the process of editing the constructed work and
  - Conclusion was summarizing all of the details about the work.

- **Component 7 – Evaluation:** This component enables the lecturer to assess the creativity of their before and after the lessons by making use of relevant assessments. Its main steps are as follows:
  - ◦ Creative Thinking assessment (the creativity assessment) and
  - ◦ Creative Production assessment (the work assessment).

The Potential Evaluation Outcomes

Table 1 illustrates an evaluation of the appropriateness of an EEL on SC Model.

In this expert level evaluation. Items are listed based on the overall appropriateness of an EEL on SC Model. The following items should especially be taken into account:

- The order of the main components in an EEL on SC Model is easy to understand.

Table 1. The appropriateness of the evaluation model for EEL on SC

Evaluation Lists	Results		Appropriateness Level
	$\bar{X}$	S.D.	
1. The principles of the system that were used as the base to synthesize an Embedded Engineering Learning on Social Cloud Model			
2. The components of the model were related an Embedded Engineering Learning on Social Cloud Model			
3. The sequences of the model's components that is clear and continuous			
4. The relations of each component towards the others			
5. The arrangement of the sequences of the components in an Embedded Engineering Learning on Social Cloud Model was suitable and easy to understand			
6. The overall of the components of an Embedded Engineering Learning on Social Cloud Model was complete as it can satisfy, the needs and accurate to the purposes of the research			
7. An Embedded Engineering Learning on Social Cloud Model that to developed a suitable of Creative Thinking			
8. An Embedded Engineering Learning on Social Cloud that to developed a suitable of Creative Product			
9. An Embedded Engineering Learning on Social Cloud Model had possibility utilization to develop the practical system			
Summary			

- EEL on SC Model enables the development of a pragmatic system.
- System principles can be considered as the basis to integrate EEL onto SC Model.

CONCLUSION

Based on the results of the evaluation of an EEL on SC Model it can be suggested whether an 'imagineering' approach to learning is and complies with design principles leading to creative products. Similarly, it can also provide an evidence for whether the SC supports co-learning environments which contributes to the efficiency of the process. Not only training institutions, but also knowledge enterprises should have a ready infrastructure for network systems to access the cloud technology.

REFERENCES

Babaoglu, O. (2014, September 22). Escape From the Data Center: The Promise of Peer-to-Peer Cloud Computing. *IEEE Spectrum*.

Babaoglu, O., Marzolla, M., & Tamburini, M. (2012). Design and Implementation of a P2P Cloud System. *Proceedings of the 27th Annual ACM Symposium on Applied Computing*, 412–417. 10.1145/2245276.2245357

Barr, M., & Massa, A. (2006). *Programming embedded systems: with C and GNU development tools*. O'Reilly Media Inc.

Center for Imagineering Leadership and Renewal. (2011). *What is Imagineering?* Retrieved from http://www.bernardfranklinphd.com/2011/04/what-is-imagineering.html

Chard, K., Bubendorfer, K., Caton, S., & Rana, O. F. (2012). Social cloud computing: A vision for socially motivated resource sharing. *IEEE Transactions on Services Computing*, 5(4), 551–563. doi:10.1109/TSC.2011.39

Chard, K., Caton, S., Rana, O., & Bubendorfer, K. (2010). Social Cloud: Cloud Computing in Social Networks. *2010 IEEE 3rd International Conference on Cloud Computing*, 99–106. 10.1109/CLOUD.2010.28

Dictionarist. (2011). *Imagineering*. Retrieved from http://www.dictionarist.com/Imagineering

Gartner. (2017). *Report "The Nexus of Forces: Social, Mobile, Cloud and Information"*. Retrieved from http://www.gartner.com/DisplayDocument?doc_cd=234840

Haas, C., Caton, S., Chard, K., & Weinhardt, C. (2013). Co-operative infrastructures: An eco- nomic model for providing infrastructures for social cloud computing. In *System Sciences (HICSS), 2013 46th Hawaii International Conference on*. IEEE. 10.1109/HICSS.2013.147

Harris, J. (2001). Structuring internetenriched learning spaces for understanding and action. *Learning and Leading with Technology, 28*(4), 50–55.

Haythornthwaite, C. (2006). Facilitating collaboration in online learning. *Journal of Asynchronous Learning Networks, 10*(1), 7 – 24. Retrieved November 20, 2006 from http://www.sloanc.org/publications/jaln/v10n1/pdf/v10n1_2haythornthwaite.pdf

Henri, F. (1992). Computer conferencing and content analysis. In A. R. Kaye (Ed.), *Collaborative learning through computer conferencing: The Najaden Papers* (pp. 117–136). Berlin: Springer Verlag. doi:10.1007/978-3-642-77684-7_8

Jacobsen, D. M. (2001). *Building different bridges: Technology integration, engaged student learning, and new approaches to professional development*. Paper presented at AERA 2001: What We Know and How We Know It, the 82nd Annual Meeting of the American Educational Research Association, Seattle, WA. Retrieved November 20, 2006, from http://www.ucalgary.ca/~dmjacobs/aera/building_bridges.html

Johnson, D. W., & Johnson, R. (1994). *Joining together: Group theory and group skills* (5th ed.). Boston: Allyn & Bacon.

Kanoun, O. (2016). *Chair for Measurement and Sensor Technology Embedded Systems*. Retrieved from https://www.tu-chemnitz.de/studium/studiengaenge/flyer/embedded_ systems_eng.pdf

McLoughlin, C., & Luca, J. (2000). Cognitive engagement and higher order thinking through computer conferencing: We know why but do we know how? In A. Herrmann & M. M. Kulski (Eds.), *Flexible Futures in Tertiary Teaching. Proceedings of the 9th Annual Teaching Learning Forum, 24 February 2000*. Perth: Curtin University of Technology. Retrieved November 20, 2006, from http://lsn.curtin.edu.au/tlf/tlf2000/mcloughlin.html

Newmann, F. M., & Wehlage, G. G. (1993). Five standards of authentic instruction. *Educational Leadership, 50*(7), 812.

Parab, J., Shinde, S. A., Shelake, V. G., Kamat, R. K., & Naik, G. M. (2008). *Practical aspects of embedded system design using microcontrollers*. Springer Science & Business Media; doi:10.1007/978-1-4020-8393-8

Scardamalia, M., & Bereiter, C. (2003). Knowledge building. In G. W. Guthrie (Ed.), *Encyclopedia of Education* (2nd ed.; pp. 1370–1373). New York: Macmillan Reference.

Schnabel, M. A., & Ham, J. J. (2014). The Social Network Learning Cloud: Architectural Educa-tion for the 21st Century. *International Journal of Architectural Computing, 12*(3), 225–241. doi:10.1260/1478-0771.12.3.225

SIPA. (2012). *SIPA Reports results of a survey software market and Software Services Thailand Year 2014*. Retrieved from http://www.sipa.or.th/th/news/2007

Slotte, V., & Tynjälä, P. (2005). Communication and collaborative learning at work: Views expressed on a crossCultural elearning course. *International Journal on E-Learning, 4*(2), 191–207.

Sonawane, H., Gupta, D., & Jadhav, A. (n.d.). Social Cloud Computing Using Social Network. *IOSR Journal of Computer Engineering, 1*(16), 15.

Swan, K. (2005). A constructivist model for thinking about learning online. In J. Bourne & J. C. Moore (Eds.), *Elements of Quality Online Education: Engaging Communities*. Needham, MA: SloanC. Retrieved November 20, 2006, from http://www.kent.edu/rcet/Publications/upload/constructivist%20theory.pdf

Thailand. (2000). *I. C. T. Policy Framework BE 2554-2563*. Ministry of Information and Communication Technology.

Vahid, F., & Givargis, T. (2002). *Embedded system design: a unified hardware/software introduction* (Vol. 4). New York, NY: John Wiley & Sons.

Watthananon, J. (2015). A Comparison of the Effectiveness of STEM Learning and Imagineering Learning by Undergraduate Student in Computer Science. *International Journal of the Computer, the Internet and Management, 23*(1), 45-52.

Wright, A. (2008). *The Imagineering Field Guide to Disneyland: An Imagineer's-eye Tour*. Disney.

Chapter 7
Brain–Computer Interface for Cyberpsychology

Yujia Peng
University of California – Los Angeles, USA

ABSTRACT

As a new way of implementing human-computer interface, brain-computer interfaces (BCI) dramatically changed the user experiences and have broad applications in cyber behavior research. This chapter aims to provide an overall picture of the BCI science and its role in cyberpsychology. The chapter starts with an introduction of the concept, components, and the history and development of BCI. It is then followed by an overview of neuroimaging technologies and signals commonly used in BCI. Then, different applications of BCI on both the clinical population and the general population are summarized in connection with cyberpsychology. Specifically, applications include communication, rehabilitation, entertainments, learning, marketing, and authentication. The chapter concludes with the future directions of BCI.

INTRODUCTION

A 73-year-old woman was in the locked-in state caused by amyotrophic lateral sclerosis (ALS) and was taken care by her family and full-time caregivers. She could only communicate with the outside world by moving eyes to send signals to an eye tracker until the presence of Brain Painting (Kübler, Halder, Furdea, & Hösle, 2008; Münßinger et al., 2010), a P300 brain-computer interfaces (BCI)-controlled application, which was facilitated and installed at the patient's home. Painting had been her favorite hobby and the device enabled her to paint again by reading her

DOI: 10.4018/978-1-5225-7128-5.ch007

brain signals extracted by electroencephalogram (EEG). The device allowed her to select a variety of tools, shapes, colors to paint on the virtual canvas. The patient stated: "I am using Brain Painting 1 to 3 times per week, but if I could, I would use it every day." In many similar examples, the device was found to significantly improve quality of life of patients (Botrel, Holz, & Kübler, 2015; Holz, Botrel, Kaufmann, & Kübler, 2015; Holz, Botrel, & Kübler, 2015).

What Is BCI?

The story described above was one of the thousands of the real stories, showing us the state-of-art use of BCI. This technology was applied to devices such as wheelchairs, cursors and so on to link human beings' brains with outside world directly and to change the way we live. Notably, it brings opportunities for paralyzed people to live a more convenient life while for healthy people more joyous.

So, what is BCI? In the review by Wolpaw, Birbaumer, McFarland, Pfurtscheller, and Vaughan (2002), the authors defined BCI as "a communication system in which messages or commands that an individual sends to the external world do not pass through the brain's normal output pathways of peripheral nerves and muscles." A more recent definition (Guger, Allison, & Müller-Putz, 2015) of BCI was "a device that reads voluntary changes in brain activity, then translates these signals into a message or command in real-time". BCI, which is also called a mind-machine interface (MMI), or sometimes direct neural interface, brain-machine interface (BMI), is a direct communication pathway between the brain and an external device.

What Are Major Components of BCI?

A BCI system starts with human brains and ends with an external device. It typically contains 4 parts between the two ends in the order of signal acquisition, digitized signals, signal processing components (e.g. feature extraction, translation algorithm), and device command. The inputs of BCI systems refer to brain activities or signals recorded from human brains, such as the electrophysiological activity from the user. Major physiological methods of recording brain activities and different kinds of signals recorded are listed in the part 2b. The output can be commands sent to control diverse devices such as a mouse or a robotic arm. Examples of external devices chosen to be used in a BCI system are listed in part 3.

History and Development of BCI

The history of BCI is not very long, spanning a century till now (Wolpaw et al., 2002). The history started with the discovery of the electrical activity of the human brain and the development of electroencephalography (EEG) by Hans Berger (1929). In 1924, the first recording of human brain activity by EEG was conducted by Berger, during which he identified oscillatory activity in the brain, such as the alpha wave, also known as Berger's wave (Wiedemann, 1994).

EEG was welcomed into our daily life only recently due to the constraints of the poor resolution and low reliability of the information detectable during the first 70 years of this history. Due to similar reasons, EEG based communication attracted little scientific attention at first. Recent scientific, technological, and societal events have changed this situation, and thus people have started to use EEG to decipher thoughts or intents. Till now, numerous research papers have been published to advance the BCI technology. There is also a considerable amount of reviews on BCI. For example, Wolpaw, McFarland, and Vaughan (2000) provided a comprehensive summary of the BCI technology prior to the first international meeting on BCI research and development; Lotte, Congedo, Lécuyer, Lamarche, and Arnaldi (2007) compared classification algorithms for EEG-based BCIs; Zander, Kothe, Jatzev, and Gaertner (2010) reviewed how to enhance human-computer interaction (HCI) with input from BCIs. For the use of BCIs in the field of assistive technology (AT), please refer to a review by Moghimi, Kushki, Marie Guerguerian, and Chau (2013). These reviews have effectively synthesized the existing literature and inspired the thinking of what, how, and why BCI can be used for cyber behavior research, an important and emerged field of research. The rest of the chapter briefly introduced the neuroimaging technologies and signals commonly used in BCI. Then, it presented the application of BCIs in the field of cyber behaviors from aspects of the clinical and the general population, such as e-learning, neuro-gaming, and neuro-surfing.

METHODS OF BCI

What Neuroimaging Technologies Are Commonly Used?

A variety of methods for monitoring brain activity currently exists and can be divided into noninvasive techniques and invasive techniques.

Noninvasive neuroimaging technologies are easy to wear but may produce poor signal resolution because the skull dampens signals. It is also more difficult to spatially localize the area of the brain that created signals compared to invasive ones. Noninvasive techniques include electrophysiological methods (e.g. EEG), magnetoencephalography (MEG) (Mellinger et al., 2007), functional magnetic resonance imaging (fMRI) (Ruiz, Buyukturkoglu, Rana, Birbaumer, & Sitaram, 2014; Sitaram et al., 2008), functional near-infrared imaging (fNIR) (Naseer & Hong, 2015) and the combinations of technologies above (e.g. EEG-fMRI, Deshpande et al.,

2017). However, not all of them were commonly used in communication and control processes due to high expenses and limited temporal resolution. EEG is currently the most convenient, safe and inexpensive, and can provide a basis for safe and uni-directional communication with acceptable resolution, and is the most commonly used nowadays (Guger, Allison, & Ushiba, 2017; Hwang, Kim, Choi, & Im, 2013).

In 1994, dry-EEG was developed by Taheri, Knight, and Smith. It is a system similar to the original EEG except that its electrodes are adapted in such a way as to establish a direct contact with the scalp without relying on the conductive gel. Dry electrodes can lower the impedance between electrodes and scalp and allow for EEG applications outside the laboratory (Wyckoff, Sherlin, Ford, & Dalke, 2015; Zander et al., 2011). Because the dry-EEG can reduce the preparation time and users don't need to wash electrode gels off their hair, this system may lead to new applications in both disabled and healthy group.

Invasive techniques, such as electrocorticogram (ECoG) recordings (i.e. implantable electrodes on or in the neocortex), measures the electrical activity of the brain taken from beneath the skull. ECoG has higher spatial resolution than EEG, broader bandwidth, higher characteristic amplitude, and far less vulnerability to artifacts such as electromyography (EMG) or ambient noise. At the same time, ECoG is likely to have greater long-term stability and to produce less tissue damage and reaction than intracortical recordings (Schalk, 2008). Invasive techniques are more commonly applied to patients in the complete locked-in state (CLIS) with the hope to establish communications (Jarosiewicz et al., 2015), though the reliability was found to be limited (Birbaumer, Gallegos-Ayala, Wildgruber, Silvoni, & Soekadar, 2014). The technique has also been widely applied in epilepsy patients to achieve spelling tasks (Leuthardt, Schalk, Wolpaw, Ojemann, & Moran, 2004) or moving the cursor (Hinterberger et al., 2008).

What Brain Signals Are Involved?

Present-day EEG-based non-invasive BCIs mainly use the following kinds of signals: visual evoked potential (VEP) or steady-state visual evoked potential (SSVEP) (Herrmann, 2001), slow cortical potentials (Birbaumer et al., 2000b; Andrea Kübler et al., 2005), P300 evoked potentials (Farwell & Donchin, 1988, for a review, see Fazel-Rezai et al., 2012), mu and beta rhythms (Wolpaw & McFarland, 2004). What these signals are and how they are used are briefly introduced below.

VEP is an evoked electrophysiological potential that can provide important diagnostic information regarding the functional integrity of the visual system (Odom et al., 2004). Sutter (1992) described a BCI system in which the VEPs produced by brief visual stimuli and recorded from the scalp over visual cortex were used. The users faced a video screen displaying 64 symbols and looked at the symbol they wanted to select. The system could determine the symbol that the users were looking at by analyzing the VEPs of the target and that of each symbol.

Slow cortical potentials (SCPs) are slow voltage changes generated in the cortex which occur over 0.5-10s. Negative SCPs are typically associated with movement and cortical activation, while positive SCPs are usually associated with cortical deactivation (Donchin & Smith, 1970; Wolpaw et al., 2002). Studies have proved that patients can successfully control the movements of a computer cursor on the screen (Birbaumer et al., 2000) or an electronic spelling device (Birbaumer et al., 1999) by learning to control SCPs.

P300 evoked potentials refer to the positive potential about 300 ms after the flash and are generated involuntarily (stimulus-feedback) when people see something they recognize and may allow BCIs to decode categories of thoughts without training patients first, which is an advantage over other methods (Wolpaw et al., 2002). Donchin et al. (2000) have used P300 in a BCI to determine users' desired choice from columns of flashes based on the fact that rare events elicit the P300 component. P300 is prominent only in the responses elicited by the desired choice. The P300-based BCI has a considerable potential for further improvement on the speed of yielding words (Donchin, Spencer, & Wijesinghe, 2000) and motor controls (Kaplan, Zhigulskaya, & Kirjanov, 2016).

The mu rhythm refers to the 8-12Hz EEG activity displayed by primary or motor cortical areas when people are awake, which is in frequency and amplitude related to the posterior alpha rhythm. Mu rhythms are usually associated with beta rhythms which have an 18–26 Hz frequency. Rhythmical beta activity is encountered chiefly over the frontal and central regions and can be found almost in all healthy adults (Niedermeyer & da Silva, 2005). These two kinds of signals can predict users' motion well. Movement or preparation for movement is typically accompanied by a decrease in mu and beta rhythms. In opposite, rhythm increase occurs after movement and with relaxation (Pfurtscheller, Stancak Jr, & Neuper, 1996). Furthermore, the changes of mu and beta rhythms occur not only with actual movement but also with motor imagery (Pfurtscheller, Neuper, Flotzinger, & Pregenzer, 1997), which is a commonly used paradigm in BCI that has a profound impact on the clinical population (Alonso-Valerdi, Salido-Ruiz, & Ramirez-Mendoza, 2015).

HOW IS BCI RELATED TO CYBER BEHAVIOR?

The Internet and computers, which connect people with each other and the outside world, are becoming more and more popular among both teenagers and adults. The Internet even becomes a necessity for some who may develop to be addicted. A study has found that the time an average person spent on the Internet only for fun and personal interest every week has a mean of 4.9 hours while those who are addicted spent a mean time 38.5 hours each week (Young, 1998).

Cyberpsychology is the study of the human mind and its behavior in the context of human interaction and communication with both men and machine. While statistical and theoretical research in this field is based around Internet usage, cyberpsychology also covers, but is not limited to the following areas: e-learning, online shopping, computer-mediated communication, and video and/or online gaming, etc. With connections between men and machines becoming stronger, BCI studies are catching more attention in the field of cyberpsychology.

BCI provides a new, direct way for humans to communicate with machines (Kumar & Sharma, 2012), making the borderline between humans and machines even blurred. Modern BCIs are sophisticated enough to serve as a kind of input device for computers, mimicking keyboards, mice, and joysticks. In clinical field, BCI-based keyboards, for example, help users surf the Internet without any physical touch. And with the emergence of dry electrode EEG systems, BCIs are ready for real-life applications outside of the laboratory (Zander et al., 2011).

The influence of BCI on cyber behavior can be seen both among the clinical and the general populations. An application of BCI often starts with an aim of improving the clinical population's life quality, and later, with the development of technologies, the application gradually catches the attention of those investors because of the potential profits in the general population.

How Does BCI Benefit Clinical Populations?

As illustrated in the story at the beginning of the chapter, individuals in clinical populations have very different lifestyles from the general population. Due to some diseases like Amyotrophic Lateral Sclerosis (ALS), brainstem stroke, brain or spinal cord injury, the neural pathways of patients that control muscles can be severely impaired. The number of people involved is very large ——nearly two million people in the United States alone (Rebsamen et al., 2010). Whether these patients can communicate with the outside world to some extent determines their life quality. One of the solutions for locked-in people to have cyber behavior is to establish communication and control channels directly from the brain, and BCI may become a promising way of giving them a chance to feel the joy of the cyber world.

In the review of Daly and Wolpaw (2008), two ways of using BCI to benefit clinical rehabilitation were proposed. The first, also the more common way is to enable people to interact with their environment through brain signals rather than through muscles, substituting for the loss of normal neuromuscular outputs. The second way attracted more attention recently, which is to use BCI to induce activity-dependent brain plasticity to restore more normal brain function. The other is to use BCI to control an external device, such as spelling devices, wheelchairs, and prosthetic devices. Empirical studies related to both ways will be mentioned below.

One way of enabling the communication is to translate brain activities into specific items. Take as an example a spelling device "The Thought Translation Device (TTD)", which has been mentioned once where slow cortical potential (SCP) was briefly introduced. It was developed to communicate with locked-in patients (Birbaumer et al., 1999; Birbaumer et al., 2000). The TTD trained locked-in patients to self-regulate SCPs of their EEG which can be taken as a paradigm for the first way of using BCI in clinical rehabilitation. After learning SCP self-control, patients selected items in a computerized language support program. Results showed that patients could write their own letters based on the TTD and demonstrated the usefulness of the TTD which may fulfill the communication between patients, computers and the Internet. The study of Mellinger, Hinterberger, Bensch, Schröder, and Birbaumer (2003) covered the history of the development of BCI communication system and presented a novel Brain Web Surfer that overcame many of the difficulties present in previous approaches such as being slow and noisy.

Another way of fulfilling the interaction between patients and the Internet is using brain signals to control a computer cursor. For instance, studies at the Wadsworth Center showed that people could learn to control the amplitude of mu or beta rhythms in EEG activity recorded from sensorimotor cortex and could use those rhythms to move a cursor on a computer screen in two dimensions. Another study was done by Karim et al. (2006) Karim et al. (2006), who developed a neural internet system controlled by the SCPs extracted through appropriate filtering. Users moved the cursor upward to reject a command by producing negative SCP shifts or move the cursor downward to select a command by producing positive SCP shifts. Another study developed an internet browser based on P300 event-related potential. This browser is available for navigation, hyperlink selection and page scrolling for standard pages by letting users select symbols on another screen. This system has been tested on the healthy group (Muglerab et al., 2008) and was later tested on patients with ALS. They achieved an average accuracy of 73% and a subsequent information transfer rate (ITR) of 8.6 bits/minute which showed the success of this system (Mugler, Ruf, Halder, Bensch, & Kubler, 2010). In Yu et al.'s study (2012), authors even considered the number of targets in a web page. They used a target filter to exclude most of those targets of no interest which were determined by inputting keywords with a P300-based speller. After the filtering, patients used their motor imagery and P300 potential to control the horizontal movement and vertical movement of a cursor respectively (Yu, Li, Long, & Gu, 2012).

Besides patients' communication with the computer and the Internet, a lot of studies focused on devices like BCI-based wheelchairs that can help locked-in people move. (Rebsamen et al., 2010) developed a brain-controlled wheelchair for the use of navigation in familiar environments. It is intended as a realistic mobility recovery tool for locked-in people. More recent studies further advanced this idea by introducing automated navigation technique (Zhang et al., 2016) and multi-sensory inputs (Kucukyildiz, Ocak, Karakaya, & Sayli, 2017).

There are also prosthetic devices designed for people with tetraplegia. The research of Hochberg et al. (2006) and the research of Pfurtscheller et al. (2003) are two examples that BCI signals are used in Neuromotor prostheses (NMPs) (Hochberg et al., 2006) and functional electrical stimulation (FES) (Pfurtscheller, Müller, Pfurtscheller, Gerner, & Rupp, 2003).

Furthermore, with the development of techniques, many BCIs are now intended not only as tools for communication but also as treatments for physical or cognitive impairments (Huggins et al., 2017). Studies have found that EEG–based motor imagery BCI technology could improve motor function by inducing activity-dependent brain plasticity on stroke patients (Ang et al., 2015; Ang et al., 2014; Pichiorri et al., 2015).

How Can BCI Do for The General Population?

BCI appears in the domain for healthy users in aspects such as entertainments, online learning, marketing, and authentication.

Entertainments

Entertainments play a vital role in the modern life and nothing stops people from pursuing more immersive entertainments experiences that interact with human beings in an online manner. Below, applications of BCI related to entertainments will be discussed from two aspects: games and musical creation.

Video games are now a media phenomenon that has entered the mainstream of many cultures and are played in many forms, both online or offline. It has been reported that there are over 60% of Americans playing some form of interactive games on a regular basis (Williams & Skoric, 2005). Because of the progress in BCI research, there is a rising interest in the application of BCI to the field of games (Nijholt, 2009). Under this trend, one main topic in this field is the possible role of BCI being used in games and some principles in developing BCI games.

In a literature of the leading expert Nijholt (Nijholt, Bos, & Reuderink, 2009), listed are reasons of why we should involve BCI into games. First, a healthy person may also meet situations where only part of his or her available skills can be used. For example, when your two hands are all occupied, brain signals can play the role of a hand. Moreover, BCI can collect information on the mental state of users, e.g. boredom, anxiousness, which may help the application to have better user experiences. As for the principles in developing, almost all literature pointed out that BCI game should contain some characteristics that no other modality can offer in order to attract players. For example, BCIs should be able to provide users' mental states in an efficient and effective way (Bos et al., 2010; Nijholt & Tan, 2007).

The group of Gürkök has developed several games based on BCI signal (Gürkök, 2012; Nijholt et al., 2009). Bacteria Hunt, taken as an example, is a multimodal, multi-paradigm game. In this game, players controlled an amoeba by the keyboard and were also influenced by the relative alpha power, which was a correlation of relaxed alertness (Mühl et al., 2010). Other examples include: "MindGame" in which a character on a three-dimensional game board was controlled to move based on the P300 event-related potential of users (Finke, Lenhardt, & Ritter, 2009); An archery game in which users made shots of arrows by controlling the focus level, with higher focus level granted closer distance between the shot and the bullseye (Liao et al., 2012); and "Thinking penguin" in which users controlled the jumping of a penguin that slides down a snowy mountain slope via BCI (Leeb, Lancelle, Kaiser, Fellner, & Pfurtscheller, 2013).

Later, the researchers started looking into the influence of adding BCI input on collaboration in a multiplayer game and developed the game "Mind the Sheep!". The game has one BCI version and one non-BCI version to investigate the social interaction between the players in BCI and non-BCI situations separately. Results showed that the BCI version could increase player's level of engagement and led to a more positive user experience (Gürkök, 2012). Other examples include: a multi-user video game called "BrainArena" in which two users could play a simple football game by means of two BCIs (Bonnet, Lotte, & Lécuyer, 2013); and a two-player ball game in which users tried to push balls by increasing attentional level measured as the theta to beta band power in EEG (Shenjie, Thomas, & Vinod, 2014).

BCIs can also be used in designing games. Researchers measured users' attention levels to identify points of high player interest in a First Person Shooter (FPS) games. Their results suggested that analysis of these points could lead to a better understanding of player interest and how to design more interesting games (Chan, Mikami, & Kondo, 2010).

Besides games, another field that recently attracts the attention of BCI researchers is music composition. Imagine a piece of melody pops up in your mind and you want to extract the tune to prevent it from slipping away or to share it with others, the state-of-art BCI technologies can help you to do that. BCIs in music can be categorized into passive control and direct control (Wadeson, Nijholt, & Nam, 2015). For passive control BCIs, the system receives input from a non-interactive user, interprets the signals based on pre-programmed algorithms and parameters and outputs music. For example, Miranda and colleagues (2008) developed Brain-Computer Music Interface (BCMI) to extract EEG signals from human brains and generate musical notes based on the power spectrum of EEG signals. Later studies followed similar ideas and developed different algorithms for both online (Miranda, 2010) and offline music generation (Wu, Li, & Yao, 2013). For direct control music composition, users have more voluntary control over what music to generate. In the study by Eaton and Miranda (2013), participants were presented with four on-screen options that flash at different frequencies. Users could gaze on one of the icons and the visually evoked SSVEP signals were extracted by EEG to allow real-time control of musical parameters.

Online Learning

The ability to acquire users' mental states also makes brain-computer interfaces powerful tools in the field of online learning. Using BCI-based devices, e-learning software could monitor learners' state and provide feedback and guidance accordingly.

Crowley, Sliney, Pitt, and Murphy (2010) tested the system NeuroSky, which was a non-invasive, gel-free, biosensor that read electrical activity in the brain to determine states of attention and relaxation while users were doing the Stroop test or the tower of Hanoi. Results showed that such BCIs were feasible to measure the attention and meditation levels of a learner.

Some researchers also used BCIs to develop an e-learning system that monitors the students' motivation and concentration status and gives students feedback on retained concentration and motivation (Yoshida et al., 2011). Other researchers proved that users could retain more information by increasing their reading engagement physiologically which may be helpful when materials were boring (Andujar & Gilbert, 2013). Thus e-learning may play an important role in helping learners to get a better result by giving neurofeedback in the future.

Marketing

Recent years have seen a dramatic increase in the importance of information technology, e.g. the Internet, both in traditional and in the emergence of electronic business. Internet-based electronic marketplaces make use of information technology to perform their functions with increased effectiveness and reduced transaction costs, resulting in more efficient "friction-free" markets (Bakos, 1998). Thus, if BCI-based markets were made possible, people could select items they want without clicking and they can search what they want by letting the computer analyses their brain waves.

Below are a few examples of consumer neuroscience. In the study of Sands and Sands (2012), they asked participants to wear EEG hats and move around in a supermarket while signals are recorded. They found hedonic items produce the largest brain responses. And there was a correlation between the brain response to the first eye fixations on an item and the decision of whether to buy it. The second example is about advertising. In the study of Silberstein and Nield (2012), steady-state topography (SST) was used to measure motivational valence (MV) changes in response to television advertising. They observed a larger approach response by the female group to an attractive male actor in the advertising compared with the male group. And the differences in MV were mediated by the left prefrontal cortex for the approach component and the right prefrontal cortex for the withdraw component. Studies focusing on exploring the possibility of future BCI based consumer market also exists. Garcia (2008) explored the use of higher stimulation frequencies steady-state visual evoked potential (high–SSVEP) in BCI application and suggested that this method could be used in the future of BCI consumer market when visual stimuli at different frequencies were under selection.

BCI can be also used in designing products. A group of researchers recorded four elementary-school-students' brain wave changes when they are reading electronic books and tested what kind of color allocating on books can bring the best reading experiences (Wu, Liu, & Tzeng, 2011).

Authentication

People facing hackers and other unfriendly organizations, maintaining internet security can be a big problem these days. People need to input passwords and verification codes to log in any accounts which made it troublesome and difficult to remember all of the numbers. Moreover, the most severe problem with textual passwords is their vulnerability to dictionary attacks (Thorpe, van Oorschot, & Somayaji, 2005). If neuron activities can be taken as a way to identify people, internet activities will become safer and more effective. For instance, the study of Thorpe et al. (2005) proposed an authentication method---pass-thought, for access to computing devices, whereby a user thought of a password. The system needed to extract high-entropy information, which made a person unique, from a user to prove that they are who they claim. Although BCI application in this field is still in its infancy, this kind of password can be taken as a substitute for passwords in the future (Saulynas, Lechner, & Kuber, 2017), the former avoiding the difficulty of memorizing and the potential observation by nearby third parties.

FUTURE RESEARCH DIRECTIONS OF BCI

The development of brain-computer interfaces has been growing at full speed with the advancement of the EEG and other neuroimaging technologies in recent years. Besides its rapid advancement from the engineering viewpoint, progress has been made to investigate the brain-computer interfaces as a methodology in the field of cyber behavior. This chapter reviewed the components, methods, and applications of the brain-computer interfaces, especially illustrating its possible usages in Cyberpsychology. The prospect of BCI is becoming even more promising, as more effort has been made to create applications for the cyber world.

For years, BCI had been limited to laboratory use, because of the heaviness and expensiveness of medical grade EEG systems. However, devices with better mobility and lower costs are quickly emerging, such as dry-electrode EEG devices which could better serve patients and also potentially bring BCIs to our daily life. Nevertheless, there are only prototypes and proofs of concepts, demonstrating the fact that these fields are still having a long way to go. It would be interesting and encouraging to port traditional BCI-based applications to low-cost consumer BCIs. The feasibility must be rigorously tested by scientific researchers and further refinements are also needed to improve performances. Thus, more studies are needed to conduct these fundamental experiments before promoting the low-cost BCI-based systems.

Meanwhile, virtually any brain-computer interface could benefit from understanding how to make better use of the brain signals acquired by the EEG devices. As mentioned above, BCIs now employ different kinds of signals to perform various tasks. The performance of BCIs largely depends on the signals and the classification algorithms. Scientists have been competing to find better ways to decode the data from brains in hopes of improving the accuracy of the BCI speller (Blankertz et al., 2004). We could expect that, in the future, BCIs of higher resolution and lower cost will make BCI-based applications, such as neuro-gaming and assistive speller, easier and more suitable for daily use.

REFERENCES

Alonso-Valerdi, L. M., Salido-Ruiz, R. A., & Ramirez-Mendoza, R. A. (2015). Motor imagery based brain–computer interfaces: An emerging technology to rehabilitate motor deficits. *Neuropsychologia*, *79*, 354–363. doi:10.1016/j. neuropsychologia.2015.09.012 PMID:26382749

Andujar, M., & Gilbert, J. E. (2013). *Let's learn!: enhancing user's engagement levels through passive brain-computer interfaces*. Paper presented at the CHI'13 Extended Abstracts on Human Factors in Computing Systems. 10.1145/2468356.2468480

Ang, K. K., Chua, K. S. G., Phua, K. S., Wang, C., Chin, Z. Y., Kuah, C. W. K., ... Guan, C. (2015). A randomized controlled trial of EEG-based motor imagery brain-computer interface robotic rehabilitation for stroke. *Clinical EEG and Neuroscience*, *46*(4), 310–320. doi:10.1177/1550059414522229 PMID:24756025

Ang, K. K., Guan, C., Phua, K. S., Wang, C., Zhou, L., Tang, K. Y., ... Chua, K. S. G. (2014). Brain-computer interface-based robotic end effector system for wrist and hand rehabilitation: Results of a three-armed randomized controlled trial for chronic stroke. *Frontiers in Neuroengineering*, 7. PMID:25120465

Bakos, Y. (1998). The emerging role of electronic marketplaces on the Internet. *Communications of the ACM*, *41*(8), 35–42. doi:10.1145/280324.280330

Berger, H. (1929). Über das elektrenkephalogramm des menschen. *European Archives of Psychiatry and Clinical Neuroscience*, *87*(1), 527–570.

Birbaumer, N., Gallegos-Ayala, G., Wildgruber, M., Silvoni, S., & Soekadar, S. R. (2014). Direct brain control and communication in paralysis. *Brain Topography*, *27*(1), 4–11. doi:10.100710548-013-0282-1 PMID:23536247

Birbaumer, N., Ghanayim, N., Hinterberger, T., Iversen, I., Kotchoubey, B., Kubler, A., ... Flor, H. (1999). A spelling device for the paralysed. *Nature*, *398*(6725), 297–298. doi:10.1038/18581 PMID:10192330

Birbaumer, N., Kubler, A., Ghanayim, N., Hinterberger, T., Perelmouter, J., Kaiser, J., ... Flor, H. (2000). The thought translation device (TTD) for completely paralyzed patients. *IEEE Transactions on Rehabilitation Engineering*, *8*(2), 190–193. doi:10.1109/86.847812 PMID:10896183

Blankertz, B., Muller, K.-R., Curio, G., Vaughan, T. M., Schalk, G., Wolpaw, J. R., ... Hinterberger, T. (2004). The BCI competition 2003: Progress and perspectives in detection and discrimination of EEG single trials. *Biomedical Engineering. IEEE Transactions on*, *51*(6), 1044–1051. PMID:15188876

Bonnet, L., Lotte, F., & Lécuyer, A. (2013). Two brains, one game: Design and evaluation of a multi-user BCI video game based on motor imagery. *IEEE Transactions on Computational Intelligence and AI in Games*, *5*(2), 185–198. doi:10.1109/TCIAIG.2012.2237173

Bos, D.-O., Reuderink, B., van de Laar, B., Gurkok, H., Muhl, C., Poel, M., . . . Nijholt, A. (2010). *Human-computer interaction for BCI games: Usability and user experience.* Paper presented at the Cyberworlds (CW), 2010 International Conference on. 10.1109/CW.2010.22

Botrel, L., Holz, E., & Kübler, A. (2015). Brain Painting V2: Evaluation of P300-based brain-computer interface for creative expression by an end-user following the user-centered design. *Brain-Computer Interfaces*, *2*(2-3), 135–149. doi:10.1080/2326263X.2015.1100038

Chan, K., Mikami, K., & Kondo, K. (2010). *Measuring interest in linear single player FPS games.* Paper presented at the ACM Siggraph Asia 2010 Sketches. 10.1145/1899950.1899953

Crowley, K., Sliney, A., Pitt, I., & Murphy, D. (2010). *Evaluating a Brain-Computer Interface to Categorise Human Emotional Response.* Paper presented at the Advanced Learning Technologies (ICALT), 2010 IEEE 10th International Conference on.

Daly, J. J., & Wolpaw, J. R. (2008). Brain–computer interfaces in neurological rehabilitation. *Lancet Neurology*, *7*(11), 1032–1043. doi:10.1016/S1474-4422(08)70223-0 PMID:18835541

Deshpande, G., Rangaprakash, D., Oeding, L., Cichocki, A., & Hu, X. P. (2017). A new generation of brain-computer interfaces driven by discovery of latent EEG-fMRI linkages using tensor decomposition. *Frontiers in Neuroscience*, *11*, 246. doi:10.3389/fnins.2017.00246 PMID:28638316

Donchin, E., & Smith, D. (1970). The contingent negative variation and the late positive wave of the average evoked potential. *Electroencephalography and Clinical Neurophysiology*, *29*(2), 201–203. doi:10.1016/0013-4694(70)90124-0 PMID:4194603

Donchin, E., Spencer, K. M., & Wijesinghe, R. (2000). The mental prosthesis: Assessing the speed of a P300-based brain-computer interface. *IEEE Transactions on Rehabilitation Engineering*, *8*(2), 174–179. doi:10.1109/86.847808 PMID:10896179

Eaton, J., & Miranda, E. (2013). *Real-time notation using brainwave control.* Paper presented at the Sound and Music Computing Conference.

Farwell, L. A., & Donchin, E. (1988). Talking off the top of your head: Toward a mental prosthesis utilizing event-related brain potentials. *Electroencephalography and Clinical Neurophysiology*, *70*(6), 510–523. doi:10.1016/0013-4694(88)90149-6 PMID:2461285

Fazel-Rezai, R., Allison, B. Z., Guger, C., Sellers, E. W., Kleih, S. C., & Kübler, A. (2012). P300 brain computer interface: Current challenges and emerging trends. *Frontiers in Neuroengineering*, 5. PMID:22822397

Finke, A., Lenhardt, A., & Ritter, H. (2009). The MindGame: A P300-based brain–computer interface game. *Neural Networks*, *22*(9), 1329–1333. doi:10.1016/j.neunet.2009.07.003 PMID:19635654

Garcia, G. (2008). *High frequency SSVEPs for BCI applications.* Paper presented at the Computer-Human Interaction.

Guger, C., Allison, B., & Ushiba, J. (2017). *Recent Advances in Brain-Computer Interface Research—A Summary of the BCI Award 2015 and BCI Research Trends. In Brain-Computer Interface Research* (pp. 131–136). Springer.

Guger, C., Allison, B. Z., & Müller-Putz, G. R. (2015). *Brain-Computer Interface Research: A State-of-the-Art Summary 4. In Brain-Computer Interface Research* (pp. 1–8). Springer. doi:10.1007/978-3-319-25190-5

Gürkök, H. (2012). *Mind the sheep! User experience evaluation & brain-computer interface games.* University of Twente.

Herrmann, C. S. (2001). Human EEG responses to 1–100 Hz flicker: Resonance phenomena in visual cortex and their potential correlation to cognitive phenomena. *Experimental Brain Research, 137*(3-4), 346–353. doi:10.1007002210100682 PMID:11355381

Hinterberger, T., Widman, G., Lal, T. N., Hill, J., Tangermann, M., Rosenstiel, W., ... Birbaumer, N. (2008). Voluntary brain regulation and communication with electrocorticogram signals. *Epilepsy & Behavior, 13*(2), 300–306. doi:10.1016/j.yebeh.2008.03.014 PMID:18495541

Hochberg, L. R., Serruya, M. D., Friehs, G. M., Mukand, J. A., Saleh, M., Caplan, A. H., ... Donoghue, J. P. (2006). Neuronal ensemble control of prosthetic devices by a human with tetraplegia. *Nature, 442*(7099), 164–171. doi:10.1038/nature04970 PMID:16838014

Holz, E. M., Botrel, L., Kaufmann, T., & Kübler, A. (2015). Long-term independent brain-computer interface home use improves quality of life of a patient in the locked-in state: A case study. *Archives of Physical Medicine and Rehabilitation, 96*(3), S16–S26. doi:10.1016/j.apmr.2014.03.035 PMID:25721543

Holz, E. M., Botrel, L., & Kübler, A. (2015). Independent home use of Brain Painting improves quality of life of two artists in the locked-in state diagnosed with amyotrophic lateral sclerosis. *Brain-Computer Interfaces, 2*(2-3), 117–134. doi:10.1080/2326263X.2015.1100048

Huggins, J. E., Guger, C., Ziat, M., Zander, T. O., Taylor, D., Tangermann, M., . . . Rupp, R. (2017). Workshops of the Sixth International Brain–Computer Interface Meeting: brain–computer interfaces past, present, and future. *Brain-Computer Interfaces*, 1-34.

Hwang, H.-J., Kim, S., Choi, S., & Im, C.-H. (2013). EEG-based brain-computer interfaces: A thorough literature survey. *International Journal of Human-Computer Interaction, 29*(12), 814–826. doi:10.1080/10447318.2013.780869

Jarosiewicz, B., Sarma, A. A., Bacher, D., Masse, N. Y., Simeral, J. D., Sorice, B., . . . Gilja, V. (2015). Virtual typing by people with tetraplegia using a self-calibrating intracortical brain-computer interface. *Science Translational Medicine, 7*(313).

Kaplan, A., Zhigulskaya, D., & Kirjanov, D. (2016). Studying the ability to control human phantom fingers in P300 brain-computer interface. *Вестник Российского государственного медицинского университета*(2 (eng)).

Karim, A. A., Hinterberger, T., Richter, J., Mellinger, J., Neumann, N., Flor, H., ... Birbaumer, N. (2006). Neural internet: Web surfing with brain potentials for the completely paralyzed. *Neurorehabilitation and Neural Repair, 20*(4), 508–515. doi:10.1177/1545968306290661 PMID:17082507

Kübler, A., Halder, S., Furdea, A., & Hösle, A. (2008). Brain painting – BCI meets art. *Proceedings of the 4th International Brain-Computer Interface Workshop and Training Course*, 361–366.

Kübler, A., Nijboer, F., Mellinger, J., Vaughan, T. M., Pawelzik, H., Schalk, G., ... Wolpaw, J. R. (2005). Patients with ALS can use sensorimotor rhythms to operate a brain-computer interface. *Neurology, 64*(10), 1775–1777. doi:10.1212/01. WNL.0000158616.43002.6D PMID:15911809

Kucukyildiz, G., Ocak, H., Karakaya, S., & Sayli, O. (2017). Design and implementation of a multi sensor based brain computer interface for a robotic wheelchair. *Journal of Intelligent & Robotic Systems*, 1–17.

Kumar, S., & Sharma, M. (2012). BCI: Next Generation for HCI. *International Journal of Advanced Research in Computer Science and Software Engineering, 2*(3), 146–151.

Leeb, R., Lancelle, M., Kaiser, V., Fellner, D. W., & Pfurtscheller, G. (2013). Thinking penguin: Multimodal brain–computer interface control of a vr game. *IEEE Transactions on Computational Intelligence and AI in Games, 5*(2), 117–128. doi:10.1109/TCIAIG.2013.2242072

Leuthardt, E. C., Schalk, G., Wolpaw, J. R., Ojemann, J. G., & Moran, D. W. (2004). A brain–computer interface using electrocorticographic signals in humans. *Journal of Neural Engineering, 1*(2), 63–71. doi:10.1088/1741-2560/1/2/001 PMID:15876624

Liao, L.-D., Chen, C.-Y., Wang, I.-J., Chen, S.-F., Li, S.-Y., Chen, B.-W., ... Lin, C.-T. (2012). Gaming control using a wearable and wireless EEG-based brain-computer interface device with novel dry foam-based sensors. *Journal of Neuroengineering and Rehabilitation, 9*(1), 5. doi:10.1186/1743-0003-9-5 PMID:22284235

Lotte, F., Congedo, M., Lécuyer, A., Lamarche, F., & Arnaldi, B. (2007). A review of classification algorithms for EEG-based brain–computer interfaces. *Journal of Neural Engineering, 4*(2), R1–R13. doi:10.1088/1741-2560/4/2/R01 PMID:17409472

Mellinger, J., Hinterberger, T., Bensch, M., Schröder, M., & Birbaumer, N. (2003). Surfing the web with electrical brain signals: the brain web surfer (BWS) for the completely paralysed. *Proc. 2nd World Congr. Int. Soc. Physical and Rehabilitation Medicine*, 731-738.

Mellinger, J., Schalk, G., Braun, C., Preissl, H., Rosenstiel, W., Birbaumer, N., & Kübler, A. (2007). An MEG-based brain–computer interface (BCI). *NeuroImage, 36*(3), 581–593. doi:10.1016/j.neuroimage.2007.03.019 PMID:17475511

Miranda, E. R. (2010). Plymouth brain-computer music interfacing project: From EEG audio mixers to composition informed by cognitive neuroscience. *International Journal of Arts and Technology, 3*(2-3), 154–176. doi:10.1504/IJART.2010.032562

Miranda, E. R., Durrant, S., & Anders, T. (2008). *Towards brain-computer music interfaces: progress and challenges.* Paper presented at the Applied Sciences on Biomedical and Communication Technologies, 2008. ISABEL'08. First International Symposium on. 10.1109/ISABEL.2008.4712626

Moghimi, S., Kushki, A., Marie Guerguerian, A., & Chau, T. (2013). A review of EEG-based brain-computer interfaces as access pathways for individuals with severe disabilities. *Assistive Technology, 25*(2), 99–110. doi:10.1080/10400435.20 12.723298 PMID:23923692

Mugler, E. M., Ruf, C. A., Halder, S., Bensch, M., & Kubler, A. (2010). Design and implementation of a P300-based brain-computer interface for controlling an internet browser. *IEEE Transactions on Neural Systems and Rehabilitation Engineering, 18*(6), 599–609. doi:10.1109/TNSRE.2010.2068059 PMID:20805058

Muglerab, E., Benschc, M., Haldera, S., Rosenstielc, W., Bogdancd, M., Birbaumerae, N., & Kübleraf, A. (2008). Control of an internet browser using the P300 event-related potential. *International Journal of Bioelectromagnetism, 10*(1), 56–63.

Mühl, C., Gürkök, H., Bos, D. P.-O., Thurlings, M. E., Scherffig, L., Duvinage, M., ... Heylen, D. (2010). Bacteria hunt. *Journal on Multimodal User Interfaces, 4*(1), 11–25. doi:10.100712193-010-0046-0

Münßinger, J. I., Halder, S., Kleih, S. C., Furdea, A., Raco, V., Hösle, A., & Kübler, A. (2010). Brain painting: First evaluation of a new brain–computer interface application with ALS-patients and healthy volunteers. *Frontiers in Neuroscience*, 4. PMID:21151375

Naseer, N., & Hong, K.-S. (2015). fNIRS-based brain-computer interfaces: A review. *Frontiers in Human Neuroscience*, 9.

Niedermeyer, E., & da Silva, F. H. L. (2005). *Electroencephalography: basic principles, clinical applications, and related fields*. Wolters Kluwer Health.

Nijholt, A. (2009). *BCI for games: A 'state of the art' survey. In Entertainment Computing-ICEC 2008* (pp. 225–228). Springer.

Nijholt, A., Bos, D. P.-O., & Reuderink, B. (2009). Turning shortcomings into challenges: Brain–computer interfaces for games. *Entertainment Computing, 1*(2), 85–94. doi:10.1016/j.entcom.2009.09.007

Nijholt, A., & Tan, D. (2007). Playing with your brain: brain-computer interfaces and games. *Proceedings of the international conference on Advances in computer entertainment technology*. 10.1145/1255047.1255140

Odom, J. V., Bach, M., Barber, C., Brigell, M., Marmor, M. F., Tormene, A. P., & Holder, G. E. (2004). Visual evoked potentials standard. *Documenta ophthalmologica, 108*(2), 115-123.

Pfurtscheller, G., Müller, G. R., Pfurtscheller, J., Gerner, H. J., & Rupp, R. (2003). 'Thought'–control of functional electrical stimulation to restore hand grasp in a patient with tetraplegia. *Neuroscience Letters, 351*(1), 33–36. doi:10.1016/S0304-3940(03)00947-9 PMID:14550907

Pfurtscheller, G., Neuper, C., Flotzinger, D., & Pregenzer, M. (1997). EEG-based discrimination between imagination of right and left hand movement. *Electroencephalography and Clinical Neurophysiology, 103*(6), 642–651. doi:10.1016/S0013-4694(97)00080-1 PMID:9546492

Pfurtscheller, G., Stancak, A. Jr, & Neuper, C. (1996). Event-related synchronization (ERS) in the alpha band—an electrophysiological correlate of cortical idling: A review. *International Journal of Psychophysiology, 24*(1), 39–46. doi:10.1016/S0167-8760(96)00066-9 PMID:8978434

Pichiorri, F., Morone, G., Petti, M., Toppi, J., Pisotta, I., Molinari, M., ... Cincotti, F. (2015). Brain–computer interface boosts motor imagery practice during stroke recovery. *Annals of Neurology, 77*(5), 851–865. doi:10.1002/ana.24390 PMID:25712802

Rebsamen, B., Guan, C., Zhang, H., Wang, C., Teo, C., Ang, M. H., & Burdet, E. (2010). A brain controlled wheelchair to navigate in familiar environments. *Neural Systems and Rehabilitation Engineering. IEEE Transactions on, 18*(6), 590–598.

Ruiz, S., Buyukturkoglu, K., Rana, M., Birbaumer, N., & Sitaram, R. (2014). Real-time fMRI brain computer interfaces: Self-regulation of single brain regions to networks. *Biological Psychology*, *95*, 4–20. doi:10.1016/j.biopsycho.2013.04.010 PMID:23643926

Sands, S. F., & Sands, J. A. (2012). Recording brain waves at the supermarket: What can we learn from a shopper's brain? *IEEE Pulse*, *3*(3), 34–37. doi:10.1109/MPUL.2012.2189170 PMID:22678838

Saulynas, S., Lechner, C., & Kuber, R. (2017). Towards the use of brain–computer interface and gestural technologies as a potential alternative to PIN authentication. *International Journal of Human-Computer Interaction*, 1–12.

Schalk, G. (2008). Brain–computer symbiosis. *Journal of Neural Engineering*, *5*(1), 1. doi:10.1088/1741-2560/5/1/P01 PMID:18310804

Shenjie, S., Thomas, K. P., & Vinod, A. (2014). *Two player EEG-based neurofeedback ball game for attention enhancement.* Paper presented at the Systems, Man and Cybernetics (SMC), 2014 IEEE International Conference on. 10.1109/SMC.2014.6974412

Silberstein, R. B., & Nield, G. E. (2012). Measuring Emotion in Advertising Research: Prefrontal Brain Activity. *IEEE Pulse*, *3*(3), 24–27. doi:10.1109/MPUL.2012.2189172 PMID:22678836

Sitaram, R., Weiskopf, N., Caria, A., Veit, R., Erb, M., & Birbaumer, N. (2008). fMRI brain-computer interfaces. *IEEE Signal Processing Magazine*, *25*(1), 95–106. doi:10.1109/MSP.2008.4408446

Sutter, E. E. (1992). The brain response interface: Communication through visually-induced electrical brain responses. *Journal of Microcomputer Applications*, *15*(1), 31–45. doi:10.1016/0745-7138(92)90045-7

Thorpe, J., van Oorschot, P. C., & Somayaji, A. (2005). Pass-thoughts: authenticating with our minds. *Proceedings of the 2005 workshop on New security paradigms.* 10.1145/1146269.1146282

Wadeson, A., Nijholt, A., & Nam, C. S. (2015). Artistic brain-computer interfaces: State-of-the-art control mechanisms. *Brain-Computer Interfaces*, *2*(2-3), 70–75. doi:10.1080/2326263X.2015.1103155

Wiedemann, H. R. (1994). Hans Berger. *European Journal of Pediatrics*, *153*(10), 705–705. doi:10.1007/BF01954482 PMID:7813523

Williams, D., & Skoric, M. (2005). Internet fantasy violence: A test of aggression in an online game. *Communication Monographs*, 72(2), 217–233. doi:10.1080/03637750500111781

Wolpaw, J. R., Birbaumer, N., McFarland, D. J., Pfurtscheller, G., & Vaughan, T. M. (2002). Brain–computer interfaces for communication and control. *Clinical Neurophysiology*, *113*(6), 767–791. doi:10.1016/S1388-2457(02)00057-3 PMID:12048038

Wolpaw, J. R., & McFarland, D. J. (2004). Control of a two-dimensional movement signal by a noninvasive brain-computer interface in humans. *Proceedings of the National Academy of Sciences of the United States of America*, *101*(51), 17849–17854. doi:10.1073/pnas.0403504101 PMID:15585584

Wolpaw, J. R., McFarland, D. J., & Vaughan, T. M. (2000). Brain-computer interface research at the Wadsworth Center. *IEEE Transactions on Rehabilitation Engineering*, *8*(2), 222–226. doi:10.1109/86.847823 PMID:10896194

Wu, C.-H., Liu, C. J., & Tzeng, Y.-L. (2011). *Brain Wave Analysis in Optimal Color Allocation for Children's Electronic Book Design*. Paper presented at the TANET 2011.

Wu, D., Li, C., & Yao, D. (2013). Scale-free brain quartet: Artistic filtering of multi-channel brainwave music. *PLoS One*, *8*(5), e64046. doi:10.1371/journal.pone.0064046 PMID:23717527

Wyckoff, S. N., Sherlin, L. H., Ford, N. L., & Dalke, D. (2015). Validation of a wireless dry electrode system for electroencephalography. *Journal of Neuroengineering and Rehabilitation*, *12*(1), 95. doi:10.118612984-015-0089-2 PMID:26520574

Yoshida, K., Sakamoto, Y., Satou, Y., Miyaji, I., Yamada, K., & Fujii, S. (2011). *Trial of a distance learning system using a brain wave sensor. In Knowledge-Based and Intelligent Information and Engineering Systems* (pp. 86–95). Springer.

Young, K. S. (1998). Internet addiction: The emergence of a new clinical disorder. *Cyberpsychology & Behavior*, *1*(3), 237–244. doi:10.1089/cpb.1998.1.237

Yu, T., Li, Y., Long, J., & Gu, Z. (2012). Surfing the internet with a BCI mouse. *Journal of Neural Engineering*, *9*(3), 036012. doi:10.1088/1741-2560/9/3/036012 PMID:22626911

Zander, T. O., Kothe, C., Jatzev, S., & Gaertner, M. (2010). *Enhancing human-computer interaction with input from active and passive brain-computer interfaces. In Brain-Computer Interfaces* (pp. 181–199). Springer.

Zander, T. O., Lehne, M., Ihme, K., Jatzev, S., Correia, J., Kothe, C., ... Nijboer, F. (2011). A dry EEG-system for scientific research and brain–computer interfaces. *Frontiers in Neuroscience*, 5. PMID:21647345

Zhang, R., Li, Y., Yan, Y., Zhang, H., Wu, S., Yu, T., & Gu, Z. (2016). Control of a Wheelchair in an Indoor Environment Based on a Brain–Computer Interface and Automated Navigation. *IEEE Transactions on Neural Systems and Rehabilitation Engineering*, *24*(1), 128–139. doi:10.1109/TNSRE.2015.2439298 PMID:26054072

Section 3
Activity–Focused Cyber Behavior

Chapter 8
Digital Behavior Change Interventions

David Messer
Arizona State University, USA

Caroline E. Shanholtz
University of Arizona, USA

Abhik Chowdhury
Arizona State University, USA

ABSTRACT

The internet holds considerable potential to improve the world's health. Noncommunicable, or so-called lifestyle, diseases are responsible for more than three-fifths of all deaths worldwide. With over half of the world's population now online, public health officials and entrepreneurs have developed a growing array of digitally mediated interventions to encourage healthy lifestyle choices. In this chapter, the authors discuss online and digitally mediated interventions, provide examples of their use, and summarize recommendations for future research and development. Particular attention is paid to online education, social media support groups, adaptive and gamified interventions, and emerging technologies such as ambient and wearable sensors and artificial intelligence.

INTRODUCTION

The internet holds considerable potential to improve the world's health. Noncommunicable, or so-called lifestyle, diseases are responsible for more than three-fifths of all deaths worldwide (World Health Organization, 2017). These diseases lower quality of life, reinforce inequality in wealth, and incur an enormous economic

DOI: 10.4018/978-1-5225-7128-5.ch008

burden (Kaiser Family Foundation, 2017). Thankfully, many can be prevented or ameliorated through behavior change. While the benefits of such changes, involving adjustments to exercise, diet, smoking and alcohol use among other activities, are widely-known, many people decline to make them (Hardcastle et al., 2015). Far-reaching, sustainable, and low-cost interventions that encourage healthy behavior are needed. The internet offers an important tool to achieve this end.

Since 2000, internet use has increased nearly tenfold, with over half of the world's population now online (Internet World Statistics, 2018). Public health officials and entrepreneurs have taken notice and developed a growing array of digitally-mediated interventions to encourage healthy lifestyle choices. In the following pages we will discuss these interventions, provide examples of their use, and summarize recommendations for future research and development.

Asynchronous Educational Modules

The term "asynchronous" refers to users' ability to access information at any time, without needing to "synchronize" their learning with an instructional source (e.g. a teacher). Most early online interventions were asynchronous, consisting of instructive text, pictures, and video presented on a webpage, essentially emulating book learning. Initially, these interventions provided an important source of information for users who lacked access to print reference materials. Today, much of the material on the internet still takes this form and is used ubiquitously to help people learn, make decisions, and change behavior. The central benefit of asynchronous interventions is the freedom to learn at one's own pace and to study, in depth, areas of interest. The drawback of such a simple presentational format is its passivity—users are required to actively seek out the intervention and return in the absence of an incentive, though newer interventions employ interactive and gamification elements to increase use, as discussed below. Thus, while well-constructed asynchronous interventions can be effective for motivated users, attrition is high for those with less motivation. The example "Effects of Internet Training in Mindfulness Meditation on Variables Related to Cancer Recovery," presented below, provides a good example of the differential effectiveness inherent in these interventions.

Synchronous Interventions

With improved video-conferencing technology, digitally-mediated interventions replicating person-to-person therapeutic interactions have become possible. Online coaching, psychotherapy, and medical encounters have been explored and real-time classroom environments developed (Tuckson, Edmunds, & Hodgkins, 2017). Unlike their asynchronous brethren, real-time interventions provide a sense of community and immediacy, prompting user engagement regardless of initial motivation, and allow for personalized feedback from the instructional source. Synchronous online interventions may be less stressful for some users than in-person interactions and thus may encourage use (Chen, Ko, & Lin, 2006). For instance, in Wolever et al. (2012), adults dealing with workplace stress received 12 weeks of either traditional (in-person) group or internet-delivered mindfulness training. The two conditions showed similar improvements on perceived stress, mindfulness, and sleep quality when compared to wait-list control condition, but the internet condition showed lower attrition and additional improvement in heart rate variability, a measure of physiological resilience.

Social Media Support Groups

Online support groups provide a venue in which individuals with similar goals can give and receive advice and encouragement. While some groups exist on free-standing platforms (the "Fitbit" (2018) community is an example of an independent behavior change support group), groups that piggyback on existing social media platforms, such as Facebook and Twitter, have received accelerating attention due to the large number of users frequenting these sites (Bennett & Glasgow, 2009). In addition to their reach, social media support groups allow users to generate and share content—increasing personal investment in the intervention—and receive advice from family and friends—potentially improving credibility and acceptance of the circulated health information (De Bruyn & Lilien, 2008). Despite these factors encouraging engagement, support group use and persistence has been lower than expected (Maher et al., 2014). Only one study (Foster et al., 2010) succeeded in enticing frequent participation and did so by grouping users with family and friends (rather than strangers) and initiating a friendly-competitive "leader-board" in which users were challenged to outdo one another in achieving their health goals. Such a strategy seems consonant with the ways that people naturally use social media—to interact with people known to them offline and to engage in entertainment (Maher et al., 2014).

Adaptive and Gamified Interventions

Foster's (2010) use of a "friendly-competitive" atmosphere suggests that engagement, fun, and community are key ingredients for user persistence in online interventions. Developers have attempted to employ these elements by creating websites that respond uniquely (i.e. adapt) to user input and provide game-like incentives, such as "badges," virtual points, and tangible rewards (Bimba et al., 2017; Sardi, Idri,

& Fernández-Alemán, 2017). The online language learning platform "Duolingo" (2018) for example, rewards regular use with virtual currency that can be used to unlock special website content and earn on-site rewards. Adaptive website responses reinforce users' perception that their work is producing meaningful results and provides a sense of connection similar to person-to-person interaction. In addition, these websites often enable connection with one's online community by the sharing of personal progress over social media. The example, "A randomized clinical trial of online stress inoculation for adult children of divorce" presented below, is an example of an intervention emphasizing interactive user involvement.

New Technologies: Ambient and Wearable Sensors

Wearable and ambient sensors continuously collect and display data about their environment. Today's smartphones can perform certain functions in this manner, for instance measuring the phone's movement and orientation in space, from which conclusions about one's walking or sleep movement can be drawn. The utility of these applications is necessarily limited, however, by a smartphone's limited hardware and computing power. In contrast, sensors manufactured for specialized use can record large amounts of live, high-quality data without the need for user interaction and then present this data via an attractive and convenient interface. Such precise and timely data can provide a foundation for personalized goal setting and progress tracking (Lyons, Lewis, Mayrsohn, & Rowland, 2014).

Problems with these devices have emerged, however. Use of consumer-grade wearables is low; a full half of people who purchase a device stop using it, permanently, and a third do so within six months of purchase (Patel, Asch, & Volpp, 2015). Unlike cell phones which serve a variety of functions, specialized electronics such as fitness trackers and posture correctors have little value outside of their specific, dedicated purpose (Piwek, Ellis, Andrews, & Joinson, 2016). Further, many devices have difficulty reaching their target market. Fitness trackers, for example, tend to be purchased by individuals well-versed in exercise who wish to quantify their progress, rather than those for whom the devices may be most useful—i.e. individuals who are older, in poorer health, or who lack motivation to exercise (Patel, Asch, & Volpp, 2015). In addition, for a sizable portion of the population, the cost of these devices is prohibitive. Lastly, companies' goals of efficiently moving wearable electronics to market often precludes the completion of rigorous efficacy studies. Claims of sensor accuracy and reliability are, therefore, often left unsubstantiated. The example, "Advances in Wearable and Ambient Sensors," presented below, further explores the potential and challenges of these technologies.

Blended Interventions

Recent interventions blend many of the elements presented above to create comprehensive programs. For instance, a weight-loss application created by Omada Health and recently profiled by National Public Radio (Aubrey, 2018) includes asynchronous diet and exercise information, synchronous support from an e-coach, social media encouragement from peers, gamification, and an internet-enabled scale to send health data to researchers. Such comprehensive interventions are likely to become more common, since they utilize the benefits of each approach in a method suited to the health outcomes targeted (Verhoeks, Teunissen, van der Stelt-Steenbergen, & Largo-Janssen, 2017).

ILLUSTRATIVE EXAMPLES

The following interventions illustrate principles described above. The first study is an example of a stand-alone asynchronous intervention, the second utilizes user interactivity and support group elements, and the third describes recent developments in the field of wearable and ambient sensors.

Example 1: Effects of Internet Training in Mindfulness Meditation on Variables Related to Cancer Recovery (Messer, Horan, Larkey, & Shanholtz, Manuscript Submitted for Publication)

For many cancer survivors, depression, anxiety, fatigue, and sleep difficulties persist after treatment, compromising quality of life and engendering further health problems. The goal of this study was to determine whether online mindfulness training could reduce these symptoms and improve recovery. Specifically, anxiety, depression, overall emotional functioning, sleep, and fatigue were assessed before and after the intervention, as outcome measures.

Mindfulness training may be particularly beneficial for this population. While, in general, stress can be overcome through active coping, for cancer survivors, stress is often caused by the ongoing, subjective, fear of recurrence rather than by a specific external stressor (Allen, Savadatti, & Levy, 2009; Koolhaas et al., 2015). Effective coping must therefore involve adaptation to the experience of anxiety. Mindfulness-based treatments, developed to help individuals cope with distressing thoughts and feelings, are uniquely suited to this need.

This study's mindfulness training, derived from Messer, Horan, Turner, & Weber's (2015) treatment, consisted of six guided meditation audio clips with accompanying textual lessons. Each week, a new exercise and lesson were presented. Participants were asked to read the lessons and listen to the exercises once a day at a time and place of their choosing. Treatment adherence was monitored by users clicking on a link that appeared only after an exercise finished playing. If not clicked within ten minutes, the link disappeared. Meanwhile, *usual care* condition participants completed all pre and post-assessments but were not provided with mindfulness lessons or exercises.

Participants were cancer survivors recruited from major hospitals and randomly assigned to either internet-delivered mindfulness training or usual care control conditions. All participants met inclusion criteria of being age 35 or older, literate in English, owning a confidential email address, and having entered remission from cancer in the previous three years. In addition, those with a current mindfulness practice, autoimmune disorder, or impaired hearing were excluded. Seventy-six percent of the sample identified as female and 80% as white, with a mean age of 51.0 years.

Results revealed clear positive results across all variables, with particularly large effects on sleep and fatigue. Sleep and fatigue are key factors affecting cancer patients' independence, quality of life, and ability to pursue life goals (Hann, Denniston, & Baker, 2000) and sleep, in particular, influences future health outcomes (Sephton & Spiegel, 2003).

In addition, we tracked user engagement and correlated this with improvement. Mindfulness-training participants completed, on average, approximately two exercises per week. Two-thirds engaged with the treatment on a weekly basis or more often. Pearson product-moment correlations indicated that for all variables, greater exercise completion was related to improved outcomes.

Mindfulness training offers health benefits and a method by which cancer patients can cope with depression and anxiety. Psychologically healthy patients can more easily manage their recovery, follow treatment protocols, access needed care, and enjoy life (Adler & Paige, 2008). Online training represents an accessible, cost-effective intervention for survivors who cannot, or prefer not to, participate in in-person mindfulness-based interventions (Fish, Brimson, & Lynch, 2016). Whether offered as a stand-alone treatment or incorporated into hospital-based medical care, online mindfulness training represents a significant emerging resource for physicians and their patients.

Example 2: A Randomized Clinical Trial of Online Stress Inoculation for Adult Children of Divorce (Shanholtz, Messer, Davidson, Randall, & Horan, 2017)

Transitions is an online program aimed at helping young adults acquire coping skills to use in the context of a recent parental divorce. The intervention targets stress and relationship-management/communication techniques for use in parent-child relationships. In addition, *Transitions* provides psychoeducation regarding parental separation, and training in relaxation, cognitive restructuring, and mindfulness meditation. The program, in its entirety, lasts four hours over the course of two weeks.

Transitions consists of lectures presented over Microsoft PowerPoint slides, interactive reflection questions, and video testimonials from other college students who have experienced parental separation or divorce while in college. Participants were encouraged to practice their newly acquired skills in their outside life and to report the amount and nature of this practice to researchers.

Participants ($N = 108$), recruited through a southwestern university and screened to be over age 18, had all experienced a parental separation or divorce within the past year, and denied seeking psychological services elsewhere at the time of the study. Participants (51% male) primarily identified as White (65%), were on average 19 years of age, and came from families with heterosexual parents. Participants were randomly assigned to participate in *Transitions* or a control group. All participants were pretested immediately before beginning treatment, received treatment, and then posttested one week after treatment completion in both the treatment and control conditions. Outcome assessments measured stress and parent-young adult relationship quality.

Participants completing *Transitions* reported significant reductions in stress in comparison with control participants but no improvement in parent-child relationship quality. Future research should further explore the reasons for this partial effectiveness. It is possible that parent-young adult relationship quality requires more time to change, and especially so, given that many young adults in college do not interact with their parent on a daily basis. Additionally, *Transitions* targets only half of the parent-child relationship; future research might provide resources to both parents and children and evaluate changes over time driven by each participant in the dyad.

Young adults who experience parental separation need services to assist them in coping with this challenging family restructuring (Bulduc, et al., 2007). *Transitions* provides evidence that an interactive online intervention can reduce family-related stress. The online format may be particularly effective for this population, since young adults are familiar with web-based services and have access to the internet on a college campus (Wantland, et al., 2004). Further online interventions can be provided and scaled at little, accessed in a convenient and private location, and pursued on a schedule matching participant needs.

Example 3: Wearable and Ambient Sensor Technologies - Past and Present

In 1993, Thad Starner created and began donning what he termed a "remembrance agent," a wearable computer that included a handheld keyboard and small head-mounted text display (Starner & Rhodes, 1996). In interactions with other people and the environment, Thad would load useful information onto the screen. Though a bit unwieldy (and, frankly, not very attractive), the remembrance agent's main drawback was its inability to cull multiple data streams (e.g. date, time, and GPS location) to provide useful contextual information. Even so, Starner's invention bridged the gap between the physical world and our vast reserves of digital information. Today, Google and select other companies use artificial intelligence (AI) systems to comb through online data and prompt users to change their behavior. For example, by accessing GPS smartphone locations, online calendars, and ambient traffic information, Google can prompt users to leave for any scheduled meetings and provide maps and driving directions. Leveraging data from a diverse set of sensors may solve the problem of wearables providing little value outside their original use case (Kennedy et al., 2012), but having access to such a wide range of data may pose privacy and security concerns.

While smartphones can act as ambient sensors, the UPRIGHT (2018) posture corrector is truly wearable. The small UPRIGHT device clings to the upper back and contains an accelerometer that works as an orientation sensor. If the user slouches, the device provides feedback in the form of a gentle buzz. In addition, UPRIGHT provides a mobile interface that tracks posture improvement over time and allows users to set long term goals and track progress.

As discussed previously, few wearable sensors provide rigorously verified health information. The Alivecor Heart Monitor (2018) is one that does. Produced by Kardina, this wearable electrocardiogram wristband is the first Apple watch accessory to obtain U.S. Food and Drug Administration approval. The device is designed to serve individuals at high risk for atrial fibrillation and stroke by providing users and doctors access to heart rhythm data. Users install an application on their iPhone and apple watch and the latter continuously collects low-fidelity heart rate data which is analyzed by AI to identify irregular patterns. If an abnormality is recognized, the application prompts the user to place their other hand on the band and take a high-fidelity reading. All readings can be immediately shared with one's doctor for review.

CONCLUSION AND FUTURE RESEARCH DIRECTIONS

Many of the examples presented above produced significant, healthful behavior change. This result argues strongly for the potential of new technologies to improve societal health. Indeed, digital behavior change interventions offer an array of benefits. First, most can be made widely availability at low-cost, benefitting individuals who may have trouble accessing in-person support (e.g. those in rural areas, with limited incomes, or with physical disabilities (Norman et al., 2007). Second, these interventions can be customized to meet the needs of unique users, thereby increasing cultural sensitivity (Yellowlees, Marks, Hilty, & Shore, 2008) and can be updated regularly to reflect emerging knowledge. Third, online interventions allow some degree of anonymity, which may be preferred by patients with sensitive health conditions (Lau, Colley, Willett, & Lynd, 2012). Fourth, the use of existing social-networking platforms allows individuals to receive information from family, peers, and other trusted sources, increasing the credibility of the information and the individual's motivation to change. (Maher et al., 2014). Fifth, these interventions can employ interactive and gamification strategies to increase involvement, learning, and sense of connection (Bimba et al., 2017). Finally, new technologies that monitor health metrics in real-time would allow patients and their doctors—who could receive such information streamed to them—to notice small declines in health and make lifestyle change before larger problems manifest. Monitoring and timely support, provided from a distance, would decrease the need for in-person medical visits and save patients time and money.

Still, challenges remain. To begin, user engagement and persistence are central concerns. To put it plainly, if people fail to use digital behavior change interventions, it will not matter how effective they are. The intervention, "Effects of Internet Training in Mindfulness Meditation on Variables Related to Cancer Recovery" (Messer, Horan, Larkey, & Shanholtz, In Press) provides a good example of this. Effectiveness correlated with frequency of use, but some users simply did not complete the intervention and thus did not benefit. Low engagement with online interventions is common and methods to encourage use and persistence should continue to be investigated (Barello, et al., 2015). As previously noted, adaptive and gamified interventions, and Foster et al.'s (2010) use of a "friendly-competitive" community-based environment seem particularly promising for online interventions. For consumer electronics, additional factors such as cost, comfort, attractiveness may impact adoption.

While engagement of some sort is clearly critical, what constitutes effective engagement may vary depending upon the intervention, health outcome targeted, and method of user engagement (e.g. via phone, computer, or ambient sensor, etc.). Some interventions may require consistent use to attain positive health effects (e.g.

the practice of mindfulness) while other, so called "just-in-time," interventions (Intille, 2004) may require only intermittent use at critical moments. Researchers should utilize both qualitative and quantitative inquiry to understand and patterns and obstacles of use and discern which interventions, in which dosages, delivered at which moments, lead to desirable outcomes for which behaviors. Given the complexity of these questions, researchers have begun using artificial intelligence to synthesize, analyze, and draw conclusions from the data of diverse studies (Michie et al., 2017a).

Second, assuring the effectiveness of interventions is an ongoing challenge. Traditional evaluation, involving randomized controlled trials and outcome analysis weeks or months after implementation, is too slow to match the quick evolution of platforms and subsequent user engagement. However, real-time data produced by digital interventions allows researchers to utilize nuanced research designs and statistical techniques, such as factorial and adaptive approaches, to refine models of behavior change and predict and evaluate outcomes (for a full description of techniques employed to evaluate digital interventions, see West & Michie, 2016). Another challenge to evaluation is the potential lack of coordination between researchers and developers, which is to say, developers may move to market before determining a product's effectiveness. While digital interventions need not show effectiveness to be marketed, it is ultimately in the best interest of developers to help users. Embedding evaluation into the design process itself, from prototype to finished product, sharing these results with the public, and allowing external research to be conducted on new technologies, will improve both commercial success and consumer safety (Michie et al., 2017b). Despite these steps, the effectiveness of many interventions may never ultimately be determined, given the continually changing landscape of intervention implementation, content, and use.

Finally, privacy is a concern with digital interventions, which generate a wealth of personal and commercially valuable data. While data gathered from FDA approved medical devices are protected by the Health Insurance Portability and Accountability Act, those collected by consumer electronics are not. Users are left to weigh the benefit of the intervention against the cost of potentially exposing health information to third parties and possibly impacting health or life insurances decisions. Governments should draft regulations concerning this data sooner rather than later.

Digital interventions also encounter challenges like those of traditional interventions, including the risk of providing incorrect or counterproductive advice to the public and the possibility that user engagement may reduce the use of more effective behavior change strategies.

The example "Wearable and Ambient Sensor Technologies: Past and Present," highlights the considerable potential of new technologies to improve preventive health care and prompt behavior change. Certain challenges are unique to these technologies, however. First, the accuracy of sensors and AI algorithms that analyze their data are difficult to ascertain. Anecdotally, such technologies continue to improve; however, unlike unlike medical devices, which are regulated by the United States Food and Drug Administration, consumer electronics are unregulated and need not voluntarily provide reliability data (only a few have. The Alivecor heart monitor, presented previously, is one). Potentially inaccurate information is a problem both for users and for doctors expected to make diagnosis and prescription decisions based on it. Assuming accurate information can be obtained, doctors will need a way of reviewing the vast amounts of information arriving from these devices daily. Artificial intelligence algorithms will be needed to analyze and draw attention to salient changes, and questions of medical liability concerning this new information remain.

Despite these challenges, digital behavior-change interventions hold enormous potential. With creativity, responsibility, and care, researchers, entrepreneurs, and the public can create a technological infrastructure that will support human health for years to come.

REFERENCES

Adler, N. E., & Page, A. E. K. (2008). *Cancer care for the whole patient: Meeting psychosocial health needs.* Institute of Medicine: Committee on Psychosocial Services to Cancer Patients/Families in a Community Setting Board on Health Care Services.

Alivecor Heart Monitor. (2018). Retrieved from https://www.alivecor.com/

Allen, J. D., Savadatti, S., & Levy, A. G. (2009). The transition from breast cancer 'patient' to 'survivor.'. *Psycho-Oncology, 18*(1), 71–78. doi:10.1002/pon.1380 PMID:18613299

Aubrey, A. (2018, March 5). This chef lost 50 pounds and reversed prediabetes with a digital program. *National Public Radio.* Retrieved from https://www.npr.org/sections/thesalt/2018/03/05/589286575/this-chef-lost-50-pounds-and-reversed-pre-diabetes-with-a-digital-program

Barello, S., Triberti, S., Graffigna, G., Libreri, C., Serino, S., Hibbard, J., & Riva, G. (2015). eHealth for Patient Engagement: A Systematic Review. *Frontiers in Psychology, 6*, 2013. doi:10.3389/fpsyg.2015.02013 PMID:26779108

Bennett, G. G., & Glasgow, R. E. (2009). The delivery of public health interventions via the Internet: Actualizing their potential. *Annual Review of Public Health, 30*(1), 273–292. doi:10.1146/annurev.publhealth.031308.100235 PMID:19296777

Bimba, A. T., Idris, N., Al-Hunaiyyan, A., Mahmud, R. B., & Shuib, N. L. B. M. (2017). Adaptive feedback in computer-based learning environments: A review. *Adaptive Behavior*, 25(5), 217–234. doi:10.1177/1059712317727590

Bulduc, J. L., Caron, S. L., & Logue, M. E. (2007). The effects of parental divorce on college students. *Journal of Divorce & Remarriage*, 46(3-4), 83–104. doi:10.1300/J087v46n03_06

Chen, N., Ko, H., Kinshuk, & Lin, T. (2006). A model for synchronous learning using the Internet. *Innovations in Education and Teaching International*, 42(2), 181–194. doi:10.1080/14703290500062599

De Bruyn, A., & Lilien, G. L. (2008). A multi-stage model of word-of-mouth influence through viral marketing. *International Journal of Research in Marketing*, 25(3), 151–163. doi:10.1016/j.ijresmar.2008.03.004

Duolingo. (2018). Retrieved from https://www.duolingo.com/

Falconier, M. K., Nussbeck, F., Bodenmann, G., Schneider, H., & Bradbury, T. (2015). Stress from daily hassles in couples: Its effects on intradyadic stress, relationship satisfaction, and physical and psychological well-being. *Journal of Marital and Family Therapy*, 41(2), 221–235. doi:10.1111/jmft.12073 PMID:24807831

Fish, J., Brimson, J., & Lynch, S. (2016). Mindfulness interventions delivered by technology without facilitator involvement: What research exists and what are the clinical outcomes? *Mindfulness*, 7(5), 1011–1023. doi:10.100712671-016-0548-2 PMID:27642370

Fitbit. (2018). Retrieved from https://www.fitbit.com/home

Foster, D., Linehan, C., Kirman, B., Lawson, S., & James, G. (2010). Motivating physical activity at work: Using persuasive social media for competitive step counting. *14th International Academic MindTrek Conference: Envisioning Future Media Environments*, 111–116.

Hann, D. M., Denniston, M. M., & Baker, F. (2000). Measurement of fatigue in cancer patients: Further validation of the fatigue symptom inventory. *Quality of Life Research: An International Journal of Quality of Life Aspects of Treatment, Care and Rehabilitation*, 9(7), 847–854. doi:10.1023/A:1008900413113 PMID:11297027

Hardcastle, S. J., Hancox, J., Hattar, A., Maxwell-Smith, C., Thøgersen-Ntoumani, C., & Hagger, M. S. (2015). Motivating the unmotivated: How can health behavior be changed in those unwilling to change? *Frontiers in Psychology*, 6, 835. doi:10.3389/fpsyg.2015.00835 PMID:26136716

Internet World Statistics. (2018). *Usage and population statistics*. Retrieved from https://www.internetworldstats.com/stats.htm

Intille, S. S. (2004). *Ubiquitous computing technology for just-in-time motivation of behavior change*. Retrieved March 15, 2018 from http://citeseerx.ist.psu.edu/viewdoc/download?doi=10.1.1.5.7011&rep=rep1&type=pdf

Kaiser Family Foundation. (2017, July). *The U.S. government and global non-communicable disease efforts*. Retrieved from https://www.kff.org/global-health-policy/fact-sheet/the-u-s-government-and-global-non-communicable-diseases/

Kennedy, C. M., Powell, J., Payne, T. H., Ainsworth, J., Boyd, A., & Buchan, I. (2012). Active Assistance Technology for Health-Related Behavior Change: An Interdisciplinary Review. *Journal of Medical Internet Research, 14*(3), e80. doi:10.2196/jmir.1893 PMID:22698679

Koolhaas, J. M., Bartolomucci, A., Buwalda, B. D., De Boer, S. F., Flügge, G., Korte, S. M., ... Richter-Levin, G. (2011). Stress revisited: a critical evaluation of the stress concept. *Neuroscience & Biobehavioral Reviews, 35*(5), 1291-1301.

Lyons, E. J., Lewis, Z. H., Mayrsohn, B. G., & Rowland, J. L. (2014). Behavior change techniques implemented in electronic lifestyle activity monitors: A systematic content analysis. *Journal of Medical Internet Research, 16*(8), e192. doi:10.2196/jmir.3469 PMID:25131661

Maher, C. A., Lewis, L. K., Ferrar, K., Marshall, S., De Bourdeaudhuij, I., & Vandelanotte, C. (2014). Are health behavior change interventions that use online social networks effective? A systematic review. *Journal of Medical Internet Research, 16*(2), e40. doi:10.2196/jmir.2952 PMID:24550083

Messer, D., Horan, J. J., Turner, W., & Weber, W. (2015). The effects of internet-delivered mindfulness training on stress, coping, and mindfulness in university students. *AERA Open, 2*(1). doi: 2332858415625188

Michie, S., Thomas, J., Johnston, M., Aonghusa, P., Shawe-Taylor, J., Kelly, M. P., ... West, R. (2017a). The human behaviour-change project: Harnessing the power of artificial intelligence and machine learning for evidence synthesis and interpretation. *Implementation Science; IS, 12*(121). doi:10.118613012-017-0641-5 PMID:29047393

Michie, S., Yardley, L., West, R., Patrick, K., & Greaves, F. (2017b). Developing and evaluating digital interventions to promote behavior change in health and health care: Recommendations resulting from an international workshop. *Journal of Medical Internet Research, 19*(6), 27–39. doi:10.2196/jmir.7126 PMID:28663162

Norman, G. J., Zabinski, M. F., Adams, M. A., Rosenberg, D. E., Yaroch, A. L., & Atienza, A. A. (2007). A review of eHealth interventions for physical activity and dietary behavior change. *American Journal of Preventive Medicine, 33*(4), 336-345. doi: 10.1016/j.amepre.2007.05.007

Patel, M. S., Asch, D. A., & Volpp, K. G. (2015). Wearable devices as facilitators, not drivers, of health behavior change. *Journal of the American Medical Association, 313*(5), 459–460. doi:10.1001/jama.2014.14781 PMID:25569175

Piwek, L., Ellis, D. A., Andrews, S., & Joinson, A. (2016). The rise of consumer health wearables: Promises and barriers. *PLoS Medicine, 13*(2), e1001953. doi:10.1371/journal.pmed.1001953 PMID:26836780

Sardi, L., Idri, A., & Fernández-Alemán, J. L. (2017). A systematic review of gamification in e-health. *Journal of Biomedical Informatics, 71*, 31–48. doi:10.1016/j.jbi.2017.05.011 PMID:28536062

Sephton, S. E., & Spiegel, D. (2003). Circadian disruption in cancer: A neuroendocrine-immune pathway from stress to disease? *Brain, Behavior, and Immunity, 17*(5), 321–328. doi:10.1016/S0889-1591(03)00078-3 PMID:12946654

Shanholtz, C. E., Messer, D., Davidson, R. D., Randall, A. K., & Horan, J. J. (2017). A randomized clinical trial of online stress inoculation for adult children of divorce. *Journal of Divorce & Remarriage, 58*(8), 599–613. doi:10.1080/10502556.2017.1354278

Starner, T., & Rhodes, B. J. (1996). *Remembrance Agent*. Retrieved March 15th, 2018 from http://alumni.media.mit.edu/~rhodes/Papers/remembrance.html

Tuckson, R. V., Edmunds, M., & Hodgkins, M. L. (2017). Telehealth. *The New England Journal of Medicine, 377*(16), 1585–1592. doi:10.1056/NEJMsr1503323 PMID:29045204

UPRIGHT. (2018). Retrieved from https://www.uprightpose.com/

Verhoeks, C., Teunissen, D., van der Stelt-Steenbergen, A., & Lagro-Janssen, A. (2017, August). Women's expectations and experiences regarding e-health treatment: A systematic review. *Health Informatics Journal*, 1–17. doi:10.1177/1460458217720394 PMID:28764600

Wantland, D. J., Portillo, C. J., Holzemer, W. L., Slaughter, R., & McGhee, E. M. (2004). The effectiveness of Web-based vs. non-Web-based interventions: A meta-analysis of behavioral change outcomes. *Journal of Medical Internet Research, 6*(4), e40. doi:10.2196/jmir.6.4.e40 PMID:15631964

West, R., & Michie, S. (2016). *A guide to development and evaluation of digital behaviour change interventions in healthcare*. London: Silverback Publishing.

Wolchik, S. A., Sandler, I. N., Millsap, R. E., Plummer, B. A., Greene, S. M., Anderson, E. R., ... Haine, R. A. (2002). Six-year follow-up of preventive interventions for children of divorce: A randomized controlled trial. *Journal of the American Medical Association, 288*(15), 1874–1881. doi:10.1001/jama.288.15.1874 PMID:12377086

Wolever, R. Q., Bobinet, K. J., McCabe, K., Mackenzie, E. R., Fekete, E., Kusnick, C. A., & Baime, M. (2012). Effective and viable mind-body stress reduction in the workplace: A randomized controlled trial. *Journal of Occupational Health Psychology, 17*(2), 246–258. doi:10.1037/a0027278 PMID:22352291

World Health Organization. (2017, June). *Noncommunicable diseases: Fact sheet*. Retrieved from http://www.who.int/mediacentre/factsheets/fs355/en/

Yellowlees, P., Marks, S., Hilty, D., & Shore, J. H. (2008). Using e-Health to Enable Culturally Appropriate Mental Healthcare in Rural Areas. *Telemedicine Journal and e-Health, 14*(5), 486–492. doi:10.1089/tmj.2007.0070 PMID:18578685

Chapter 9

Predicting Shoppers' Acceptance of E-Shopping on the Internet

Chandra Sekhar Patro
Gayatri Vidya Parishad College of Engineering, India

ABSTRACT

The emergence and rapid escalation of e-retailing has triggered many changes in daily life of the shoppers as well as the marketers. E-retailing is playing a major role in the Indian economy and is expected to change the current scenario of shopping from physical stores to e-stores. Similarly, changes in consumers' attitudes along with the availability of cheaper and reliable technology have led to a significant growth in online sales around the world. The chapter aims to examine the shoppers' attitudes towards e-shopping and also to find the critical reasons for not shopping through online. The results reveal that the shoppers are still hesitating to purchase online. The most important reasons for not shopping online are preferring to buy by touching and feeling, online security and privacy, and customer service quality. The factors influencing to buy online are being able to get detailed product information, product delivery, convenience, product quality, and competitive prices. These results also have some practical implications for managers and strategists of e-stores.

INTRODUCTION

E-shopping is a fast growing area of technology and establishing a virtual store on the internet allows the retailers to expand their market and reach out to consumers who may not otherwise visit the physical store.Internet has very differentiated impact along the various stages of the consumer decision-making process and the

DOI: 10.4018/978-1-5225-7128-5.ch009

true value-added of the Internet to consumers materializes at very specific points in the purchase process (Zeng & Reinartz, 2003). Retailers are doing business online and trade has become more easy and fast. The e-vendors have become the essence of e-business as to show their services and products. Internet gathers all competitors and consumers in one place. It brings new lane to promote, advertise products and services in market (Silverstein, 2002).

Online shopping attitudes refer to consumers' psychological state in terms of making purchase in the internet (Li & Zang, 2002). In the existing circumstances, many companies have started using internet with the aim of cutting marketing costs, thus, reducing the price of their products and services in order to hang about further on highly competitive markets. Companies also use internet to convey, communicate and disseminate the information, to sell product, to take feedback, to compare prices, product features and after sale service facilities they will receive if they purchase the product from a particular store (Shergill & Chen, 2005). Most of the physical retail stores have expanded their market by using the internet to get the best of both worlds. Stores that are marketing their products in both areas can take advantage of the high demand for e-shopping availability.

Online buyers are always seeking new items, new magnetism and the most important thingbeing price compatibility with their budget. The internet is the best way to save time and moneythrough purchasing online within their range of budget from home or anywhere. They also useinternet for comparison of prices and items, news, visit social networks and search information and so on (Katta & Patro, 2017). Culture, social, personal, psychological behaviour also affects the buyers' attitude in online shopping. E-shoppers always want to seek information within few clicks and reach to themost relevant information according to their requirements such as competitive brands, best priceoffers, product specification and consumer word-of-mouth (Gao, 2005). To enhance and attract the buyerit is very important to know about their attitude and understand what they require and need. Sincee-shopping is the new medium of shopping with new demands of buyers. All buyers have their owndesires and demands for products so, that it is crucial for all e-retailers to identify and know about their consumers (Hasslinger, 2007). The main barrier in the process of e-shopping is the safety andprivacy issue. Due to which the buyers are reluctant to make online purchasing, another most familiarbarrier is the low level of trust on e-stores therefore the e-retailers have to make proper strategies toincrease the buyer's level of trust on them.

In order to remain competitive the online marketers need to adopt effective strategies to satisfy their customers' needs and wants. But the shoppers' behaviour in a virtual environment often seems to be a complex, as their expectations change with the change in time and technological advancements (Patro, 2016). Moreover, in a virtual environment where next web store is just a mouse click away, it becomes extensively difficult to understand the consumers' behaviour and take effective measures to attract them to make purchases online and from the same store (Tanadi, Samadi, & Gharleghi, 2015). Thus, researchers and managers have often acknowledged that the source of competitive advantage is closely related to the long-term relationships between customers and the e-retailers.

E-tailing has emerged as a new avenue for consumers to shop in. With the Internet spreading worldwide at a fast rate, online selling is becoming attractive for e-retailers. It is referred as a synonymous with business-to-consumer (B2C) transactions in online stores, where a customer can shop for apparel, cell phones, cameras, computers, books, magazines, music CDs and DVDs, shoes, furniture, health equipment, flowers, etc. Companies like Amazon and Dell were the first to create the online retail industry by putting the entire customer experience-from browsing products to placing orders to paying for purchases on the Internet (Ruby, 2016). The success of these and other companies encouraged traditional retailers to create an online presence to augment their brick-and-mortar outlets. This revolutionary way of selling goods and services has also gained popularity in India.

With the initiation of technology, e-tailers are devising attractive delivery options such as same-day delivery or delivery within an hour, easy-to-use check out process, buying through mobile apps, and try at home or your door, etc., for improved customer experience (Chaturvedi & Gupta, 2014). As e-tailing is a relatively new trading channel, a majority of online retailers still lack in the digital marketing skills and does not have proper governance structure in place. Security remains one of the major concerns for consumers as the complexity of online fraud attacks continue to increase. Despite being mired in many issues, the e-tailing industry is rising and changing in a rapid manner. The constantly changing dynamics of the online retail industry has put pressure on all the stakeholders to redesign their business models, if they desire to stay competitive and grow (Capgemini, 2013). The growth of E-Tailing in India will be complementary to the growth of traditional retail, and in no way be at cross purposes. On the contrary, it will improve efficiencies and reduce transaction costs in retailing and thereby boost the productivity of manufacturers and service providers.

SIGNIFICANCE OF E-SHOPPING

E-shopping is a fast growing area of technology and establishing a virtual store on the internet allows the retailers to expand their market and reach out to consumers who may not otherwise visit the physicalstore. E-shopping has become the third most popular internet activity following the e-mail usage andweb browsing. Internet is changing the way how consumers shop and buy the goods and services.The convenience of e-buying is the major desirability factor for the consumers. Unique e-payment systems offer simple and safe purchasing from other individuals. The benefits of e-shopping also come with potential risks and dangers that the consumers must be aware of. In future, we can expectthe e-stores to enhance their technology enormously, allowing for much easier and a more realisticbuying experience.

Many entrepreneurs have been taking advantage of this opportunity and established e-stores onthe internet namely, Flipkart, Amazon, Snapdeal, Shopclues, Ebay, Askmebazar, Jabong, Yepme, Yebhi, Myntra, Bigbasket, Localbanya, etc. At present there is also rise in popularity of e-websites, which allow consumers to sell and purchase to each other such as Quikr, OLX, etc. In Andhra Pradesh the e-commerce market has been continually escalating and this aspect can be noticed by taking intoaccount both the increasing number of e-stores and the number of visitors that is gradually increasing, visitors that change into buyers of goods on the internet. Due to the busy schedules, heavy traffic, easy access to internet, availability of wide range of products and services on the internet, competitive prices, and home delivery services after working hours, have curved most of the customers attention towards e-stores (Katta & Patro, 2016). One of the biggest challenges of e-stores is attracting enough online customers to be profitable and survive. If they are not able to attract and retain enough customers, they cannot survive in the market. That is why a shift in buying behaviour and attitude of consumers toward e-shopping is a key to success of e-stores.

BACKGROUND

Many studies have focused on identifying the factors which affect the willingness ofshoppers to buy online or to engage in internet shopping. The researchers focused on the different perceived advantage and risk aspects of e-shopping that influence the attitudes of the buyers. E-retailing has evolved rapidly to meet the needs of today'shighly competitive and fast paced market and this can be attributed to improvements and advancements in technology (Baršauskas, Šarapovas, & Cvilikas, 2008). More specifically, consumers' perceptions of the customer service, commitment and web security of online purchasing exhibit significant relationships with their online buying intention (Jusoh & Ling, 2012). Gupta and Khincha (2015) identified that time saving and cash on delivery facility are major factors that influence online shopping behaviour of buyers. Sorce, Perotti, and Widrick (2005) identified that older online shoppers search for significantly fewer products than their younger counterparts, theyactually purchase as much as younger consumers. Younger consumers were more likely to agreethat online shopping was more convenient than older consumers do. Case and Dick (2001) found that internet knowledge, income and education level are especially important predictors of online purchases among university students. Richa (2012) also identified that e-shopping in India is significantly affected by various demographic factors like age, gender, marital status, family size and income.

Online shopping and online buyer attitude depend on the factors such as shopping motives, personality variables, internet knowledge and experience, shopping incentives, website visibility, e-store credibility, information comparison, payment security, privacy, and convenient time (Wang, Liu, & Cheng, 2008). Keisidou, Sarigiannidis, and Maditinos (2011); Lian and Lin (2008) found that Personal Innovativeness of Information Technology (PIIT), perceived security and product involvement have an effect on the buyers attitude towards online shopping, yet the results vary among the different product types. Tassabehji (2003) identified the advantages of B2C e-tailing as, cheap product choices, price comparison opportunities and improved delivery processes. Nayak and Debashish (2017) examined the factors that influence the online shopping decisions of young consumers in Indian context. The results of the study show that the factors influencing the consumers' decision of online shopping are convenience, security & privacy on website, time and cost efficiency, online product information availability and website interface. Yörük, Dündar, Moga, and Neculita (2011) examined the shopping behaviour of consumers and their attitudes toward internet shopping, and found that the shoppers are still hesitating to shop online. The most important reasons for not shopping online are security, preference to shop traditional way, prefer to buy by touching and feeling and willing to use products immediately (Katta & Patro, 2016).

Goswami, Baruah, and Borah (2013) stated that the online marketer should give more importance on price factor and after sale factor. Saravanan, Yoganandan, and Ruby (2013) have identified seven factors namely information, company and product perception, safety, purchase intension, easiness, value and assurance which has significant influence the online shopping behaviour of teachers. Liu, He, Gao, and Xie (2008) have identified that customer services are strongly predictive of online shopping customer satisfaction. Further complete product information, design of website, delivery, security and privacy has very important role in customer satisfaction. Nuseir, Arora, Al-Masri, and Gharaibeh (2010) found that lack of high quality e-promotion will restrict consumer's decision to purchase though internet and will not motivate a consumer to follow the purchase decision process from top to bottom. Kim and Stoel (2004) stated that consumers need additional satisfaction while purchasing from e-stores otherwise the customers switch to other e-stores. Consumers' seek satisfaction and new ways to solve their problems through innovative services and greater service innovativeness requires more intensive interaction between the service provider and customers for effective service delivery (Ribbink, van Riel, Liljander, & Streukens, 2004). Moreover, effective service delivery leads to improved consumer perception of innovative service benefit (Bonnin, Segard, & Vialle, 2005). Consumers' who trust an innovation or a new technology feel that they have more control over their behavior and shows low emotional resistance towards it (Patro, 2017).

E-shopping adopters have higher expectations from online shopping on issues relating to privacy policy and risk (Saprikis, Chouliara, & Vlachopoulou, 2010). It could help firms better understand their particular needs and consequently, analogous marketing policies could be applied, as the better understanding of online consumer behaviour. Osman, Yin-Fah and Choo (2010) stated that purchase perception and website quality have significant relationship with attitude towards online purchasing behaviour. Delafrooz, Paim, Haron, Sidin, and Khatibi, (2009) found that gender, education background, purchase perception and website quality have directly influence on attitude towards online purchasing behaviour. Dai, Luo, Liao, and Cao (2015) found that consumer innovativeness and emotion are significant antecedents of trust, risk perception of service, perceived benefits, and service quality. Online retailers with excellent service quality have the advantage of learning about their customers' expectation, thus improving their satisfaction (Khristianto, Kertahadi, & Suyadi, 2012). Guo, Ling and Liu (2012) explicate service quality as the level of assistance for online retailers in providing an efficient, as well as effective shopping, purchasing and delivery of products and services. Christodoulides and Michaelidou (2011) state that online retailers that are able to provide and exchange information via formal or informal platform with customers would most likely improve customer satisfaction and add value to shopping experience.

The studies found that reputation of the e-retailer, website design, perceived ease of usefulness, perceived ease of use, offline-online integration has positive relation in influencing consumer satisfaction.

FORCES DRIVING THE GROWTH OF E-RETAILING

Online retail is likely to be driven primarily by an increase in the number of broadband connections and smart phone usage in developing economies. According to Capgemini (2013), the forces driving e-retail growth across all major geographies include:

1. **Advancements in Technology:** The availability of fast, secure, and cheap technology has enabled many new players to enter the e-commerce market, making it highly competitive and price-effective. Over the last 20 years, technology has evolved from command-line interface to drop-down menus

to apps, making it simpler and easier to use. Consumers now have a higher level of comfort in using technology and this has positively impacted online commerce.

2. **Evolving Consumer Needs:** Online retailers are now focusing on identifying consumer needs and understanding their shopping behaviour to better serve them with innovative products and services. Retailers are not only targeting customers on the basis of demographics, but are analyzing their spending patterns to better market their products. This precise target helps online retailers to convert more leads into sales.

3. **An Increase in Internet and Smart Phone Users:** The sale of smart phones and tablets exceeded those of desktops and laptops. More consumers are expected to access the internet through their mobile devices than from their desktop computers. Miniaturization of components and wireless technology has allowed consumers to shop and interact over the internet while they are on the move.

4. **Social Media:** Social networking platforms have opened a new channel for online retailers to promote and raise awareness for their products. Social media is mainly used by the population in the age group of 18-34 years, which has made it an important medium for branding and loyalty. Social marketing programs are a must-have for today's user experience, and they provide an excellent platform for retailers to get customer feedback.

CHALLENGES FACED BY E-RETAIL INDUSTRY

The bottom line is that capturing customers' product and payment preferences in order to deliver an enhanced online shopping experience is driving e-commerce growth. But there are certain challenges that the e-commerce industry is facing. Without tackling these issues it will be difficult for the industry to continue on this growth path (Rao & Patro, 2016; Capgemini, 2013). The key challenges include:

1. **Security Concerns:** The number of online fraud incidents decreased but cost of combating fraud has increased as incidents increase in volume and occur in more lucrative sectors. This indicates that the complexity and sophistication of online fraud attacks is on the rise and still weighs heavily on many consumers choosing not to shop or transact online.

2. **Poor Digital Marketing Expertise:** E-commerce is a new concept and marketing teams of online retailers are still exploring relevant ways of reaching out to consumers. Unlike traditional media (purchased airtime or ad space), social media such as Facebook and Twitter are free. However, the learning curve to

use them effectively has been steep for online retailers. Poor marketing skills are negatively impacting the firm's brand equity, sales, customer acquisition, and retention.

3. **Lack of Appropriate Governance:** In the face of changing market dynamics, new product lines, and new sales channels, online retailers are struggling with governance of their e-commerce efforts. As firms move from traditional retail to online retail, improper governance and a flawed control structure can lead to inefficient processes.

4. **ProperIntegration of Technology:** Improper, or lack of, integration of systems and business processes (such as order-to-cash management and customer relationship management) has had a negative impact on the customer experience.

For online retailers, it will be difficult to retain customers if they do not integrate their back-end systems seamlessly with their front- end systems. Many online retailers do not provide a multi-channel payment option which has also negatively impacted their businesses.

KEY FOCUS AREAS FOR E-RETAILERS

The e-retail industrial leaders need to manage technological and physical requirements for cross-border commerce. In order to keep up with the trajectory, there are four key areas that cross-border retailers should focus on to continue global expansion across the world (Martin, 2016; Rao & Patro, 2016).

1. **Localization Matters:** Expanding globally is not simply standing up a website. Every country has cultural nuances, consumer expectations, and compliance regulations that require attention. International customers in the digital age expect a personal shopping experience and if the web store they're visiting feels foreign, they likely won't be inclined to engage or buy. Going global isn't a luxury – if you're in the retail game, it's a channel that must be explored. Online merchants need to consider both present and future expectations and trends to build a meaningful presence within new markets they're planning to enter.

2. **Shipping is the New Black:** While delivery may not be the most glamorous aspect of the ecommerce experience, it may have the biggest influence on brand perception and customer satisfaction which as retailers know, is the heart of the operation. As global e-commerce sales continue to rise, guaranteeing reliable and timely delivery is harder than ever to ensure. With online retail only becoming more commonplace, especially around winter holidays, customers

aren't going to simply accept stumbles in service quality as the new normal. An online retailer's shipping capabilities need to keep pace with demand if they want to keep customers happy.

3. **Omni channel - Window Shopping Transformed:** While ecommerce may have changed buyers' relationships with brick-and-mortar retail, that doesn't mean a web store is the one-stop shop for their needs. Ads on desktops, research on mobile, shopping cart conversion on tablet, ship-to-store delivery and coupons by mail all play a part in converting a sales strategy into bottom-line profits. Retailers need to be present and consistent for the entire customer journey, respond to customer preferences, and ensure continuity across all purchasing and delivery channels.

4. **The Mobile Necessity**: For years marketers have been challenged to figure out the right game plan for mobile e-retailing. Until recently the opportunity has sat on the back burner with little data to prove impact and true ROI. But today mobile makes up at least 45 percent of total ecommerce sales and retailers don't have a choice but to include this channel in their strategy. Retailers need to reconcile experiences across traditional and mobile-friendly web stores, and help customers easily navigate a transaction in a way that is sensitive to the nuances of their local market.

In this competitive and ever changing business environment, the key focus areas for merchants include:

1. **To improve purchase conversion rate:** Most consumers use the internet for comparison purposes and for choosing their products, hence firms are investing heavily in digital marketing and data analytics to convert consumers into customers.

2. **To enhance fraud control:** Security is the main concern for many online customers, therefore controlling fraud is one of the key focus areas for retailers. Retailers can use third-party vendors for fraud control, but they need to clearly identify their risk areas.

3. **To improve ease of use:** Retailers are focusing on improving their web portals and are making them easy to explore. This will help in reducing customer dropout rates due to the inflexible structure of the website. Easy navigation and efficient check-out services are also key focus areas for retailers.

4. **To diversify payment channels:** Retailers have realized that they have to improve their payment services or customers will move out. Firms, big or small, are partnering with payment service provider s to provide their customers with different payment channels at an affordable price.

5. **To optimize the business model:** Most retail firms are focusing on defining their online business model to foster customer engagement and loyalty. Firms have realized that there is no one model that fits all, and they need to find out what works best for them.

Going forward, investments in enhancing the user experience are likely to remain a top priority, followed by investment in developing mobile and commerce platforms. Investments in enhancing the user experience are seen as the largest opportunity to drive additional revenue. Merchants are also investing in rewards and loyalty programs to attract and retain customers. Retailers who do not have an online sales channel are looking to invest in developing their e-commerce platforms and integrating them with their offline sales channels. Retailers are likely to invest more of their resources in developing value-for-money products and also in providing new payment methods such as e-invoicing.

OBJECTIVES OF THE CHAPTER

1. To study the demographic profile of the shoppers, and their awareness towards internet and e-shopping.
2. To examine the factors influencing the selected shoppers' attitude towards e-shopping.
3. To analyze the main reasons showing impact on the shoppers' for not shopping through online mode.

RESEARCH METHODOLOGY

The research study was carried out to examine selected shoppers' attitude, overall satisfaction and experiences towards online shopping. The preliminary research and review of literature was carried out by referring articles and research papers on use and spread of online buying of products or services. The information is collected from both primary and secondary sources. The secondary data was collected from different websites, libraries, magazines, conference proceedings, journals and newspaper publications. The primary data was collected with the help of structured questionnaire. The important aspects covered in the questionnaire were, demographic profile of shoppers, shoppers' awareness towards internet and e-shopping, categories of items purchased through online and offline, shoppers' perception towards online shopping, and the reasons for not shopping through online. For the survey purpose the students of various colleges from Andhra Pradesh, India were selected to know their opinions regarding e-shopping and their buying experiences. The sample consisted of students pursuing bachelors and masters degrees at different. The questionnaires were distributed to the students and were asked to fill out the survey. A total of 255 valid responses were received and used for the analysis. The respondents were asked to rate on an agreement scale of Strongly Disagree to Strongly Agree. The frequency percentages, mean values, standard deviation is computed for the data. To evaluate the relative significance of each variable on the shoppers' attitude, ANOVA test is conducted using SPSS 20.0 software.

STATISTICAL ANALYSIS

The respondents were asked demographic questions which include gender, age, education, internet usage, and whether they shop online or not. If they have never shopped online, they were asked the reasons for not shopping online. If they shopped online, what kind of products did they buy? In addition to these questions, respondents were asked to rate ten indicators concerning the reasons to shop online. The collected data was tabulated and analyzed to draw inferences on selected assumptions relating to consumers' responses and their overall opinion on online buying of items. The overall findings and opinion of selected buyers are discussed in the chapter.

Demographic Profile of the E-Shoppers

The demographic profile of the respondents is exhibited in Table 1. It shows that 57 per cent of the respondents are male while 43 per cent of them are female. Since our sample consists of bachelor's and master's students, 78 per cent of respondents

Table 1. Demographic profile of respondents

Demographic Factor	Frequency	Percentage
Gender		
Male	146	57%
Female	109	43%
Age		
18 - 20	47	18%
21 - 25	197	78%
26 - 30	11	4%
Education		
Bachelor's	170	67%
Master's	85	34%

are in the age group of 21 to 25 years and 18 per centare in the age group of 18-20 years. It is observed that 67 per cent of the respondents are bachelors and 34 per cent are master's students.

Internet Accessibility for Shoppers'

As indicated in Table 2, 70 per cent of respondents have internet access intheir college premises and 30 per cent responded that they are not having internet accessibility at their college. 92 per centof the respondents said that they have internet access at their homes or hostels. It is found that majority of the respondents using internet

Table 2. Summary of internet accessibility for respondents

Indicator	Frequency	Percentage
Can you use internet at College?		
Yes	179	70%
No	76	30%
Can you use internet at Home/Hostel?		
Yes	235	92%
No	20	8%
How long have you been using Internet?		
1 - 2 years	40	16%
3 - 4 years	104	41%
5 - 6 years	70	27%
7 - 8 years	29	11%
Above 8 years	12	5%
How many times a week do you browse Internet?		
Never	8	3%
Daily	129	51%
2-3 days	79	31%
4-5 days	23	9%
6-7 days	16	6%
How many times did you shop online?		
Never	78	31%
1-2 times	78	31%
3-4 times	47	18%
5-6 times	33	13%
7 times and more	19	7%

for online shopping are for a period of 3-4 years (41 per cent), 5-6 years (27 per cent), and 1-2 years (16 per cent). The analysis also specifies that 51 per centof the respondents browse internet daily and 31 per cent for 2 to 3 days.While internet access and usage is very high, about 31 per cent of the respondents in did not purchase products online. 31 per cent of respondents purchased products online for 1-2 times and 18 per cent purchased 3-4 times. It basically shows that the shoppers' in Andhra Pradesh are reluctant to shop online even if they spend long hours on internet.

Categories of Items Purchased Online

An attempt is made to know the items purchased only online, only offline and the combination of online and offline. The shoppers' were asked about their opinions on the items they purchased online and what they would buy among the different categories of items available in the e-stores. The data shown in Table 3 presents a list of 16 categories and the purchase habits of the respondents. The consumers mostly purchased or like to buy travel and movie tickets, mobiles, clothing or fashion items, and electronic items through online.

Table 3. Categories of items purchased

Sl. No.	Items	Only Online		Only Offline		Online and Offline	
		#	%	#	%	#	%
1	Clothing/Fashion	145	57	62	24	48	19
2	Electronics	136	53	54	21	65	25
3	Mobiles	165	65	49	19	41	16
4	Computers	114	45	53	21	88	35
5	Toys/Gift Items	88	35	77	30	90	35
6	Books/Magazines	123	48	56	22	76	30
7	Music/Video CDs	61	24	108	42	86	34
8	Sports Equipment	18	7	167	65	70	27
9	Games/Software	28	11	117	46	110	43
10	Cosmetics	123	48	68	27	64	25
11	Groceries	39	15	136	53	80	31
12	Flowers	29	11	178	70	48	19
13	Movie Tickets	165	65	41	16	49	19
14	Travel Tickets	166	65	43	17	46	18
15	Hotel Reservations	70	27	98	38	87	34
16	Other Items	83	33	82	32	90	35

Travel ticket bookings is the product category where the majority of the respondents representing 65 per cent revealed that they pay only online while 18 per cent of the respondents revealed that they make travel ticket bookings both online as well as offline as per the situational convenience. However, there are 17 per cent of the respondents who revealed that they make travel ticket bookings only offline. With regard to movie ticket bookings and mobiles, majority of the respondents representing 65 per cent revealed that they purchaseonly online. 19 per cent of the respondents book movie ticket both online and offline while 17 per cent of the respondents revealed that they book movie ticket only offline.In the case of mobiles, 16 per cent of the respondents revealed that they buy both online and offline whereas, 19 per cent revealed that they purchase mobiles only offline.

In the case of clothing/fashion 57 per cent of the respondents revealed that they buy through online, whereas for electronic items, 53 per cent of the respondents revealed that they buy through online websites. With regard to cosmetics, books and magazines, 48 per cent of the respondents buy only through online. As many as 45 per cent of the respondents buy computers only online while 35 per cent of the respondents revealed that they buy toys/gift items only online. In case of hotel reservations category, 27 per cent of the respondents revealed that they purchase through online and 24 per cent of the respondents revealed that they purchase Music/Video CDsonly through online. There are 15 per cent of the respondents who revealed that they purchase groceries only online. In the case of games/software items and flowers 11 per cent of the respondents revealed that they buy only online. Regarding sports equipment 7 per cent of the respondents revealed that they buy through online.With reference to other items 33 per cent of the respondents revealed that they only online. Thus, it reveals that the most advantageous items to purchase online are travel and movie tickets, mobiles and fashion items. Groceries, sports equipments and flowers are the most unsuitable items for online purchases. Because especially inspection of these items before purchase are important, and returning these items is also a major issue for these items.

Factors Influencing Shoppers' Toward E-Shopping

The opinion of sample population has been ascertained on likert scale and the descriptive statistics related to the fifteen factors that are influencing the shoppers towards shopping online is shown in Table 4.

The analysis indicates that 'convenience in buying (24/7)' secured highest rating ($\mu=3.92$; t=13.975, p=0.000<0.01). The factors 'offers competitive and low prices ($\mu=3.91$; t=13.766, p=0.000<0.01)' and 'get on-time product delivery ($\mu=3.88$; t=12.838, p=0.000<0.01)' are the second the third highly rated. The other factors influencing the shoppers to shop online are 'wide variety of products ($\mu=3.87$;

Table 4. Descriptive statistics (n=255)

Sl. No.	Factors	Mean	Std. Deviation	Std. Error Mean	t	Sig. (2-tailed)
1	Convenience in buying (24/7)	3.92	1.049	.066	13.975	.000
2	Get detailed Product Information	3.77	1.145	.072	10.777	.000
3	Online buying saves time	3.85	1.067	.067	12.680	.000
4	Offers competitive and low Prices	3.91	1.055	.066	13.766	.000
5	Wide Variety of Products	3.87	1.098	.069	12.723	.000
6	Get on-time Product Delivery	3.88	1.093	.068	12.838	.000
7	Website Design and Features	3.78	1.128	.071	11.104	.000
8	Availability of various Payment Modes	3.76	1.171	.073	10.373	.000
9	Safe and Secure in Transactions	3.66	1.206	.076	8.725	.000
10	Supply Quality Products	3.69	1.195	.075	9.226	.000
11	Trustworthiness of Website	3.59	1.226	.077	7.715	.000
12	Compare the Products and Items	3.87	1.101	.069	12.682	.000
13	Better than catalogue shopping	3.69	1.214	.076	9.133	.000
14	Eliminates Intermediaries	3.72	1.189	.074	9.689	.000
15	Customer and Product Service	3.51	1.210	.076	6.368	.000

Source: Primary Data; All the t-values are significant at 0.01 level

$t=12.723$, $p=0.000<0.01$)', 'compare the products and items ($\mu=3.87$; $t=12.682$, $p=0.000<0.01$)', 'online buying saves time($\mu=3.85$; $t=12.680$, $p=0.000<0.01$)', 'website design and features ($\mu=3.78$; $t=11.104$, $p=0.000<0.01$)', 'get detailed product information ($\mu=3.77$; $t=10.777$, $p=0.000<0.01$)', 'availability of various payment modes ($\mu=3.76$; $t=10.373$, $p=0.000<0.01$)','eliminates intermediaries ($\mu=3.72$; $t=9.689$, $p=0.000<0.01$)','supply quality products ($\mu=3.69$; $t=9.226$, $p=0.000<0.01$)', 'better than catalogue shopping ($\mu=3.69$; $t=9.133$, $p=0.000<0.01$)', 'safe and secure in transactions ($\mu=3.66$; $t=8.725$, $p=0.000<0.01$)', 'trustworthiness of website ($\mu=3.59$; $t=7.715$, $p=0.000<0.01$)',customer and product service ($\mu=3.51$; $t=6.368$, $p=0.000<0.01$)'. It is pertinent to note that all the fifteen variables have positive ratings by the respondents as the mean values of each variable is higher than 3.5 and all the t-statistic values are significant in influencing the shoppers towards online shopping.

The inter-item correlation coefficient matrix also shows that all the factors have significant influence on the shoppers at 0.01 significant levels (2-tailed) as shown in Table 5. Therefore, the validity of the research has been achieved to a satisfactory level. The ANOVA test with reference to the factors influencing the shoppers to shop online and gender is shown in Table 6.

Table 5. Inter - Item correlation coefficient matrix

Factor Constructs	1	2	3	4	5	6	7	8	9	10	11	12	13	14	15
1 Convenience in buying (24/7)	1.00														
2 Get detailed Product Information	0.75	1.00													
3 Online buying saves time	0.78	0.90	1.00												
4 Offers competitive and low Prices	0.72	0.92	0.87	1.00											
5 Wide Variety of Products	0.81	0.83	0.91	0.79	1.00										
6 Get on-time Product Delivery	0.72	0.95	0.90	0.93	0.87	1.00									
7 Website Design and Features	0.78	0.95	0.95	0.88	0.87	0.91	1.00								
8 Availability of various Payment Modes	0.79	0.82	0.88	0.76	0.96	0.86	0.87	1.00							
9 Safe and Secure in Transactions	0.80	0.86	0.85	0.88	0.84	0.87	0.86	0.82	1.00						
10 Supply Quality Products	0.83	0.88	0.88	0.87	0.83	0.87	0.88	0.82	0.94	1.00					
11 Trustworthiness of Website	0.75	0.92	0.88	0.89	0.85	0.94	0.89	0.85	0.88	0.87	1.00				
12 Compare the Products and Items	0.77	0.85	0.93	0.80	0.94	0.87	0.89	0.95	0.85	0.84	0.86	1.00			
13 Better than catalogue shopping	0.74	0.86	0.85	0.88	0.79	0.88	0.86	0.77	0.93	0.92	0.88	0.80	1.00		
14 Eliminates Intermediaries	0.76	0.88	0.85	0.88	0.86	0.91	0.86	0.84	0.92	0.90	0.92	0.85	0.93	1.00	
15 Customer and Product Service	0.81	0.91	0.88	0.87	0.87	0.90	0.92	0.86	0.87	0.91	0.89	0.86	0.88	0.87	1.00

Correlation is significant at the 0.01 level (2-tailed).

Table 6. ANOVA: Factors influencing online shoppers'

Factors		Sum of Squares	df	Mean Square	F	Sig.
Convenience in buying (24/7)	Between Groups	171.819	1	171.819	404.556	.000
	Within Groups	107.452	253	.425		
	Total	279.271	254			
Get detailed Product Information	Between Groups	242.381	1	242.381	678.148	.000
	Within Groups	90.426	253	.357		
	Total	332.808	254			
Online buying saves time	Between Groups	208.143	1	208.143	650.986	.000
	Within Groups	80.893	253	.320		
	Total	289.035	254			
Offers competitive and low Prices	Between Groups	195.573	1	195.573	566.439	.000
	Within Groups	87.353	253	.345		
	Total	282.925	254			
Wide Variety of Products	Between Groups	212.456	1	212.456	574.706	.000
	Within Groups	93.528	253	.370		
	Total	305.984	254			
Get on-time Product Delivery	Between Groups	217.668	1	217.668	643.619	.000
	Within Groups	85.563	253	.338		
	Total	303.231	254			
Website Design and Features	Between Groups	217.051	1	217.051	517.633	.000
	Within Groups	106.086	253	.419		
	Total	323.137	254			
Availability of various Payment Modes	Between Groups	242.833	1	242.833	581.926	.000
	Within Groups	105.575	253	.417		
	Total	348.408	254			
Safe and Secure in Transactions	Between Groups	248.200	1	248.200	518.461	.000
	Within Groups	121.117	253	.479		
	Total	369.318	254			
Supply Quality Products	Between Groups	237.045	1	237.045	477.940	.000
	Within Groups	125.481	253	.496		
	Total	362.525	254			
Trustworthiness of Website	Between Groups	235.147	1	235.147	406.265	.000
	Within Groups	146.437	253	.579		
	Total	381.584	254			

continued on following page

Table 6. Continued

Factors		Sum of Squares	df	Mean Square	F	Sig.
Compare the Products and Items	Between Groups	216.466	1	216.466	598.413	.000
	Within Groups	91.518	253	.362		
	Total	307.984	254			
Better than catalogue shopping	Between Groups	246.832	1	246.832	490.525	.000
	Within Groups	127.309	253	.503		
	Total	374.141	254			
Eliminates Intermediaries	Between Groups	238.668	1	238.668	500.839	.000
	Within Groups	120.564	253	.477		
	Total	359.231	254			
Customer and Product Service	Between Groups	217.257	1	217.257	355.964	.000
	Within Groups	154.414	253	.610		
	Total	371.671	254			

All the f-values are significant at 0.01 level

The analytical results show that all the factors have a significant influence on the shoppers to shop online. The most significantly related factors with reference to gender of the respondents are: get detailed product information (F=678.14, p=0.000<0.01), online buying saves time (F=650.98, p=0.000<0.01), get on-time product delivery (F=643.61, p=0.000<0.01), compare the products and items (F=598.41, p=0.000<0.01), availability of various payment modes (F=581.92, p=0.000<0.01), and wide variety of products (F=574.70, p=0.000<0.01).The other factors driving the shoppers towards e-shopping are: offers competitive and low prices (F=566.43, p=0.000<0.01), website design and features (F=517.63, p=0.000<0.01), safe and secure in transactions (F=518.46, p=0.000<0.01), better than catalogue shopping (F=490.52, p=0.000<0.01), and eliminates intermediaries (F=500.83, p=0.000<0.01).The least significantly related factors with regard to gender of the respondents are: customer and product service (F=355.96, p=0.000<0.01), convenience in buying 24/7 (F=404.55, p=0.000<0.01), trustworthiness of website (F=406.26, p=0.000<0.01), and supply quality products (F=477.94, p=0.000<0.01). Therefore, the e-retailers need to focus on these factors to enhance the online shopping experience of the shoppers.

Reasons for Not Shopping Online

The descriptive statistics related to the ten factors that are influencing the shoppers' for not shopping online is shown in Table 7.

The statisticsshows that 'lack of proficiency with the internet' got highest rating (μ=3.98; t=14.151, p=0.001<0.01). The factors 'complex, compared to traditional shopping (μ=3.93; t=12.387, p=0.001<0.001)' and 'difficulty in returning products/ items (μ=3.87; t=12.289, p=0.000<0.001)' are the second the third highly rated. The other reasonsshowing impact on the shoppers for not shopping online are 'need and want to use products immediately (μ=3.69; t=9.873, p=0.000<0.001)', 'lack of trust on e-retailers (μ=3.60; t=7.662, p=0.000<0.001)', 'previous purchase bad experience (μ=3.58; t=7.872, p=0.000<.001)', 'risk of credit/debit card transactions (μ=3.47; t=6.404, p=0.000<0.001)', 'lack of customer service (μ=3.42; t=5.691, p=0.000<0.001)', 'lack of online security and privacy (μ=3.27; t=3.522, p=0.000<0.001)', 'like to see and feel while buying (μ=3.27; t=3.513, p=0.000<0.001)'. It is pertinent to note that all the ten factors have positive ratings by the respondents as the mean values of each variable is higher than 3 and all the t-statistic values are significant in influencing the shoppers for not shopping through online medium.

Table 7. Descriptive statistics (n=255)

Sl. No.	Factor	Mean	Std. Deviation	Std. Error Mean	t	Sig. (2-tailed)
1	Lack of Online Security and Privacy	3.27	1.227	.077	3.522	.001
2	Like to see and feel while buying	3.27	1.230	.077	3.513	.001
3	Need and want to use products immediately	3.69	1.123	.070	9.873	.000
4	Risk of Credit/Debit card transactions	3.47	1.183	.074	6.404	.000
5	Lack of trust on e-Retailers	3.60	1.251	.078	7.662	.000
6	Complex, compared to Traditional Shopping	3.93	1.193	.075	12.387	.000
7	Previous purchase bad experience	3.58	1.177	.074	7.872	.000
8	Lack of proficiency with the Internet	3.98	1.106	.069	14.151	.000
9	Difficulty in returning products/items	3.87	1.136	.071	12.289	.000
10	Lack of customer service	3.42	1.177	.074	5.691	.000

Source: Primary Data; All the t-values are significant at 0.01 level

The inter-item correlation coefficient matrix also shows that all the factors have significant impact on the shoppers for not shopping online at 0.01 significant levels (2-tailed) as shown in Table 8. Therefore, the validity of the research has been achieved to a satisfactory level. The ANOVA test with reference to the reasons for not shopping online and gender is shown in Table 9.

The ANOVA results reveal that all the factors have a significant impact on the shoppers for not shopping online. The most significantly related factors with reference to gender of the respondents are: lack of trust on e-retailers (F=617.388, p=0.000<0.01), need and want to use products immediately (F=569.74, p=0.000<0.01), previous purchase bad experience (F=540.332, p=0.000<0.01), like to see and feel while buying (F=523.31, p=0.000<0.01), lack of online security and privacy (F=504.818, p=0.000<0.01), and risk of credit/debit card transactions (F=495.505, p=0.000<0.01).The least significantly related factors with regard to gender of the respondents are: complex, compared to traditional shopping (F=358.385, p=0.000<0.01), lack of proficiency with the internet (F=374.808, p=0.000<0.01), difficulty in returning products/items (F=465.265, p=0.000<0.01), lack of customer service (F=479.533, p=0.000<0.01). Therefore, the e-retailers need to focus on these factors to enhance the online shopping experience of the shoppers.

Table 8. Inter - Item correlation coefficient matrix

	Factor Constructs	1	2	3	4	5	6	7	8	9	10
1	Lack of Online Security and Privacy	1									
2	Like to see and feel while buying	0.87	1								
3	Need and want to use products immediately	0.91	0.79	1							
4	Risk of Credit/Debit card transactions	0.9	0.93	0.87	1						
5	Lack of trust on e-Retailers	0.95	0.88	0.87	0.91	1					
6	Complex, compared to Traditional Shopping	0.88	0.76	0.96	0.86	0.87	1				
7	Previous purchase bad experience	0.85	0.88	0.84	0.87	0.86	0.82	1			
8	Lack of proficiency with the Internet	0.88	0.87	0.83	0.87	0.88	0.82	0.94	1		
9	Difficulty in returning products/items	0.85	0.88	0.86	0.91	0.86	0.84	0.92	0.9	1	
10	Lack of customer service	0.88	0.87	0.87	0.9	0.92	0.86	0.87	0.91	0.89	1

Table 9. ANOVA: Reasons for not shopping online

Factors		Sum of Squares	df	Mean Square	F	Sig.
Lack of Online Security and Privacy	Between Groups	254.688	1	254.688	504.818	.000
	Within Groups	127.642	253	.505		
	Total	382.329	254			
Like to see and feel while buying	Between Groups	259.076	1	259.076	523.310	.000
	Within Groups	125.253	253	.495		
	Total	384.329	254			
Need and want to use products immediately	Between Groups	221.695	1	221.695	569.740	.000
	Within Groups	98.446	253	.389		
	Total	320.141	254			
Risk of Credit/Debit card transactions	Between Groups	235.394	1	235.394	495.505	.000
	Within Groups	120.190	253	.475		
	Total	355.584	254			
Lack of trust on e-Retailers	Between Groups	281.744	1	281.744	617.388	.000
	Within Groups	115.456	253	.456		
	Total	397.200	254			
Complex, compared to Traditional Shopping	Between Groups	211.955	1	211.955	358.385	.000
	Within Groups	149.629	253	.591		
	Total	361.584	254			
Previous purchase bad experience	Between Groups	239.814	1	239.814	540.332	.000
	Within Groups	112.288	253	.444		
	Total	352.102	254			
Lack of proficiency with the Internet	Between Groups	185.612	1	185.612	374.808	.000
	Within Groups	125.290	253	.495		
	Total	310.902	254			
Difficulty in returning products/items	Between Groups	212.456	1	212.456	465.265	.000
	Within Groups	115.528	253	.457		
	Total	327.984	254			
Lack of customer service	Between Groups	230.494	1	230.494	479.533	.000
	Within Groups	121.608	253	.481		
	Total	352.102	254			

All the f-values are significant at 0.01 level

The results of the survey explicate that the attitudes of e-shoppers in the case of graduate students, more experienced internet users and buyers who have internet access at their homes are more positive than attitudes of non e-shoppers, less experienced internet users, consumers who don't have internet access in their homes. The shoppers also have positive attitude towards convenience, time constraints, competitive prices, and product delivery factors of e-shopping. The primary obstacles of the e-shopping have to be eliminated so, that more buyers will tend to shift from traditional stores to e-stores. Finally, it is determined that both e-shoppers and non e-shoppers have a positive attitude towards e-shopping.

MEASURES TO IMPROVE E-SHOPPING EXPERIENCE

Generally speaking, web shopping in India has been increasing day by day and is in a good form. According to the survey, most of the respondents are satisfied with the current conditions available in the online shopping. Based on the comments and suggestions by the respondents, there still are certain areas in which the e-retailers need to make some improvements to make a better shopping experience.

1. The e-retailers in order to increase the sales and create a more comfortable web shopping environment should pay more attention on the shopper's security and privacy indicators.
2. Provide the e-shoppers with a more attractive and contented environment while shopping online.
3. The online shoppers should be able to classify the products more clearly and take much less time to choose the products which they like.
4. Undertake rigorous efforts to further enhance the areas like payment structure and logistics.
5. Proper and valid information regarding the products/itemsshould be provided in the vendors' online websites.
6. The e-retailers should provide much better customer services to their shoppers which will change their stance towards web shopping.
7. Display valid feedback, ratings and reviews from the previous users of the products which will be helpful to minimize the risk of the shoppers.

Finally, e-retailers must adapt to all types of browsers and devices, as customers use all of them to make e-purchases and at the same time, the mobile devices are also increasingly gaining importance in e-shopping. The challenge is not only to make sure that shopping applications work on each device, but also that they make the best use of the features of each platform. In addition, the shopper's expectations are always growing from time to time with a change in the marketing conditions. Savvy retailers will embrace the challenges and constantly improve the online shopping experience.

FUTURE RESEARCH DIRECTIONS AND LIMITATIONS

The outcome of the study expell that the consumers' who rated these factors high, their attitudes toward e-shopping are also high. There are some direct implications of these results and findings for the e-retailers. The e-retailers should have good quality website, provide high service and product quality, and provide better prices for their customers to positively influence their satisfaction and behaviour. This leads the potential consumers to shop online and the marketers to retain the existing customers. On the further research, information can be collected from consumers to generalize the results for the entire population of different major states of India and also the data should also be collected from the shoppers of specific e-stores to be able to measure the quality of goods and services of these e-stores. Further, the researchers can also focus on the consumers' online purchase decision making process.

As with most research, this study has certain limitations. Firstly, the information collected for the study was only from bachelor and master's graduate students of different colleges in Andhra Pradesh, India. Secondly, there are many factors affecting on buyer's e-shopping attitude. But in this study, only certain important factors influencing on online shopping attitude and reasons for not shopping online are examined. Taking these issues into consideration, the results are to be interpreted in light of the limitations outlined here. Despite these limitations, the results of the study are informative and important for global e-tailing research.

CONCLUSION

E-shopping has become extremely trendy over the past decade. Although e-shopping can be very convenient and beneficial there are also some potential problems that can arise. Shoppers' have been seen to exhibit different purchasing attitudes when shopping online than shopping in a physical store. This makes it crucial that e-retailers know the attitudes of buyers and make changes in order to remain profitable and successful. Another potential problem may be addiction to e-shopping which can also lead to an unhealthy addictive pattern of behaviour and as a result causes financial damage.

Online purchasing has a potential to growth but proper boosting is needed which can be effectively done through social media, because this is the only medium of sales promotions which can be in low cost and maximum reach. This indicates that the e-marketers should give more importance on price factor and after sale factor. Also, a variety of payment options must be provided to the consumer in this case and technically the payment gateways must be strong enough to avoid any security breach and there must be marketing activities on increasing awareness about their offerings. In future, it can be expected the e-stores to improve their technology enormously, allowing for an easier and a more realistic e-shopping experience. The technology of e-shopping websites will continue to grow and, as a result, will expand the e-market and benefiting thousands of shoppers' worldwide.

REFERENCES

Baršauskas, P., Šarapovas, T., & Cvilikas, A. (2008). The evaluation of e-commerce impact on business efficiency. *Baltic Journal of Management*, *3*(1), 71–91. doi:10.1108/17465260810844275

Bonnin, G., Segard, O., & Vialle, P. (2005). Relationship marketing and innovation: The case of the launch of wireless local loop telecommunication services in France. *Journal of Services Research*, 149–171.

Capgemini. (2013). *Evolving E-Commerce Market Dynamics: Changing Merchant Payment Needs and the Impact on Banks*. Retrieved on September 8, 2017, from http://www.capgemini.com/cards

Case, T., Burns, O. M., & Dick, G. N. (2001). Drivers of Online Purchases among U.S. Students. *Proceedings of 7th American conference on Information Systems*, 900-907.

Chaturvedi, S., & Gupta, S. (2014). Effect of Social Media on Online Shopping Behaviour of Apparels in Jaipur City- An Analytical Review. *Journal of Business Management, Commerce & Research*, *2*(7), 1–8.

Christodoulides, G., & Michaelidou, N. (2011). Shopping motives as antecedents of e-satisfaction and e-loyalty. *Journal of Marketing Management*, *27*(1-2), 181–197. doi:10.1080/0267257X.2010.489815

Dai, H., Luo, X., Liao, Q., & Cao, M. (2015). Explaining consumer satisfaction of services: The role of innovativeness and emotion in an electronic mediated environment. *Decision Support Systems*, *70*, 97–106. doi:10.1016/j.dss.2014.12.003

Delafrooz, N., Paim, L. H., Haron, S. A., Sidin, S. M., & Khatibi, A. (2009). Factors affecting students' attitude toward online shopping. *African Journal of Business Management, 3*(5), 200–209.

Gao, Y. (Ed.). (2005). *Web systems design and online consumer behavior*. IGI Global. doi:10.4018/978-1-59140-327-2

Goswami, A., Baruah, P., & Borah, S. (2013). Customer Satisfaction towards Online Shopping with Special Reference to Teenage Group of Jorhat Town. *PARIPEX - Indian Journal of Research, 3*(4), 239-241.

Guo, X., Ling, K. C., & Liu, M. (2012). Evaluating factors influencing customer satisfaction towards online shopping in China. *Asian Social Science, 8*(13), 40–50. doi:10.5539/ass.v8n13p40

Gupta, D. K., & Khincha, P. K. (2015). Factors Influencing Online Shopping Behavior of Customers: An Empirical Study. *Common Wealth Journal of Commerce & Management Research, 2*(7), 39–50.

Hasslinger, A., Hodzic, S., & Obazo, C. (2007). *Consumer behaviour in online shopping* (Master's Thesis). Department of Business Studies, Kristianstaad University.

Jusoh, Z. M., & Ling, G. H. (2012). Factors Influencing Consumers' Attitude Towards E-Commerce Purchases Through Online Shopping. *International Journal of Humanities and Social Science, 2*(4), 223–230.

Katta, R. M. R., & Patro, C. S. (2016). Online Shopping Behavior: A Study of Factors Influencing Consumer Satisfaction on Online viz-a-viz Conventional Store Shopping. *International Journal of Sociotechnology and Knowledge Development, 8*(4), 21–36. doi:10.4018/IJSKD.2016100102

Katta, R. M. R., & Patro, C. S. (2017). Influence of Web Attributes on Consumer Purchase Intentions. *International Journal of Sociotechnology and Knowledge Development, 9*(2), 1–16. doi:10.4018/IJSKD.2017040101

Keisidou, E., Sarigiannidis, L., & Maditinos, D. (2011). Consumer characteristics and their effect on accepting online shopping in the context of different product types. *International Journal of Business Science and Applied Management, 6*(2), 31–51.

Khristianto, W., Kertahadi, I., & Suyadi, I. (2012). The influence of information, system and service on customer satisfaction and loyalty in online shopping. *International Journal of Academic Research, 4*(2), 28–32.

Kim, S., & Stoel, L. (2004). Apparel retailers: Website quality dimensions and satisfaction. *Journal of Retailing and Consumer Services*, *11*(2), 109–117. doi:10.1016/S0969-6989(03)00010-9

Li, N., & Zhang, P. (2002). Consumer Online Shopping Attitudes and Behavior: An Assessment of Research. *Proceedings of Eight American Conference on Information Systems*, 508-517.

Lian, J., & Lin, T. (2008). Effects of consumer characteristics on their acceptance of online shopping: Comparisons among different product types. *Computers in Human Behavior*, *24*(1), 48–65. doi:10.1016/j.chb.2007.01.002

Liu, X., He, M., Gao, F., & Xie, P. (2008). An empirical study of online shopping customer satisfaction in China: A holistic perspective. *International Journal of Retail & Distribution Management*, *36*(11), 919–940. doi:10.1108/09590550810911683

Martin, R. (2016). *Ready for More: Four Key Focus Areas for Global Ecommerce in 2016*. Retrieved on August 12, 2017, from http://blogs.pb.com/ecommerce/2016/01/04/four-key-focus-areas-for-global-ecommerce-in-2016

Nayak, P. K., & Debashish, S. S. (2017). Young consumers' online shopping decision influencers: A study on university students of Odisha. *Effulgence*, *15*(1), 45–50.

Nuseir, M. T., Arora, N., Al-Masri, M. M., & Gharaibeh, M. (2010). Evidence of Online Shopping: A Consumer Perspective. *International Review of Business Research Papers*, *6*(5), 90–106.

Osman, S., Yin-Fah, B. C., & Choo, B. H. (2010). Undergraduates and online purchasing behavior. *Asian Social Science*, *6*(10), 133. doi:10.5539/ass.v6n10p133

Patro, C. S. (2016). Attitudes of E-Shoppers and Non E-Shoppers towards E-Shopping: A Comparative Study. *International Journal of Cyber Behavior, Psychology and Learning*, *6*(2), 96–108. doi:10.4018/IJCBPL.2016040106

Patro, C. S. (2017). Consumer Attitude and Loyalty in Online Shopping Environments: A Study of Facets Driving Shoppers Towards E-Stores. *International Journal of Cyber Behavior, Psychology and Learning*, *7*(3), 57–72. doi:10.4018/IJCBPL.2017070105

Rao, K. R. M., & Patro, C. S. (2016). Online Marketing-The Powerful Astra in the Strategic Armory of Marketers. *Mizoram University Journal of Humanities and Social Sciences*, *2*(2), 1–17.

Rao, K. R. M., & Patro, C. S. (2017). Shopper's Stance towards Web Shopping: An Analysis of Students Opinion of India. *International Journal of Online Marketing*, *7*(3), 42–54. doi:10.4018/IJOM.2017070104

Ribbink, D., van Riel, A. C. R., Liljander, V., & Streukens, S. (2004). Comfort your online customer: Quality, trust and loyalty on the internet. *Managing Service Quality*, *14*(6), 446–456. doi:10.1108/09604520410569784

Richa, D. (2012). Impact of demographic factors of consumers on online shopping behaviour: A study of consumers in India. *International Journal of Engineering and Management Sciences*, *3*(1), 43–52.

Ruby, K. (2016). E-tailing in India- Growth, Challenges and Opportunities. *Journal of Marketing and HR*, *2*(1), 102–112.

Saprikis, V., Chouliara, A., & Vlachopoulou, M. (2010, December). Perceptions towards online shopping: Analyzing the Greek University students' attitude. *Communications of the IBIMA*, 1-13.

Saravanan, R., Yoganandan, G., & Ruby, N. (2013). A Study on Online Shopping Behaviour of Teachers Working in Self-Financing Colleges in Namakkal District With Special Reference to K.S.R College of Arts And Science, Tiruchengode, Namakkal District. *International Journal of Research in Commerce, IT & Management*, *3*(6), 31–37.

Shergill, G. S., & Chen, Z. (2005). Web-Based Shopping: Consumers' attitudes Towards Online Shopping in New Zealand. *Journal of Electronic Commerce Research*, *6*(2), 78.

Silverstein, B. (2002). *Business to Business internet marketing*. Jim Hoskins.

Sorce, P., Perotti, V., & Widrick, S. (2005). Attitude and Age Differences in Online Buying. *International Journal of Retail & Distribution Management*, *33*(2), 122–132. doi:10.1108/09590550510581458

Tanadi, T., Samadi, B., & Gharleghi, B. (2015). The Impact of Perceived Risks and Perceived Benefits to Improve an Online Intention among Generation-Y in Malaysia. *Asian Social Science*, *11*(26), 226. doi:10.5539/ass.v11n26p226

Tassabehji, R. (2003). *Applying E-commerce in Business*. New Delhi, India: Sage Publications.

Wang, N., Liu, D., & Cheng, J. (2008). Study on the influencing factors of online shopping. In *Proceedings of the 11th Joint Conference on Information Sciences.* Atlantis Press.

Yörük, D., Dündar, S., Moga, L.M., & Neculita, M. (2011). Drivers and Attitudes towards Online Shopping: Comparison of Turkey with Romania. *Communications of the IBIMA*, 1-13. DOI: 10.5171/2011.575361

Zeng, M., & Reinartz, W. (2003). Beyond online search: The road to profitability. *California Management Review*, *45*(2), 107–130. doi:10.2307/41166168

Chapter 10
Cyberbullying:
Prevalence, Characteristics, and Consequences

Michelle F. Wright
Pennsylvania State University, USA & Masaryk University, Czech Republic

ABSTRACT

Children and adolescents are actively engaged in a digital world in which blogs, social networking sites, watching videos, and instant messaging are a typical part of their daily lives. Their immersion in the digital world has occurred for as long as they remember, with many not knowing a world without our modern technological advances. Although the digital age has brought us many conveniences in our daily lives, there is a darker side to children's and adolescents' involvement with these technologies, such as cyberbullying. This chapter draws on research from around the world, utilizing a variety of research designs, to describe the nature, extent, causes, and consequences associated with children's and adolescents' involvement in cyberbullying. Concluding the chapter is a solutions and recommendations section in which it is argued that cyberbullying is a global concern, affecting all aspects of society, requiring a whole-community approach.

INTRODUCTION

Millions of youths have fully embraced digital technologies (e.g., mobile phones, the Internet), utilizing these digital technologies daily (Lenhart, 2015). Digital technologies provide many benefits to youths, including the ability to communicate with just about anyone, access to information for leisure and school purposes, and

DOI: 10.4018/978-1-5225-7128-5.ch010

entertainment (e.g., watching videos). Although there are many benefits associated with youths' digital technology use, they are also at risk for a variety of negative experiences, such as receiving unwanted electronic content via videos, images, and text, identity theft, using fake or untrue information for schoolwork, and sexual predators. Another risk associated with their digital technology use is cyberbullying.

Defined as an extension of traditional bullying involving bullying behaviors using electronic technologies, including email, instant messaging, Facebook, and text messaging through mobile devices, cyberbullying involves malicious intent to cause harm to a victim or victims (Bauman, Underwood, & Card, 2013; Grigg, 2012).

The ability to remain anonymous in the cyber context offers flexibility to cyberbullies as they can harm their victims without much concern for the consequences of their actions, due to their ability to mask or hide their identity (Wright, 2014b). Anonymity can trigger the online disinhibition effect which leads some youths to do or say things that they would typically never do or say in the offline world (Suler, 2004; Wright, 2014a). Bullying through digital technologies allows cyberbullies to harm victims in a shorter amount of time. For example, cyberbullies can spread a rumor in the online world in a matter of minutes, while it could take hours for a rumor to spread in the offline world. Cyberbullies can also target victims as often as they like. Victims of offline bullying are able to escape bullying in the sanctuary of their homes, while cyberbullying often follows victims into their homes and other places they perceive as safe. Additionally, cyberbullying can involve the bully and victim only, one bystander, or multiple bystanders. For example, posting a video making fun of someone can receive thousands of watches, whereas being bullied in the lunchroom might only be visible to the individuals paying attention to what is happening. Therefore, the nature of the cyberbullying is somewhat distinctive from face-to-face traditional bullying.

The aim of this chapter is to examine cyberbullying among youths in elementary, middle, and high schools. The studies reviewed in this chapter are from various disciplines, including psychology, education, media studies, communication, social work, sociology, and computer science. This chapter reviews literature with cross-sectional, longitudinal, qualitative, and quantitative research designs to describe cyberbullying. In addition, the chapter draws on studies from a variety of different countries in an effort to provide a more thorough review of the literature. The chapter is organized into the following six sections:

1. Description and definition of cyberbullying: review of the definition of cyberbullying, the types of digital technologies used, the role of anonymity, and the prevalence rates of cyberbullying perpetration and victimization

2.   Characteristics and risk factors related to youths' involvement in cyberbullying: review of the research on the predictors associated with cyberbullying among youths

3.   Consequences associated with youths' involvement in cyberbullying: review of the research findings regarding the social, psychological, behavioral, and academic consequences related to youths' cyberbullying involvement

4.   Solutions and recommendations: provides suggestions for prevention and intervention programs and recommendations for public policy development

5.   Future research directions: provides recommendations for future research aimed at understanding and preventing children's and adolescents' involvement in cyberbullying

6.   Conclusion: concluding remarks regarding the current nature of the literature on cyberbullying.

BACKGROUND

Define as youths' use of digital technologies to hostilely and intentionally harass, embarrass, and intimidate others, cyberbullying can sometimes involve repetition and an imbalance of power, like traditional forms of face-to-face bullying (Smith et al., 2013). Instrumental to the definition of cyberbullying is the hostility and intentionality of the act, which highlights the requirement that these behaviors must be intentionally and maliciously harmful to qualify as cyberbullying. Repetitiveness of cyberbullying behavior involves cyberbullies targeting a victim or victims multiple times by sharing humiliating video or text messages to one person or multiple people (Bauman et al., 2013). It is easier for bullies to perpetuate the cycle of cyberbullying. For example, cyberbullies can share a humiliating video or text message with one person who can then turn around and share the content additional times and with other people, and then these people can then share the video or text message.

The use of digital technologies to harm others is what separates the definition of cyberbullying from the traditional face-to-face bullying definition (Curelaru, Iacob, & Abalasei, 2009). Cyberbullying behaviors can occur through a variety of digital technologies and involve different behaviors, including sending unkind text messages and emails, theft of identity information, pretending to be someone else, making anonymous phone calls, sharing secrets about the victim by posting or sending the secret to someone else, spreading nasty rumors using social networking websites, threatening to harm someone, or uploading an embarrassing picture or video of the victim with malicious intent (Bauman et al., 2013). Other examples of cyberbullying involvement behaviors that are similar to those carried out in the offline world, such as harassment, insults, verbal attacks, teasing, physical threats, social exclusion, and humiliation. Furthermore, cyberbullying can involve also the distribution of explicit or embarrassing videos through a variety of mediums, such as social networking sites, text messages, and online gaming sites, creating websites to defame someone else, and making fake social networking profiles using someone else's identity (Rideout et al., 2005).

There are also cyberbullies behaviors that have no offline equivalent, such as happy slapping and flaming (Rideout et al., 2005). Happy slapping is defined as a group of people who randomly insult another person while filming the incident on a mobile phone, and then these individuals will post the image(s) or video(s) online for others to see. Flaming involves posting provocative or offensive messages in a public forum with the intention of provoking an angry response or argument from members of the forum. Cyberbullying behaviors can take place through a variety of digital technologies, with the most frequently used technologies to harm others including gaming consoles, instant messaging tools, and social networking sites (Ybarra et al., 2007).

Prevalence of Cyberbullying Behaviors in the United States and Other Countries

Understanding the prevalence rates of youths' cyberbullying involvement is important as it highlights how frequency youths are exposed to these behaviors. In one of the earliest studies on cyberbullying, Patchin and Hinduja (2006) found that 29% of children and adolescents in their sample reported that they had experienced cyber victimization and 47% indicated that they had witnessed cyberbullying. Similar rates were found by Kowalski and Limber (2007). There were 3,767 middle school students, ages 11 through 14, included in their study. Their findings indicated that 11% of the sample were cyberbullied, 4% bullied others, and 7% were classified as both cybervictim and cyberbully. Using a slightly older sample (grades 9-12th), Goebert et al. (2011) found that 56.1% of youths in their sample from Hawaii were victims of cyberbullying. In a more recent investigation, Hinduja and Patchin (2012) examined cyberbullying behaviors within the past 30 days among 6th through 12th graders. Findings revealed that 4.9% of these youths perpetrated cyberbullying in the past 30 days. Among Canadian 10th graders, Cappadocia et al. (2013) found that 2.1% of adolescents in their study reported to perpetrating cyberbullying, 1.9% were classified as cybervictims, and 0.6% explained that they were both cyberbullies and cyber victims. In a sample of 8th through 10th graders, Bonnanno and Hymel (2013) found that 6% of their sample admitted to being cyberbullies, 5.8% were classified as cybervictims only, and 5% were cyberbullies and cybervictims.

Cyberbullying involvement is a global problem and increasing evidence indicates that cyberbullying occurs among youths in Africa, Asia, Australia, Europe, and South

America. In one study, Laftman, Modin, and Ostberg (2013) found that 5% of their large Swedish sample ($N = 22,544$, ages 15-18) were victims of cyberbullying, 4% were perpetrators of cyberbullying, and 2% were classified as both cyberbullies and cybervictims. Using a younger sample of Swedish adolescents, Beckman et al. (2012) found that 1.9% of their sample from 7th through 9th grade were classified as cybervictims, 2.9% as cyberbullies, and 0.6% as both cyberbullies and cybervictims. These rates were similar to those found among adolescents in Ireland. In particular, Corcoran et al. (2012) found that 6% of youths, between the ages of 12 through 17, in their study reported that they were victimized by cyberbullying. Higher rates were found in Brighi et al.'s (2012) study. They found that 12.5% of Italian adolescents in their sample were classified as cybervictims. Similar prevalence rates were found by Festl et al. (2013). In their sample of German adolescents, Festl et al. (2013) found that 13% were classified as cyberbullies and 11% as cybervictims. Research has also focused on the prevalence rates of cyberbullying perpetration and victimization among children and adolescents from Israel. Rates are generally higher than some European countries, but not as high as those found in India. Olenik-Shemesh et al. (2010) found that 16.5% of their participants ($N = 242$; 13-16 year olds) were cybervictims. The rate of Israeli adolescents identified as cybervictims or witnesses of cyberbullying was 32.4% of the sample ($N = 355$; 13 to 17 year olds; Lazuras et al., 2013).

A lot of research attention has focused on prevalence rates among Turkish youths. Estimates of cyberbullying victimization among Turkish youths vary, from 18% to 32% (Eruder-Baker, 2010; Yilmaz, 2011). Cyberbullying perpetration rates among Turkish youths also varies from 6% through 9% (Ayas & Horzum, 2012; Yilmaz, 2011). Aricak et al. (2008) found some of the highest rates of cyberbullying perpetration. In their sample of Turkish secondary school students, they found that 36% reported that they were cyberbullies.

Research on cyberbullying bullying involvement among youths in Asian countries has been slower to develop. In one of the first studies on cyberbullying in Asia, Huang and Chou (2010) found that 63.4% of the Taiwanese youths in their sample had witnessed cyberbullying, 34.9% were classified as cybervictims, and 20.4% admitted to being cyberbullies. Jang, Song, and Kim (2014) examined cyberbullying involvement among 3,238 Korean adolescents. In this study, 43% of the sample classified as perpetrators or victims of cyberbullying. These prevalence rates are similar to those of youths in China. In particular, Zhou et al. (2013) found that 34.8% of the 1,438 youths in their sample were classified as cyberbullies and 56.9% as cybervictims. Focusing exclusively on Facebook cyberbullying, Kwan and Skoric (2013) reported that 59.4% of Singaporean adolescents in their study experienced cyber victimization through this social media website, while 56.9%

perpetrated cyberbullying. In addition, Wong et al. (2014) found that 12.2% of adolescents in their sample ($N = 1,912$) were cybervictims and 13.1% were classified as cyberbullying perpetrators.

Some of the research on the prevalence of cyberbullying has focused on cross-cultural differences in youths' cyberbullying involvement. This research usually classified countries according to an independent self-construal or an interdependent self-construal. Someone with an independent self-construal views the self as separate from the social context, while someone with an interdependent self-construal views themselves within the context of their social environment or society. Usually people from Western countries, like the United States, Canada, and England, are reinforced and primed for behaving in ways aligned with an independent self-construal. On the other hand, people from Eastern countries, like China, Korea, and Japan, are reinforced and primed for behavior consistently in regards to an interdependent self-construal. Differences in these self-construals affect people's social behaviors, particularly bullying and cyberbullying. Therefore, independent and interdependent self-construals have been used to explain these behaviors.

In the research on cross-cultural differences in cyberbullying, Barlett et al. (2013) found that youths from the United States self-reported higher levels of cyberbullying involvement when compared to youths from Japan. These results were also corroborated in a study examining differences in cyberbullying involvement rates among Japanese and Austrian adolescents such that Austrian adolescents reported more cyberbullying perpetration and victimization than Japanese adolescents (Strohmeier, Aoyama, Gradinger, & Toda, 2013). In addition, Li (2008) found that Chinese youths engaged in less cyberbullying perpetration when compared to Canadian children and adolescents. However, Li found little differences between Chinese and Canadian youths when it came to cyberbullying victimization. In an earlier study, with a different sample, Li (2006) found that Chinese youths self-reported more cyberbullying victimization in comparison to Canadian youths. Focused on differences in reactive (i.e., response to provocation) and proactive (i.e., to obtain some sort of goal) forms of cyberbullying, Shapka and Law found that East Asian adolescents from Canada reported more proactive cyberbullying perpetration while Canadian adolescents reported engaging in more reactive forms of cyberbullying.

Little attention has been given to understanding cyberbullying involvement among youths from Africa, India, and South America. In one of the few studies to investigate cyberbullying involvement in India, Wright et al. (2015) found that Indian adolescents reported more cyberbullying perpetration and victimization when compared to adolescents from China and Japan, with Chinese adolescents reporting more of these behaviors in comparison to Japanese adolescents. Gender differences in cyberbullying involvement are also found to vary across countries as well. In particular, Genta et al. (2012) found that Italian males perpetrated more cyberbullying when compared to Spanish and English males. In Wright and colleagues' (2015) research, they found boys from India were more often involved in cyberbullying when compared to boys from China and Japan.

Taken together, this research indicates that cyberbullying perpetration and cyber victimization is a global concern, warranting additional investigations. Variations in prevalence rates are due to differences in samples, sampling techniques, and measures used.

CHARACTERISTICS ASSOCIATED WITH CYBERBULLYING

After much of the prevalence of cyberbullying research indicates that researchers should be considered with these behaviors, other research focused on the characteristics associated with youths' involvement in cyberbullying. Age is one variable examined as having a role in cyberbullying. Research focused on age and cyberbullying typically reveals that cyberbullying victimization is more prevalent among early adolescents, while cyberbullying perpetration is more often carried out by older adolescents. Williams and Guerra (2007) examined cyberbullying perpetration among adolescents between 6th through 8th grades. They delineated different types of cyberbullying, with findings revealing that physical forms of cyberbullying, like hacking, peaked in middle school, while rates of physical forms of cyberbullying declined in high school. Other research has indicated that 9th graders had the highest risk of cyberbullying involvement when compared to adolescents in middle school (Wade & Beran, 2011). Consequently, age was not found to be a reliable predictor of youths' cyberbullying involvement.

Gender has also been examined as a predictor of cyberbullying involvement among youths. Some researchers have found that boys reported that they were more often the perpetrators of cyberbullying when compared to girls (Boulton et al., 2012; Li, 2007; Ybarra et al., 2007). Girls reported more cyber victimization than boys in other studies (Hinduja & Patchin, 2007; Kowalski & Limber, 2007). In contrast, some researchers

some researchers (e.g., Dehue, Bolman, & Vollink, 2008; Pornari & Wood, 2010) reported that girls engaged in more cyberbullying perpetration, while boys experienced more cyber victimization (e.g., Huang & Chou, 2010; Sjurso, Fandrem, & Roland, 2016). Other researchers (e.g., Stoll & Block, 2015; Wright & Li, 2013b) have found no gender differences in children's and adolescents' involvement in these behaviors. In a recent study on the role of digital technologies and behavior in girls' and boys' cyberbullying perpetration, Wright (in press) found that it is important to consider the type of technology used and the behaviors perpetrated. In particular, boys were more likely to experience cyberbullying via gaming consoles, while girls were more likely to perpetrate relational and verbal forms of cyberbullying. Therefore, like age, gender has proven to be an inconsistent predictor of cyberbullying involvement as well.

Youths' involvement in traditional forms of bullying typically examined as a risk factor associated with cyberbullying involvement. In this research, relationships are usually found between cyberbullying perpetration and traditional face-to-face bullying perpetration, cyber victimization and traditional face-to-face victimization, and traditional face-to-face victimization and cyberbullying perpetration (Barlett & Gentile, 2012; Mitchell et al., 2007; Wright & Li, 2013a, 2013b).

Digital technology use is another characteristic associated with cyberbullying perpetration and victimization among youths. In this research, youths' greater use of the internet is positively correlated with their cyberbullying perpetration and victimization (Ang, 2016; Aricak et al., 2008). In addition, cybervictims are more likely to use instant messaging tools, email, blogging sites, and online game when compared to nonvictims, another finding suggesting the role of digital technology use in cyberbullying involvement (Smith et al., 2008). The link between digital technology use and cyberbullying involvement might be explained by some youths' greater likelihood to disclose personal information online. Disclosing personal information online, like one's geographical location or school name, increases youths' risk for cyberbullying victimization.

Both internalizing difficulties, such as depression and loneliness, and externalizing difficulties, such as alcohol and drug use, are factors related to youths' involvement in cyberbullying. To explain these associations, researchers propose that internalizing and externalizing problems reduce youths' coping strategies, which makes them more vulnerable to cyberbullying (Cappadocia et al., 2013; Mitchell et al., 2007). Alcohol and drug use are both associated with youths' involvement in cyberbullying as the perpetrator and victim (Cappadocia et al., 2013; Wright, in press).

Researchers have also investigated a variety of variables in relation to youths' cyberbullying involvement. In some research, higher normative beliefs (i.e., beliefs about the acceptability of behavior or behaviors) regarding face-to-face bullying and cyberbullying were related positively to cyberbullying perpetration (e.g., Burton, Florell, & Wygant, 2013; Wright, 2014b). Consequently, cyberbullies often hold favorable attitudes toward engaging in bullying behaviors, leading them to believe these behaviors are acceptable to perpetrate. In addition, holding lower levels of provictim attitudes, defined as the belief that bullying is unacceptable and that defending victims is valuable, lower peer attachment, less self-control and empathy, and greater moral disengagement were each correlated positively with cyberbullying perpetration (e.g., Sevcikova, Machackova, Wright, Dedkova, & Cerna, 2015; Wright, Kamble, Lei, Li, Aoyama, & Shruti, 2015).

Little attention has been given to understanding the longitudinal relationships between various characteristics and youths' cyberbullying involvement. In one of the few studies to investigate these behaviors utilizing a longitudinal design, Fanti et al. (2012) examined children's and adolescents 'exposure to violent media, their callous and unemotional traits, and their cyberbullying involvement one year later. Media violence exposure was positively linked to adolescents' cyber victimization one year later. Wright (2014a) found that perceived stress from parents, peers, and academics/school were related to adolescents' cyberbullying perpetration one year later. Taken together, the research in this section highlights the various risk factors that increases youths' vulnerability to cyberbullying perpetration and victimization. This section also described the individual predictors associated with youths' cyberbullying involvement. The rest of this section will focus on the role of parents, schools/teachers, and peers in youths' involvement in cyberbullying.

Parents

Some parents choose to monitor their children's activities in the online world. Mason (2008) found that 50% of children and adolescents reported that their parents did not monitor their online activities, while 80% of parents reported monitoring their children's online activities. In another study, 93% of parents reported that they set limits on their children's online activities (McQuade, Colt, & Meyer, 2009). However, only 37% of their children reported that they were given rules from their parents concerning their online activities. This could mean that parents are over reporting the amount of monitoring they engage in or that their strategies for monitoring are ineffective such that their children believe no strategies have been implemented. Parents have an important role in protecting their children against online risks. More attention should be given to have parents navigate having conversations with their children about online risks and opportunities.

Wright (2015) examined the person, either parents, teachers, or friends, who most frequently mediated youths' digital technology use. She found that parents were more likely to mediate youths' digital technology use and when they did their children reported less cyber victimization and negative adjustment difficulties. Consequently she concluded that parental mediation buffers against these negative psychological consequences. A possible explanation for these relationships is that parents who monitor their children's digital technology use provide more opportunities to discuss the risks associated with technology use. Furthermore, it might even increase youths' awareness that negative online behaviors are not acceptable. It could also make them think about what their parents might do if they engaged in negative online behaviors. This proposal is consistent with research finding that youths who believed that their parents would punish them for participating in negative online behaviors, like cyberbullying, were less likely to perpetrate cyberbullying (Hinduja & Patchin, 2013; Wright, 2013a). Other research has revealed that parental monitoring has no impact on youths' online risk exposure. In this research, Aoyama et al. (2011) found that parental mediation and monitoring of children's online activities were unrelated to youths' involvement in cyberbullying. They explained that some parents lack the technological skills to understand how to effectively monitor their children's online activities. Because parents lack these skills, they are not sure of how and when to intervene. Such a proposal is consistent with previous research findings in which parents reported that they were not sure how to discuss online activities with their children (Rosen, 2007). This uncertainty might lead some parents to not know to talk to their children about appropriate online behaviors.

Some parents do not follow-up on the strategies they implement for making the Internet safer for their children. Youths might develop the perception that their parents are not concerned with their online behaviors, and this could subsequently increase their risk of engaging in cyberbullying. In addition, it is important for parents to not only enforce the strategies they implement regarding digital technology use but to also update the strategies they use as their children become older and desire more independence and privacy.

Family characteristics have also been examined in association with youths' cyberbullying involvement. Ybarra and Mitchell (2004) found that family income, parental education, and marital status of caregivers were unrelated to youths' cyberbullying perpetration or victimization. However, Arslan et al. (2012) found that parental unemployment was related to youths' cyberbullying perpetration and victimization. Neglectful parenting increased youths' risk of cyberbullying involvement when compared to uninvolved youths (Dehue, Bolman, Vollink, & Pouwelse, 2012). Furthermore, authoritarian parenting style increased youths' experience of cyberbullying as cybervictims.

In sum, the literature reviewed in this section suggests that parents have an important role in mitigating their children's involvement in cyberbullying and other negative online behaviors. The research reviewed in the next section focuses on the role of schools and peers in youths' cyberbullying perpetration and victimization.

Schools

The schools' role in monitoring and providing sanctions for youths' cyberbullying is a topic of great debate. This is because many cyberbullying incidences occur off school grounds, making it difficult for the school to know about these cases and how to deal with such situations (deLara, 2012; Mason, 2008). Although most cyberbullying incidences occurs off school grounds, many of these incidences involve youths who attend the same school. This further complicates the schools' role in handling cyberbullying. Because cyberbullying typically involves youths who know each other at school, it is likely that knowledge of the incidence might spread across the school or that these individuals might engage in negative interactions while on school grounds, which could disrupt the learning process.

Although cyberbullying incidences have the potential to "spill over" onto school grounds, administrators' and teachers' perceptions of cyberbullying vary, leading some school staff to perceive these behaviors as problematic while others do not (Kochenderfer-Ladd & Pelletier, 2008). Oftentimes administrators and teachers will not perceive cyberbullying or any form of covert bullying behavior as serious and harmful (Sahin, 2010). Some teachers are more likely to encourage prevention programs designed to reduce physical forms of face-to-face bullying (Tangen & Campbell, 2010). They do not understand the harmful consequences associated with relational bullying and cyberbullying. Some teacher training does not properly inform teachers on how to recognize cyberbullying or how to deal with it. Sometimes teachers are unfamiliar with newer technologies (Cassidy et al., 2012a). This unfamiliarity makes it difficult for teachers to deal with cyberbullying as they were unsure of how to respond to the incident or which strategies to implement to alleviate the situation. If teachers are concerned about cyberbullying, there are usually few policies and programs at the school level, making it difficult to implement solutions (Cassidy, Brown, & Jackson, 2012b).

Schools must recognize the importance of implement effective policies and professional development designed to deal effectively with cyberbullying as these behaviors impact learning (Shariff & Hoff, 2007). When youths are involved in cyberbullying, as perpetrators or victims, they are less likely to perceived their school and teachers positively when compared to uninvolved youths (Bayar & Ucanok, 2012). Many victims of cyberbullying fear that their classmates might be cyberbullies, which disrupts their ability to concentrate on learning (Eden, Heiman, & Olenik-Shemesh, 2013). Such disruptions might reduce their academic attainment and performance. Furthermore, lower school commitment and perceptions of a negative school climate increase youths' perpetration of cyberbullying as they feel less connected to their school (Williams & Guerra, 2007).

Administrators and teachers require training to increase their awareness of cyberbullying. They also need to work together to develop policies at the school level to reduce these behaviors and implement strategies to handle cyberbullying incidences. Confidence in one's teaching abilities and having a stronger commitment to their school increases teachers' likelihood of learning about cyberbullying (Eden et al., 2013). When teachers learn about cyberbullying, they increase their awareness of these behaviors and how to effectively deal with these incidences. This awareness could help to prevent youths' involvement in cyberbullying. In particular, when teachers feel more confident, they intervene in cyberbullying incidences more often, which protects adolescents' from experiencing these behaviors (Elledge et al., 2013). Teachers' motivation for learning about cyberbullying varies such that elementary school teachers are more concerned with this behavior than middle school students. This is problematic as cyberbullying involvement increases from elementary school to middle school (Ybarra et al., 2007). Therefore, there is a need for educator training programs aimed at raising awareness of cyberbullying, particularly in the middle school years.

Peers

Peer relationships help youths learn about the social norms dictating acceptable and unacceptable behaviors within the peer group; as a consequence of this learning, youths will engage in more of these acceptable behaviors, as dictated by their peers, even if they are negative. In one study, the best predictor of cyberbullying involvement was the climate of the classroom in which these behaviors were encouraged (Festl et al., 2013). Furthermore, believing that one's friends engaged in cyberbullying predicts youths' perpetration of these behaviors (Hinduja & Patchin, 2013). The peer contagion effect potentially explains these associations, which suggests that the engagement in negative behaviors perpetrated by one's friends "spread" to other children and adolescents within their social network (Sijtsema, Ashwin, Simona, & Gina, 2014).

Peer attachment is another variable which has been examined in relation to youths' involvement in cyberbullying. Peer attachment refers to youths' beliefs that their peers will be or will not be there for them when they need it. This variable directly relates to peer interactions. In one study, Burton et al. (2013) found that lower of peer attachment were associated positively with cyberbullying perpetration and victimization. Peer rejection also increase youths' cyberbullying perpetration and cyber victimization (Sevcikova et al., 2015; Wright & Li, 2013b). To explain the connection between peer rejection and cyberbullying involvement, Wright and Li (2012) propose that peer rejection triggers negative emotional responses that leads to cyberbullying perpetration and victimization. Other research has explored the potential of cyberbullying to promote youths' social standing in their peer group, both online and offline. With digital technologies having such a prominent role in youths' lives, these technologies might be used as tools to promote or maintain youths' social standing in the peer group. Wright (2014c) found that higher levels of perceived popularity, a reputational type of popularity in the peer group, was associated positively with cyberbullying perpetration six months later among adolescents. The literature in this section suggests that it is important to consider the role of peers in youths' cyberbullying involvement.

CONSEQUENCES ASSOCIATED WITH CYBERBULLYING INVOLVEMENT

Parents, schools, and researchers' concerns with cyberbullying involvement among youths are triggered by the various negative social, psychological, behavioral, and academic consequences associated with youths' exposure to these behaviors. Much of the research on cyberbullying reveals that this experience disrupts youths' emotional experiences. Cybervictims report lower levels of global happiness, general school happiness, school satisfaction, family satisfaction, and self-satisfaction (Toledano, Werch, & Wiens, 2015). Furthermore, cybervicitms also report that they experience anger, sadness, and fear more often than uninvolved youths (Dehue et al., 2008; Machackova, Dedkova, Sevcikova, & Cerna, 2013; Patchin & Hinduja, 2006).

Cyberbullying involvement also disrupts youths' academic performance. In particular, cyberbullies and cybervictims experience more academic difficulties, including less motivation for school, poor academic performance, lower academic attainment, and more school absences (Belae & Hall, 2007; Yousef & Bellamy, 2015). Lower school functioning, such as disruptive classroom behaviors, lower grades, and lower test scores, is associated with cyberbullying perpetration and cyber victimization (Wright, in press).

Cyberbullies and cybervictims are also at risk for a variety of internalizing and externalizing difficulties (e.g., Mitchell, Ybarra, & Finkelhor, 2007; Patchin & Hinduja, 2006; Wright, 2014b; Ybarra, Diener-West, & Leaf, 2007). Youths involved in cyberbullying report more suicidal thoughts and attempts when compared to uninvolved youths (Bauman, Toomey, & Walker 2013). Experiencing or perpetrating cyberbullying increases youths' risk of mental health problems (Beckman et al., 2012) and psychiatric and psychosomatic problems (Sourander et al., 2010).

The research on psychological and behavioral consequences related to cyberbullying involvement usually do not take into account youths' involvement in traditional forms of bullying and victimization. Studies that consider youths' involvement in both cyber and face-to-face forms of bullying is important because these variables are highly correlated (Williams & Guerra, 2007; Wright & Li, 2013b). In one of the few studies to take into these high correlations, Bonanno et al. (2013) controlled for face-to-face bullying and victimization, and found that youths involved in cyberbullying experienced greater depressive symptoms and suicidal ideation. Other researchers have focused on the conjoint effects of cyber and face-to-face bullying on youths' psychological and behavioral adjustment. Gradinger et al. (2009) and Perren et al. (2012) found that victims of both traditional face-to-face bullying and cyberbullying reported higher levels of internalizing symptoms when compared to children and adolescents who experienced only one type of victimization. Thus, a combination of various bullying behaviors exacerbates children's and adolescents' experience of depression, anxiety, and loneliness. Such findings further support the importance of considering children's and adolescents' involvement in bullying behaviors both offline and online in an effort to understand more about these relationships and how to best intervene.

SOLUTIONS AND RECOMMENDATIONS

Everyone in our communities should be concerned with youths' involvement in cyberbullying. School curriculum should include elements that teach youths about cyberbullying, digital literacy, and digital citizenship (Cassidy et al., 2012b). Such curriculum should also discuss the many positive uses of digital technology, provictim attitudes, empathy, self-esteem, and social skills. Schools should also aim to improve school climate by learning students' names, praising good behavior, and staying technologically up-to-date (Hinduja & Patchin, 2012). A code of conduct should also be developed and adopted which addresses appropriate digital technology use. Not only is it important to implement this code of conduct but for administrators, teachers, and other school staff to enforce these policies.

Parents also have a role in helping to address cyberbullying. They should partner with educators from their children's school and increase their awareness and knowledge of digital technologies (Cassidy et al., 2012a; Diamanduros & Downs, 2011). Furthermore, parents should develop more knowledge of digital technologies in an effort to understand their children's desire to be involved in the cyber context and to have an awareness of the potential risks that their children might be exposed to via digital technologies. Such knowledge can help them develop and implemental parental monitoring strategies to reduce their children's vulnerability to cyberbullying. They should also maintain an open dialogue with their children regarding appropriate digital technology use. Some parents engage in poor digital technology habits, such as using mobile phones and texting while driving or using mobile phones during dinner or special events. Therefore, should model appropriate online behavior in order to serve as appropriate role models for their children.

FUTURE RESEARCH DIRECTIONS

The purpose of this literature review was to describe cyberbullying behaviors and the role of various characteristics and risk factors associated with youths' involvement in these behaviors. This review of the literature on cyberbullying involvement suggests some noticeable limitations and future directions for research. Anonymity is a prominent factor found to relate to youths' perpetration of cyberbullying.

Despite such awareness, little attention has been given to this topic, particularly how anonymous beliefs about the cyber context development and how such beliefs relate to cyberbullying. Other research should focus on non-anonymous of cyberbullying versus anonymous forms of cyberbullying in order to understand more about the motivators underlying these behaviors, and whether victims might experience differential adjustment difficulties following victimization by anonymous versus non-anonymous forms of cyberbullying. More specifically, non-anonymous cyberbullying, perpetrated by a known peer, might have more of an impact on an adolescent's depressive symptoms than if he or she were to experience the same behaviors from an anonymous perpetrator.

More attention is needed to understand more about the long-term impact of cyberbullying perpetration and cyber victimization across multiple age groups, particularly among young children and adults. Most studies on cyberbullying involvement focus on early and late adolescents, with little attention given to cyberbullying perpetration and cyber victimization among elementary school-aged children (Madden et al., 2013; Ybarra et al., 2007). Focusing on this younger age group makes it easier to understand the developmental trajectory of traditional face-to-face bullying and cyberbullying involvement, and it could help to answer questions about the temporal order of these bullying behaviors. This research will help to shed light on whether there is an age at which youths are most vulnerable to cyberbullying involvement. Intervention and prevention programs could be developed which specific consideration to the specific age group identified as at the most risk for cyberbullying involvement.

CONCLUSION

The findings from the literature on cyberbullying underscores the need for continued investigations on cyberbullying. The earlier research on cyberbullying focused on prevalence rates of cyberbullying to understand how many youths were at risk for these behaviors. From this early research, researchers directed their attention to the causes and consequences of youths' cyberbullying involvement. Most of the research focused on the "causes" of cyberbullying utilize concurrent research designs and on the role of parents, schools, and peers in youths' involvement in these behaviors. More investigations need to focus on these individuals and entities as cyberbullying is a global concern. This is important as cyberbullying affects all aspects of our society, undermining ethical and moral values. It is imperative that we unite and do our part to reduce children's and adolescents' involvement in cyberbullying together.

REFERENCES

Ang, R. P. (2016). Cyberbullying: Its prevention and intervention strategies. In D. Sibnath (Ed.), *Child safety, welfare and well-being: Issues and challenges* (pp. 25–38). Springer. doi:10.1007/978-81-322-2425-9_3

Aoyama, I., Utsumi, S., & Hasegawa, M. (2011). Cyberbullying in Japan: Cases, government reports, adolescent relational aggression and parental monitoring roles. In Q. Li, D. Cross, & P. K. Smith (Eds.), *Bullying in the global playground: Research from an international perspective*. Oxford, UK: Wiley-Blackwell.

Aricak, T., Siyahhan, S., Uzunhasanoglu, A., Saribeyoglu, S., Ciplak, S., Yilmaz, N., & Memmedov, C. (2008). Cyberbullying among Turkish adolescents. *Cyberpsychology & Behavior*, *11*(3), 253–261. doi:10.1089/cpb.2007.0016 PMID:18537493

Arslan, S., Savaser, S., Hallett, V., & Balci, S. (2012). Cyberbullying among primary school students in Turkey: Self-reported prevalence and associations with home and school life. *Cyberpsychology, Behavior, and Social Networking*, *15*(10), 527–533. doi:10.1089/cyber.2012.0207 PMID:23002988

Ayas, T., & Horzum, M. B. (2010). *Cyberbullg / victim scale development study*. Retrieved from: http://www.akademikbakis.org

Barlett, C. P., & Gentile, D. A. (2012). Long-term psychological predictors of cyber-bullying in late adolescence. *Psychology of Popular Media Culture*, *2*, 123–135. doi:10.1037/a0028113

Barlett, C. P., Gentile, D. A., Anderson, C. A., Suzuki, K., Sakamoto, A., Yamaoka, A., & Katsura, R. (2013). Cross-cultural differences in cyberbullying behavior: A short-term longitudinal study. *Journal of Cross-Cultural Psychology*, *45*(2), 300–313. doi:10.1177/0022022113504622

Bauman, S., Toomey, R. B., & Walker, J. L. (2013). Associations among bullying, cyberbullying, and suicide in high school students. *Journal of Adolescence*, *36*(2), 341–350. doi:10.1016/j.adolescence.2012.12.001 PMID:23332116

Bauman, S., Underwood, M. K., & Card, N. A. (2013). Definitions: Another perspective and a proposal for beginning with cyberaggression. In S. Bauman, D. Cross, & J. Walker (Eds.), *Principles of cyberbullying research: Definitions, measures, methodology* (pp. 26–40). New York, NY: Routledge.

Bayar, Y., & Ucanok, Z. (2012). School social climate and generalized peer perception in traditional and cyberbullying status. *Educational Sciences: Theory and Practice*, *12*, 2352–2358.

Beckman, L., Hagquist, C., & Hellstrom, L. (2012). Does the association with psychosomatic health problems differ between cyberbullying and traditional bullying? *Emotional & Behavioural Difficulties*, *17*(3-4), 421–434. doi:10.1080/13632752. 2012.704228

Bonanno, R. A., & Hymel, S. (2013). Cyber bullying and internalizing difficulties: Above and beyond the impact of traditional forms of bullying. *Journal of Youth and Adolescence*, *42*(5), 685–697. doi:10.100710964-013-9937-1 PMID:23512485

Boulton, M., Lloyd, J., Down, J., & Marx, H. (2012). Predicting undergraduates' self-reported engagement in traditional and cyberbullying from attitudes. *Cyberpsychology, Behavior, and Social Networking*, *15*(3), 141–147. doi:10.1089/cyber.2011.0369 PMID:22304402

Brighi, A., Guarini, A., Melotti, G., Galli, S., & Genta, M. L. (2012). Predictors of victimisation across direct bullying, indirect bullying and cyberbullying. *Emotional & Behavioural Difficulties*, *17*(3-4), 375–388. doi:10.1080/13632752.2012.704684

Burton, K. A., Florell, D., & Wygant, D. B. (2013). The role of peer attachment and normative beliefs about aggression on traditional bullying and cyberbullying. *Psychology in the Schools*, *50*(2), 103–114. doi:10.1002/pits.21663

Cappadocia, M. C., Craig, W. M., & Pepler, D. (2013). Cyberbullying: Prevalence, stability and risk factors during adolescence. *Canadian Journal of School Psychology*, *28*(2), 171–192. doi:10.1177/0829573513491212

Cassidy, W., Brown, K., & Jackson, M. (2012a). "Making kind cool": Parents' suggestions for preventing cyber bullying and fostering cyber kindness. *Journal of Educational Computing Research*, *46*(4), 415–436. doi:10.2190/EC.46.4.f

Cassidy, W., Brown, K., & Jackson, M. (2012b). "Under the radar": Educators and cyberbullying in schools. *School Psychology International*, *33*(5), 520–532. doi:10.1177/0143034312445245

Corcoran, L., Connolly, I., & O'Moore, M. (2012). Cyberbullying in Irish schools: An investigation of personality and self-concept. *The Irish Journal of Psychology*, *33*(4), 153–165. doi:10.1080/03033910.2012.677995

Curelaru, M., Iacob, I., & Abalasei, B. (2009). *School bullying: Definition, characteristics, and intervention strategies*. Lumean Publishing House.

Dehue, F., Bolman, C., & Vollink, T. (2008). Cyberbullying: Youngsters' experiences and parental perception. *CyberPscyhology & Behavior*, *11*(2), 217–223. doi:10.1089/cpb.2007.0008 PMID:18422417

Dehue, F., Bolman, C., Vollink, T., & Pouwelse, M. (2012). Cyberbullying and traditional bullying in relation to adolescents' perceptions of parenting. *Journal of Cyber Therapy and Rehabilitation, 5*, 25–34.

deLara, E. W. (2012). Why adolescents don't disclose incidents of bullying and harassment. *Journal of School Violence, 11*(4), 288–305. doi:10.1080/15388220 .2012.705931

Diamanduros, T., & Downs, E. (2011). Creating a safe school environment: How to prevent cyberbullying at your school. *Library Media Connection, 30*(2), 36–38.

Eden, S., Heiman, T., & Olenik-Shemesh, D. (2013). Teachers' perceptions, beliefs and concerns about cyberbullying. *British Journal of Educational Technology, 44*(6), 1036–1052. doi:10.1111/j.1467-8535.2012.01363.x

Elledge, L. C., Williford, A., Boulton, A. J., DePaolis, K. J., Little, T. D., & Salmivalli, C. (2013). Individual and contextual predictors of cyberbullying: The influence of children's provictim attitudes and teachers' ability to intervene. *Journal of Youth and Adolescence, 42*(5), 698–710. doi:10.100710964-013-9920-x PMID:23371005

Erdur-Baker, O. (2010). Cyberbullying and its correlation to traditional bullying, gender and frequent and risky usage of internet-mediated communication tools. *New Media & Society, 12*(1), 109–125. doi:10.1177/1461444809341260

Fanti, K. A., Demetriou, A. G., & Hawa, V. V. (2012). A longitudinal study of cyberbullying: Examining risk and protective factors. *European Journal of Developmental Psychology, 8*(2), 168–181. doi:10.1080/17405629.2011.643169

Festl, R., Schwarkow, M., & Quandt, T. (2013). Peer influence, internet use and cyberbullying: A comparison of different context effects among German adolescents. *Journal of Children and Media, 7*(4), 446–462. doi:10.1080/17482798.2013.781514

Goebert, D., Else, I., Matsu, C., Chung-Do, J., & Chang, J. Y. (2011). The impact of cyberbullying on substance use and mental health in a multiethnic sample. *Maternal and Child Health Journal, 15*(8), 1282–1286. doi:10.100710995-010-0672-x PMID:20824318

Gradinger, P., Strohmeier, D., & Spiel, C. (2009). Traditional bullying and cyberbullying. *The Journal of Psychology, 217*, 205–213.

Grigg, D. W. (2012). Definitional constructs of cyberbullying and cyber aggression from a triangulatory overview: A preliminary study into elements. *Journal of Aggression, Conflict and Peace Research, 4*(4), 202–215. doi:10.1108/17596591211270699

Hinduja, S., & Patchin, J. W. (2007). Offline consequences of online victimization. *Journal of School Violence, 6*(3), 89–112. doi:10.1300/J202v06n03_06

Hinduja, S., & Patchin, J. W. (2012). Cyberbullying: Neither and epidemic nor a rarity. *European Journal of Developmental Psychology, 9*(5), 539–543. doi:10.10 80/17405629.2012.706448

Hinduja, S., & Patchin, J. W. (2013). Social influences on cyberbullying behaviors among middle and high school students. *Journal of Youth and Adolescence, 42*(5), 711–722. doi:10.100710964-012-9902-4 PMID:23296318

Huang, Y., & Chou, C. (2010). An analysis of multiple factors of cyberbullying among junior high school students in Taiwan. *Computers in Human Behavior, 26*(6), 1581–1590. doi:10.1016/j.chb.2010.06.005

Jang, H., Song, J., & Kim, R. (2014). Does the offline bully-victimization influence cyberbullying behavior among youths? Application of general strain theory. *Computers in Human Behavior, 31*, 85–93. doi:10.1016/j.chb.2013.10.007

Kochenderfer-Ladd, B., & Pelletier, M. (2008). Teachers' views and beliefs about bullying: Influences on classroom management strategies and students' coping with peer victimization. *Journal of School Psychology, 46*(4), 431–453. doi:10.1016/j.jsp.2007.07.005 PMID:19083367

Kowalski, R. M., & Limber, S. P. (2007). Electronic bullying among middle school students. *The Journal of Adolescent Health, 41*(6), 22–30. doi:10.1016/j.jadohealth.2007.08.017 PMID:18047942

Kwan, G. C. E., & Skoric, M. M. (2013). Facebook bullying: An extension of battles in school. *Computers in Human Behavior, 29*(1), 16–25. doi:10.1016/j.chb.2012.07.014

Laftman, S. B., Modin, B., & Ostberg, V. (2013). Cyberbullying and subjective health: A large-scale study of students in Stockholm, Sweden. *Children and Youth Services Review, 35*(1), 112–119. doi:10.1016/j.childyouth.2012.10.020

Lazuras, L., Barkoukis, V., Ourda, D., & Tsorbatzoudis, H. (2013). A process model of cyberbullying in adolescence. *Computers in Human Behavior, 29*(3), 881–887. doi:10.1016/j.chb.2012.12.015

Lenhart, A. (2015). *Teens, social media & technology overview 2015*. Retrieved from: http://www.pewinternet.org/2015/04/09/teens-social-media-technology-2015/

Li, Q. (2007). Bullying in the new playground: Research into cyberbullying and cybervictimization. *Australian Journal of Educational Technology, 23*, 435–454.

Li, Q. (2008). A cross-cultural comparison of adolescents' experience related to cyberbullying. *Educational Research, 50*(3), 223–234. doi:10.1080/00131880802309333

Machackova, H., Dedkova, L., & Mezulanikova, K. (2015). Brief report: The bystander effect in cyberbullying incidents. *Journal of Adolescence, 43*, 96–99. doi:10.1016/j.adolescence.2015.05.010 PMID:26070168

Machackova, H., Dedkova, L., Sevcikova, A., & Cerna, A. (2013). Bystanders' support of cyberbullied schoolmates. *Journal of Community & Applied Social Psychology, 23*(1), 25–36. doi:10.1002/casp.2135

Mason, K. (2008). Cyberbullying: A preliminary assessment for school personnel. *Psychology in the Schools, 45*(4), 323–348. doi:10.1002/pits.20301

McQuade, C. S., Colt, P. J., & Meyer, B. N. (2009). *Cyber bullying: Protecting kids and adults from online bullies*. Westport, CT: Praeger.

Mitchell, K. J., Ybarra, M., & Finkelhor, D. (2007). The relative importance of online victimization in understanding depression, delinquency, and substance use. *Child Maltreatment, 12*(4), 314–324. doi:10.1177/1077559507305996 PMID:17954938

Patchin, J. W., & Hinduja, S. (2006). Bullies move beyond the schoolyard: A preliminary look at cyberbullying. *Youth Violence and Juvenile Justice, 4*(2), 148–169. doi:10.1177/1541204006286288

Perren, S., Dooley, J., Shaw, T., & Cross, D. (2010). Bullying in school and cyberspace: Associations with depressive symptoms in Swiss and Australian adolescents. *Child and Adolescent Psychiatry and Mental Health, 4*(1), 1–10. doi:10.1186/1753-2000-4-28 PMID:21092266

Pornari, C. D., & Wood, J. (2010). Peer and cyber aggression in secondary school students: The role of moral disengagement, hostile attribution bias, and outcome expectancies. *Aggressive Behavior, 36*(2), 81–94. doi:10.1002/ab.20336 PMID:20035548

Rideout, V. J., Roberts, D. F., & Foehr, U. G. (2005). *Generation M: Media in the lives of 8-18-year-olds: Executive summary*. Menlo Park, CA: Henry J. Kaiser Family Foundation.

Rosen, L. D. (2007). *Me, Myspace, and I: Parenting the Net Generation*. New York: Palgrave Macmillan.

Sahin, M. (2010). Teachers' perceptions of bullying in high schools: A Turkish study. *Social Behavior and Personality, 38*(1), 127–142. doi:10.2224bp.2010.38.1.127

Sevcikova, A., Machackova, H., Wright, M. F., Dedkova, L., & Cerna, A. (2015). Social support seeking in relation to parental attachment and peer relationships among victims of cyberbullying. *Australian Journal of Guidance & Counselling, 15*, 1–13. doi:10.1017/jgc.2015.1

Shapka, J. D., & Law, D. M. (2013). Does one size fit all? Ethnic differences in parenting behaviors and motivations for adolescent engagement in cyberbullying. *Journal of Youth and Adolescence, 42*(5), 723–738. doi:10.100710964-013-9928-2 PMID:23479327

Shariff, S., & Hoff, D. L. (2007). Cyber bullying: Clarifying legal boundaries for school supervision in cyberspace. *International Journal of Cyber Criminology, 1*, 76–118.

Sijtsema, J. J., Ashwin, R. J., Simona, C. S., & Gina, G. (2014). Friendship selection and influence in bullying and defending. *Effects of moral disengagement. Developmental Psychology, 50*(8), 2093–2104. doi:10.1037/a0037145 PMID:24911569

Sjurso, I. R., Fandream, H., & Roland, E. (2016). Emotional problems in traditional and cyber victimization. *Journal of School Violence, 15*(1), 114–131. doi:10.1080/15388220.2014.996718

Smith, P. K., Del Barrio, C., & Tokunaga, R. S. (2013). Definitions of bullying and cyberbullying: How useful are the terms? In S. Bauman, D. Cross, & J. Walker (Eds.), *Principles of cyberbullying research: Definitions, measures, methodology* (pp. 26–40). New York, NY: Routledge.

Smith, P. K., Mahdavi, J., Carvalho, M., Fisher, S., Russell, S., & Tippett, N. (2008). Cyberbullying: Its nature and impact in secondary school pupils. *Journal of Child Psychology and Psychiatry, and Allied Disciplines, 49*(4), 376–385. doi:10.1111/j.1469-7610.2007.01846.x PMID:18363945

Sourander, A., Brunstein, A., Ikonen, M., Lindroos, J., Luntamo, T., Koskelainen, M., ... Helenius, H. (2010). Psychosocial risk factors associated with cyberbullying among adolescents: A population-based study. *Archives of General Psychiatry, 67*(7), 720–728. doi:10.1001/archgenpsychiatry.2010.79 PMID:20603453

Stoll, L. C., & Block, R. Jr. (2015). Intersectionality and cyberbullying: A study of cybervictimization in a Midwestern high school. *Computers in Human Behavior, 52*, 387–391. doi:10.1016/j.chb.2015.06.010

Strohmeier, D., Aoyama, I., Gradinger, P., & Toda, Y. (2013). Cybervictimization and cyberaggression in Eastern and Western countries: Challenges of constructing a cross-cultural appropriate scale. In S. Bauman, D. Cross, & J. L. Walker (Eds.), *Principles of cyberbullying research: Definitions, measures, and methodology* (pp. 202–221). New York: Routledge.

Suler, J. (2004). The online disinhibition effect. *Cyberpsychology & Behavior, 7*(3), 321–326. doi:10.1089/1094931041291295 PMID:15257832

Tangen, D., & Campbell, M. (2010). Cyberbullying prevention: One primary school's approach. *Australian Journal of Guidance & Counselling, 20*(02), 225–234. doi:10.1375/ajgc.20.2.225

Toledano, S., Werch, B. L., & Wiens, B. A. (2015). Domain-specific self-concept in relation to traditional and cyber peer aggression. *Journal of School Violence, 14*(4), 405–423. doi:10.1080/15388220.2014.935386

Wade, A., & Beran, T. (2011). Cyberbullying: The new era of bullying. *Canadian Journal of School Psychology, 26*(1), 44–61. doi:10.1177/0829573510396318

Wong, D. S., Chan, H. C. O., & Cheng, C. H. (2014). Cyberbullying perpetration and victimization among adolescents in Hong Kong. *Children and Youth Services Review, 36*, 133–140. doi:10.1016/j.childyouth.2013.11.006

Wright, M. F. (2013). The relationship between young adults' beliefs about anonymity and subsequent cyber aggression. *Cyberpsychology, Behavior, and Social Networking, 16*(12), 858–862. doi:10.1089/cyber.2013.0009 PMID:23849002

Wright, M. F. (2014a). Cyber victimization and perceived stress: Linkages to late adolescents' cyber aggression and psychological functioning. *Youth & Society.*

Wright, M. F. (2014b). Predictors of anonymous cyber aggression: The role of adolescents' beliefs about anonymity, aggression, and the permanency of digital content. *Cyberpsychology, Behavior, and Social Networking, 17*(7), 431–438. doi:10.1089/cyber.2013.0457 PMID:24724731

Wright, M. F. (2014c). Longitudinal investigation of the associations between adolescents' popularity and cyber social behaviors. *Journal of School Violence, 13*(3), 291–314. doi:10.1080/15388220.2013.849201

Wright, M. F. (2015). Cyber victimization and adjustment difficulties: The mediation of Chinese and American adolescents' digital technology usage. *Cyberpsychology (Brno), 1*(1), 1. Retrieved from http://cyberpsychology.eu/view.php?cisloclanku=2015051102&article=1

Wright, M. F. (in press). Adolescents' cyber aggression perpetration and cyber victimization: The longitudinal associations with school functioning. *Social Psychology of Education*.

Wright, M. F., Kamble, S., Lei, K., Li, Z., Aoyama, I., & Shruti, S. (2015). Peer attachment and cyberbullying involvement among Chinese, Indian, and Japanese adolescents. *Societies (Basel, Switzerland)*, *5*(2), 339–353. doi:10.3390oc5020339

Wright, M. F., & Li, Y. (2012). Kicking the digital dog: A longitudinal investigation of young adults' victimization and cyber-displaced aggression. *Cyberpsychology, Behavior, and Social Networking*, *15*(9), 448–454. doi:10.1089/cyber.2012.0061 PMID:22974350

Wright, M. F., & Li, Y. (2013a). Normative beliefs about aggression and cyber aggression among young adults: A longitudinal investigation. *Aggressive Behavior*, *39*(3), 161–170. doi:10.1002/ab.21470 PMID:23440595

Wright, M. F., & Li, Y. (2013b). The association between cyber victimization and subsequent cyber aggression: The moderating effect of peer rejection. *Journal of Youth and Adolescence*, *42*(5), 662–674. doi:10.100710964-012-9903-3 PMID:23299177

Ybarra, M. L., Diener-West, M., & Leaf, P. (2007). Examining the overlap in internet harassment and school bullying: Implications for school intervention. *The Journal of Adolescent Health*, *1*(6), 42–50. doi:10.1016/j.jadohealth.2007.09.004 PMID:18047944

Ybarra, M. L., & Mitchell, K. J. (2004). Online aggressor/targets, aggressors, and targets: A comparison of associated youth characteristics. *Journal of Child Psychology and Psychiatry, and Allied Disciplines*, *45*(7), 1308–1316. doi:10.1111/j.1469-7610.2004.00328.x PMID:15335350

Yousef, W. S. M., & Bellamy, A. (2015). The impact of cyberbullying on the self-esteem and academic functioning of Arab American middle and high school students. *Electronic Journal of Research in Educational Psychology*, *23*(3), 463–482.

Zhou, Z., Tang, H., Tian, Y., Wei, H., Zhang, F., & Morrison, C. M. (2013). Cyberbullying and its risk factors among Chinese high school students. *School Psychology International*, *34*(6), 630–647. doi:10.1177/0143034313479692

ADDITIONAL READING

Bauman, S. (2011). *Cyberbullying: What counselors need to know*. Alexandria, VA: American Counseling Association.

Bauman, S., Cross, D., & Walker, J. (2013). *Principles of cyberbullying research: Definitions, measures, and methodology*. New York, NY: Routledge.

Hinduja, S., & Patchin, J. W. (2015). *Bullying beyond the schoolyard: Preventing and responding to cyberbullying*. Thousand Oaks, CA: Sage Publications.

Li, Q., Cross, D., & Smith, P. K. (2012). *Cyberbullying in the global playground*. Malden, MA: Blackwell Publishing. doi:10.1002/9781119954484

Menesini, E., & Spiel, C. (2012). *Cyberbullying: Development, consequences, risk and protective factors*. New York, NY: Psychology Press.

Tokunaga, R. S. (2010). Following you home from school: A critical review and synthesis of research on cyberbullying victimization. *Computers in Human Behavior*, *26*(3), 277–287. doi:10.1016/j.chb.2009.11.014

KEY TERMS AND DEFINITIONS

Anonymity: The quality of being unknown or unacknowledged.

Anxiety: A mental health disorder which includes symptoms of worry, anxiety, and/or fear that are intense enough to disrupt one's daily activities.

Collectivism: A cultural value that stressed the importance of the group over individual goals and cohesion within social groups.

Cyberbullying: Children's and adolescents' usage of electronic technologies to hostilely and intentionally harass, embarrass, and intimidate others.

Empathy: The ability to understand or feel what another person is experiencing or feeling.

Externalizing Difficulties: Includes children's and adolescents' failure to control their behaviors.

Individualism: The belief that each person is more important than the needs of the whole group or society.

Loneliness: An unpleasant emotional response to isolation or lack of companionship.

Normative Belief: Beliefs about the acceptability and tolerability of a behavior.

Parental Mediation and Monitoring: The strategies that parents use to manage the relationship between their children and media.

Parenting Style: The standard strategies that parents use in their child rearing.

Peer Attachment: The internalization of the knowledge that their peers will be available and responsive.

Peer Contagion: The transmission or transfer of deviant behavior from one adolescent to another.

Provictim Attitudes: The belief that bullying is unacceptable and that defending victims is valuable.

Social Exclusion: The process involving individuals or groups of people block or deny someone from the group.

Traditional Face-to-Face Bullying: The use of strength or influence to intimidate or physically harm someone.

Chapter 11

The Cyber Acumen:
An Integrative Framework to Understand Average Users' Decision-Making Processes in Cybersecurity

Xiang Michelle Liu
Marymount University, USA

ABSTRACT

The major purpose of this chapter is to understand average user's decision-making process in cybersecurity by reviewing and integrating several major theoretical frameworks discussed and applied in decision making processes in cybersecurity. The average users are the ones who do not realize or understand when or how to perform security-critical decisions, the ones who are unmotivated to comply with company and school cybersecurity policies and procedures due to inconvenience, and the ones who do not have sufficient knowledge in cybersecurity to make sound security decisions. It is important to discuss and understand the role of such users and their behaviors based on systematic analysis so that we can identify potential factors causing "poor" security decisions and find ways to reduce the likelihood of being victims of cyber-attacks. The ultimate goal is to provide insights and make recommendations on how to foster individual's cyber acumen and cultivate a more effective decision-making process.

DOI: 10.4018/978-1-5225-7128-5.ch011

INTRODUCTION

Only amateurs attack machines; professionals target people. (Schneier, 2015)

Background

Juniper Research predicted that rapid digitization of consumers' lives as well as organizational and government records will increase the cost of cybercrimes to $2.1 trillion globally by 2019, quadrupling the estimated cost of cybercrimes in 2015 (Juniper Research, 2015). Another report released by the Centre for Strategic and International Studies (CSIS) disclosed that, in the U.S. alone, cybercrime caused the loss of at least one half million jobs annually as companies struggle with the loss of intellectual property and suffer reputational harm (Center for Strategic and International Studies, 2013). According to the FBI's Internet Crime Complaint Center (IC3), a federal agency providing the public with a reporting system and monitoring trending scams, significant amount of complaints were filed by the public in 2016 centered around business email compromise (BEC), ransomware, tech support fraud, and extortion (Internet Crime Complaint Center, 2017). The report disclosed that among various types of cybercrimes, the top three crime types by reported loss were BEC, romance and confidence fraud, and non-payment and non-delivery scams; while the top three crime types reported by victims were non-payment and non-delivery, personal data breach, and payment scams in 2016. IC3 received a total of 298,728 complaints with reported losses in excess in $1.3 billion in 2016 alone.

Hundreds of thousands of people fall victim to cyber attacks and cybercrimes each year, ranging from a local Virginia supermarket phished by an individual posing as the company founder (see Bryan, 2017) to the Anthem data breach started by a phishing campaign and ending with 78.8 million consumers' personal data potentially exposed (see Snell, 2017). Cybercriminals have been persistently engaged in exploiting vulnerabilities known and/or unknown to the public, from various devices, networks and systems. More often, they succeed by taking advantage of inherent natures or weakness of human beings such as curiosity, credulousness, wanting to be helpful, greed, and trading security measures for convenience. For instances, as early as 2000, ILOVEYOU letter virus quickly swept through banks, securities firms, and tech companies worldwide by luring users to open an email with the subject line ILOVEYOU and download attached files with virus embedded (see Strickland, 2018). As almost two decades passed since ILOVEYOU spreading, it is becoming more and more conspicuous that humans are a major cause of cybersecurity failures. One of the latest astonishing data breach case in Equifax, which was caused by the company's IT and cybersecurity team's decision not to patch a known vulnerability in the Apache Struts web application software on time (Newman, 2017, Septemeber 14), further corroborates that humans are "the weakest link in the chain" (Schneier, 2015) in the context of cyberspace.

The Research Question and Objectives

Social engineering attacks facilitated by the Internet and Social Media Networks websites combined with lack of awareness and compliance with organizational security policies are frequently cited as security concerns. The cases enumerated in the Background section pose a haunting puzzle to both practitioners and scholars in cybersecurity for a long time: why humans tend to make poor security decisions in the domain of cybersecurity such as clicking a forgery link in a phishing email (e.g., Grazioli, 2004), reusing passwords across different websites (e.g., Das et al., 2014), or choosing not to patch systems and applications even when the patches and updates are available (e.g., Mathur & Chetty, 2017)? Have the perceived anonymity and disinhibition created by the virtual environment and cyberspace (Suler, 2004) been hotbeds for such poor decisions? Is the "wicked" nature of the cyberspace which the average users interact with every day the root cause of the problem and if so, what approach(es) and mitigations can be done to mediate the decision process for a more desirable result?

The "wicked problem" refers to class of social system problems which are "ill-formulated, where the information is confusing, where there are many clients and decision makers with conflicting values, and where the ramification is in the whole system are thoroughly confusing" (Churchman, 1967, p.141). When examining the cyberspace as a system, the author argues that problems generated by such chaotic, complex system are inherently "wicked" due to the pervasive nature of cyberspace, which is characterized by numerous interactive transactions occurring near the speed of light (Churchman, 1967; Rittel & Webber, 1973). Vigilance, basic knowledge and awareness of security and privacy in the cyberspace, detection, and acumen are the cornerstones of circumventing and thwarting the cyber "wicked problems". Therefore, the major purpose of this article is to understand average user's decision making process in cybersecurity by reviewing and integrating several major theoretical frameworks discussed and applied in decision making processes in cybersecurity. This article aims to understand what factors influence user's behavior online and identify the key factors or processes impact their decision making and ensued behavior. The ultimate goal is to provide insights and make recommendations on how to foster individual's cyber acumen and cultivate a more effective decision-making process.

Human Factors in Cybersecurity

There have been various studies conducted to analyze possible roles for human factors in the cybersecurity realm (e.g., Boyce et al., 2011; Dutt, Ahn & Gonzalez, 2013; Proctor & Chen, 2015). However, the "numerous interdependencies, and complexities that arise based on the interaction of humans and technology (Mancuso, 2014, p.415)" demands greater involvement of experts from different disciplines including human factors specialists, psychologists and criminologists in cybersecurity. The complexity of human interactions with technology in the cyberspace as a "wicked problem" is consistent with the definition of human factors by Human Factors and Ergonomics Society (HFES), which is "the scientific discipline concerned with the understanding of interactions among humans and other elements of a system" (HFES, 2018). As illustrated in the next section of this chapter, the author takes an interdisciplinary approach to integrate theories from different disciplines for analyses of cybersecurity issues involving humans.

Even though Artificial Intelligence (AI) and machine learning have been employed in different industry sectors as frontier cybersecurity defense mechanisms (Dietterich & Horvitz, 2015; Mittu & Lawless, 2015), they are still in the nascent stage and far from being implemented to their full potentials. For some tasks and cases, we do not seem to be able to avoid relying on humans to make wise judgement, decisions, and perform security-critical functions (Yampolskiy, 2017). When examining the cyberspace including the Internet, corporation networks, home LANS (local area networks), IoT (Internet of Things) devices, and more, humans in the loop must play various roles and make decisions (sometimes implicit) in performing security-related functions. The average users (i.e., non-malicious humans) are the ones who do not realize or understand when or how to perform security-critical decisions, the ones who are unmotivated to comply with organization cybersecurity policies and procedures due to inconvenience or no foreseen consequences, and the ones who do not have sufficient knowledge in cybersecurity to make sound security decisions. It is important to discuss and understand the role of such users and their behaviors based on systematic analysis so that we can identify potential factors causing "poor" security decisions and find ways to reduce the likelihood of their and their organizations being victims of cyber attacks.

REVIEW OF MAJOR AREAS

An Overview of Decision-Making Processes in Cybersecurity

Due to the fact that humans are often cited as "the weakest link of the chain", the study on decision-making processes and actions in cybersecurity is rooted in principles of communication-human information-processing (Proctor & Chen, 2015). More specifically, one of the major pillars of this study is to apply scientific knowledge of human cognition to understanding perceptions of cybersecurity risks, cybersecurity-related decisions, and the actual actions that humans make resulting in safeguard or imperil of system security (Networking and Information Technology Research and Development Program, 2014).

One of the widely recognized model to depict and outline the decision-making process in security-related functions is the human-in-the-loop security framework (HITL) proposed by Lorrie Cranor (2008). The HITL is designed to understand the behavior of non-malicious users instead of cybercriminals with malicious intentions, which fits the focus of this chapter well. The HITL is a process-based model to analyze and provide insights to system developers and designers regarding how to incorporate users' traits, attitude, knowledge and their possible interactions with the system (i.e., human factors) into design to avoid security problems that might arise from the interaction between humans and software systems (Bravo-Lillo et al., 2011). This framework is based on a more general model of human cognition, the communication-human information processing (C-HIP) from the warnings science literature (Wogalter, 2006). As Cranor (2008) pointed out, the HITL framework is a conceptual framework that can be used to capture a series of sequential stages with feedback loops that users may experience. Further, it facilitates systematic analysis of the human role in secure system by modeling factors and information processing stages that will impact security-related behaviors. The HITL framework is as shown in Figure 1 and Table 1 summarizes each component of the framework with respective factors to consider.

Review of Three Major Decision-Making Theories and Frameworks

The HITL framework is used as the baseline model guiding the review process. The author has conducted an extensive literature search and found that three theories from different disciplines provide further insights and elaborations on some of the components in the HITL framework. The three conceptual theories will be ed as follows.

Figure 1. The HITL framework (adapted from Bravo-Lillo et al., 2011)

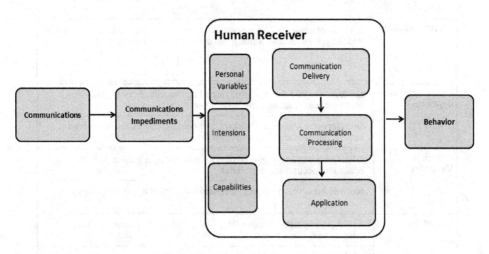

The Theory of Planned Behavior (TPB)

The component of "Intentions" in the HITL framework has its theoretical anchor in the well-known theory of TPB. Firstly, we need to understand what factors are likely to drive a user's violation of security policy or make poor security decision. They occur in response to the environment and past behavior and are reinforced by the lack of consequences of the behavior such as a low number of prosecutions. Everyone responds to the environment from their own perspective. It is necessary to identify and investigate the precipitating factors of one's intention to comply with or violate the security policy or ignoring warning signs or notices. The TPB provides solid theoretical foundation for such context (Bulgurcu,Cavusoglu & Benbasat, 2010; Guo et al., 2011).

The TPB has been one of the most widely cited and applied theories in explaining and predicting a wide range of behaviors (Sheppard,Hartwick & Warshaw, 1988). The theory posits that individuals' behavior is guided by three main constructs: attitude toward the behavior, subjective norm, and perceived behavioral control (Ajzen & Madden, 1986). In combination, the above three constructs lead to the formation of a behavioral intention, which is considered to be the immediate antecedent of behavior (Ajzen & Icek, 1991). Attitude toward behavior reflects one's favorable or unfavorable feelings of performing a behavior. In this study, it refers to the degree to which the average users value the security behavior. Subjective norm reflects one's perception of social pressure to engage or not to engage in a particular behavior. It can be defined as one's "perceived social pressure about compliance with the requirements of the information security policy caused by behavioral

Table 1. Components of the HITL security framework

Communication	Severity of hazard, frequency with which hazard is encountered, extent to which appropriate user action is necessary to avoid hazard
Communication impediments	**Environmental Stimuli**: Other related and unrelated communications, user's primary task, ambient light, noise
	Interference: Malicious attackers, technology failures, environmental stimuli that obscure the communication
Personal Variables	**Demographics and personal characteristics:** Age, gender, culture, education, occupation, disabilities
	Knowledge and experience: Education, occupation, prior experience
Intentions	**Attitudes and beliefs:** Reliability, conflicting goals, distraction from primary task, risk perception, self-efficacy, response efficacy
	Motivation: Conflicting goals, distraction from primary task, convenience, risk erception, consequences, incentives/disincentives
Capabilities	Knowledge, cognitive or physical skills, memorability, required software or devices
Communication delivery	**Attention switch:** Environmental stimuli, interference, format, font size, length, delivery channel, habituation
	Attention maintenance: Environmental stimuli, format, font size, length, delivery channel, habituation
Communication processing	**Comprehension:** Symbols, vocabulary and sentence structure, conceptual complexity, personal variables
	Knowledge acquisition: Exposure or training time, involvement during training, personal characteristics
Application	**Knowledge retention**: Frequency, familiarity, long term memory, involvement during training, personal characteristics
	Knowledge transfer: Involvement during training, similarity of training, personal characteristics
Behavior	Type of behavior, ability of people to act randomly in this context, usefulness of prediction to attacker

(Adapted from Cranor, 2008)

expectations of such important referents as executives, colleagues, and managers (Bulgurcu, Cavusoglu & Benbasat, 2010, p.529). Perceived behavioral control reflects one's perceptions of the ability to perform a given behavior. Ajzen (2002) further suggested that the construct of perceived behavior control comprises two distinct dimensions: perceived self-efficacy and perceived controllability. Perceived self-efficacy is defined as individual judgments of a person's capabilities to perform a behavior. Controllability is defined as individual beliefs about the extent to which performing the behavior is up to the actor. Self-efficacy has been regarded as one of the major cognitive factors guiding behavior (Bandura, 1997). A higher degree of self-efficacy to comply with security policies and guidelines, in our case, reflects that a user's evaluation of her own personal skills and competency about fulfilling the security-related functions are higher. This suggests that an frequent, effective security education, training, and awareness program are necessary mechanism to control system misuse (D'Arcy, Hovav & Galletta, 2009).

The Theory of Deception Detection

Although the TPB has been used to explain human behavior in different contexts, it does not fully capture the information processing and evaluation aspects of the decision process, especially for the emerging phenomenon of user falling victims for various online social engineering attacks including phishing and Internet scams. In the HITL framework, information processing of communications consists of three steps: communication delivery, communication processing, and application. It is noted that communications in the HITL were discussed in the context of security warnings, notices, status indicators, policies and trainings, thus, is more suitable for scenarios in an organizational setting.

The author selects an information-processing model of deception detection for this review as it has been used in different studies (Grazioli, 2004; Johnson et al., 2001; Proctor & Chen, 2015) to understand the reasons underlying average users' success and failure at detecting different forms intentional deception on the Internet, therefore, aligns with the unit of analysis of this chapter–individual level decision making. In summary, the Theory of Deception states that individuals detect deception by capturing and interpreting anomalies in their environment. This model depicts four processing stages that affect whether a receiver will detect the deception: activation, hypothesis generation, hypothesis evaluation, and global assessment, which shown as in Figure 2.

According to Grazioli (2004) and Proctor and Chen (2015), in the activation stage, the user notices cues that signal anomalies from expectations or past experiences, suggesting "something may be wrong." At the stage of hypothesis generation, the user generates hypotheses to explain the anomalies. The next stage is hypothesis evaluation, in which the user decides whether to accept the deception hypothesis based on his or her evaluations of hypotheses. In the global assessment stage, the user assigns different weights to the individual hypotheses in order to obtain an

Figure 2. Model of deception detection (adapted from (Proctor & Chen, 2015))

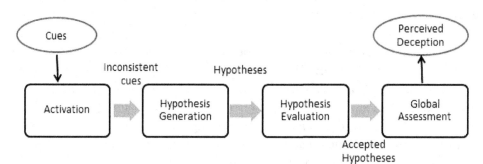

overall assessment of deception. This model provides insights on the major factor differentiating users who were able to detect a deceptive website or a phishing email, which is their ability to evaluate cues (hypothesis evaluation) based on their domain-specific knowledge (Grazioli, 2004).

One major limitation of this model lies in that the four information processing stages only focus on explicit processes of decision making, not the implicit process. However, both explicit and implicit process are indispensable for a person's final decision for the action. This was depicted by Kahneman's (2011) that explicit processes allocate "attention to the effortful mental activities that demand it," implicit processes operate "automatically and quickly, with little or no effort" (p. 20–21). And the average users tend to minimize effort and rely on experiences and heuristics to simplify decisions (Kahneman, 2011; Wickens, 2014). Therefore, the model may play less important role in predicting implicit aspect of individual decision making process and actual behaviors.

"OODA" Loop Theory

OODA (Observe → Orient → Decide → Act) loop theory has been mainly discussed and applied in the military command and control or cyber warfare fields. However, its main components and constructs are generic enough to be externalized in different domains and settings for additional insights on individual's decision making process in the cyberspace. This four-stage model depicts continuous decision cycle in which the decision-maker interacts with the environment over short time scale (Boyd, 1986; Brehmer, 2005). The OODA model emphasizes the important role of environment in the decision-making process and interactions as well as feedback loops between the decision-maker, the environment, and different stages. OODA loop is shown as in Figure 3.

Figure 3. Boyd's (1986) original OODA loop model

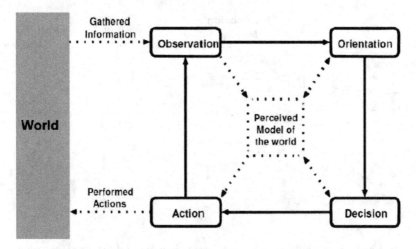

It is noted that adding cognitive components enhances the capability of the explanation power of the model for the decisional activities of individuals when processing "wicked problems" (Builder,Bankes & Nordin, 1999). An individual's mental model of the world is influenced by previous experience, cultural traditions, genetic heritage, as well as cognitive analysis and synthesis (Brumley,Kopp & Korb, 2006). The orientation stage also accounts the cultural and social aspects of decision-making as human factors.

This model is especially relevant when examining the decision making processes average users make in the cyberspace, both explicitly and implicitly. The environment in the OODA loop model is inherently complex, constantly changing, and requires quick reactions and decisions. The OODA loop can provide insights and guidelines for users to make effective decisions in the complex, dynamic, ubiquitous, and uncertain environment that characterizes the cyberspace domain (Brehmer, 2005; Brumley,Kopp & Korb, 2006).

Integrative Theoretical Framework

Based on the review, discussions, and evaluation of the three major models on decision making from different domains, the author proposes an integrative framework on decision making in the cyberspace: Cyber Acumen Model. The proposed framework overarches the average users' decision making processes in the cyberspace, in which the core elements are Pre-decision making (attitude, subject norm, knowledge, etc.), rationalization/judgment (identifying alternatives, weighing the evidence, etc.) leading to the security decision, and post-decision making (actual behavior). The model is illustrated in Figure 4.

Figure 4. Cyber Acumen Model (CAM)

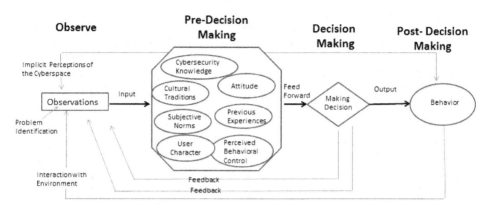

It is worthy to note that user characteristics is a critical factor affecting security attitudes and behaviors, which have not been covered in the three theoretical frameworks reviewed. Due to the fact that various experimental studies (Egelman & Peer, 2015; Herrero et al., 2017; Mathur & Chetty, 2017; Sheng et al., 2010; Wash & Rader, 2015; Whitty et al., 2015) corroborated the importance of user characteristics and personal traits in the decision-making process, the CAM includes this factor in as one of the components in the Orient stage. For example, user characteristics can influence computer security attitudes and behaviors such as sensation seeking (Herrero et al., 2017) and self-monitoring and perseverance (Whitty et al., 2015) influence users' decision to or not to download updates for Android (Mathur & Chetty, 2017).

DISCUSSION

This chapter starts with a fundamental question: what difference does cyberspace/virtual world make for an individual's decision-making process and online behavior? The cyberspace enables and facilitate average user to multi-task and conduct numerous interactive transactions in short time scale. It also fosters false perceptions of anonymity, disinhibition, and no immediate consequences when users violate security policy, for instance. The author argues that all of these inherent natures of the cyberspace cause "wicked" problems (Churchman, 1967), which add complexity and chaos to the decision making process that needs further reflection and discussion from their reality/physical world counterparts. Decision making and choice are central to various areas in the domain of cybersecurity such as strong/weak passwords to use (Das et al., 2014), the privacy offered by websites (Vu et al., 2010), phishing detection (Grazioli, 2004) and mobile app selection (Kelley,Cranor & Sadeh, 2013). There is a need for research to integrate these areas of cybersecurity and the proposed integrative framework responds to this call as a start point.

Researchers have found that individuals are generally aware of what constitutes good cybersecurity practices and what is regarded inapproprate behavior (Tam,Glassman & Vandenwauver, 2010). However, users are motivated to engage in these bad security practices because they do not see any immediate negative consequences and/or because of the convenience–security tradeoff. Futher, previous studies pointed out that psychology plays an important role in providing answers to why individuals engage in risky cybersecurity practice (e.g., Wiederhold, 2014). A number of variables including age, perseverance, and self-monitoring were found to be significant when predicting the risky practice of sharing passwords.

The CAM framework that the author proposes in this chapter integrates user characteristics along with psychology component (intention, attitudes, and subject norms), domain knowledge and past experiences as the factors impacting decisions. The relationships between the various components are intentionally vague in that the interactions among those components are complex and needs further analysis.

FUTURE RESEARCH DIRECTIONS

There are several future research directions summarized as follows. First, the author will refine the CAM framework and extend the current review to a theoretical paper with testable hypotheses. Second, quantitative studies will be conducted such as interviews and case studies, focusing on teenager users. Third, the long-term plan is to design and implement an empirical study to validate the CAM. Future work is also needed to provide more concrete guidance on how to operationalize the human threat identification and mitigation process. Future work can also be conducted in an interdisciplinary setting with security engineers and human factor specialists collaborating on developing more specific guidelines and design patterns for usable security to mitigate human threats and better support average users.

REFERENCES

Ajzen, I. (1991). The Theory of Planned Behavior. *Organizational Behavior and Human Decision Processes*, *50*(2), 179–211. doi:10.1016/0749-5978(91)90020-T

Ajzen, I. (2002). Perceived Behavioral Control, Self-Efficacy, Locus of Control, and the Theory of Planned Behavior. *Journal of Applied Social Psychology*, *32*(4), 665–683. doi:10.1111/j.1559-1816.2002.tb00236.x

Ajzen, I., & Madden, T. J. (1986). Prediction of goal-directed behavior: Attitudes, intention and perceived behavioral control. *Journal of Experimental Social Psychology, 22*(5), 453–474. doi:10.1016/0022-1031(86)90045-4

Bandura, A. (1997). *Self-efficacy: the Exercise of Control.* New York: Freeman.

Boyce, M. W., Duma, K. M., Hettinger, L. J., Malone, T. B., Wilson, D. P., & Lockett-Reynolds, J. (2011). *Human performance in cybersecurity: A research agenda.* Paper presented at the the Human Factors and Ergonomics Society Annual Meeting, Santa Monica, CA. 10.1177/1071181311551233

Boyd, J. R. (1986). *Patterns of conflict.* Retrieved from http://www.dnipogo.org/boyd/patterns_ppt.pdf

Bravo-Lillo, C., Cranor, L. F., Downs, J. S., & Komanduri, S. (2011). Bridging the Gap in Computer Security Warnings: A Mental Model Approach. *IEEE Security and Privacy, 9*(2), 18–26. doi:10.1109/MSP.2010.198

Brehmer, B. (2005). *The dynamic OODA loop: Amalgamating Boyd's OODA loop and the cybernetic approach to command and control.* Paper presented at the the 10th International Command and Control Research and Technology Symposium: The Future of C2, McLean, VA.

Brumley, L., Kopp, C., & Korb, K. (2006). *The Orientation Step of the OODA Loop and Information Warfare.* Paper presented at the 7th Australian Information Warfare & Security Conference 2006 Proceedings, Clayton School of Information Technology, Monash University, Perth, Australia.

Bryan, A. (2017). *Ellwood THompasson's falls for phishing scam; data compromised.* Retrieved from http://wtvr.com/2017/02/23/ellwood-thompsons-falls-for-phishing-scam-1/

Builder, C. H., Bankes, S. C., & Nordin, R. (1999). *Command concepts: A Theory Derived from the Practice of Command and Control.* Santa Monica, CA: RAND Corporation.

Bulgurcu, B., Cavusoglu, H., & Benbasat, I. (2010). Information Security Policy Compliance: An Empirical Study of Rationality-Based Beliefs and Information Security Awareness. *Management Information Systems Quarterly, 34*(3), 523–A527. doi:10.2307/25750690

Center for Strategic and International Studies. (2013). *The Economic Impact of Cybercrime and Cyber Espionage.* Retrieved from https://www.mcafee.com/us/resources/reports/rp-economic-impact-cybercrime.pdf

Churchman, C. W. (1967). Wicked problems. *Management Science, 14*(4), 141–142.

Cranor, L. F. (2008). A framework for reasoning about the human in the loop. *Proceedings of the 1st Conference on Usability, Psychology, and Security.*

D'Arcy, J., Hovav, A., & Galletta, D. (2009). User Awareness of Security Countermeasures and Its Impact on Information Systems Misuse: A Deterrence Approach. *Information Systems Research, 20*(1), 79–98. doi:10.1287/isre.1070.0160

Das, A., Bonneau, J., Caesar, M., Borisov, N., & Wang, X. (2014). The Tangled Web of Password Reuse. *Symposium on Network and Distributed System Security (NDSS).* Retrieved from https://www.cs.cmu.edu/~anupamd/paper/NDSS2014.pdf

Dietterich, T. G., & Horvitz, E. J. (2015). Rise of concerns about AI: Reflections and directions. *Communications of the ACM, 58*(10), 38–40. doi:10.1145/2770869

Dutt, V., Ahn, Y.-S., & Gonzalez, C. (2013). Cyber Situation Awareness: Modeling Detection of Cyber Attacks with Instance-based Learning Theory. *Human Factors, 55*(3), 605–618. doi:10.1177/0018720812464045 PMID:23829034

Egelman, S., & Peer, E. (2015). The Myth of the Average User: Improving Privacy and Security Systems through Individualization. *Proceedings of the 2015 New Security Paradigms Workshop.* 10.1145/2841113.2841115

Grazioli, S. (2004). Where Did They Go Wrong? An Analysis of the Failure of Knowledgeable Internet Consumers to Detect Deception Over the Internet. *Group Decision and Negotiation, 13*(2), 149–172. doi:10.1023/B:GRUP.0000021839.04093.5d

Guo, K. H., Yuan, Y., Archer, N. P., & Connelly, C. E. (2011). Understanding Nonmalicious Security Violations in the Workplace: A Composite Behavior Model. *Journal of Management Information Systems, 28*(2), 203–236. doi:10.2753/MIS0742-1222280208

Herrero, J., Urueña, A., Torres, A., & Hidalgo, A. (2017). My computer is infected: The role of users' sensation seeking and domain-specific risk perceptions and risk attitudes on computer harm. *Journal of Risk Research, 20*(11), 1466–1479. doi:10.1080/13669877.2016.1153504

Human Factors and Ergonomics Society (HFES). (2018). *What is Human Factors/Ergonomics?* Retrieved from https://www.hfes.org/Security/ContentPages/?Id=40

Internet Crime Complaint Center. (2017). *2016 Internet Crime Report.* Retrieved from https://pdf.ic3.gov/2016_IC3Report.pdf

Johnson, P. E., Grazioli, S., Jamal, K., & Berryman, G. (2001). Detecting deception: Adversarial problem solving in a low base rate world. *Cognitive Science, 25*(3), 355–392. doi:10.120715516709cog2503_2

Juniper Research. (2015). *Cybercrime will Cost Businesses Over $2 Trillion by 2019.* Retrieved from https://www.juniperresearch.com/press/press-releases/cybercrime-cost-businesses-over-2trillion

Kahneman, D. (2011). *Thinking, fast and slow.* New York, NY: Farrar, Straus and Giroux.

Kelley, P. G., Cranor, L. F., & Sadeh, N. (2013). Privacy as Part of the App Decision-making Process. *Proceedings of the 2013 ACM Annual Conference on Human Factors in Computing Systems.* 10.1145/2470654.2466466

Mancuso, V. F. (2014). *Human factors in cyber warfare II: Emerging perspectives.* Paper presented at the Human Factors and Ergonomics Society 58th Annual Meeting, Santa Monica, CA. 10.1177/1541931214581085

Mathur, A., & Chetty, M. (2017). *Impact of User Characteristics on Attitudes Towards Automatic Mobile Application Updates.* Paper presented at the Thirteenth Symposium on Usable Privacy and Security (SOUPS 2017), Santa Clara, CA.

Mittu, R., & Lawless, W. I. (2015). *Human factors in cybersecurity and the role for AI.* Paper presented at the Foundations of Autonomy and Its (Cyber) Threats: From Individual to Interdependence, AAAI Spring Symposium Series.

Networking and Information Technology Research and Development Program. (2014). *Federal cybersecurity game—change R&D: Science of security.* Retrieved from https://www.nitrd.gov/cybersecurity/

Newman, L. H. (2017, September 14). Equifax Officially Has No Excuse. *Wired.* Retrieved from https://www.wired.com/story/equifax-breach-no-excuse/

Proctor, R. W., & Chen, J. (2015). The Role of Human Factors/Ergonomics in the Science of Security: Decision Making and Action Selection in Cyberspace. *Human Factors, 57*(5), 721–727. doi:10.1177/0018720815585906 PMID:25994927

Rittel, H. W. J., & Webber, M. M. (1973). Dilemmas in a General Theory of Planning. *Policy Sciences, 4*(2), 155–169. doi:10.1007/BF01405730

Schneier, B. (2015). *Secrets and Lies: Digital Security in a Networked World* (1st ed.). John Wiley and Sons. doi:10.1002/9781119183631

Sheng, S., Holbrook, M., Kumaraguru, P., Cranor, L. F., & Downs, J. (2010). Who falls for phish?: a demographic analysis of phishing susceptibility and effectiveness of interventions. *Proceedings of the SIGCHI Conference on Human Factors in Computing Systems*, 373-382. 10.1145/1753326.1753383

Sheppard, B. H., Hartwick, J., & Warshaw, P. (1988). The theory of reasoned action: A meta-analysis of past research with recommendations for modifications and future research. *The Journal of Consumer Research*, *15*(3), 325–343. doi:10.1086/209170

Snell, E. (2017). *Anthem Data Breach Reportedly Caused by Foreign Nation Attack*. Retrieved from https://healthitsecurity.com/news/anthem-data-breach-reportedly-caused-by-foreign-nation-attack

Strickland, J. (2018). *10 Worst Computer Viruses of All Time*. Retrieved from https://computer.howstuffworks.com/worst-computer-viruses2.htm

Suler, J. (2004). The Online Disinhibition Effect. *Cyberpsychology & Behavior*, *7*(3), 321–326. doi:10.1089/1094931041291295 PMID:15257832

Tam, L., Glassman, M., & Vandenwauver, M. (2010). The psychology of password management: A tradeoff between security and convenience. *Behaviour & Information Technology*, *29*(3), 233–244. doi:10.1080/01449290903121386

Vu, K.-P. L., Chambers, V., Creekmur, B., Cho, D., & Proctor, R. W. (2010). Influence of the Privacy Bird® user agent on user trust of different web sites. *Computers in Industry*, *61*(4), 311–317. doi:10.1016/j.compind.2009.12.001

Wash, R., & Rader, E. (2015). *Too Much Knowledge? Security Beliefs and Protective Behaviors Among United States Internet Users*. Paper presented at the Eleventh Symposium On Usable Privacy and Security (SOUPS 2015), Ottawa, Canada.

Whitty, M., Doodson, J., Creese, S., & Hodges, D. (2015). Individual Differences in Cyber Security Behaviors: An Examination of Who Is Sharing Passwords. *Cyberpsychology, Behavior, and Social Networking*, *18*(1), 3–7. doi:10.1089/cyber.2014.0179 PMID:25517697

Wickens, C. D. (2014). Effort in Human Factors Performance and Decision Making. *Human Factors*, *56*(8), 1329–1336. doi:10.1177/0018720814558419 PMID:25509817

Wiederhold, B. K. (2014). The Role of Psychology in Enhancing Cybersecurity. *Cyberpsychology, Behavior, and Social Networking*, *17*(3), 131–132. doi:10.1089/cyber.2014.1502 PMID:24592869

Wogalter, M. S. (2006). Communication-Human Information Processing (C-HIP) Model. In M. S. Wogalter (Ed.), *Handbook of Warnings* (pp. 51–61). Mahwah, NJ: CRC Press.

Yampolskiy, R. V. (2017). AI Is the Future of Cybersecurity, for Better and for Worse. *Harvard Business Review*. Retrieved from https://hbr.org/2017/05/ai-is-the-future-of-cybersecurity-for-better-and-for-worse

Section 4
Effect–Focused Cyber Behavior

Chapter 12
Deviant Pornography Use:
Linkages to Individual Differences and Early-Onset Adult Pornography Use

Kathryn C. Seigfried-Spellar
Purdue University, USA

ABSTRACT

The impact of both intentional and unintentional exposure to internet pornography on adolescents has been debated in the literature for decades. However, the differences in the operational definitions of pornography and exposure, not to mention the differences in methodology and sampling, make it difficult to synthesize findings and identify patterns across studies. In addition, the majority of the research has employed a rather broad measure of "exposure to general pornography" by adolescents in order to understand the impact of early exposure to pornography; however, internet pornography includes a wide range of sexually explicit materials, not just adult pornography. Thus, the goal of this chapter is to explore the relationship between nondeviant pornography use and deviant pornography use (e.g., child pornography) by discussing the Seigfried-Spellar study which examined the role of individual differences and age of onset in deviant pornography use.

INTRODUCTION

The globalization of technology, specifically the Internet, has profoundly influenced pornography consumption as a result of the Triple-A engine (i.e., affordable, accessible, anonymous; Cooper, 1998). In a study by Wolak, Mitchell, and Finkelhor (2007), 42% of internet users aged 10-17 years reported being exposed to online

DOI: 10.4018/978-1-5225-7128-5.ch012

pornography within the last year, with 66% of them reporting only unintentional exposure to internet pornography. In addition, males and youths between 13 to 17 years of age were 9x more likely to report intentional exposure to internet pornography (Wolak et al., 2007). The impact of both intentional and unintentional exposure to Internet pornography on adolescents has been debated in the literature for decades (Bloom & Hagedorn, 2015; Dombrowski et al., 2007; Flood, 2009; Flood & Hamilton, 2003; Owens, Behun, Manning, & Reid, 2012; Peter & Valkenburg, 2016; Sabina, Wolak, & Finkelhor, 2008; Springate & Omar, 2013; Svedin, Akerman, & Prieve, 2011; Tsitsika et al., 2009). However, this debate is biased in that the majority of the research focuses on the negative impact of adolescents viewing pornography (see Harper & Hodgins, 2016; Peter & Valkenburg, 2016).

In addition, the definition of pornography, or sexually explicit material (SEM), varies in the literature (Owens et al., 2012). Owens et al. (2012) defined pornography according to the 1986 Attorney General Commission on Pornography "as any material that is predominately sexually explicit and intended primarily for the purpose of sexual arousal" (p. 103). However, Peter and Valkenburg (2011) provided a more descriptive definition of pornography, specifically sexually explicit internet materials (SEIM), as:

Professionally produced or user-generated pictures or videos (clips) on or from the internet that are intended to arouse the viewer... and depict sexual activities, such as masturbation as well as oral, anal, and vaginal penetration, in an unconcealed way, often with a close-up on genitals. (p. 1015-1016)

The definition of *exposure* also differs in the literature as intentional (deliberate, wanted), unintentional (unwanted, accidental), or not specified (any exposure; see Peter & Valkenburg, 2016). Overall, differences in the operational definitions of pornography, not to mention the differences in methodology and sampling, make it difficult to synthesize findings and identify patterns across studies in the literature (see Bloom & Hagedorn, 2015; Dombrowski et al., 2007; Owens et al., 2012; Peter & Valkenburg, 2016; Short, Black, Smith, Wetterneck, & Wells, 2012; Springate & Omar, 2013).

Overall, the majority of the research has employed a rather broad measure of "exposure to *general* pornography," by adolescents (i.e., self-reported pornography use; Seigfried-Spellar, 2016) in order to understand the impact of early exposure to pornography. However, internet pornography includes a wide-range of sexually explicit materials, not just adult pornography. In addition, research indicates there are personality differences between consumers and non-consumers of Internet pornography. Thus, the goal of this chapter is to explore the relationship between nondeviant pornography use (adult-only pornography) and deviant pornography use (e.g., child pornography) by discussing the Seigfried-Spellar (2016) study which examined the role of individual differences and age of onset in deviant pornography use. Please note that the goal of this chapter is not to make any moral judgments about the use of mainstream pornography.

LITERATURE REVIEW

Exposure to Pornography

Most recently, Peter and Valkenburg (2016) published a review of the literature from 1995 to 2015 on the implications of adolescents' use of pornography. First, the authors concluded that although the exact prevalence rates are difficult to determine for both intentional and unintentional exposure, at least a "sizeable minority" of all adolescents use pornography (Peter & Valenburg, 2016, p. 515). In addition, research consistently shows that adolescents' use of pornography is related to stronger permissive sexual attitudes (Lo, Neilan, Sun, & Chiang, 1999; Lo & Wei, 2005; Peter & Valkenburg, 2006b, 2008, 2010; To, Iu Kan, & Ngai, 2015; To, Ngai, & Iu Kan, 2012); although, Brown and L'Engle (2009) and Doornwaard, Bickham, Rich, ter Bogt, and van den Eijnden (2015) reported this relationship only for male adolescents.

The literature is less clear about the relationship between pornography use and sexual behaviors for adolescents (Peter & Valkenburg, 2016). Some research suggests a relationship between pornography use and the occurrence of sexual intercourse (Atwood et al., 2012; Bogale & Seme, 2014; Brown & L'Engle, 2009; Cheng et al., 2014; Donevan & Mattebo, 2017; Kastbom, Sydsjö, Bladh, Priebe, & Svedin, 2015; Manaf et al., 2014; Vandenbosch & Eggermont, 2013) and increased casual sex behaviors (Cheng et al., 2014; Lim, Agius, Carrotte, Vella, Hellard, 2017; Lo et al., 1999; Lo & Wei, 2005; Mattebo et al., 2014). However, other studies suggest no relationship between adolescents' pornography use and early sexual debut (Luder et al., 2011) or greater experience with different sexual behaviors (Doornwaard et al., 2015; Mattebo, Tydén, Häggström-Nordin, Nilsson, & Larsson, 2014). Finally, Peter and Valkenburg (2016) and Ortiz and Thompson (2017) argue the current body of knowledge is less consistent regarding the relationship between risky sexual behaviors (e.g., unprotected sex, multiple sex partners) and adolescents' pornography use (see Braun-Courville & Rojas, 2009; Donevan & Mattebo, 2017; Luder et al., 2011).

Finally, the literature suggests that individual differences exist between adolescent consumers and non-consumers of pornography. Specifically, adolescents who used pornography exhibited sensation-seeking (Beyens, Vandenbosch, & Eggermont, 2015; Luder et al., 2011; Peter & Valkenburg, 2006b, 2011; Ševčíková et al., 2014), low self-control (Holt, Bossler, & May, 2012), less life satisfaction (Peter & Valkenburg, 2006a, 2011), less perceived autonomy (Weber, Quiring, & Daschmann, 2012), and greater self-efficacy (Kim, 2001, 2011) compared to their counterparts. However, the results are inconsistent regarding the relationship between self-esteem and adolescent pornography use (see Kim, 2001, 2011; Mesch & Maman, 2009).

Overall, the majority of the literature focuses on the impact of exposure to Internet pornography on adolescents. However, Internet pornography includes a wide range of sexually explicit materials, both deviant and nondeviant, and few studies have examined the use of different types or categories of pornography (Denney & Tewksbury, 2017; Hald & Štulhofer, 2016; Seigfried-Spellar & Rogers, 2013; Seigfried-Spellar, 2016). In addition, deviant (e.g., child pornography) and nondeviant pornography are readily available on the Internet, yet few empirical studies analyze the relationship between the two (Seigfried-Spellar & Rogers, 2013). The question, then, becomes what factors put someone at risk for transitioning from a nondeviant pornography user to a deviant pornography user?

Deviant Pornography

Pornography or sexually explicit materials is a board term that includes a wide-range of sexual activities and behaviors, which may be summarized in four categories (Denny & Tewksbury, 2017; Döring. 2009): soft core/erotic, 2) hardcore, 3) deviant/paraphilia, and 4) illegal pornography. Softcore or erotic pornography often includes nudity and the images are sexually arousing, but they do not portray real sexual acts (i.e., they may portray simulated sex). Hardcore pornography refers to images that include real sex acts and usually some form of penetration (e.g., oral, vaginal, or anal). Hardcore pornography is sometimes referred to as "mainstream pornography," which is what most people who report watching pornography are referring to (Paul, 2009). Paraphilia/deviant pornography includes fetishes or sexual activities that may be considered atypical or socially nonconforming, but are not necessarily illegal (see Denny & Tewksbury, 2017; Seigfried-Spellar, 2013), such as BDSM (i.e., bondage and discipline, dominance and submission, sadism and masochism), amputee pornography, coprophilia or scat pornography (i.e., feces), or barely legal pornography (i.e., actors appear to be barely above the age of consent).

Finally, illegal pornography refers to images that depict criminally-sanctioned acts or actors; although what is considered to be "illegal" may differ by jurisdiction, this form of pornography usually refers to child pornography (i.e., sexually explicit images of minors), also referred to as child sex abuse images or child sexual exploitation material. In addition, bestiality or animal pornography (sexually explicit acts with animals) and animal crush videos (i.e., fetish that derives sexual arousal from crushing or torturing animals to death; see *Animal Crush Video Prohibition*

Act, 2010) may be included in this category as they are considered illegal in many jurisdictions (Perdue & Lockwood, 2014). Although hardcore pornography is considered mainstream, deviant and illegal pornography are readily available on the internet (Seigfried-Spellar & Rogers, 2013).

According to the Internet Watch Foundation (IWF; 2017), 57,335 webpages, hosted on 2,416 domains worldwide, contained child sex abuse images or videos and were removed in 2016. In 2016, the Canadian Centre for Child Protection reported the estimated age of the child, using the sexual maturation rating (SMR), in 43,597 child sex abuse images, and found that 49.6% of the children appeared to be under the age of 8 years (Canadian Centre for Child Protection, 2016). According to PornHub (2017), "teen" was the 4th most searched term in 2016; and although "teen" refers to 18 or 19-year olds, this term could also include actors who are under the age of consent depending on jurisdiction, which is why "young adult" has been suggested to replace the search term, "teen" (Pegg, 2016).

Overall, internet pornography includes a wide-range of sexually explicit materials. A few studies have shown that adolescents are exposed to deviant pornography, specifically boys are more likely to see extreme images (e.g., rape, child pornography; Sabina, Wolak, & Finkelhor, 2008), and frequent pornography users are more likely to view deviant pornography (e.g., violent, animal, and child pornography; Svedin, Åkerman, & Priebe, 2011). However, few empirical studies have analyzed the relationship between nondeviant (e.g., adult pornography) and deviant (bestiality, child) pornography use. Essentially, when are individuals who consume nondeviant forms of pornography (e.g., mainstream adult pornography) at a greater risk for consuming more deviant or illegal forms of pornography (e.g., animal or child pornography)?

NONDEVIANT VS. DEVIANT PORNOGRAPHY USER

Individual Differences

Empirical research is slowly uncovering the factors related to people's decisions to consume various genres of Internet pornography. As previously discussed, research suggests that adolescents who use pornography exhibited sensation-seeking (Beyens et al., 2015; Luder et al., 2011; Peter & Valkenburg, 2006b, 2011; Ševčíková et al., 2014), low self-control (Holt, Bossler, & May, 2012), less life satisfaction (Peter & Valkenburg, 2006a, 2011), less perceived autonomy (Weber et al., 2012), and greater self-efficacy (Kim, 2001, 2011) compared to their counterparts. Using adult samples (mostly college students), research suggests individuals exhibiting psychopathic (Barnes, Malamuth, & Check, 1984; Paul, 2009; Williams, Cooper,

Howell, Yuille, & Paulhus, 2009), antisocial (Fisher & Barak, 2001; Shim, Lee, & Paul, 2007), or sensation-seeking dispositions (Hald, Kuyper, Adam, & de Wit, 2013; Sinković, Štulhofer, & Božić, 2013; Weisskirch & Murphy, 2004) may be more likely to consume pornographic materials. Personality characteristics are also predictive of Internet child pornography consumption. Bogaert (2001) found that men who prefer sexualized images of children were more likely to possess aggressive and dominant personality traits. Seigfried, Lovely, and Rogers (2008) found Internet child pornography users were more manipulative, dishonest, and less likely to make decisions based on personal moral values compared to non-users of child pornography.

Previous research (Williams, Howell, Cooper, Yuille, & Paulhus, 2004, 2009; Seigfried, 2007; Seigfried-Spellar, Lovely, & Rogers, 2011) suggests Bandura's (1977) theory of reciprocal determinism may explain why some people intentionally consume pornography when others do not. According to Bandura (1977), the theory of reciprocal determinism states behavioral (B), psychological and cognitive (P), and environmental (E) factors all interact and exert bidirectional influences on human nature. The strength and influence of each factor varies and depends on different situations and settings. In addition, people are not only influenced by their environment but are active participants in their surroundings, as well (Bandura, 1977, 1978, 1994).

According to Bandura (1986), "when situational constraints are weak, personal factors serve as the predominant influence in the regulatory system" (p. 35). There is a disconnect between the social and environmental constraints of Internet pornography (see Seigfried-Spellar et al., 2011). Deviant and nondeviant sexually explicit materials have always existed; however, the regulations of such materials are inconsistent (Akdeniz, 2008). For example, the possession of Internet child pornography is legal in some countries (e.g., Russia) and illegal in others (e.g., United States; see International Centre for Missing & Exploited Children, 2016). Although the production, distribution, and possession of child pornography are illegal in the United States, the Internet has created an environment with "weak constraints" because child pornography is accessible, affordable, and anonymous (Cooper, 1998). Thus, with weak environmental limits, individual differences and biological factors should be predictors of whether a person will engage in deviant pornography (see Seigfried-Spellar, 2011).

For example, Williams et al. (2004, 2009) found that college students who met the subclinical definition of psychopathy were more likely to actively seek out pornographic materials. In addition, Seigfried (2007) found a relationship between Internet child pornography use (B), online communication environments (E), and the individual's personality and decision-making traits (P). That is to say, the more online communication networks utilized by the individual (i.e., engaging in chat rooms, bulletin boards, and instant messaging), the greater the risk for engaging in Internet child pornography – especially for individuals with an exploitive-manipulative personality (Seigfried, 2007). Overall, research has shown a relationship between individual differences and preferences in sexual media. Based on Bandura's triadic model, one can expect a theoretical relationship between individual differences and intentional pornography use as a result of the Internet's social and environmental constraints (see Seigfried-Spellar et al., 2011).

Guttman-Like Progression

A Guttman-Like Progression was first applied to computer criminal behavior by Hollinger (1988). Hollinger (1988) interviewed a small number of computer hackers and computer science students to determine if involvement in computer deviance (e.g., guessing passwords, unauthorized file modification) followed a particular pattern of progression. Based on the interviews, Hollinger (1988) concluded that the activities of computer hackers followed a Guttman-like progression. Using Hollinger's work as a foundation, Seigfried-Spellar and Rogers (2013) explored the literature to determine if pornography use, from nondeviant to deviant, also followed a Guttman-like progression. According to the literature, desensitization to mainstream pornography has been reported with some pornography consumers.

Specifically, child pornography users may experience a level of desensitization to mainstream pornography which results in a need to collect more extreme pornographic materials (see Merdian et al., 2013; Quayle & Taylor, 2002; Quayle & Taylor, 2003; Young, 2001). In addition, some child pornography users may collect sexual images of children, not because of an underlying paraphilia or sexual interest in children, but because the images are easily accessible via the Internet (Basbaum, 2010) or as part of a preference for sexually deviant content (Kettleborough & Merdian, 2017). According to McCarthy (2010), there are significant differences in the ratio of adult to child pornography in the pornography collections of contact vs. non-contact child pornography offenders; specifically, individuals who possess more child pornography than adult pornography are more likely to be contact offenders compared to non-contact child pornography offenders (McCarthy, 2010). Finally, Endrass et al. (2009) studied the pornography collections of 231 men charged with child pornography possession; the results indicated the collections included a wide range of sexually explicit materials, including other deviant forms of pornography, such as bestiality. Overall, there may be a relationship between desensitization to nondeviant pornography and the need to compulsively collect more novel and usual forms of pornography.

In the first study to assess the Guttman-like progression for nondeviant (adult-only) and deviant (child and/or animal) pornography use, Seigfried-Spellar and

Rogers (2013) explored whether the age of onset for *intentional* adult-pornography use discriminated between adult-only and adult + deviant pornography users (i.e., adult + deviant users self-reported intentionally using both mainstream and child/animal pornography)[1]. Seigfried-Spellar and Rogers (2013) found individuals who consumed both "adult + deviant" pornography reported a significantly younger "age of onset" for adult pornography use compared to adult-only users. In other words, adult and animal/child pornography (adult + deviant) users reported intentionally searching for and accessing adult pornography at a younger age than individuals who only consumed adult pornography (adult-only users). In addition, no one reported the sole consumption of child pornography (Seigfried-Spellar & Rogers, 2013); these findings suggested that deviant pornography use follows a Guttman-like progression (see Hollinger, 1988).

SEIGFRIED-SPELLAR (2016) STUDY

The Seigfried-Spellar and Rogers (2013) study was limited by its sample in that sex representation was disproportionate, for 80% ($n = 502$) were women and 20% ($n = 128$) were men. However, a younger "age of onset" for adult pornography use was still a statistically significant predictor of later deviant pornography use even after controlling for sex. To better understand the relationship between "age of onset" and adult-only versus adult + deviant pornography use, the Seigfried-Spellar (2016) study used a different sampling methodology and assessed whether individual differences discriminated between adult-only and adult + deviant pornography users. The overall goal was to develop a predictive risk model to determine if age of onset for adult pornography use and individual differences discriminated between adult-only and adult + deviant pornography use.

The Seigfried-Spellar (2016) study had three primary objectives. The first aim was to replicate the Seigfried-Spellar and Rogers (2013) study using a different sampling methodology. Instead of a panel sample, Seigfried-Spellar (2016) employed a snowballing methodology using an anonymous Internet-based survey. The second aim of this study was to determine whether deviant pornography use (e.g., Internet child pornography and/or animal pornography) followed a Guttman-like progression, meaning no one would report the sole consumption of animal or child pornography. The final aim of this study was to assess whether personality traits and cognitive dispositions discriminated between adult-only and adult + deviant pornography users. By measuring age of onset for adult pornography use, as well as individual differences, the current study attempted to develop a predictive model which discriminated between adult-only and adult + deviant pornography users.

Method and Data

272 respondents completed an anonymous Internet-based survey advertised as "attitudes toward adult websites" using a snowball sampling methodology; 142 (54.6%) were women and 127 (46.7%) were men. The majority of the sample was white ($n = 243$, 89.3%), between the ages of 18 and 35 years ($n = 209$, 76.8%). The survey was posted on a variety of sites, including chat rooms, discussion forums, and social media websites (e.g., Facebook). In order to participate in the study, the respondents had to indicate on the demographics questionnaire that they were at least 18 years of age or older and were currently permanent residents of either the United States, United Kingdom, Australia, or Canada. These countries were included because they have the similar laws criminalizing child pornography. The survey included three scales: Online Pornography Survey (Seigfried, 2007), Five-Factor Model Rating Form (Widiger, 2004), and Moral Decision-Making Scale (cf., Rogers, Smoak, & Liu, 2006).

The respondent's Internet pornography behavior and age of onset were measuring using the Online Pornography Survey (OPS; Seigfried, 2007; Seigfried-Spellar, 2011). The OPS included 54 questions that assessed the respondents' pornography behaviors, including intentional searching, accessing, downloading, and exchanging of sexually explicit Internet images. In the OPS, adult pornography was defined as pornographic images "featuring individuals *over* the age of 18 years," whereas child pornography was defined as pornographic materials "featuring individuals *under* the age of 18 years." Animal pornography or bestiality was defined as pornographic images "featuring individuals *over* the age of 18 years *with* an animal." 15 items from the Online Pornography Survey measured the respondent's age of onset for online pornography use. The following is a sample question related to age of onset from the OPS: "How old were you the first time you knowingly accessed a website in order to view pornographic materials featuring individuals *under* the age of 18 years?" The respondents' choices for age of onset items were: does not apply to me, under 12 years of age, 12 to under 16 years of age, 16 to under 19 years of age, 19 to under 24 years of age, 24 years of age or older, and decline to respond. Based on item endorsement, the respondents were classified as either self-reported users or non-users of adult, animal (bestiality), or child pornography.

The Five-Factor Model Rating Form (FFMRF) measured the following individual differences, which are considered to be the five key traits of personality: Neuroticism (emotional instability), Extraversion (positive affect), Openness to Experience (unconventionality), Agreeableness (vs. antagonism), and Conscientiousness (constraint; Widiger, 2004; Widiger & Lowe, 2007; Mullins-Sweatt et al., 2006). The FFMRF displays 30 polar opposites on a Likert scale of 1 (extremely low) to 5 (extremely high). For example, the openness to experience item, ideas, was measured with "pragmatic, rigid" at one end of the spectrum and "strange, odd, peculiar, creative" on the polar end. In this study, the Cronbach's alphas for the FFMRF were: Neuroticism = .72, Extraversion = .76, Openness to Experience = .72, Agreeableness = .60, and Conscientiousness = .81.

The cognitive disposition of the individual was assessed using the Moral Decision-Making Scale (MDKS), which focuses on the respondents' "moral compass," meaning whether or not decisions are based on Hedonistic, Internal, or Social Values (c.f., Rogers et al., 2006). The MDKS included 15 items, which were scaled from 1 (not important in my decisions) to 8 (very important in my decisions) for statements such as, "if my choice is consistent with my own moral beliefs." The Cronbach's alphas for the Moral Decision-Making subscales were low but acceptable: Social Values (α = .65), Internal Values (α = .71), and Hedonistic Values (α = .69).

Statistical significance was set at the alpha level of .05 prior to any analyses. In order to identify the relationship between individual differences (FFMRF, MDKS) and pornography use (adult-only vs. adult + deviant), a zero-order correlation was conducted. Next, the Fisher-Freeman-Halton Exact Test examined the relationship between age of onset for adult pornography and adult-only vs. adult + deviant pornography use. The Fisher-Freeman-Halton Exact Test approximates the chi-square test when expected cell counts are small and extends the Fisher's Exact Test to the $R \times C$ case (cf., Freeman & Halton, 1951). Finally, those variables identified as statistically significant were entered into a backward stepwise (Wald) logistic regression in order to determine if individual differences and age of onset for adult pornography use predicted group membership for adult-only versus adult + deviant Internet pornography use.

Results

Of the 272 respondents, only 16.9% (n = 46) indicated that they were non-consumers of adult, animal, or child pornography. Of the 226 (83.1%) consumers of pornography, all of them reported using adult pornography. This finding supported the author's expectation, as well as the Seigfried-Spellar and Rogers (2013) findings, that no one would be a *sole* consumer of child pornography. 25.2% (n = 57) of the pornography consumers reported using bestiality/animal pornography, and 6.6% (n = 15) of the pornography users consumed Internet child pornography. Of the 137 male consumers of pornography, 12 (8.8%) consumed child pornography; of the 86 female consumers of pornography, 2 (2.3%) consumed child pornography. Finally, 11 (4.9%) of the pornography users consumed all three pornography genres (adult, animal, *and* child). See Table 1 for a detailed breakdown of the respondents by their self-reported sex and type of pornography consumed (none, adult, animal, and/or child).

Table 1. Classification of respondents by self-reported use of adult, animal, and/ or child pornography

| Porn User Type | Sex | | | Total |
	Male ($n = 142$)	Female ($n = 127$)	Decline ($n = 3$)	($N = 272$)
None	5 (1.8)	41 (15.1)	0 (0.0)	46 (16.9)
Adult-Only	96 (35.3)	68 (25.0)	1 (0.4)	165 (60.7)
Animal-Only	0 (0.0)	0 (0.0)	0 (0.0)	0 (0.0)
Child-Only	0 (0.0)	0 (0.0)	0 (0.0)	0 (0.0)
Adult & Animal	29 (10.6)	16 (5.9)	1 (0.4)	46 (16.9)
Adult & Child	3 (1.1)	1 (0.4)	0 (0.0)	4 (1.5)
Animal & Child	0 (0.0)	0 (0.0)	0 (0.0)	0 (0.0)
Adult, Animal, & Child	9 (3.3)	1 (0.4)	1 (0.4)	11 (4.0)

Note. Values represent frequencies with percentages in parentheses.

A zero-order correlation examined the relationship between sex and self-reported pornography use (i.e., adult, animal, and child pornography). Based on item responses, a dichotomous variable was created for each pornography category: adult, animal, and child. The respondents were coded as either non-users (0) or users (1) for each category of pornography. There was a statistically significant relationship between adult pornography use and animal pornography use, $r_\phi (272) = .22, p < .01$, and animal pornography use and child pornography use, $r_\phi (272) = .31, p < .01$. However, there was only a moderately significant relationship between adult and child pornography use, $r_\phi (272) = .11, p = .09$. Thus, individuals who consumed adult pornography were statistically more likely to also consume animal (bestiality) pornography, and animal pornography users were significantly more likely to consume child pornography. However, self-reported adult pornography use was not significantly correlated with self-reported child pornography use. Finally, consistent with previous research, men were significantly more likely to self-report the use of adult, $r_\phi (269) = -.38, p < .01$, animal/bestiality, $r_\phi (269) = -.17, p < .01$, and child pornography, $r_\phi (269) = -.16, p = .01$.

Next, respondents were categorized as either: adult-only or adult and animal/ child (adult + deviant) pornography users. Of the 226 pornography users, 165 (73%) were classified as adult-only consumers and 61 (27%) were classified as "adult + deviant" pornography users. The author then compared the self-reported age at which the respondents first *intentionally* searched for and viewed adult pornography (i.e., "age of onset" for adult pornography use) to determine if age of onset differentiated between adult-only and adult + deviant pornography users. Based on the Fisher-Freeman-Halton Exact Test ($p = .026$), adult + deviant pornography users reported a significantly younger "age of onset" compared to adult-only pornography users (see Table 2). This finding supported previous research and the author's hypothesis that deviant pornography users were more likely to report the *intentional* use (i.e., does not include accidental exposure) of adult pornography at a younger age than the adult-only pornography users.

As shown in Table 2, 41% of the adult + deviant pornography users reported an "age of onset" under 16 years of age, compared to only 30% of the adult-only respondents. 5% of the adult + deviant users reported engaging in adult pornography use under the age of 12 years, compared to only 1% of the adult-only group. Finally, 32% ($n = 51$) of the adult-only pornography users reported an age of onset of 25 years of age or older, compared to only 13% ($n = 8$) for the adult + deviant pornography group.

To assess whether adult + deviant pornography use followed a Guttman-like progression, the author analyzed the 11 respondents who reported engaging in all three types of pornography (adult, animal, and child) to determine their "age of onset" for each category of pornography. As shown in Table 3, 54.5% of the consumers self-reported engaging in adult pornography under the age of 16 years, and 63.6% reported that they began accessing child pornography after the age of 19 years. Although only a few individuals reported using all types of pornography ($n = 11$), preliminary findings suggest a trend towards a Guttman-like progression in that the majority of users began consuming adult and animal pornography at a younger age, prior to their use of child pornography.

The next set of analyses determined if personality (openness to experience, conscientiousness, extraversion, agreeableness, neuroticism) and cognitive

Table 2. Adult-only vs. adult and deviant pornography use by age of onset cross-tabs

	Type of Porn User	
Age of Onset	Adult-Only $n = 159$	Adult & Deviant $n = 61$
< 12	2 (1.3%)	3 (4.9%)
12 < 16	46 (28.9%)	22 (36.1%)
16 < 19	30 (18.9%)	15 (24.6%)
19 < 24	30 (18.9%)	13 (21.3%)
24 <	51 (32.1%)	8 (13.1%)

Note. Six adult-only pornography users were dropped from this analysis due to missing data.
Fisher-Freeman-Halton Exact Test, $p = .026$
Effect Size, Cramer's $V = .214$

Table 3. Age of onset for consumers of adult, animal, and child pornography

Age of Onset	Type of Pornography		
	Adult	Animal	Child
< 12	1 (9.1)	1 (9.1)	1 (9.1)
12 < 16	5 (45.5)	2 (18.2)	2 (18.2)
16 < 19	2 (18.2)	2 (18.2)	1 (9.1)
19 < 24	2 (18.2)	4 (36.4)	3 (27.3)
24 <	1 (9.1)	2 (18.2)	4 (36.4)

$N = 11$

Note. Values represent frequencies with percentages in parentheses.

characteristics (internal, social, and hedonistic moral values) discriminated between adult-only and adult + deviant pornography users. There was a statistically significant relationship between adult-only versus adult + deviant pornography use and Openness to Experience, $r_{pb} = 0.16$, $p = .02$. There was a moderately significant correlation between adult-only versus adult + deviant pornography use and Extraversion, $r_{pb} = 0.12$, $p = .07$, and social moral values, $r_{pb} = -0.12$, $p = .09$. However, there was no evidence to suggest a significant relationship between adult-only versus adult + deviant pornography use and the following individual difference variables: Agreeableness, Neuroticism, Conscientiousness, Internal Values, and Hedonistic Values.

Based on the significant findings from the zero-order correlations and Fisher-Freeman-Halton Exact Test, the author conducted a backward stepwise (Wald) logistic regression to determine if "age of onset" and Openness to Experience were significant predictors of adult-only versus adult + deviant pornography use. As shown in Table 4, the best predictive model for adult-only versus adult + deviant

Table 4. Exploratory backward (wald) logistic regression differentiating between adult-only vs. adult + deviant pornography users by individual differences and age of onset

Variable	B	SE B	Exp (B)
Step 1			
Age of Onset	-0.34	0.13	0.72**
Openness	0.58	0.26	1.79*

$**p < .01$, $*p < .05$

Note. $R^2 = .05$ (Hosmer & Lemeshow) .06 (Cox & Snell) .08 (Nagelkerke).

pornography use included both variables, Openness to Experience ($W = 5.18$, $p = .02$) and Age of Onset ($W = 6.76$, $p < .01$).

Adult + Deviant pornography users had a significantly younger "age of onset" for adult pornography use compared to adult-only pornography users. Using the reciprocal of the odds ratio[2], individuals with an older age of onset for adult pornography use were 1.4x less likely to engage in deviant pornography. In addition, adult + deviant pornography users were significantly higher on openness to experience (i.e., more unconventional) than adult-only pornography users. Thus, respondents who scored high on openness to experience were 1.8x more likely to be adult + deviant pornography users compared to adult-only pornography users.

Discussion

The main premise of the Seigfried-Spellar (2016) study was to assess whether age of onset and individual differences significantly distinguished between individuals who self-reported as adult-only pornography users vs. self-reported users of both adult and deviant (i.e., animal and/or child) pornography users. The results suggested that age of onset for adult pornography and individual differences were significantly related to adult-only vs. adult + deviant pornography users. In addition, child pornography users were more likely to consume both adult and animal pornography, rather than just solely consuming child pornography. Overall, the Seigfried-Spellar (2016) study was able to replicate the findings of Seigfried-Spellar and Rogers (2013) using a different sampling methodology, and assess the role of individual differences between adult-only and adult + deviant pornography users, as well as the age of onset for individuals who consumed adult, animal, and child pornography.

Consistent with Seigfried-Spellar and Rogers (2013), the current study suggested men were more likely to self-report the use of adult, animal, and child pornography compared to women. The results also suggested adult pornography use was significantly correlated with animal pornography use, and animal pornography use was significantly correlated with child pornography use. However, in the current study, adult pornography use was not significantly correlated with child pornography use, which is contrary to the Seigfried-Spellar and Rogers (2013) findings. Even after controlling for sex, the relationships between adult, animal, and child pornography use remained the same (Adult and Animal: $r = .17$, $p < .01$; Animal and Child: $r = .28$, $p < .01$; Adult and Child: $r = .05$, $p > .05$). In addition, none of the respondents were animal-only, child-only, or deviant-only (animal and child) pornography users. Instead, individuals who engaged in deviant pornography use also reported the use of nondeviant adult pornography.

Finally, the respondents' self-reported age of onset for adult pornography significantly predicted adult-only vs. adult + deviant pornography use. That is to say, adult + deviant pornography users self-reported a younger age of onset for nondeviant (adult-only) pornography compared to the adult-only pornography users. Overall, these findings support the conclusion drawn by Seigfried-Spellar and Rogers (2013) that Internet pornography use may follow a Guttman-like progression in that deviant pornography use is more likely to occur after the use of nondeviant adult pornography. In addition, individuals with higher scores on openness to experience were significantly more likely to be adult + deviant pornography users compared to adult-only pornography users. High scores on openness to experience, often referred to as intellect or unconventionality, are associated with being "open-minded, unusual, weird, creative, peculiar, and unconventional" (Trull & Widiger, 2013, p. 137). Thus, individuals with high openness to experience and a younger age of onset for adult pornography use may be at greater risk for engaging in deviant pornography.

Merdian, Wilson, Thakker, Curtis, and Boer (2013) studied the motivations of child pornography offenders (with and without hands-on contact offenses) to start viewing Internet child pornography. A number of themes were identified, including initial trigger, sexual identity, progression from legal material, detached/passive emotions, and positive emotions. According to Merdian et al. (2013), child pornography offenders were more likely to endorse the theme "progression from legal material" compared to mixed offenders (child pornography users with hands-on contact offenses). In addition, all of the offenders who endorsed this theme reported the consumption of other deviant pornography. This theme was also linked to the "source of positive emotions" theme in that child pornography offenders collected a wide variety of pornography genres as a coping mechanism for life stressors (Merdian et al., 2013). Thus, for some child pornography users, desensitization may occur with nondeviant pornography use to more deviant pornography genres (Merdian et al., 2013; Quayle & Taylor, 2002, 2003; Young, 2001), and the likelihood of desensitization may be influenced by the age of onset for nondeviant adult pornography and individual differences, such as openness to experience.

Although the Seigfried-Spellar (2016) study extended the previous findings of Seigfried-Spellar and Rogers (2013), it is not without limitations. First, the sample was not representative of the entire population of Internet users; although, the choice to employ a snowball sampling methodology was an attempt to replicate the findings of the Seigfried-Spellar and Rogers (2013) study using a different sampling procedure. In addition, it is possible that the individuals who self-selected to participate in the current study are different from those who chose not to participate; however, volunteer bias is a common concern that presents itself in many survey-based research designs.

There may also be concerns of whether the respondents over- or under-reported their pornography use; however, research suggests Internet-based research designs decrease the respondent's level of socially desirable responding (see Joinson, 1999; Chang & Krosnick, 2009) while self-disclosure of sensitive topics is increased due to the Internet's perceived anonymity (see Gosling, Vazire, Srivastava, & John, 2004; Mueller et al., 2000). In a recent meta-analysis, Dodou and de Winter found the scores on social desirability in online, offline, and paper-based surveys to be the same (2015). Finally, only two forms of deviant pornography were included in this study, animal (bestiality) and child pornography; future studies should include other forms of deviant, but legal, adult-only pornography, such as fetish pornography (e.g., amputee pornography, BDSM).

CONCLUSION

Overall, the impact of both intentional and unintentional exposure to Internet pornography on adolescents has been debated in the literature for decades. This author emphasizes that the purpose of this chapter was not to make any moral judgements about the use of mainstream pornography; instead, this chapter explored the relationship between nondeviant and deviant pornography consumption. As mentioned previously, the majority of the literature focuses on the negative impact of being exposed to pornography during adolescence, with fewer studies examining the potential benefits of pornography use or exposure (see Harper & Hodgins, 2016). In addition, internet pornography includes a wide range of sexually explicit materials, both deviant and nondeviant; however, few studies have examined the use of different types or categories of pornography (Denney & Tewksbury, 2017; Hald & Štulhofer, 2016; Seigfried-Spellar & Rogers, 2013; Seigfried-Spellar, 2016).

The Seigfried-Spellar (2016) study was the first to assess whether individual differences and age of onset for adult pornography use discriminated between adult-only and adult + deviant pornography users. Preliminary findings suggest that deviant pornography use, specifically child pornography, may follow a Guttman-like progression for some individuals in that they become desensitized and progress from nondeviant forms of pornography to more extreme genres (see Seigfried-Spellar & Rogers, 2013). In addition, for some individuals, with specific personality characteristics, intentional early exposure to adult pornography may be a risk factor for later consumption of deviant pornography.

However, more research is needed to understand this Guttman-like progression from nondeviant to deviant forms of pornography and the role of individual differences and age of onset for adult pornography use. The Seigfried-Spellar (2016) study only focused on two forms of deviant pornography, animal (bestiality) and child pornography; however, future research should assess the relationship between child pornography and other forms of pornography defined as socially deviant (e.g., fetish pornography). Since Internet pornography is easily accessible, affordable, and anonymous (see Cooper, 1998), future research is needed to understand why some individuals *intentionally* consume deviant pornography when others do not.

REFERENCES

Akdeniz, Y. (2008). *Internet child pornography and the law: National and international responses*. Burlington, VT: Ashgate Publishing Co.

Animal Crush Video Prohibition Act (2010), Pub. L. 111–294, 124 Stat. 3177

Atwood, K. A., Zimmerman, R., Cupp, P. K., Fongkaew, W., Miller, B. A., Byrnes, H. F., ... Chookhare, W. (2012). Correlates of precoital behaviors, intentions, and sexual initiation among Thai adolescents. *The Journal of Early Adolescence*, *32*(3), 364–386. doi:10.1177/0272431610393248

Bandura, A. (1977). *Social Learning Theory*. Englewood Cliffs, NJ: Prentice Hall.

Bandura, A. (1978, April). The self system in reciprocal determinism. *The American Psychologist*, *33*(4), 344–358. doi:10.1037/0003-066X.33.4.344

Bandura, A. (1986). *Social Foundations of Thought and Action: A Social Cognitive*. Englewood Cliffs, NJ: Prentice-Hall.

Bandura, A. (1994). Social Cognitive Theory of Mass Communication. In J. Bryant & D. Zillmann (Eds.), *Media Effects: Advances in Theory and Research* (pp. 61–90). Hillsdale, NJ: Erlbaum.

Barnes, G. E., Malamuth, N. M., & Check, J. (1984). Personality and sexuality. *Personality and Individual Differences*, *5*(2), 159–172. doi:10.1016/0191-8869(84)90048-5

Basbaum, J. P. (2010). Sentencing for possession of child pornography: A failure to distinguish voyeurs from pederasts. *The Hastings Law Journal*, *61*, 1–24.

Beyens, I., Vandenbosch, L., & Eggermont, S. (2015). Early adolescent boys' exposure to internet pornography Relationships to pubertal timing, sensation seeking, and academic performance. *The Journal of Early Adolescence*, *35*(8), 1045–1068. doi:10.1177/0272431614548069

Bloom, Z. D., & Hagedorn, W. B. (2015). Male adolescents and contemporary pornography: Implications for marriage and family counselors. *The Family Journal (Alexandria, Va.)*, *23*(1), 82–89. doi:10.1177/1066480714555672

Bogaert, A. F. (2001). Personality, individual differences, and preferences for the sexual media. *Archives of Sexual Behavior*, *30*(1), 29–53. doi:10.1023/A:1026416723291 PMID:11286004

Bogale, A., & Seme, A. (2014). Premarital sexual practices and its predictors among in-school youths of Shendi town, West Gojjam zone, north western Ethiopia. *Reproductive Health*, *11*(1), 49. doi:10.1186/1742-4755-11-49 PMID:24961239

Braun-Courville, D. K., & Rojas, M. (2009). Exposure to sexually explicit web sites and adolescent sexual attitudes and behaviors. *The Journal of Adolescent Health*, *45*(2), 156–162. doi:10.1016/j.jadohealth.2008.12.004 PMID:19628142

Brown, J. D., & L'Engle, K. L. (2009). X-Rated: Sexual attitudes and behaviors associated with US. Early adolescents' exposure to sexually explicit media. *Communication Research*, *36*(1), 129–151. doi:10.1177/0093650208326465

Canadian Centre for Child Protection. (2016, January). *Child sexual abuse images on the internet: A cybertip.ca analysis*. Retrieved December 18, 2018 from https://www.cybertip.ca/pdfs/CTIP_CSAResearchReport_2016_en.pdf

Chang, L., & Krosnick, J. A. (2009). Winter. National surveys via RDD telephone interviewing versus the internet: Comparing sample representativeness and response quality. *Public Opinion Quarterly*, *73*(4), 641–678. doi:10.1093/poq/nfp075

Davies, H. T. O., Crombie, I. K., & Tavakoli, M. (1998). When can odds ratios mislead? *British Medical Journal*, *316*(7136), 989–991. doi:10.1136/bmj.316.7136.989 PMID:9550961

Denney, A. S., & Tewksbury, R. (2017). ICTs and Sexuality. In M. R. P. McGuire & T. J. Holt (Eds.), *Handbook of Technology, Crime, and Justice* (pp. 113–133). New York, NY: Routledge.

Dodou, D., & de Winter, J. C. F. (2014, July). Social desirability is the same in offline, online, and paper surveys: A meta-analysis. *Computers in Human Behavior*, *36*, 487–495. doi:10.1016/j.chb.2014.04.005

Dombrowski, S. C., Gischlar, K. L., & Durst, T. (2007). Safeguarding young people from cyber pornography and cyber sexual predation: A major dilemma of the Internet. *Child Abuse Review*, *16*(3), 153–170. doi:10.1002/car.939

Donevan, M., & Mattebo, M. (2017). The relationship between frequent pornography consumption, behaviors, and sexual preoccupancy among male adolescents in Sweden. *Sexual & Reproductive Healthcare: Official Journal of the Swedish Association of Midwives, 12*, 82–87. doi:10.1016/j.srhc.2017.03.002 PMID:28477937

Doornwaard, S. M., Bickham, D. S., Rich, M., ter Bogt, T. F. M., & van den Eijnden, R. J. J. M. (2015). Adolescents' use of sexually explicit Internet material and their sexual attitudes and behavior: Parallel development and directional effects. *Developmental Psychology, 51*(10), 1476–1488. doi:10.1037/dev0000040 PMID:26376287

Döring, N. M. (2009). The internet's impact on sexuality: A critical review of 15 years of research. *Computers in Human Behavior, 25*(5), 1089–1101. doi:10.1016/j. chb.2009.04.003

Endrass, J., Urbaniok, F., Hammermeister, L. C., Benz, C., Elbert, T., Laubacher, A., & Rossegger, A. (2009). The consumption of internet child pornography and violent and sex offending. *BMC Psychiatry, 9*(1), 43. doi:10.1186/1471-244X-9-43 PMID:19602221

Fisher, W. A., & Barak, A. (2001). Internet pornography: A social psychological perspective on internet sexuality. *Journal of Sex Research, 38*(4), 312–323. doi:10.1080/00224490109552102

Flood, M. (2009). The harms of pornography exposure among children and young people. *Child Abuse Review, 18*(6), 384–400. doi:10.1002/car.1092

Flood, M., & Hamilton, C. (2003, February). *Youth and pornography in Australia: Evidence on the extent of exposure and likely effects.* The Australian Institute.

Freeman, G. H., & Halton, J. H. (1951). Note on exact treatment of contingency, goodness of fit and other problems of significance. *Biometrika, 38*(1-2), 141–149. doi:10.1093/biomet/38.1-2.141 PMID:14848119

Gosling, S. D., Vazire, S., Srivastava, S., & John, O. P. (2004). February/March. Should we trust web-based studies? A comparative analysis of six preconceptions about internet questionnaires. *The American Psychologist, 59*(2), 93–104. doi:10.1037/0003-066X.59.2.93 PMID:14992636

Häggström-Nordin, E., Hanson, U., & Tydén, T. (2005). Association between pornography consumption and sexual practices among adolescents in Sweden. *International Journal of STD & AIDS, 16*(2), 102–107. doi:10.1258/0956462053057512 PMID:15807936

Hald, G. M., Kuyper, L., Adam, P. C. G., & de Wit, J. B. F. (2013). Does viewing explain doing? Assessing the association between sexually explicit materials use and sexual behaviors in a large sample of Dutch adolescents and young adults. *Journal of Sexual Medicine*, *10*(12), 2986–2995. doi:10.1111/jsm.12157 PMID:23621804

Hald, G. M., & Štulhofer, A. (2016). What types of pornography do people use and do they cluster? Assessing types and categories of pornography consumption in a large-scale online sample. *Journal of Sex Research*, *53*(7), 849–859. doi:10.1080/00224499.2015.1065953 PMID:26445007

Harper, C., & Hodgins, D. C. (2016). Examining correlates of problematic internet pornography use among university students. *Journal of Behavioral Addictions*, *5*(20), 179–191. doi:10.1556/2006.5.2016.022 PMID:27156383

Hollinger, R. C. (1988). Computer hackers follow a guttman-like progression. *Sociology and Social Research*, *72*(3), 199–200.

Holt, T. J., Bossler, A. M., & May, D. C. (2012). Low self-control, deviant peer associations, and juvenile cyberdeviance. *American Journal of Criminal Justice*, *37*(3), 378–395. doi:10.100712103-011-9117-3

International Centre for Missing and Exploited Children. (2016). *Child pornography: Model legislation and global review* (8th ed.). Author. Retrieved from www.icmec.com

Internet Watch Foundation. (2017, April 3). *IWF Annual Report 2016*. Retrieved December 18, 2017 from iwf.org.uk

Joinson, A. (1999, August). Social desirability, anonymity, and internet-based questionnaires. *Behavior Research Methods, Instruments, & Computers: A Journal of the Psychonomic Society, 31*(3), 433-438.

Kastbom, A. A., Sydsjö, G., Bladh, M., Priebe, G., & Svedin, C.-G. (2015). Sexual debut before the age of 14 leads to poorer psychosocial health and risky behaviour in later life. *Acta Paediatrica (Oslo, Norway)*, *104*(1), 91–100. doi:10.1111/apa.12803 PMID:25213099

Kettleborough, D. G., & Merdian, H. L. (2017). Gateway to offending behaviour: Permission- giving thoughts of online users of child sexual exploitation material. *Journal of Sexual Aggression*, *23*(1), 19–32. doi:10.1080/13552600.2016.1231852

Kim, Y.-H. (2001). Korean adolescents' health risk behaviors and their relationships with the selected psychological constructs. *The Journal of Adolescent Health*, *29*(4), 298–306. doi:10.1016/S1054-139X(01)00218-X PMID:11587914

Kim, Y.-H. (2011). Adolescents' health behaviours and its associations with psychological variables. *Central European Journal of Public Health*, *19*(4), 205–209. PMID:22432395

Lim, M. S. C., Agius, P. A., Carrotte, E. R., Vella, A. M., & Hellard, M. E. (2017). Young Australians' use of pornography and associations with sexual risk behaviours. *Australian and New Zealand Journal of Public Health*, *41*(4), 438–443. doi:10.1111/1753-6405.12678 PMID:28664609

Lo, V., Neilan, E., Sun, M., & Chiang, S. (1999). Exposure of Taiwanese adolescents to pornographic media and its impact on sexual attitudes and behaviour. *Asian Journal of Communication*, *9*(1), 50–71. doi:10.1080/01292989909359614

Lo, V., & Wei, R. (2005). Exposure to Internet pornography and Taiwanese adolescents' sexual attitudes and behavior. *Journal of Broadcasting & Electronic Media*, *49*(2), 221–237. doi:10.120715506878jobem4902_5

Luder, M.-T., Pittet, I., Berchtold, A., Akré, C., Michaud, P.-A., & Surís, J.-C. (2011). Associations between online pornography and sexual behavior among adolescents: Myth or Reality? *Archives of Sexual Behavior*, *40*(5), 1027–1035. doi:10.100710508-010-9714-0 PMID:21290259

Manaf, M. R. A., Tahir, M. M., Sidi, H., Midin, M., Nik Jaafar, N. R., Das, S., & Malek, A. M. A. (2014). Pre-marital sex and its predicting factors among Malaysian youths. *Comprehensive Psychiatry*, *55*(Suppl. 1), S82–S88. doi:10.1016/j.comppsych.2013.03.008 PMID:23587530

Mattebo, M., Tydén, T., Häggström-Nordin, E., Nilsson, K. W., & Larsson, M. (2014). Pornography and sexual experiences among high school students in Sweden. *Journal of Developmental and Behavioral Pediatrics*, *35*(3), 179–188. doi:10.1097/DBP.0000000000000034 PMID:24695119

McCarthy, J. A. (2010, June). Internet sexual activity: A comparison between contact and non-contact child pornography offenders. *Journal of Sexual Aggression*, *16*(2), 181–195. doi:10.1080/13552601003760006

McHugh, M. L. (2009). The odds ratio: Calculation, usage, and interpretation. *Biochemia Medica*, *19*(2), 120–126. doi:10.11613/BM.2009.011

Merdian, H. L., Wilson, N., Thakker, J., Curtis, C., & Boer, D. P. (2013). "So why did you do it?": Explanations provided by child pornography users. *Sexual Offender Treatment*, *8*(1). Retrieved from http://www.sexualoffender-treatment.org/117.html

Mesch, G. S., & Maman, T. L. (2009). Intentional online pornographic exposure among adolescents: Is the Internet to blame? *Verhaltenstherapie & Verhaltensmedizin*, *30*(3), 352–367.

Mueller, J., Jacobsen, D., & Schwarzer, R. (2000). What are computing experiences good for?: A case study in online research. In M. H. Birnbaum (Ed.), *Psychological experiments on the internet* (pp. 195–216). New York, NY: Academic Press. doi:10.1016/B978-012099980-4/50009-5

Mullins-Sweatt, S. N., Jamerson, J. E., Samuel, D. B., Olson, D. R., & Widiger, T. A. (2006). Psychometric properties of an abbreviated instrument of the five-factor model. *Assessment*, *13*(2), 119–137. doi:10.1177/1073191106286748 PMID:16672728

Ortiz, R. R., & Thompson, B. (2017). Content effects: Pornography and sexually explicit content. In P. Rossler (Ed.), *The International Encyclopedia of Media Effects* (pp. 246–257). Malden, MA: John Wiley & Sons. doi:10.1002/9781118783764. wbieme0122

Owens, E. W., Behun, R. J., Manning, J. C., & Reid, R. C. (2012). The impact of internet pornography on adolescents: A review of the research. *Sexual Addiction & Compulsivity*, *19*(1-2), 99–122. doi:10.1080/10720162.2012.660431

Paul, B. (2009). Predicting internet pornography use and arousal: The role of individual difference variables. *Journal of Sex Research*, *46*(4), 344–357. doi:10.1080/00224490902754152 PMID:19219657

Pegg, S. (2016, January 15). Could your taste for 'teen' porn land you in legal trouble? *The Conversation*. Retrieved December 18, 2017 from theconversation.com

Perdue, A., & Lockwood, R. (2014). *Animal cruelty and freedom of speech: When worlds collide*. West Lafayette, IN: Purdue University Press.

Peter, J., & Valkenburg, P. M. (2006a). Adolescents' exposure to sexually explicit material on the internet. *Communication Research*, *533*(2), 178–204. doi:10.1177/0093650205285369

Peter, J., & Valkenburg, P. M. (2006b). Adolescents' exposure to sexually explicit online material and recreational attitudes toward sex. *Journal of Communication*, *56*(4), 639–660. doi:10.1111/j.1460-2466.2006.00313.x

Peter, J., & Valkenburg, P. M. (2008). Adolescents' exposure to sexually explicit Internet material, sexual uncertainty, and attitudes toward uncommitted sexual exploration: Is there a link? *Communication Research*, *35*(5), 579–601. doi:10.1177/0093650208321754

Peter, J., & Valkenburg, P. M. (2010). Processes underlying the effects of adolescents' use of sexually explicit Internet material: The role of perceived realism. *Communication Research*, *37*(3), 375–399. doi:10.1177/00936502103362464

Peter, J., & Valkenburg, P. M. (2011). The use of sexually explicit internet material and its antecedents: A longitudinal comparison of adolescents and adults. *Archives of Sexual Behavior*, *40*(5), 1015–1025. doi:10.100710508-010-9644-x PMID:20623250

Peter, J., & Valkenburg, P. M. (2016). Adolescents and pornography: A review of 20 years of research. *Journal of Sex Research*, *53*(4-5), 509–531. doi:10.1080/002 24499.2016.1143441 PMID:27105446

PornHub. (2017). *Pornhub's 2016 year in review*. Retrieved December 18, 2017 from pornhub.com.

Quayle, E., & Taylor, M. (2002). Child pornography and the internet: Perpetuating a cycle of abuse. *Deviant Behavior: An Interdisciplinary Journal*, *23*(4), 331–361. doi:10.1080/01639620290086413

Quayle, E., & Taylor, M. (2003). Model of problematic internet use in people with a sexual interest in children. *Cyberpsychology & Behavior*, *6*(1), 93–106. doi:10.1089/109493103321168009 PMID:12650567

Rogers, M., Smoak, N. D., & Liu, J. (2006). Self-reported computer criminal behavior: A big-5, moral choice and manipulative exploitive behavior analysis. *Deviant Behavior*, *27*(3), 1–24. doi:10.1080/01639620600605333

Sabina, C., Wolak, J., & Finkelhor, D. (2008). The nature and dynamics of internet pornography exposure for youth. *Cyberpsychology & Behavior*, *11*(6), 1–3. doi:10.1089/cpb.2007.0179 PMID:18771400

Seigfried, K. (2007). *Self-reported online child pornography behavior: A psychological analysis* (Unpublished master's thesis). John Jay College of Criminal Justice, New York, NY.

Seigfried, K. C., Lovely, R. W., & Rogers, M. K. (2008). Self-reported consumers of internet child pornography: A psychological analysis. *International Journal of Cyber Criminology*, *2*(1), 286–297.

Seigfried-Spellar, K. C. (2011). *The role of individual differences in predicting the type of images collected by internet child pornography consumers* (Unpublished Dissertation). Purdue University, West Lafayette, IN.

Seigfried-Spellar, K. C. (2016). Deviant pornography use: The role of early-onset adult pornography use and individual differences. *International Journal of Cyber Behavior, Psychology and Learning,6*(3), 34–47. doi:10.4018/IJCBPL.2016070103

Seigfried-Spellar, K. C., Lovely, R. W., & Rogers, M. K. (2011). Self-reported internet child pornography consumers: A personality assessment using Bandura's theory of reciprocal determinism. In K. Jaishankar (Ed.), *Cyber Criminology: Exploring Internet Crimes and Criminal Behavior* (pp. 65–77). Boca Raton, FL: Taylor and Francis. doi:10.1201/b10718-8

Seigfried-Spellar, K. C., & Rogers, M. K. (2013). Does deviant pornography use follow a guttman-like progression? *Computers in Human Behavior,29*(5), 1997–2003. doi:10.1016/j.chb.2013.04.018

Shim, J. W., Lee, S., & Paul, B. (2007). Who responds to unsolicited sexually explicit materials on the Internet?: The role of individual differences. *Cyberpsychology & Behavior, 10*(1), 71–79. doi:10.1089/cpb.2006.9990 PMID:17305451

Short, M. B., Black, L., Smith, A. H., Wetterneck, C. T., & Wells, D. E. (2012). A review of internet pornography use research: Methodology and content from the past 10 years. *Cyberpsychology, Behavior, and Social Networking, 15*(1), 13–23. doi:10.1089/cyber.2010.0477 PMID:22032795

Sinković, M., Štulhofer, A., & Božić, J. (2013). Revisiting the association between pornography use and risky sexual behaviors: The role of early exposure to pornography and sexual sensation seeking. *Journal of Sex Research, 50*(7), 633–641. doi:10.10 80/00224499.2012.681403 PMID:22853694

Springate, J., & Omar, H. A. (2013). The impact of the Internet on the sexual health of adolescents: A brief review. *International Journal of Child and Adolescent Health, 6*(4), 469–471.

Svedin, C. G., Åkerman, I., & Priebe, G. (2011). Frequent users of pornography. A population based epidemiological study of Swedish male adolescents. *Journal of Adolescence, 34*(4), 779–788. doi:10.1016/j.adolescence.2010.04.010 PMID:20888038

To, S., Iu Kan, S., & Ngai, S. S. (2015). Interaction effects between exposure to sexually explicit online materials and individual, family, and extrafamilial factors on Hong Kong high school students' beliefs about gender role equality and body-centered sexuality. *Youth & Society, 47*(6), 747–768. doi:10.1177/0044118X13490764

To, S., Ngai, S. S., & Iu Kan, S. (2012). Direct and mediating effects of accessing sexually explicit online materials on Hong Kong adolescents' attitude, knowledge, and behavior relating to sex. *Children and Youth Services Review, 34*(11), 2156–2163. doi:10.1016/j.childyouth.2012.07.019

Trull, T. J., & Widiger, T. A. (2013). Dimensional models of personality: The five factor model and the DSM-5. *Dialogues in Clinical Neuroscience, 15*(2), 135–146. PMID:24174888

Tsitsika, A., Critselis, E., Kormas, D., Konstantoulaki, E., Constantopoulos, A., & Kafetzis, D. (2009). Adolescent pornographic internet site use: A multivariate regression analysis of the predictive factors of use and psychosocial implications. *Cyberpsychology & Behavior, 12*(5), 545–550. doi:10.1089/cpb.2008.0346 PMID:19772438

Weber, M., Quiring, O., & Daschmann, G. (2012). Peers, parents, and pornography: Exploring adolescents' exposure to sexually explicit material and its developmental correlates. *Sexuality & Culture, 16*(4), 408–427. doi:10.100712119-012-9132-7

Weisskirch, R., & Murphy, L. (2004, Summer). Friends, porn, and punk: Sensation seeking in personal relationships, internet activities, and music preference among college students. *Adolescence, 39*(154), 189–201. PMID:15563033

Widiger, T. (2004). *Five Factor Model Rating Form (FFMRF).* Retrieved October 13, 2010 from www.uky.edu/~widiger/ffmrf.rtf

Widiger, T. A., & Lowe, J. R. (2007). Five-factor model assessment of personality disorder. *Journal of Personality Assessment, 89*(1), 16–29. doi:10.1080/00223890701356953 PMID:17604531

Williams, K., Cooper, B., Howell, T., Yuille, J., & Paulhus, D. (2009). Inferring sexually deviant behavior from corresponding fantasies: The role of personality and pornography consumption. *International Journal of Criminal Justice and Behavior, 36*(2), 198–222. doi:10.1177/0093854808327277

Williams, K., Howell, T., Cooper, B., Yuille, J., & Paulhus, D. (2004, May). *Deviant sexual thoughts and behaviors: The roles of personality and pornography use.* Poster Sessions presented at the 16th Annual American Psychology Society, Chicago, IL.

Wolak, J., Mitchell, K., & Finkelhor, D. (2007). Unwanted and wanted exposure to online pornography in a national sample of youth internet users. *Pediatrics, 119*(2), 247–257. doi:10.1542/peds.2006-1891 PMID:17272613

Young, K. S. (2001). *Tangled in the Web: Understanding Cybersex from Fantasy to Addiction.* Bloomington, IN: AuthorHouse.

ENDNOTES

[1]   In this study, deviant referred to materials deemed illegal through formal social controls (laws) rather than informal social controls (personal morals). Bestiality and child pornography are examples of deviant pornography in the United States.

[2]   Since the odds ratio for "age of onset" in Table 4 is less than one, we use the reciprocal of the odds ratio, which is 1 divided by Exp(B), in order to ease its interpretation (Davies, Crombie, & Tavakoli, 1998; McHugh, 2009).

Chapter 13
Adolescent Victim Experiences of Cyberbullying:
Current Status and Future Directions

Minghui Gao
Arkansas State University, USA

Tonja Filipino
Arkansas State University, USA

Xu Zhao
The University of Calgary, Canada

Mark McJunkin
Arkansas State University, USA

ABSTRACT

This chapter started by introducing a recent research study that disclosed adolescent victim experiences across seven major types of cyberbullying, significant gender and age differences, and reasons for not reporting incidents of cyberbullying to adults. The chapter then related the research findings to major areas in the literature on the nature and forms of cyberbullying in contrast to traditional forms of bullying, its prevalence among school-aged youths, the effects of gender and age on adolescent victim experiences of cyberbullying, and the factors that contribute to adolescent attitude toward reporting cyberbullying incidents to adults. The chapter suggested that future research should further explore issues such as how various types of cyberbullying affect adolescent mental wellbeing, how age and gender affect school-aged youth victim experiences of various forms of cyberbullying, and how professionals and other adults may help adolescents counter cyberbullying.

DOI: 10.4018/978-1-5225-7128-5.ch013

INTRODUCTION

Cyberbullying is "a unique form of bullying" (Patchin & Hinduja, 2010, p. 614) that involves "sending or posting harmful or cruel text or images using the Internet or other digital communication devices" (Willard, 2004, p.1). The rapidly evolving information technology provides numerous easy avenues for spreading negative messages, and thus enables various forms of cyberbullying behaviors. Willard (2004) has identified the following forms of cyberbullying:

1. **Flaming:** Sending angry, rude, vulgar messages directed at a person or persons privately or to an online group;
2. **Denigration (put-downs):** Sending or posting harmful, untrue, or cruel statements about a person to the person or other people;
3. **Online harassment:** Repeatedly sending a person offensive messages;
4. **Cyberstalking:** Harassment that include threats of harm or is highly intimidating;
5. **Outing:** Sending or posting material about a person that contains sensitive, private, or embarrassing information, including forwarding private messages or images. Engag[ing] in tricks to solicit embarrassing information that is then made public;
6. **Masquerade:** Pretending to be someone else and sending or posting material that makes that person look bad or places that person in potential danger;
7. **Exclusion:** Actions that specifically and intentionally exclude a person from an online group.

In the following sections, we will first introduce a recent research study that we conducted to explore adolescent experience as victims of various forms of cyberbullying as well as their explanations of why they decide to report or not to report their victim experience of cyberbullying. We will then relate our main findings to major research areas in the literature on the nature and forms of cyberbullying and its prevalence among school-aged youths, the effects of gender and age on adolescent victim experiences of cyberbullying, and the factors that contribute to adolescent attitude toward reporting cyberbullying incidents to adults. Finally, we will end this chapter by pinpointing future directions pertaining to the understanding and intervention of school-aged youth's victim experiences of cyberbullying.

INTRODUCING A RECENT STUDY

Recently, we conducted a survey research to explore adolescent victim experiences of cyberbullying (Gao, Zhao, & McJunkin, 2016). The study aimed to answer the following research questions: 1) to what extent are adolescents exposed to different types of cyberbullying? 2) Is there any gender difference in adolescent victim experiences of cyberbullying? 3) Is there any age- or grade-related difference in adolescent victim experiences of cyberbullying? 4) To what extents are adolescent victims of cyberbullying willing to report their incidents to adults, and what factors contribute to their decision-makings about whether to report their experiences?

To collect both quantitative and qualitative information about respondents' experiences of cyberbullying, the first author devised the Adolescent Victims of Cyberbullying Questionnaire (AVCQ; see Appendix A). The AVCQ contains 15 questions that fall into three sections. The first section includes six questions that aim to solicit respondents' demographic information. The second section contains seven questions that address respondents' victim experiences with seven forms of cyberbullying behaviors identified by Willard (2004), including cyberstalking, denigration, exclusion, flaming, harassment, masquerade, and outing. The third section entails two questions that tap into respondents' decision-making and justifications regarding whether to report incidents of cyberbullying. The questionnaire was piloted, and Cronbach's alpha was calculated. The reliability coefficient for each item was high ($\alpha \geq .75$), which suggests that the AVCG was reliable. Students participating in the pilot study commented that the definitions of the various cyberbullying forms overall helped them understand the meanings of these terms while also giving suggestions for rewording. The questionnaire was revised by accommodating the students' feedbacks and then was employed as data collection tool for this study.

The researchers sent invitation to more than 300 students in Northeastern Arkansas schools and received 74 signed consent forms to participate in the study. The participants were directed to understand meanings of the seven cyberbullying types before responding to the questionnaire. Of the 74 completed questionnaires, 61 were valid and thus included in data analysis. The study sample (n= 61) included 21 tenth graders (12 girls and 9 boys), 20 eleventh graders (10 girls and 10 boys), and 20 twelfth graders (10 girls and 10 boys). Difference in the sample's gender-grade composition is not significant, $\chi^2 (2, N = 61) = 0.28, p = .87$. Quantitative data were analyzed using descriptive statistics, Chi-square analysis, Fisher's exact test (when the cell count is less than 5), and residual analysis (by calculating standardized residuals, or Std. Res). An alpha level of .05 was used for all statistical tests. Qualitative data were analyzed using thematic coding, and case and cross-case analysis. The results include four aspects as follows.

First of all, adolescent victim experiences varied across the seven types of cyberbullying. Table 1 presents the results. Sitting atop the list is flaming, with nearly half of the respondents indicating having been flamed (46%). Around one third of the respondents reported having been denigrated (34%), harassed online

Table 1. Frequency (%) of adolescents being cyberbullied (n = 61)

Type of Cyberbullying	Frequency (%)
1. Flaming	28 (46%)
2. Denigration	21 (34%)
3. Online Harassment	20 (33%)
4. Cyberstalking	19 (31%)
5. Outing	17 (28%)
6. Masquerade	12 (20%)
7. Exclusion	8 (13%)

(33%), cyberstalked (31%), or outed (28%). At the bottom of the list are masquerade (20%) and exclusion (13%).

Secondly, a Pearson's Chi-square test for a 2 (gender) × 2 (cyberbullying) contingency table revealed that gender had significant impact on adolescent victim experiences of cyberstalking and online harassment. Table 2 shows the results. As can be seen, significant gender differences existed in the participants' experiences of cyberstalking ($\chi^2 = 4.99$, $p = .03$); more girls (44%) than boys (17%) reported having been victims of cyberstalking. In addition, marginally significant gender difference was also identified in adolescent victim experience of online harassment ($\chi^2 = 3.67$, $p = .06$); more girls (44%) than boys (21%) reported having been victims of online harassment. The analyses did not show significant gender differences in flaming ($\chi^2 = 2.90$, $p = .09$), denigration ($\chi^2 = 0.29$, $p = .60$), masquerade ($\chi^2 = 0.21$, $p = .65$), outing ($\chi^2 = 0.38$, $p = .54$), and exclusion (Fisher's exact test statistic value = 0.14, $p > .05$).

Table 2. Frequency and chi-square statistics of cyberbullying by gender (n = 61)

Type of Cyberbullying	Gender		χ^2 p Value (df = 1)
	Female (n = 32)	Male (n = 29)	
1. Flaming	18 (56%)	10 (34%)	2.90 .09
2. Denigration	12 (37%)	9 (31%)	0.29 .60
3. Online harassment	14 (44%)	6 (21%)	3.67 .06
4. Cyberstalking	14 (44%)	5 (17%)	4.98 **.03**
5. Outing	10 (32%)	7 (24%)	0.38 .54
6. Masquerade	7 (23%)	5 (17%)	0.21 .65
7. Exclusion	2 (6%)	6 (21%)	0.14 >.05*

Note. * Fisher's exact test statistic value for cell(s) with expected frequency < 5.

Thirdly, a Pearson's Chi-square test for a 2 (cyberbullying) × 3 (grade level) contingency table disclosed that 10th, 11th, and 12th graders differed significantly in their victim experiences of cyberbullying. When a significant Chi-square statistic value was identified, residual analysis was conducted by calculating *standardized residuals* (Std. Res) to find out the specific cell (i.e., grade level) that makes the greatest contribution to the Chi-square test result (Sharpe, 2015). Table 3 reveals the results.

As found out, significant grade differences existed in the participants' victim experiences of cyberstalking ($\chi^2 = 11.63$, $p = .003$). Residual analysis indicated that 12th graders (Std. Res = 2.31) were significantly more likely to be victims of cyberstalking than 10th graders (Std. Res = -.99) and 11th graders (Std. Res = -1.29). In addition, significant grade differences were also found in the participants' victim experiences of online exclusion ($\chi^2 = 8.34$, $p = .02$). Residual analysis suggested that 12th graders (Std. Res = 2.09) were more likely to be victims of online exclusion than their counterparts in 10th grade (Std. Res = -1.66) and 11th grade (Std. Res = -0.38). The same analysis, however, suggested that students from the different grades do not differ significantly in their victim experiences of flaming ($\chi^2 = 0.22$, $p = .90$), denigration ($\chi^2 = 0.60$, $p = .74$), online harassment ($\chi^2 = 3.47$, $p = .18$), masquerade ($\chi^2 = 4.53$, $p = .10$), and outing ($\chi^2 = 4.35$, $p = .11$).

The fourth aspect of the results was about whether young people, as victims (and/ or witnesses) of cyberbullying, would report the incidents to adults (e.g., school personnel, health professionals, parents, etc.), and how they justify their decision. As Table 4 shows, regardless of gender, grade level, and types of cyberbullying, an overwhelming majority (70-90%) of the respondents mentioned that they would tackle the issue on their own rather than reporting incidents of cyberbullying to adults. Three common themes were identified from their justifications, including: (1)

Table 3. Frequency and chi-square statistics of cyberbullying by grade level (n = 61)

Type of Cyberbullying	Grade Level			χ^2 p Value (df = 2)
	10th (n = 21)	11th (n = 20)	12th (n = 20)	
1. Flaming	9 (43%)	9 (45%)	10 (50%)	0.22 .90
2. Denigration	6 (29%)	8 (40%)	7 (35%)	0.60 .74
3. Online harassment	4 (19%)	8 (40%)	9 (45%)	3.47 .18
4. Cyberstalking	4 (19%)	3 (15%)	12 (60%)	11.63 **.003***
5. Masquerade	3 (14%)	2 (10%)	7 (35%)	4.53 .10
6. Outing	4 (19%)	4 (20%)	9 (45%)	4.35 .11
7. Exclusion	0 (0%)	2 (10%)	6 (30%)	8.34 **.02***

Note. * Standardized residuals were calculated when chi-square results were significant.

unawareness or underestimate of the negative effect of cyberbullying (e.g., "I don't care"; "It's no big deal" or "it is funny"); (2) fear of adult overreactions including restrictions on their Internet access (e.g., "the school staff will overreact"); and (3) determination to deal with cyberbullying on one's own (e.g., "I will deal with it"; "I can handle it myself.").

Specifically, among the 10th graders (n = 21), nine out of 12 girls (75%) and seven out of nine boys (78%) said they would not report. In regard to their justifications for not reporting their experiences, the girls either said they do not care, or mentioned that victims of cyberbullying should toughen up and not care about it. In contrast, the boys wrote that "the school counselor makes too big of a deal out of it", "the school counselor is not getting into the drama," or "I don't care enough," with one boy writing that his normal response to cyberbullying is "sometimes I laugh – it is funny."

Among the 11th graders (n = 20), seven girls (70%) and eight boys (80%) said they would not report, or if they witness any incident of cyberbullying, they would watch what is going on but would not participate in it. The girls did not want to report incidents of cyberbullying due to considerations of the potential negative consequences of doing so. The most common considerations they mentioned were either their parents might restrict their Internet access if they were aware of the issue, or they might get themselves into trouble by reporting the incidents, even though they had done nothing wrong themselves. The boys' justifications often emphasized the need/desire to deal with the issue by themselves. For example, some boys mentioned, "I'll deal with it," "[I] would fight them," and "the school staff would overreact." Others mentioned, "I do things on my own," and "I can handle myself."

Table 4. Frequency (%) of not reporting and justifications for behavioral decision

Grade	Gender	Not Reporting	Example of Justification
10th	F (n = 12)	9 (75%)	"Don't care"; "Toughen up"
	M (n = 9)	7 (78%)	"The school counselor makes too big of a deal out of it"; "not getting into the drama"; "I don't care enough"; "sometimes I laugh – it is funny"
11th	F (n = 10)	7 (70%)	"Parents would restrict Internet access"; "get oneself into trouble"
	M (n = 10)	8 (80%)	"I'll deal with it"; "would fight them"; "the school staff would overreact"; "I do things on my own"; "I can handle it myself"
12th	F (n = 10)	8 (80%)	"I don't care"; "grow up"; "it's no big deal"
	M (n = 10)	9 (90%)	"No big deal"; "just ignore it"
Total	N = 61	48 (79%)	—

Note. F = Girls, M = Boys

Among the 12th graders (n = 20), eight girls (80%) and nine boys (90%) said that, when being the target of cyberbullying or witnessing it, they would not report the incidents to adults. Some girls said that as witnesses they would join in and cheer on the bullies. Others said they would just watch but not participate in it. Still others said they would try to help or befriend the victims. Very few boys responded to this question in the survey, but one boy mentioned that when being the target or witness of cyberbullying, his typical response would be to "go on with my life." With respect to their justification, a variety of responses were given. One girl said, "I don't care," and "grow up, it's no big deal!" Five boys answered that cyberbullying is "no big deal," and that people should "just ignore it."

To sum up, limited by its small sample size (n = 61) and geographical homogeneity of the group of participants (one high school in a small town), findings of this study may not reflect national or even regional patterns in adolescents' experience of cyberbullying and thus should be interpreted with great caution. Therefore, its findings should be related to those of the large literature in this field so as to shed light on the way various forms of cyberbullying occur to adolescents in and perhaps beyond the participating school, the small town, or the state of Arkansas, for the reason that adolescents' access to the cyber world is not limited by their geographical location, and often not by their racial and social economic backgrounds.

MAJOR THEMES IN THE LITERATURE

With the recent study findings in mind, we reviewed the relevant literature in purpose of assessing the current status of knowledge about adolescent victim experiences of cyberbullying. It was found that although researchers have extensively explored cyberbullying and its impact on adolescent victims, few have investigated adolescent victim experiences of particular types of cyberbullying and, importantly, when and why the victims report their experience to adults. Therefore, starting with clarifying the nature of cyberbullying in contrast to traditional forms of bullying, our review focused on disclosing harms cyberbullying inflicts to youth wellbeing and major factors that affect school-aged youth experience of cyberbullying.

Cyberbullying vs. Traditional Bullying

Cyberbullying became a noticed phenomenon in the late 20th century following advances in information and electronic technologies such as the Internet and cell phones (Olweus, 1993). It has become prevalent among adolescents due to the distancing effect of technological devices that makes it easier for youth to say and do cruel things to others compared to what is typical in traditional face-to-face bullying situations (Donegan, 2012; National Center for Education Statistics, 2013; Center for Disease Control and Prevention, 2014). Cyberbullying involves individuals' spreading harsh, hostile, or simply negative messages via electronic devices and communication tools. Cyberbullying can take place on the Internet, through instant messaging (IM), chat rooms, on social networking sites, blogs, or gaming sites. According to Grigonis (2017), cyberbullying happens more often on Instagram at 42% than any other platforms, with Facebook following close behind at 37%, Snapchat at 31%, and YouTube at 10%. It can also crop up on mobile phones, through short message service (SMS), multimedia messaging service (MMS), or other technologies (Smith et al., 2008). By posting words and images online or sending messages via cell phones, harsh comments travel much quicker than they once did and can stick around much longer if not forever.

Comparing to traditional forms of bullying, what used to be verbal or physical is now viral. Rather than name-calling on the playground in front of a few people, harsh messages can now be posted online or sent to one person or a group of 100 or more in a matter of seconds. Unlike traditional bullies who are usually physically strong and fast, and who involve in face-to-face confrontations with their victims, cyberbullies can be anyone who has a desire to inflict "willful and repeated" harms by using computers, cell phones, and other electronic devices (Hinduja & Patchin, 2010, p. 208). Different from traditional bullying that usually occurs in school settings, cyberbullying can continue outside school and go beyond school hours (Smith et al., 2008). In fact, it can happen among youth wherever and whenever a respected adult is not present (Haber & Daley, 2011). That is, while past generations of youth would be safe from peer judgment and abuse once they arrive home from school, students today have only their wits to protect them from teasing, harassment, and threats that reach them online, anytime and anywhere (Mustacchi, 2009).

In the course of a few decades, there has been a sharp spike in the number of cyberbullying incidents among school-aged youth, with electronic bullying peaking in middle and high schools (Dehue, Bolman, & Völlink, 2008; Mendez-Baldwin, Cirillo, Ferrigno, & Argento, 2015; Patchin & Hinduja, 2010). A 2009 AP-MPV survey of 1,274 people aged 14-24 found that 50% of those surveyed experienced cyberbullying to some extent, and according to the 2011 AP-MPV survey, this figure has grown to 56% (Associated Press, 2011). According to statistics by the 2010-2011 School Crime Supplement, a total of 9% of students in grades 6–12 experienced cyberbullying (National Center for Education Statistics, 2013). The 2013 Youth Risk Behavior Surveillance Survey showed that 15% of high school students (grades 9-12) were electronically bullied in the year 2012 (Center for Disease Control and Prevention, 2014). According to Reportlinker (2017), 71% of young generations say they are concerned about cyberbullying. Among Internet users of Canadian between ages 15-29, one in five said they had been victims of cyberstalking or cyberbullying in the past five years (Hango, 2016). According to a 2016 report from the Cyberbullying Research Center, 33.8% of students between 12 and 17 were victims of cyberbullying in their lifetime (Enough.org, 2017). As Algar (2017) has revealed, cyberbullying has soared 351% in New York City schools in just two years.

Cyberbullying happens for many of the same reasons as traditional face-to-face bullying (Notar, Padget, & Roden, 2013). Bullies' behavior usually stems from psychosocial problems such as having too much or too little self-esteem, having inadequate parental care and supervision, lack of interest in school, depression or anxiety, having difficulty in controlling their emotions and impulses, and difficulty in following rules (Dombeck, 2007). According to a document published by the US federal government, two types of children are more likely to bully. The children who are popular may bully because they see it as a way to stay popular, and hurting others makes them feel powerful. The children who are less socially successful may bully because it may help them cope with their own low self-esteem or fit in with their peers, or because they have difficulty empathizing with those they hurt (Stopbullying.gov, n.d.). Research also shows that victims of traditional forms of bullying also tend to be victims of cyberbullying (Raskauskas & Stoltz, 2007).

However, compared to traditional forms of bullying, it is easier for young people to engage in cyberbullying due to several reasons. First, the distancing effect of technological devices allows cyberbullies to avoid facing their victims and also provides the illusion that cyberbullies will not get caught (Donegan, 2012). According to a survey of adolescents aged 13 to 17, most teens think people cyberbully others because cyberbullying is no big deal or has any tangible consequences, or because it is anonymous (National Crime Prevention Council, 2007). Second, cyberbullying provides the psychological experience that other forms of bullying do not. According to the same federal government document on Stopcyberbullying. org (n.d.), cyberbullies do harms as a form of entertainment when they are bored, have too much time on their hands, and have too many tech toys available to them. Many do it for laughs or to get a reaction. Furthermore, cyberbullying is also found to be significantly associated with factors such as the use of proactive aggression, justification of violence, exposure to violence, and less perceived social support of friends (Calvete, Orue, Estévez, Villardón, & Padilla, 2010). Other factors that contribute to cyberbullying include envy, prejudice, intolerance for disability, religion, gender, and negative emotions such as shame, guilt, and anger (Hoff & Mitchell, 2009; Jones, Manstead, & Livingstone, 2011). All this increases the harmful impact of cyberbullying on its victims; in extreme cases, it has also led to tragic suicide incidents (CBSNews, 2010; Friedman, 2010; Kennedy, 2010; Maag, 2007).

Harmful Impact of Cyberbullying on Youth Well-Being

Cyberbullying has harmful impact on its adolescent victims. On one hand, it is easier for the offender to strike blows against a victim without having to see the victim's physical response, and on the other hand, it is harder for responsible adults to detect and contain the situation. Cyberbullying can result in the lasting negative impact on its victims, including harming their mental health, social well-being, experience of schooling, and the quality of their future life and career as adults (Hoff & Mitchell, 2009; Mesch, 2009; Sahin, 2012).

School-aged youth are at a developmental stage where they develop social relationships outside family, and the quality of their peer relationships is significantly related to their behavioral outcomes (Mesch, 2009). Young people's social interactions with peers, including their experience of online socialization, provide opportunities for learning to develop their socio-emotional skills. Through interactions with peers, young people learn to negotiate relationships, take perspectives, and to meet their growing need for intimacy in peer relationship. Youth who report having high-quality peer relationships are found to be more confident, less aggressive, and more academically engaged; those who report having low-quality peer relationships are subject to loneliness, fear, and depression (Bukowski, Newcomb, & Hartup, 1996).

Cyberbullying has become an "emerging public health problem" (King, 2010, p. 849). As a manifestation of peer relationship problems such as break-ups, envy, intolerance, and ganging up (Mesch, 2009), cyberbullying has a pervasive influence on youth mental health, often leading the victims to feel depressed, sad, angry, frustrated, have low self-esteem and even suicidal thoughts. Victims of cyberbullying are found to be twice as likely to need help from a mental health professional and three times more likely to drop out of school than peers who do not report being cyberbullied (Connolly & Giouroukakis, 2012). Contrary to some naïve belief that the impact of cyberbullying is limited to initial responses and tends to fade soon, research indicates that the harm caused by cyberbullying has enduring negative impact on its victims, especially on their social well-being (Hoff & Mitchell, 2009; Mesch, 2009). Significant correlations have been found between adolescents' experience of cyberbullying and their feeling of loneliness (Sahin, 2012). In a research involving approximately 2,000 randomly selected middle school students from one of the largest school districts in the United States, Patchin and Hinduja (2010) found that cyberbullying victims and offenders both had significantly lower self-esteem than those who have not been subject to cyberbullying. This relationship persisted even controlling for gender, race, and age.

Cases of cyberbullying occur every day, but most real-life cyberbullying incidents contain more than one form of cyberbullying and few exemplify exactly a certain type of cyberbullying as defined previously. To shed light on the nature of real-life cyberbullying, however, let's take a look at a few high profile incidents. The story of Megan Meier is a noteworthy case that broke on national news about cyberbullying (Maag, 2007). Megan was a thirteen-year-old girl from Missouri who ended her own life after a MySpace romance ended online with a boy named Josh. Megan developed a crush on Josh until things suddenly went bad and he began insulting her. His final message to her was, "The world would be a better place without you." It was on that same day that Megan hanged herself in her room with a belt.

Another young female who chose to end her own life after becoming victim to cyberbullying, following a move to the United States from Ireland, was fifteen-year-old Phoebe Prince. According to Helen Kennedy of the New York Daily News (Kennedy, 2010), Phoebe Prince was cyberbullied by a number of students at her new school in Massachusetts. The students set out to humiliate Phoebe and make her feel unwelcomed. It was reported that Phoebe was called 'Irish slut' and 'whore' on Twitter, Craigslist, Facebook, and Formspring. Phoebe hanged herself after walking home from school and being hit by a Red Bull drink can thrown from a passing bus by the "Mean Girls."

Still another case that also gained major news attention is the tragedy of Tyler Clementi, an eighteen-year-old, Rutgers University college student. According to CBSNews (2012), Tyler was a freshman that jumped to his death from the George Washington Bridge after his roommate, Dhraun Ravi, recorded his intimate encounter with a man in the dorm room they shared. Ravi used a webcam to record Tyler and his partner from another room in the dormitory. Tyler jumped from the bridge a few days after the video was posted online (Friedman, 2010).

Gender and Age Differences in Cyberbullying

Researchers have not reached a consensus regarding gender and age differences in adolescents' experiences of cyberbullying. It has been argued that boys are more likely to bully in person, in the forms of physical, verbal, and relational bullying, whereas girls are more likely to bully online, and that cyberbullying is a higher risk for girls (Notar et al., 2013). This argument is supported by multiple studies. One study found that adolescent girls are more likely to be victims of cyberbullying than boys (25.8% girls versus 16% boys) (Adams, 2010 as cited in Notar et al., 2013). According to the website Enough.org (2017) which has amassed cyberbullying statistics from various sources, girls (40.6%) are more likely to be victims of cyberbullying than boys (28.8%), and girls dominate social media while boys tend to play video games (Cyberbullying Research Center, 2015); 54% of teens surveyed have witnessed online bullying; and 60% of teens who admit to being bullied online have told an adult, compared to 40% in 2013 (Cox, 2014). Another study found that girls reported feeling less safe at school and suffer more relational bullying (Humphrey & Symes, 2010).

Still another study showed that compared to girls, boys are more likely to be both offenders and victims of cyberbullying (Erdur-Baker, 2010). However, a study by Didden et al. (2009) found no evidence showing significant associations between cyberbullying and gender. In addition, existing literature suggests that overall students are bullied at all grade levels, in and away from school, but compared with younger kids, older students reported feeling safer at school and experiencing less relational victimizations (Humphrey & Symes, 2010). However, Didden et al. (2009) have also argued that there is no association between cyberbullying and age. These mixed findings raise the question of whether gender and age differences may be found when particular types of cyberbullying are examined. Certainly, according to our study (Gao, Zhao, & McJunkin, 2016) as introduced previously, gender and age differences do exist in several types of cyberbullying.

FUTURE RESEARCH DIRECTIONS

First of all, future research should further explore adolescent victim experiences of cyberbullying for better understanding and intervention of positive youth development. As mentioned earlier, the rapidly evolving information technology provides numerous easy avenues for spreading negative messages (Li, 2008; Notar, Padgett, & Roden, 2013). Being anonymous, cyberbullies can do tremendous harms to a large number of victims without taking a high risk of being punished (Snakenborg, Van Acker, & Gable, 2011). As a consequence, cyberbullies have invented multiple ways to harm their victims, including cyberstalking, denigration, exclusion, flaming, harassment, masquerade, and outing.

While there are cases of cyberbullying occurring multiple times a day, how young people may experience these different forms of cyberbullying largely remains unknown in the existing literature, despite the fact that research on cyberbullying in general has rapidly increased in recent years. Moreover, the current literature on cyberbullying victims, as previously discussed, has not reached a consensus regarding significant gender and age differences in the way young people experience of cyberbullying, pointing to the necessity of investigating whether gender and age differences exist in young people's experiences of particular forms of cyberbullying.

Most importantly, a key characteristic of cyberbullying, as noted earlier, is that it can happen anytime and anywhere, making it very hard for adults to detect and contain the situation itself and its impact on the victim. Furthermore, while cyberbullying victims often need help from health professionals, they may not want to report their experiences to adults and seek help. To increase our understanding of how to stop cyberbullying and reduce its negative impact on youth, social scientists need to investigate not only young people's experiences of various forms of cyberbullying but also the reasons behind their decisions on whether to report their experiences. Knowledge in this regard will help school officials, health professionals, and other responsible adults better understand the nature of cyberbullying and inform them of ways to support the victims and stop the bullies.

Second, future research should further explore how various types of cyberbullying affect adolescent mental wellbeing so as to find out coping strategies that might help prevent adolescents from conducting, and becoming victims of, cyberbullying. Recent research has pointed to both the prevalence of cyberbullying among school-aged youth (Dehue et al., 2008; Donegan, 2012; Mendez-Baldwin et al., 2015; Patchin & Hinduja, 2010) and its multiple and lasting negative effects on its victims (Connolly & Giouroukakis, 2012; King, 2010; Hoff & Mitchell, 2009; Mesch, 2009; Patchin & Hinduja, 2010; Sahin, 2012). Our recent study (Gao, Zhao, & McJunkin, 2016) contributes to the literature by looking into the extents to which adolescents either have witnessed or have been the targets of various forms of cyberbullying. It also explored their choices on whether to report incidents of cyberbullying to adults and their justifications for making the decision.

Consistent with the existing literature, results of our recent study suggest that the majority of the participants have experienced cyberbullying, either as witnesses or victims, further supporting the argument that cyberbullying in general is prevalent among school-aged youth (Dehue et al., 2008; Donegan, 2012; Mendez-Baldwin et al., 2015; Patchin & Hinduja, 2010). In addition, the present study contributes specific knowledge about the various extents to which adolescents are exposed to different forms of cyberbullying, including flaming (46%), denigration (34%), online harassment (33%), cyberstalking (31%), Outing (28%), masquerade (20%), and exclusion (13%). This finding provides a possible explanation to why the existing literature has documented a puzzling wide range of proportions (ranging from 9 through 15% to nearly 50%) of middle and high school students who reported having experienced cyberbullying (Center for Disease Control and Prevention, 2014; Associated Press, 2011; National Center for Education Statistics, 2013). With this being said, research up to date has provided very limited evidence regarding how different cyberbullying types may affect youth mental wellbeing and needs to explore further in this regard.

Third, future research should investigate further into how age and gender affect school-aged youth victim experiences of various forms of cyberbullying. Our recent study reveals that while school-aged youth are subject to all forms of cyberbullying, the factors of gender and age may make some adolescents more vulnerable than others to particular forms of cyberbullying. Girls were significantly more likely than boys to be victims of cyberstalking (44% versus 17%). Girls are also more likely to be subject to threats of harm or intimidation from the Internet. This finding is consistent with findings in the existing literature that females reported feeling less safe and more relational victimization (Humphrey & Symes, 2010). However, our recent study also challenges Humphrey and Symes's finding that in general older students reported feeling safer and less relational victimization than younger students. Results of our recent study suggest that grade-related differences in adolescents' experiences of cyberbullying vary by forms of cyberbullying. Specifically, compared to 10th and 11th graders, 12th graders are significantly more likely to experience two particular forms of cyberbullying: cyberstalking and exclusion. These findings all point to the necessity of investigating the mechanisms underlying the gender and grade-level difference in adolescents' experiences of particular forms of cyberbullying.

Last but not the least, future research should explore effective means to help adolescent counter cyberbullying. Our recent study provides strong evidence showing that adolescents' unwillingness to report incidents of cyberbullying is a key factor contributing to the prevalence of cyberbullying among school-aged youth and an important barrier against early detection and intervention to stop cyberbullying and mitigate its negative impact on youth. Cross gender and grade levels, an overwhelming majority of students would not report incidents of cyberbullying to adults. The present study identified several reasons that explain this phenomenon, including: adolescents' unawareness or underestimate of the negative effect of cyberbullying on themselves or on others, their concerns about school staff's overreaction and parents' restrictions on their Internet access, and above all, the belief that they should deal with situations of cyberbullying by themselves.

The finding that young people are either unaware of or underestimate the negative impact of cyberbullying is not surprising. The existing literature has documented that most teens think that cyberbullying is no big deal nor has any tangible consequences, or even that it is fun (National Crime Prevention Council, 2007). However, this seemingly simple finding, together with the finding of adolescents' fear of adults' overreaction and their determination to deal with cyberbullying themselves all deserve close attention and further investigation. Questions such as what makes adolescents perceive cyberbullying as harmless and even fun, where do they draw the line between friendly teasing and malicious attack and manipulation, what information help them make judgments about the nature of online behavior, how should adults deal with situations of cyberbullying in order to gain trust from adolescents are complicated psychological, legal, and ethical questions. Adding to the complexity is the fact that in the world of online socialization, individuals may be both bullies and victims. Some adolescents have been bullies themselves and are now receiving the cruelty of being bullied (Notar et al., 2013). Reporting one's cybervictim experiences means potentially disclosing one's online behaviors and, as a result, getting oneself into trouble.

The present study contributes to our knowledge of how school-aged youth experience different forms of cyberbullying and how factors such as gender, age, and perceptions of the nature of cyberbullying are related to their experiences. This knowledge has two important implications for educational and counseling practice. First, it informs educators, parents, and helping professionals of the multifarious nature of cyberbullying but also the groups of youth who are particularly vulnerable to the various forms of cyberbullying. Second, it points to the importance of preventive intervention in the efforts to stopping cyberbullying. Adults need to communicate effectively with young people, starting from early adolescence, about the nature of cyberbullying, its various forms, potential harms on the victims, and ethical ways of responding to situations of cyberbullying. This requires adults' knowledge of cyberbullying, good judgment of its nature, and strategies to have open conversations with adolescents to gain their trust.

Educators, parents, and helping professionals should not feel powerless facing the powerfully penetrating influences of the cyber world. After all, how young people behave in the cyber world themselves and how they respond to others' online behavior is ultimately shaped by the real world in which they are socialized by parents, teachers, and other important adults to think and act in ethical and responsible ways.

REFERENCES

Adams, C. (2010). Cyberbullying: How to make it stop. *Instructor, 120*(2), 44–49.

Algar, S. (2017, February 1). *Cyberbullying in city schools soars 351% in just two years*. Retrieved from www.nypost.com

Associated Press. (2011). *Executive summary: 2011 AP-MTV digital abuse study*. Retrieved from http://www.athinline.org/pdfs/MTV-AP_2011_Research_Study-Exec_Summary.pdf

Bukowski, W. M., Newcomb, A. F., & Hartup, W. (Eds.). (1996). *The company they keep*. Cambridge, UK: Cambridge University Press.

Calvete, E., Orue, I., Estévez, A., Villardón, L., & Padilla, P. (2010). Cyberbullying in adolescents: Modalities and aggressors' profile. *Computers in Human Behavior, 26*(5), 1128–1135. doi:10.1016/j.chb.2010.03.017

CBSNews. (2012, September 30). Tyler Clementi suicide sparks outrage, remorse. *CBSNews*. Retrieved from http://www.cbsnews.com/news/tyler-clementi-suicide-sparks-outrage-remorse/

Center for Disease Control and Prevention. (2014). *Youth risk behavior surveillance — United States 2013*. Washington, DC: U.S. Department of Health and Human Services. Retrieved from http://www.cdc.gov/mmwr/pdf/ss/ss6304.pdf

Connolly, M., & Giouroukakis, V. (2012). Cyberbullying: Taking control through research-based letter writing. *English Journal, 101*(6), 70–74.

Cox. (2014). *Cox 2014 Internet Safety Survey (conducted by The Futures Company)*. Retrieved from http://docplayer.net/16377341-2014-teen-internet-safety-survey-conducted-by-the-futures-company.html

Cyberbullying Research Center. (2015). *2015 Cyberbullying Data*. Retrieved from https://cyberbullying.org/2015-cyberbullying-data

Cyberbullying Research Center. (2016). *2016 Cyberbullying Data*. Retrieved from https://cyberbullying.org/2016-cyberbullying-data

Dehue, F., Bolman, C., & Völlink, T. (2008). Cyberbullying: Youngsters' experiences and parental perception. *CyberPscyhology & Behavior, 11*(2), 217–223. doi:10.1089/cpb.2007.0008 PMID:18422417

Didden, R., Scholte, R. H. J., Korzilius, H., de Moor, J. M. H., Vermeulen, A., O'Reilly, M., ... Lancioni, G. E. (2009). Cyberbullying among students with intellectual and developmental disability in special education settings. *Developmental Neurorehabilitation, 12*(3), 146–151. doi:10.1080/17518420902971356 PMID:19466622

Dombeck, M. (2007, July 24). *The long-term effects of bullying*. Retrieved from https://www.mentalhelp.net/articles/the-long-term-effects-of-bullying/

Donegan, R. (2012). Bullying and cyberbullying: History, statistics, law, prevention and analysis. *The Elon Journal of Undergraduate Research in Communications, 3*(1), 33–42.

Enough.org. (2017, November 10). *Cyberbullying Statistics*. Retried from http://enough.org/stats_cyberbullying

Erdur-Baker, Ö. (2010). Cyberbullying and its correlation to traditional bullying, gender, and frequent and risky usage of internet-mediated communication tools. *New Media & Society, 12*(1), 109–125. doi:10.1177/1461444809341260

Friedman, E. (2010, September 29). Victim of secret dorm sex tape posts Facebook goodbye, jumps to his death. *ABC News*. Retrieved from http://abcnews.go.com/US/ victim-secret-dorm-sex-tape-commits-suicide/story?id=11758716

Gao, M., Zhao, X., & McJunkin, M. (2016). Adolescents' experiences of cyberbullying: Gender, age, and reasons for not reporting to adults. *International Journal of Cyber Behavior, Psychology and Learning, 6*(4), 13–27. doi:10.4018/IJCBPL.2016100102

Grigonis, H. (2017, July 20). *Cyberbullying happens more often on Instagram*. Retrieved from https://www.digitaltrends.com/social-media/cyberbullying-statistics-2017-ditch-the-label/

Haber, J. D., & Daley, L. A. (2011). A cyberbullying protection plan. *Camping Magazine, 84*(2), 32–37.

Hango, D. (2016). *Insights on Canadian Society: Cyberbullying and cyberstalking among Internet users aged 15 to 29 in Canada*. Retrieved from https://www.statcan. gc.ca/pub/75-006-x/2016001/article/14693-eng.htm

Hinduja, S., & Patchin, J. (2010). Bullying, cyberbullying, and suicide. *Archives of Suicide Research, 14*(3), 206–221. doi:10.1080/13811118.2010.494133 PMID:20658375

Hoff, D. L., & Mitchell, S. N. (2009). Cyberbullying: Causes, effects, and remedies. *Journal of Educational Administration, 47*(2), 652–665. doi:10.1108/09578230910981107

Humphrey, N., & Symes, W. (2010). Responses to bullying and use of social support among pupils with autism spectrum disorders (ASDs) in mainstream schools: A qualitative study. *Journal of Research in Special Educational Needs, 10*(2), 82–90. doi:10.1111/j.1471-3802.2010.01146.x

Jones, S. E., Manstead, A. S. R., & Livingstone, A. G. (2011). Ganging up or sticking together? Group processes and children's responses to text-message bullying. *British Journal of Psychology, 102*(1), 71–96. PMID:21241286

Kennedy, H. (2010, March 29). Phoebe Prince, South Hadley High School's 'new girl,' driven to suicide by teenage cyber bullies. *New York Daily News*. Retrieved from http://www.nydailynews.com/news/national/phoebe-prince-south-hadley-high-school-new-girl-driven-suicide-teenage-cyber-bullies-article-1.165911

King, A. V. (2010). Constituency of cyberbullying laws: Keeping the online playground safe for both teens and free speech. *Vanderbilt Law Review, 63*(3), 845–884.

Li, Q. (2008). Cyberbullying in schools: An examination of preservice teacher's perception. *Canadian Journal of Learning and Technology*, *34*(2). Retrieved from http://www.cjlt.ca/index.php/cjlt/article/view/494/225

Maag, C. (2007, November 28). A hoax turned fatal draws anger but no charges. *The New York Times*. Retrieved from http://www.nytimes.com/2007/11/28/us/28hoax.html?_r=0

Mendez-Baldwin, M., Cirillo, K., Ferrigno, M., & Argento, V. (2015). Cyberbullying among teens. *Journal of Bullying and Social Aggression*, *1*(1). Retrieved from http://sites.tamuc.edu/bullyingjournal/cyber-bullying-among-teens/

Mesch, G. S. (2009). Parental mediation, online activities, and cyberbullying. *Cyberpsychology & Behavior*, *12*(4), 387–393. doi:10.1089/cpb.2009.0068 PMID:19630583

Mustacchi, J. (2009). R U Safe? *Educational Leadership*, *66*(6), 78–82.

National Center for Education Statistics. (2013). *Student reports of bullying and cyberbullying: Results from the 2011 school crime supplement to the National Crime Victimization Survey*. Washington, DC: U.S. Department of Education. Retrieved from https://nces.ed.gov/pubs2013/2013329.pdf

National Crime Prevention Council. (2007). *Teens and cyberbullying: Executive summary of a report on research*. Retrieved from http://www.ncpc.org/resources/files/pdf/bullying/Teens%20and%20Cyberbullying%20Research%20Study.pdf

Notar, C. E., Padgett, S., & Roden, J. (2013). Cyberbullying: A review of the literature. *Universal Journal of Educational Research*, *1*(1), 1–9. doi:10.12189/ujer.2013.010101

Olweus, D. (1993). *Bullying at school: What we know and what we can do*. Cambridge, MA: Blackwell.

Patchin, J. W., & Hinduja, S. (2010). Cyberbullying and self-esteem. *The Journal of School Health*, *80*(12), 614–621. doi:10.1111/j.1746-1561.2010.00548.x PMID:21087257

Raskauskas, J., & Stoltz, A. D. (2007). Involvement in traditional and electronic bullying among adolescents. *Developmental Psychology*, *43*(3), 564–575. doi:10.1037/0012-1649.43.3.564 PMID:17484571

Reportlinker. (2017, June). *For America's youth, standing up to the cyberbully is now a life skill*. Retrieved from https://www.reportlinker.com/insight/americas-youth-cyberbully-life-skill.html

Şahin, M. (2012). The relationship between the cyberbullying/cybervictmization and loneliness among adolescents. *Children and Youth Services Review, 34*(4), 834–837. doi:10.1016/j.childyouth.2012.01.010

Sharpe, D. (2015). Your chi-square test is statistically significant: Now what? *Practical Assessment, Research & Evaluation, 20*(8). Retrieved from http://pareonline.net/getvn.asp?v=20&n=8

Smith, P. K., Mahdavi, J., Carvalho, M., Fisher, S., Russell, S., & Tippett, N. (2008). Cyberbullying: Its nature and impact in secondary school pupils. *Journal of Child Psychology and Psychiatry, and Allied Disciplines, 49*(4), 376–385. doi:10.1111/j.1469-7610.2007.01846.x PMID:18363945

Snakenborg, J., Van Acker, R., & Gable, R. A. (n.d.). Cyberbullying: Prevention and intervention to protect our children and youth. *Preventing School Failure, 55*(2), 88-95. doi: .10.1080/1045988X.2011.539454

Stopbullying.gov. (n.d.). *Effects of bullying.* Retrieved from http://www.stopbullying.gov/at-risk/effects/index.html

StopCyberBullying.org. (n.d.). *What is cyberbullying, exactly?* Retrieved from http://www.stopcyberbullying.org/what_is_cyberbullying_exactly.html

Willard, N. (2004). *Educator's guide to cyberbullying: Addressing the harm caused by online social cruelty.* Retrieved from http://cyberbully.org

Chapter 14
Cyber–Victimization and Cyber–Aggression:
Personal and Situational Factors

Maria José D. Martins
*Polytechnic Institute of Portalegre,
Portugal & University of Lisbon, Portugal*

Ana Margarida Veiga Simão
University of Lisbon, Portugal

Ana Paula Caetano
University of Lisbon, Portugal

Isabel Freire
University of Lisbon, Portugal

Armanda Matos
University of Coimbra, Portugal

Cristina C. Vieira
University of Lisbon, Portugal

Teresa Pessoa
University of Lisbon, Portugal

João Amado
University of Lisbon, Portugal

ABSTRACT

This chapter review some of the principal personal and situational factors established through recent international research that contribute to explain the phenomenon of cyber-victimization and cyber-aggression among adolescents, as well as its relations with socio-demographic variables (age, sex, grade level). Personal factors, like emotions, motives, normative beliefs, and moral disengagement were discussed jointly with situational factors, as the role of peers, friends, school and family environments, in addition to the possible interactions of these variables on cyber-bullying. The chapter ends with a discussion of future directions about the research on this phenomenon, namely in what concern educational programs that can use digital technology to help adolescents, schools and families to deal with cyber-bullying.

DOI: 10.4018/978-1-5225-7128-5.ch014

INTRODUCTION

In the last decade cyberbullying has been the focus of attention of several researchers that emphasize the transcultural and transnational nature of the phenomenon (e.g., Kowalski, Giummetti, Schroeder, & Lattanner, 2014; Menesini, Smith, & Zukauskiene, 2010; Paladino, Menesini, Nocentini, Luik, Naruskov, Ucanok, … & Sheithauer, 2017) as well as its association with the proliferation of digital technologies use among children and youth (e.g., Livingstone, Haddon, Gorzig, & Olafsson, 2011; Twyman, Saylor, Taylor, & Comeaux, 2010).

Several studies (Beran & Li, 2007; Li, 2007; Ortega, Calmaestra, & Mora-Merchan, 2008; Ortega, Elipe, Mora-Merchan, Calmaestra, & Vega, 2009) suggested that cyberbullying is not a new type of bullying, but it's rather a new manifestation of bullying through digital means. Cyberbullying has been generally defined as repeated aggressive and intentional actions (as was bullying) but with the use of electronic devices (e.g., cell phones and computers) and associated programs (e.g., e-mail, social networks, and other Internet tools), by means of sending messages and/or creating websites that insult, denigrate, threaten, or harass others in some way (Amado, Freire, Matos, Vieira, & Pessoa, 2012; Amado, Matos, & Pessoa, 2009; Li, 2007; Kowalski, Limber, & Agaston, 2008; Martins, Veiga Simão, Freire, Caetano, & Matos, 2016; Smith, 2009; Willard, 2005). So it consists of an indirect form of bullying and frequently represents continuations of face-to-face bullying situations that amplify the roles played on face-to-face bullying or change those roles (Caetano, Amado, Martins, Veiga-Simão, Freire, & Pessoa, 2017; Kowalski, Giummetti, Schroeder, & Lattanner, 2014; Ortega, Calmaestra, & Mora-Merchan, 2008; Ortega, Elipe, Mora-Merchan, Calmaestra, & Vega, 2009; Twyman et al., 2010). Paladino et al. (2017) in study aimed to examine the role of different criteria in the perceived severity of cyberbullying incidents, and the differences between four countries (Estonia, Turley, Germany and Italy) found that the criteria used by adolescents are the same across the four countries, and include imbalance of power, intentionality, repetition and anonymity. However, the specific level of severity associated with each factor differs from country to country.

In contrast with other types of bullying, cyberbullying does not tend to decrease with age or grade level; generally it is found a pattern of increase from elementary to secondary education, and this tendency can also be found in college and university students (Francisco, Veiga Simão, Ferreira, Martins, 2015; Kowalski et al., 2014; Souza, Veiga Simão, Ferreira, & Ferreira, 2017; Walker, Sockman, & Koehn, 2011).

The enormous amount of research done in the last decade about cyberbullying allowed to identify several variables that are associated either with cyber-aggression as well as cyber-victimization and these variables can be grouped in three types:

socio-demographic (sex, grade level, age); personal (emotions, motives, moral beliefs, moral disengagement); and situational variables (role of peers and friends, family education and support, school climate) (Kowalski et al., 2014).

SOCIO-DEMOGRAPHIC AND PERSONAL FACTORS ASSOCIATED WITH CYBER-VICTIMISATION AND CYBER-AGGRESSION

In what concerns the prevalence of cyberbullying, the studies reveal some diversity from country to country and from school to school. For example, Li (2010) and Bartlett (2015) indicate values of 30% of adolescents that had been victimized. In a meta-analysis study on cyberbullying research conducted by Kowalski et al. (2014) it was estimated a prevalence of approximately 10% to 40% for cyber-victimization. A more recent literature review conducted by Aboujaoude, Savage, Starcevic, and Salame (2015) revealed that most cyber-victimization rates have ranged between 20% and 40%. Several authors (Matos, Vieira, Amado, Pessoa, & Martins, 2018; Smith, 2015) pointed out that this diversity reflects not just differences in the behavior itself but also some variations in the methodology used in the different studies, namely the definition of cyberbullying adopted.

In the exploratory study carried out in a private school (Freire, Alves, Breia, Conceição & Fragoso, 2013) in the frame of the research project "Cyberbullying – A diagnosis of the situation in Portugal", with participation of 87 students of the 8th grade (44 males and 43 females, aged 13 to 14 years), from middle-class / high-middle-class with diverse nationalities, almost 20% considered themselves victims of cyberbullying, and the most said they were observers, particularly of the victims. Only less than half of the students reported feelings of well-being in this school, with 17% explicitly expressing feelings of malaise (discrimination, fear, humiliation, exclusion and indifference), which they justified through the difficulty of living with the difference, namely cultural differences, in which predominate tensions linked to different national and cultural identities. These results alerted for better understanding of the relation between school climate and cyber-bullying.

In what concern the large sample used in the frame of the "Cyberbullying– A diagnosis of the situation in Portugal" project, with 3525 pupils from 6th, 8th, and 11th grades (mean age 13.6 years; 47,9% males and 52,1% females) from 23 middle schools and high schools located in Portugal, results showed that 7.6% (267) of the participants admitted to be cyber-victims sometimes and 2.6% (90) of these participants admitted to be cyber-victims at least once a month in the previous year. The percentage of cyber- aggressors was 3.9% (138 participants), with 1.5% (51) admitting to be involved in cyberbullying as aggressors at least once a month in the previous year (Martins et al., 2016; Matos et al., 2018). Websites were the most frequent medium used to cyber-bully, whilst sending insulting and harmful messages was the most frequently reported type of behavior. This study also aimed to understand the strategies used by students to deal with cyber-bullying. The strategies most frequently cited by the participants were technological strategies (e.g., changing passwords, blocking the bully), data that are in line with other studies (Parris et al., 2012). Active strategies like talking to the bully and becoming more careful were also reported by high percentages of students. Social strategies were cited by varying percentages of victims (Matos et al., 2018), although these are recommended as effective strategies in the literature (McGuckin et al., 2013).

Matos et al. (2018) also examined if victims knew the identity of those who cyber-bullied them and whether or not they are colleagues. Contrary to the spread idea that cyberbullying is mainly anonym (Ortega et al., 2008; Smith, 2009) this study reveals that just 26,8% of the victims stated they didn't know who was the bully, while 39,3% of the victims identify the aggressors as a classmate and 33,8% stated they knew they were not classmates.

In general studies revealed that boys are usually more involved in physical bullying but when sex are compared in terms of cyberbullying practices these differences don't emerge with the same consistence and this trend is not always found (Barlett & Coyne, 2014; Vieira et al., 2018).

Barlett and Coyne (2014) in a meta-analyses study about sex differences in cyberbullying found that males are usually more involved in cyber-aggression than females but this was not a big difference and it was moderated by age in the sense that females were more likely to report cyber-aggression during early adolescence and males were more likely to be cyber-aggressors during late adolescence. The authors consider that the interactive effect of sex and age could suggest the fact that cyberbullying is an indirect form of bullying, although not in a conclusive way (Barlett & Coyne, 2014).

In the project "Cyberbullying – A diagnosis of the situation in Portugal", rates of victimization were higher for females as well as for students in the 11th grade when compared to 6th grade and 8th grade. A two-way Anova on victimization frequency scores showed no significant interaction between sex and school grade. Regarding cyber-aggression, the interaction between sex and school grade was statistically significant, suggesting that that incidences of cyberbullying others are more frequent among boys in the 11th grade (Matos et al., 2018; Pessoa, Matos, Amado, Freire, & Caetano, 2017). As in other studies (Olweus, 2012; Ortega et al., 2009), data of the study cited above showed that, in both sexes, the tendency to become a cyber-perpetrator correlated positively with cyber victimization, revealing that some of adolescents played both roles (Matos et al., 2018; Vieira et al., 2016).

Motives most frequently mentioned for experiencing and engaging in cyber-aggression by girls, in the above cited study, were the breakdown of friendships and social rejection by peers and they were more able than boys to disclose the motives and emotions involved in cyber-acts. Taking gender socialization values and norms and the characteristics of this stage of development into consideration, we found that the motives for cyberbullying perceived by both groups of victims and the aggressors revealed two common sex differences, reflecting what tends to be valued more by girls than boys in their relationships with peers: the breakdown of emotional ties in friendships and fears of social rejection by others. These findings are consistent with the characteristics of relationships established by adolescent females with their same-sex peers, which tend to foster self-disclosure with their friends more than boys and display emotionally deeper interactions with them. Adolescent boys, who practise cyber-aggression, reported they do it because they were upset with the victim, as a justification of their behaviour, more than girls (Vieira et al., 2016).

The cited research also analysed the emotions associated with the experiences of cyber-aggressor or cyber-victim and data reveal that those experiences are different accordingly with the role played in cyber-bullying. So, cyber-victims feel more frequently the emotions of sadness, anger with will of revenge, and fear and cyber-aggressors feel more frequently happiness, indifference and relieve. It was also found that there were significant differences between the emotions experienced by cyber-victims and those that cyber-aggressors attribute to them, revealing that they have difficulties in understanding the impact of their behaviour on victims. Contrarily with what usually happened in studies in face-to-face bullying, guilty was not frequent in cyber-victims. In some of the schools it was also noticed the presence of emotions related to impotence and feelings of lack of support in cyber-victims and some feelings of guilty in cyber-aggressors, revealing the importance that moral ambience of schools could have on these behaviours (Caetano, Freire, Veiga-Simão, Martins, & Pessoa, 2016). These data are congruent with those from other studies (e.g. König, Golwitzer, & Steffegen, 2010; Li, 2010; Ortega et al., 2009; Ortega et al., 2012) that also found that negative emotions of sadness, anger with will of revenge, and fear were more experienced by cyber-victims and that positive emotions like satisfaction, relive, pleasure, amusement, and lack of empathy for victims were frequent in cyber-aggressors, even when adolescents play both roles, as cyber-aggressor and cyber-victim (with revenge mediating the transition of the role of cyber-victim to cyber-aggressor for some of the adolescents).

Ak, Özdemir and Kuzucu (2015) in a study about the mediating role of anger in cyberbullying with undergraduate Turkish students found that cyber-victimization had both direct effects on cyber-aggression and indirect effects mediated by anger-in (emotion of anger experienced inward). More recently, Görzig (2016) also report that suicidal ideation is associated with nasty web exposure and that this incident had a bigger impact if the adolescents were being targeted as cyber-victims.

In what concern motives attribute to display cyber-aggression, in the study cited above there were divergences in the perceptions of cyber-aggressors and cyber-victims. The most frequent motives reported by cyber-aggressors were pleasure, amusing, escape to boring, affiliation with groups, friendship rupture, and revenge in reaction to previous aggression. Cyber-victims perceive as the most frequent motives of cyber-aggressors envy, jealousy, lack of respect, immaturity, and a need to exercise power of cyber-aggressors over others (Caetano et al., 2017; Li, 2010). As noted above motives were different for both sexes: girls use more affiliation motives and boys use more hedonistic motives (Caetano et al., 2017; Vieira, et al., 2016). Motives were also related with age, with younger adolescents reporting more reactive motives as affiliation and envy, while the oldest ones reported more proactive motives, as amusing and enjoyment. These results are congruent with other studies that found that the youngest ones used more reactive motives for bullying (Caetano et al., 2017; Salmivalli & Niemenen, 2002). Other studies also report that cyber-victims can also experience stress and suicidal ideation (Gôrzig, 2015; Kowalski et al., 2014; Ortega et al., 2012).

Motives and emotions related with cyberbullying seem to be coherent, in the sense that enjoyment and amusing emotions were associated with hedonistic motives and emotions of revenge were associated with reactive motives as friendship rupture and reaction to previous aggressions (Caetano et al, 2017). These data seem to fit some theoretical suggestions about aggression that propose to divide it in reactive aggression and proactive aggression in face-to-face situations, accordingly to its nature and actuation. So amusement and hedonistic motives can be associated with proactive cyber-aggression and friendship rupture and revenge can be associated with reactive cyber-aggression, suggesting that the two types of aggression found in face–to-face situations are also valid in cyberspace (Caetano et al, 2016; Poulin & Boivin, 2000; Salmivalli & Niemenen, 2002).

Peluchette, Karl, Wood and Williams (2015) in a study with American and Australian young adults, about the risky social network behaviors that could contribute to cyber-victimization, concluded that extroversion, openness, and self-disclosure in social networks, as facebook, could be predictors of cyber-victimization, results that suggest some lines of action in order to help adolescents to learn about how to protect themselves on social networks.

In the meta-analysis study referred above about cyber-bullying, Kowalski et al. (2014) concluded that the strongest associations with cyberbullying perpetration were normative beliefs about aggression and moral disengagement, and the strongest associations with cyber-victimization were stress and suicidal ideation. Perren and Gutzwiller-Heltenfinger (2012) in a study with Suisse adolescents found that: bullying was highly predictable of cyberbullying; moral disengagement justifications were more predictive of bullying compared to cyber-bullying; and moral emotions, as reduced feelings of guilt and lack of remorse, predicted both bullying and cyber-bullying. The authors concluded that moral standards and moral affect are important to understand individual differences in involvement in bullying and cyberbullying conducts.

SITUATIONAL FACTORS ASSOCIATED WITH CYBER-VICTIMISATION AND CYBER-AGGRESSION

In reference to situational factors, the results of several authors' research suggest that group of peers; family; and school variables can be associated with cyberbullying phenomenon. Variables as parental support, parental monitoring, school ethos, and pressure of the peer group influence both cyber-aggression and cyber-victimization (Hinduja, & Patchin, 2013; Kowalski et al., 2014; Martins et al, 2016; Veiga Simão, Ferreira, Freire, Caetano, Martins, & Vieira, 2017). In the meta-analyses research of Kowalski et al. (2014), the strongest associations with situational variables were related with school and family and suggested that school variables that were inversely linked to engagement in cyberbullying included positive school climate and school safety. Regarding family variables, it seems that less frequent cyber-victimization is associated with parental discussion about online behavior and that cyber-bullies had weaker emotional bonds with their parents and less frequent monitoring of online activities (Kowalski et al., 2014).

Specifically concerning relationships between cyber-bullying, family and peers Fanti, Demetriou and Hawa (2012) posited that Cyprus peers aged 11 to 14 influenced cyberbullying involvement, but parent support significantly decreased the probability of involvement in such conducts. The authors concluded that their results highlight the role of parents in protection against cyber-bullying, because adolescences that reported more family support also had fewer incidents of cyber-aggression and cyber-victimization a year later (Fanti et al., 2012). Hinduja and Patchin (2013) revealed that American adolescent' peers influenced cyberbullying but the expectation of punishment for such conducts from adults reduced the likelihood of involvement. According to Hinduja and Patchin (2013), cyberbullying offences are associated with the perceptions teenagers have of their peers' similar behavior, as well as the probability of adults' reprimands. What is more, respondents who were less likely to participate in cyberbullying believed that significant adults in their life would punish them.

Sasson and Mesch (2014, 2017) in a study with 495 Israelis adolescents try to understand how peers' norms and family mediation (active guidance, restrictive supervision and non-intervention) could influence involvement in cyberbullying. The results showed that restrictive parent supervision and active guidance could be effective in minimizing several on-line risks, however peers injunctive' norms about on-line activities seem to had a stronger influence on on-line risky behaviors when compared to parent mediation, confirming the idea that in adolescence the peer group has more influence on adolescent's behaviors than parents. The results also suggested that the likelihood of being bullied on the Internet is associated with both risky behavior online and the norms prevalent within the adolescent peer group, and that just restrictive parental supervision had a significant effect on behaviors. The authors conclude that adolescents that exhibit on-line risky behaviors are older boys with frequent use of platforms that facilitate communication with strangers, came from families with little cohesion and parents that don't supervise their internet use, and simultaneously are connected with peers that give support to those behaviors (Sasson & Mesch, 2014; 2017).

Wegge, Vendebosch, Eggermont, and Pabian (2016) conduct a longitudinal study, with Belgian early adolescents, to assess the reciprocal effects of cyberbullyingand traditional bullying on social status, assessed with two measures: sociometric popularity and perceived popularity. The authors evidenced that cyberbullying perpetration predicted perceived popularity over time but not sociometric status, although traditional bullying was not associated with subsequent popularity, neither with sociometric status. However perceived popularity didn't precede cyber-bulling perpetration. The authors conclude that cyberbullying can function as a tool to eventually change the hierarchy of perceived popularity at school and may explain why this behavior increases in the secondary. These data suggested that schools must deal and prevent this phenomena because even it doesn't happen inside the schools its antecedents and specially its consequences often occur in schools (Weege et al., 2016).

The role of peers has been also evidenced in studies (Ferreira, Veiga Simão, Ferreira, Souza, & Francisco, 2016; Olenik-Shemesh, Heiman, & Segal, 2015) that focus specially on the actions that bystanders display when they face cyber-bullying. Olenik et al. (2015) in a study with Israelis adolescents identified passive bystanders and active bystanders and noticed that just 36% of the bystanders of cyberbullying offered direct help to the cyber-victims. The authors identified the active bystanders as being more often older girls, having socio-emotional support from significant others and experiencing lower levels of loneliness, when compared to the passive bystanders.

Li (2010) in a study with Canadian children and adolescents found that victims often don't tell anybody because they were afraid of an escalation of the problem and also noticed that most of bystanders didn't do nothing about it, because they think nobody would do nothing, teachers included, and also because they were afraid of being cyberbullied.

Ferreira et al. (2016) in a study comparing Portuguese and Brazilian college studies tried to assess if the fact of being an active bystander of cyberbullying that intervene could influence the probability of becoming a victim or an aggressor later. The results showed that being a passive bystander of cyberbullying (with no intervention) predisposes more to be a victim or an aggressor of cyberbullying later, especially in the Brazilian sample were students also noticed more incidents of cyberbullying than the Portuguese. Bystander active intervention seems to be less associated with future active involvement in cyberbullying, as a victim or an aggressor.

In what concern the study cited above about cyberbullying in Portugal ("Cyberbullying– A diagnosis of the situation in Portugal"), the study had also as main objectives to examine the relation between family and school environments and cyberbullying conducts (as cyber-aggressor or as cyber-victim). After a hierarchical regression analysis it was evidenced that school climate was more predictive of conducts of cyber-victimization and family dimensions were more predictive of cyber-aggression. Although both variables have an effect on both behaviors, adolescent's perceptions of bad family environment were more associated to cyber-aggression and perceptions of bad school environment were more associated with cyber-victimization. When considering just the various family dimensions, assessed in the study, it was also evidenced that both perceptions of family support and family rules were situational factors that could protect against cyberbullying. Results showed that lack of family support was more predictive for cyber-victimization and lack of family rules together with lack of family support was more predictive for cyber-aggression or of the simultaneous condition (both cyber-victim and cyber-aggressor). These data suggested that schools can have a role in preventing these behaviors, investing in media education, and promoting safe and healthy environments that could prevent cyberbullying. Also parents that promote rules to use Internet, through dialogue with adolescents, under a warm and supportive relationship seem to provide a protection factor against cyberbullying (Martins et al., 2016).

The above-cited study intended also to explore how the perception of school climate could influence the reporting of episodes of cyberbullying by adolescents to teachers and school staff. Results showed that even though cyber-victims reported cyber-victimization more to friends and parents, those who told teachers about their experience, tended to report more positive perceptions of their school climate. Sex and age did not play a significant role in the relationship between cyber-victimization and perceived school climate. These data evidenced the important role of school because it focused on whether adolescent cyber-victims' perceived school climate was related to whom they turned to report the incident. Specifically, this study was able to provide an understanding of how these adolescents perceived their school climate and how teachers played an important role in these perceptions, when adolescents experiencing cyber-victimization need their help (Veiga Simão et al., 2017). Climate university campus seems also to affect the practices of cyberbullying of Portuguese and Brazilian college students, with more incidence in the Brazilian sample (Sousa et al, 2017).

FUTURE RESEARCH DIRECTIONS

The results from research on cyberbullying that were synthesized in this chapter show the complexity of the phenomenon, its interactive nature and the challenges that researchers face when it comes to find a consensual definition and suitable way to measure cyber-victimization and cyber-aggression behaviors. The difficulties became ever greater if we think about what distinguishes those who were born in the age of technology – digital natives – and older generations, that are now considered digital immigrants (Prensky, 2001).

Livingstone et al. (2011), in a study with 25 000 adolescents about usage of Internet in several European countries, emphasize that one third of the families of these adolescents knew less about digital devices and Internet than their sons and daughters. Nguyên and Mark (2014) noticed, in a research about parents and educators perspectives about digital devices and Internet, that they have different knowledge about how adolescents use those devices, with parents having more difficulties keeping up to date the progress of technology and its use by their adolescents.

The complex and evolving world of digital technologies and Internet seem to require more effort in developing programs and manuals to parents and teachers in view to understand and deal with the phenomenon of cyber-bullying, as well as to the exposure to nasty themes on the Internet and diverse risky behaviors associated with it. In future it should be important to know better what knowledge parents have of what their sons and daughters do with mobiles devices and Internet and how they deal with on-line risky behaviors from their adolescents.

Although cyberbullying does not necessarily happen at school, because many adolescents have access to the Internet at home and other spaces (Festl, 2016; Livingstone et al., 2011), several studies (Twyman et al., 2010; Veiga Simão et al., 2017; Weege et al., 2016) highlight that school variables (as for example the fact that good school climate is important to deal with cyber-victimization) play a role in cyber-bullying. Furthermore, since cyberbullying can be a continuation of bullying at school, as various studies have already indicated (Olweus, 2012; Ortega et al., 2009, 2012; Twyman et al., 2010), the teachers are of special importance in aiding these students to deal with this phenomenon and prevent cyber-bullying. Also more studies about the bystander behavior when facing cyberbullying incidents, especially about their motives to intervene or not, could better clarify the role of peers in the interruption or escalate of cyberbullying behavior.

Some manuals (e.g., Jäger, 2010; Jäger, Stelter, Amado, Matos, & Pessoa, 2012) have been developed to help parents and teachers to deal with cyberbullying incidents, but these could be not enough. Educational programs could be designed to embrace a whole community approach, including schools, families and peers. These three domains are the main sources of efficacy information for children and adolescents and therefore, should be considered as part of the focus for effective intervention programmes (Paul, Smith, & Blumberg, 2012). Programmes could be developed and preview software to include in digital devices to help adolescents to detect, be alert and block nasty messages. Educational games with themes that include bullying and cyberbullying could also be developed in view to attract adolescents to use for educational purposes the same devices they use in a diary and routine base.

Cyberbullying specifically represents a phenomenon of social interaction (Souza et al., 2017) and studying the intentional and conscious use of language to harm others online offers prospects of an enriched psychological understanding of the cyberbullying phenomenon. We believe that the examining of adolescents' written expressions in incidents of cyberbullying and their perceived management of this language could be better identified by future innovative technological resources in online platforms. So for future research, greater use should be made of qualitative research strategies to listen and read to what adolescent, boys and girls, say about matters that researchers are still unaware of and therefore cannot apprehend using quantitative instruments. Cross-cultural issues may also play an important role in language usage, so future studies should include adolescent participants from several countries.

Although often been practiced in private rooms cyberbullying seems to be highly influenced by peers, family and school climates and the contribution and interaction of these factors should be considered in future research.

ACKNOWLEDGMENT

This study was conducted in the frame of the project "Cyberbullying – a diagnosis of the situation in Portugal," financed by The Foundation for Science and Technology (program PTDC/CPE-CED/108563/2008) in a partnership with the University of Coimbra and the University of Lisbon, coordinated by professor João Amado.

REFERENCES

Aboujaoude, E., Savage, M. W., Starcevic, V., & Salame, W. O. (2015). Cyberbullying: Review of an old problem gone viral. *The Journal of Adolescent Health*, *57*(1), 10–18. doi:10.1016/j.jadohealth.2015.04.011 PMID:26095405

Ak, S., Özdemir, Y., & Kuzucu, Y. (2015). Cybervictimization and cyberbullying: The mediating role of anger, don't anger me! *Computers in Human Behavior*, *49*, 437–443. doi:10.1016/j.chb.2015.03.030

Amado, J., Freire, I., Matos, A., Vieira, C., & Pessoa, T. (2012). O cyberbullying e a escola: uma análise da situação em Portugal [The cyberbullying and the school: analysis of the situation in Portugal]. In *Atas do III Colóquio Luso-Brasileiro de Sociologia da Educação - Problemas contemporâneos da educação no Brasil e em Portugal: desafios à pesquisa* [Proceedings of the III Congress Luso-brasilien of Socioloy of Education – Contemporary problems of education in Portugal and Brasil: challenges to research]. Rio de Janeiro, Brazil: Academic Press.

Amado, J., Matos, A., & Pessoa, T. (2009). Cyberbullying: Um novo campo de investigação e de formação [Cyberbullying: A new field of research and training]. In B. Silva, A. Lozano, L. Almeida, & M. Uzquiano (Eds.), *Atas do Congresso Galeco-Português de Psicopedagogia* [Proceedings of the X International Congress Galician-Portuguese of Psychopedagogy] (pp. 262-373). Academic Press. Retrieved from http://www.educacion.udc.es/grupos/gipdae/documentos/congreso/Xcongreso/pdfs/t1/t1c11.pdf

Barlett, C. (2015). Predicting adolescent's cyberbullying: A longitudinal risk analysis. *Journal of Adolescence*, *41*, 86–95. doi:10.1016/j.adolescence.2015.02.006 PMID:25828551

Barlett, C., & Coyne, S. (2014). A meta-analysis of sex differences in cyberbullyingbehavior: The moderating role of age. *Aggressive Behavior*, *40*(5), 474–488. doi:10.1002/ab.21555 PMID:25098968

Beran, T., & Li, Q. (2007). The relationship between cyberbullying and school bullying. *Journal of Student Well-being*, *1*(2), 15–33.

Caetano, A. P., Amado, J., Martins, M. J. D., Veiga-Simão, A. M., Freire, I., & Pessoa, M. T. (2017). Cyberbullying: motivos da agressão na perspectiva de jovens portugueses [Cyberbullying: aggression motives in the perspective of young Portuguese]. *Education and Society*, *38*(141), 1017–1034. doi:10.1590/es0101-73302017139852

Caetano, A. P., Freire, I., Veiga-Simão, A. M., Martins, M. J. D., & Pessoa, M. T. (2016). Emoções no Cyberbullying: um estudo com adolescentes portugueses [Emotions in Cyberbullying: a study with Portuguese adolescents]. *Education and Research, 42*(1), 199–212.

Fanti, K., Demetriou, A., & Hawa, V. (2012). A longitudinal study of cyberbullying: Examining risk and protective factors. *European Journal of Developmental Psychology, 9*(2), 168–181. doi:10.1080/17405629.2011.643169

Ferreira, P., Veiga Simão, A. M., Ferreira, A., Souza, S., & Francisco, S. (2016). Student bystander behavior and cultural issues in cyberbullying: When actions speak louder than words. *Computers in Human Behavior, 60,* 301–311. doi:10.1016/j. chb.2016.02.059

Festl, R. (2016). Perpetrors on the internet. Analysing individual and structural explanation factors of cyberbullying in school context. *Computers in Human Behavior, 59,* 237–248. doi:10.1016/j.chb.2016.02.017

Francisco, S., Veiga Simão, A. M., Ferreira, P. C., & Martins, M. J. D. (2015). Cyberbullying: The hidden side of college students. *Computers in Human Behavior, 43,* 167–182. doi:10.1016/j.chb.2014.10.045

Freire, I., Alves, M. M., Breia, A. P., Conceição, D., & Fragoso, L. (2013). Cyberbullying e Ambiente Escolar: Um Estudo Exploratório e Colaborativo entre a Escola e a Universidade [Cyberbullyingand school climate: An exploratory and collaborative study between school and university]. *Revista Portuguesa de Pedagogia, 47*(1), 43–64. doi:10.14195/1647-8614_47-2_3

Görzig, A. (2016). Adolescents' viewing of suicide-related web content and psychological problems: Differentiating the roles of cyberbullying involvement. *Cyberpsychology, Behavior, and Social Networking, 19*(8), 502–509. doi:10.1089/ cyber.2015.0419 PMID:27448043

Hinduja, S., & Patchin, J. (2013). Social influences on cyberbullying behaviours among middle and high school students. *Journal of Youth and Adolescence, 42*(5), 711–722. doi:10.100710964-012-9902-4 PMID:23296318

Jäger, T. (Ed.). (2010). *Taking action against cyberbullying – Training Manual.* Landau: Verlag Empirische Padagogik. Retrieved from http://www.cybertraining-project.org/book/

Jäger, T., Stelter, C., Amado, J., Matos, A., & Pessoa, T. (Eds.). (2012). *Cyberbullying - Um manual de formação de pais* [Cyberbullying: a Parents' training manual]. Retrieved from http://ct4p.zepf.eu/CT4P_Training_manual_PT.pdf

König, A., Golwitzer, M., & Steffegen, G. (2010). Cyberbullying as an act of revenge? *Journal of Australian of Guidance and Counselling, 20*(2), 210–224. doi:10.1375/ajgc.20.2.210

Kowalski, R., Giummetti, G., Schroeder, A., & Lattanner, M. (2014). Bullying in the digital age: A critical review and meta-analysis of cyberbullying research among youth. *Psychological Bulletin*, 1–61. doi:10.1037/a0035618 PMID:24512111

Kowalski, R., Limber, S., & Agaston, P. (2008). *Cyberbullying*. Oxford, UK: Blackwell P.

Li, Q. (2007). New bottle but old wine: A research of cyberbullying in schools. *Computers in Human Behavior, 23*(4), 1777–1791. doi:10.1016/j.chb.2005.10.005

Li, Q. (2010). Cyberbullying in high schools: A study of students' behavior and beliefs about this phenomenon. *Journal of Aggression, Maltreatment & Trauma, 19*(4), 372–392. doi:10.1080/10926771003788979

Livingstone, S., Haddon, L., Gorzig, A., & Olafsson, K. (2011). *Risks and safety on the Internet: the perspective of European children. Full findings*. Retrieved from www.eukidsonline.net

Martins, M. J. D., Veiga Simão, A., Freire, I., Caetano, A. P., & Matos, A. (2016). Cyber-victimization and cyber-aggression among Portuguese adolescents: The relation to family support and family rules. *International Journal of Cyber Behavior, Psychology and Learning, 6*(3), 65–78. doi:10.4018/IJCBPL.2016070105

Matos, A., Vieira, C., Amado, J., Pessoa, T., & Martins, M. J. D. (2018). Cyberbullying in Portuguese Schools: Prevalence and Characteristics. *Journal of School Violence, 17*(1), 123-137. DOI: 10.1080/15388220.2016.1263796

McGukin, C., Perren, S., Corcoran, L., Cowie, H., Dehue, F., Sevcikova, A., ...Volink, T. (2013). Coping with cyberbullying: How can we prevent cyberbullying and how victims can cope with it. In P. K. Smith & G. Steffengen (Eds.), Cyberbullying: through the new media. Findings from an international network (pp. 121-135). East Sussex, UK: Psychology Press.

Menesini, E., Smith, P., & Zukauskiene, R. (Eds.). (2010). Cyberbullying. COST IS 0801. Vilnius, Lithuania: Mylolas Romeris University Publishing Center.

Nguyên, T. T., & Mark, L. (2014). Cyberbullying, sexting, and on-line sharing a comparison of parent and school faculty perspectives. *Journal of Cyber Behavior, Psychology and Learning, 4*(1), 76-86.

Olenik-Shemesh, D., Heiman, T., & Segal, E. (2015). Bystander's behavior in cyberbullying episodes: Active and passive patterns in the context of socio-emotional factors. *Journal of Interpersonal Violence*, 1–26. doi:10.1177/0886260515585531 PMID:25948644

Olweus, D. (2012). Cyberbullying: An overrated phenomenon? *European Journal of Developmental Psychology*, *9*(5), 520–538. doi:10.1080/17405629.2012.682358

Ortega, R., Calmaestra, J., & Mora-Merchan, J. (2008). Cyberbullying. *International Journal of Psychology & Psychological Therapy*, *8*(2), 183–192.

Ortega, R., Elipe, P., Mora-Merchan, J., Calmaestra, J., & Vega, E. (2009). The emotional impact on victims of tradicional bullying and cyberbullying. *Journal of Psychology, 217*(4), 197-204. doi: 10.27/0044-3409.217.4.197

Ortega, R., Elipe, P., Mora-Merchán, J. A., Genta, M. L., Brighi, A., Guarini, A. K., ... Tippett, N. (2012). The Emotional impact of bullying and cyberbullying on victims: A European cross-national study. *Aggressive Behavior*, *38*(5), 342–356. doi:10.1002/ab.21440 PMID:22782434

Paladino, B., Menesini, E., Nocentini, A., Luik, P., Naruskov, K., Ucanok, Z., ... Sheithauer, H. (2017). Perceived severity of cyberbullying: Differences and similarities across four countries. *Frontiers in Psychology*, *8*, 1–12. doi:10.3389/fpsyg.2017.01524 PMID:28197108

Parris, L., Varjas, K., Meyers, J., & Cutts, H. (2012). High school students' perceptions of coping with cyberbullying. *Youth & Society*, *44*(2), 284–306. doi:10.1177/0044118X11398881

Paul, S., Smith, P., & Blumberg, H. (2012). Revisiting cyberbullyingin schools using the quality circle approach. *School Psychology International*, *33*(5), 492–504. doi:10.1177/0143034312445243

Peluchette, J. V., Karl, K., Wood, C., & Williams, J. (2015). Cyberbullying victimization: Do victims' personality and risky social network contribute to the problem? *Computers in Human Behavior*, *52*, 424–435. doi:10.1016/j.chb.2015.06.028

Peren, S., & Gutzwiller-Heltenfinger, E. (2012). Cyberbullying and traditional bullying in adolescence: Differential roles of moral disengagement, moral emotions and moral values. *European Journal of Developmental Psychology*, *9*(2), 195–209. doi:10.1080/17405629.2011.643168

Pessoa, T., Matos, A., Amado, J., Freire, I., & Caetano, A. P. (2017). Cyberbullying entre adolescentes y jóvenes portugueses. Contribución para una definición de los perfiles de víctimas y de agresores [Cyberbullying among Portuguese adolescents and youth. Contributions for a description of victims and aggressors profiles]. *Communication Education*, *297/298*, 11–19.

Poulin, F., & Boivin, M. (2000). Reactive and proactive aggression: Evidence of a two factor model. *Psychological Assessment*, *12*(2), 115–122. doi:10.1037/1040-3590.12.2.115 PMID:10887757

Prensky, M. (2001). Digital natives, digital immigrants. *On the Horizon, 9*(5). Retrieved from: http://www.marcprensky.com/writing/Prensky%20-%20Digital%20Natives,%20Digital%20Immigrants%20-%20Part1.pdf

Salmivalli, C., & Niemenen, E. (2002). Proactive and reactive aggression among school bullies, victims, and bully-victims. *Aggressive Behavior*, *28*(1), 30–44. doi:10.1002/ab.90004

Sasson, H., & Mesch, G. (2017). The role of parental mediation and peer norms on likelihood of cyberbullying. *The Journal of Genetic Psychology*, *178*(1), 15–27. doi:10.1080/00221325.2016.1195330 PMID:27391950

Sasson, H., & Mesch, G. S. (2014). Parental mediation, peer norms and risky online behaviors among adolescents. *Computers in Human Behavior*, *33*, 32–38. doi:10.1016/j.chb.2013.12.025

Smith, P. (2009). Cyberbullying – Abusive relationships in cyberspace. *The Journal of Psychology*, *217*(4), 180–181. doi:10.1027/0044-3409.217.4.180

Smith, P. K. (2015). The nature of cyberbullying and what we can do about it. *Journal of Research in Special Educational Needs*, *15*(3), 176–184. doi:10.1111/1471-3802.12114

Souza, S. B., Veiga Simão, A. M., Ferreira, A. I., & Ferreira, P. C. (2017). University students' perceptions of campus climate, cyberbullying and cultural issues: Implications for theory and practice. *Studies in Higher Education*, 1–16. doi:10.1080/03075079.2017.1307818

Twyman, W., Saylor, C., Taylor, A., & Comeaux, C. (2010). Comparing children and adolescents engaged in cyberbullying to matched peers. *Cyberpsychology, Behavior, and Social Networking*, *13*(2), 195–200. doi:10.1089/cyber.2009.0137 PMID:20528278

Veiga Simão, A. M., Ferreira, P. C., Freire, I., Caetano, A. P., Martins, M. J. D., & Vieira, C. (2017). Adolescent cybervictimization – Who they turn to and their perceived school climate. *Journal of Adolescence*, *58*, 12–23. doi:10.1016/j. adolescence.2017.04.009 PMID:28475930

Vieira, C. C., Matos, A., Amado, J., Freire, I., & Veiga-Simão, A. M. (2016). Boys' and girls' cyberbullying behaviours in Portugal: exploring sex differences in adolescence using gender lenses. *Ex aequo*, *34*, 143-159. Retrieved from: http://www. scielo.mec.pt/scielo.php?script=sci_arttext&pid=S0874-55602016000200011&ln g=pt&nrm=iso&tlng=en

Walker, C., Sockman, B., & Koehn, S. (2011). An exploratory study of cyberbullying with undergraduate university students. *TechTrends*, *55*(2), 31–38. doi:10.100711528-011-0481-0

Wegge, D., Vendebosch, V., Eggermont, S., & Pabian, S. (2016). Popularity through on-line harm: The longitudinal associations between cyberbullying and sociometric status in early adolescence. *The Journal of Early Adolescence*, *36*(1), 86–107. doi:10.1177/0272431614556351

WillardN. (2005). *Educator' guide to cyberbullying and cyberthreats*. Retrieved from http://www.accem.org/pdf/cbcteducator.pdf

Compilation of References

Abbott, H. (2002). *The Cambridge introduction to narrative*. Cambridge, UK: Cambridge University Press.

Aboujaoude, E., Savage, M. W., Starcevic, V., & Salame, W. O. (2015). Cyberbullying: Review of an old problem gone viral. *The Journal of Adolescent Health*, *57*(1), 10–18. doi:10.1016/j.jadohealth.2015.04.011 PMID:26095405

Adams, C. (2010). Cyberbullying: How to make it stop. *Instructor*, *120*(2), 44–49.

Adan, A., Archer, S. N., Hidalgo, M. P., Di Milia, L., Natale, V., & Randler, C. (2012). Circadian typology: A comprehensive review. *Chronobiology International*, *29*(9), 1153–1175. doi:10.3109/07420528.2012.719971 PMID:23004349

Adan, A., & Natale, V. (2002). Gender differences in morningness-eveningness preference. *Chronobiology International*, *19*(4), 709–720. doi:10.1081/CBI-120005390 PMID:12182498

Adler, N. E., & Page, A. E. K. (2008). *Cancer care for the whole patient: Meeting psychosocial health needs*. Institute of Medicine: Committee on Psychosocial Services to Cancer Patients/Families in a Community Setting Board on Health Care Services.

Ajzen, I. (1991). The Theory of Planned Behavior. *Organizational Behavior and Human Decision Processes*, *50*(2), 179–211. doi:10.1016/0749-5978(91)90020-T

Ajzen, I. (2002). Perceived Behavioral Control, Self-Efficacy, Locus of Control, and the Theory of Planned Behavior. *Journal of Applied Social Psychology*, *32*(4), 665–683. doi:10.1111/j.1559-1816.2002.tb00236.x

Ajzen, I., & Madden, T. J. (1986). Prediction of goal-directed behavior: Attitudes, intention and perceived behavioral control. *Journal of Experimental Social Psychology*, *22*(5), 453–474. doi:10.1016/0022-1031(86)90045-4

Akashi, M., Soma, H., Yamamoto, T., Tsugitomi, A., Yamashita, S., Yamamoto, T., ... Node, K. (2010). Noninvasive method for assessing the human circadian clock using hair follicle cells. *Proceedings of the National Academy of Sciences of the United States of America*, *107*(35), 15643–15648. doi:10.1073/pnas.1003878107 PMID:20798039

Akdeniz, Y. (2008). *Internet child pornography and the law: National and international responses.* Burlington, VT: Ashgate Publishing Co.

Ak, S., Özdemir, Y., & Kuzucu, Y. (2015). Cybervictimization and cyberbullying: The mediating role of anger, don't anger me! *Computers in Human Behavior, 49,* 437–443. doi:10.1016/j.chb.2015.03.030

Algar, S. (2017, February 1). *Cyberbullying in city schools soars 351% in just two years.* Retrieved from www.nypost.com

Alivecor Heart Monitor. (2018). Retrieved from https://www.alivecor.com/

Allen, J. D., Savadatti, S., & Levy, A. G. (2009). The transition from breast cancer 'patient' to 'survivor.'. *Psycho-Oncology, 18*(1), 71–78. doi:10.1002/pon.1380 PMID:18613299

Alonso, A., & Oiarzabal, P. J. (2010). *Diasporas in the new media age: Identity, politics and community.* University of Nevada Press.

Alonso-Valerdi, L. M., Salido-Ruiz, R. A., & Ramirez-Mendoza, R. A. (2015). Motor imagery based brain–computer interfaces: An emerging technology to rehabilitate motor deficits. *Neuropsychologia, 79,* 354–363. doi:10.1016/j.neuropsychologia.2015.09.012 PMID:26382749

Amado, J., Freire, I., Matos, A., Vieira, C., & Pessoa, T. (2012). O cyberbullying e a escola: uma análise da situação em Portugal [The cyberbullying and the school: analysis of the situation in Portugal]. In *Atas do III Colóquio Luso-Brasileiro de Sociologia da Educação - Problemas contemporâneos da educação no Brasil e em Portugal: desafios à pesquisa* [Proceedings of the III Congress Luso-brasilien of Socioloy of Education – Contemporary problems of education in Portugal and Brasil: challenges to research]. Rio de Janeiro, Brazil: Academic Press.

Amado, J., Matos, A., & Pessoa, T. (2009). Cyberbullying: Um novo campo de investigação e de formação [Cyberbullying: A new field of research and training]. In B. Silva, A. Lozano, L. Almeida, & M. Uzquiano (Eds.), *Atas do Congresso Galeco-Português de Psicopedagogia* [Proceedings of the X International Congress Galician-Portuguese of Psychopedagogy] (pp. 262-373). Academic Press. Retrieved from http://www.educacion.udc.es/grupos/gipdae/documentos/congreso/Xcongreso/pdfs/t1/t1c11.pdf

American Academy of Pediatrics. (2011). *Clinical report: The impact of social media on children, adolescents, and families.* Retrieved from www.pediatrics.org/cgi/doi/10.1542/peds.2011-0054

Amichai–Hamburger, Y., Lamdan, N., Madiel, R., & Hayat, T. (2008). Personality characteristics of Wikipedia members. *Cyberpsychology & Behavior, 11*(6), 679–681. doi:10.1089/cpb.2007.0225 PMID:18954273

Andujar, M., & Gilbert, J. E. (2013). *Let's learn!: enhancing user's engagement levels through passive brain-computer interfaces.* Paper presented at the CHI' 13 Extended Abstracts on Human Factors in Computing Systems. 10.1145/2468356.2468480

Ang, K. K., Chua, K. S. G., Phua, K. S., Wang, C., Chin, Z. Y., Kuah, C. W. K., ... Guan, C. (2015). A randomized controlled trial of EEG-based motor imagery brain-computer interface robotic rehabilitation for stroke. *Clinical EEG and Neuroscience*, *46*(4), 310–320. doi:10.1177/1550059414522229 PMID:24756025

Ang, K. K., Guan, C., Phua, K. S., Wang, C., Zhou, L., Tang, K. Y., ... Chua, K. S. G. (2014). Brain-computer interface-based robotic end effector system for wrist and hand rehabilitation: Results of a three-armed randomized controlled trial for chronic stroke. *Frontiers in Neuroengineering*, 7. PMID:25120465

Ang, R. P. (2016). Cyberbullying: Its prevention and intervention strategies. In D. Sibnath (Ed.), *Child safety, welfare and well-being: Issues and challenges* (pp. 25–38). Springer. doi:10.1007/978-81-322-2425-9_3

Animal Crush Video Prohibition Act (2010), Pub. L. 111–294, 124 Stat. 3177

Antonopoulous, N., Veglis, A., Gardikiotis, A., Kotsakis, R., & Kalliris, G. (2015). Web third-person effect in structural aspects of the information on media websites. *Computers in Human Behavior*, *44*, 48–58. doi:10.1016/j.chb.2014.11.022

Aoyama, I., Utsumi, S., & Hasegawa, M. (2011). Cyberbullying in Japan: Cases, government reports, adolescent relational aggression and parental monitoring roles. In Q. Li, D. Cross, & P. K. Smith (Eds.), *Bullying in the global playground: Research from an international perspective*. Oxford, UK: Wiley-Blackwell.

Appadurai, A. (1997). Fieldwork in the Era of Globalization. *Anthropology and Humanism*, *22*(1), 1. doi:10.1525/ahu.1997.22.1.115

Aricak, T., Siyahhan, S., Uzunhasanoglu, A., Saribeyoglu, S., Ciplak, S., Yilmaz, N., & Memmedov, C. (2008). Cyberbullying among Turkish adolescents. *Cyberpsychology & Behavior*, *11*(3), 253–261. doi:10.1089/cpb.2007.0016 PMID:18537493

Arslan, S., Savaser, S., Hallett, V., & Balci, S. (2012). Cyberbullying among primary school students in Turkey: Self-reported prevalence and associations with home and school life. *Cyberpsychology, Behavior, and Social Networking*, *15*(10), 527–533. doi:10.1089/cyber.2012.0207 PMID:23002988

Associated Press. (2011). *Executive summary: 2011 AP-MTV digital abuse study*. Retrieved from http://www.athinline.org/pdfs/MTV-AP_2011_Research_Study-Exec_Summary.pdf

Atwood, K. A., Zimmerman, R., Cupp, P. K., Fongkaew, W., Miller, B. A., Byrnes, H. F., ... Chookhare, W. (2012). Correlates of precoital behaviors, intentions, and sexual initiation among Thai adolescents. *The Journal of Early Adolescence*, *32*(3), 364–386. doi:10.1177/0272431610393248

Aubrey, A. (2018, March 5). This chef lost 50 pounds and reversed prediabetes with a digital program. *National Public Radio*. Retrieved from https://www.npr.org/sections/thesalt/2018/03/05/589286575/this-chef-lost-50-pounds-and-reversed-pre-diabetes-with-a-digital-program

Augner, C., & Hacker, G. W. (2012). Associations between problematic mobile phone use and psychological parameters in young adults. *International Journal of Public Health, 57*(2), 437–441. doi:10.100700038-011-0234-z PMID:21290162

Ayas, T., & Horzum, M. B. (2010). *Cyberbullg / victim scale development study*. Retrieved from: http://www.akademikbakis.org

Babaoglu, O., Marzolla, M., & Tamburini, M. (2012). Design and Implementation of a P2P Cloud System. *Proceedings of the 27th Annual ACM Symposium on Applied Computing*, 412–417. 10.1145/2245276.2245357

Babaoglu, O. (2014, September 22). Escape From the Data Center: The Promise of Peer-to-Peer Cloud Computing. *IEEE Spectrum.*

Bachrach, Y., Kosinski, M., Graepel, T., Kohli, P., & Stillwell, D. (2012, June). Personality and patterns of Facebook usage. In *Proceedings of the 4th Annual ACM Web Science Conference* (pp. 24-32). ACM. 10.1145/2380718.2380722

Baik, J., Lee, K., Lee, S., Kim, Y., & Choi, J. (2016). Predicting personality traits related to consumer behavior using SNS analysis. *New Review of Hypermedia and Multimedia, 22*(3), 189–206. doi:10.1080/13614568.2016.1152313

Baker, J. R., & Moore, S. M. (2008). Distress, coping, and blogging: Comparing new Myspace users by their intention to blog. *Cyberpsychology & Behavior, 11*(1), 81–85. doi:10.1089/cpb.2007.9930 PMID:18275317

Bakos, Y. (1998). The emerging role of electronic marketplaces on the Internet. *Communications of the ACM, 41*(8), 35–42. doi:10.1145/280324.280330

Bandura, A. (1977). *Social Learning Theory*. Englewood Cliffs, NJ: Prentice Hall.

Bandura, A. (1978, April). The self system in reciprocal determinism. *The American Psychologist, 33*(4), 344–358. doi:10.1037/0003-066X.33.4.344

Bandura, A. (1986). *Social Foundations of Thought and Action: A Social Cognitive*. Englewood Cliffs, NJ: Prentice-Hall.

Bandura, A. (1994). Social Cognitive Theory of Mass Communication. In J. Bryant & D. Zillmann (Eds.), *Media Effects: Advances in Theory and Research* (pp. 61–90). Hillsdale, NJ: Erlbaum.

Bandura, A. (1997). *Self-efficacy: the Exercise of Control*. New York: Freeman.

Barello, S., Triberti, S., Graffigna, G., Libreri, C., Serino, S., Hibbard, J., & Riva, G. (2015). eHealth for Patient Engagement: A Systematic Review. *Frontiers in Psychology, 6*, 2013. doi:10.3389/fpsyg.2015.02013 PMID:26779108

Barlett, C. (2015). Predicting adolescent's cyberbullying: A longitudinal risk analysis. *Journal of Adolescence, 41*, 86–95. doi:10.1016/j.adolescence.2015.02.006 PMID:25828551

Barlett, C. P., & Gentile, D. A. (2012). Long-term psychological predictors of cyber-bullying in late adolescence. *Psychology of Popular Media Culture, 2*, 123–135. doi:10.1037/a0028113

Barlett, C. P., Gentile, D. A., Anderson, C. A., Suzuki, K., Sakamoto, A., Yamaoka, A., & Katsura, R. (2013). Cross-cultural differences in cyberbullying behavior: A short-term longitudinal study. *Journal of Cross-Cultural Psychology, 45*(2), 300–313. doi:10.1177/0022022113504622

Barlett, C., & Coyne, S. (2014). A meta-analysis of sex differences in cyberbullyingbehavior: The moderating role of age. *Aggressive Behavior, 40*(5), 474–488. doi:10.1002/ab.21555 PMID:25098968

Barnes, G. E., Malamuth, N. M., & Check, J. (1984). Personality and sexuality. *Personality and Individual Differences, 5*(2), 159–172. doi:10.1016/0191-8869(84)90048-5

Barr, M., & Massa, A. (2006). *Programming embedded systems: with C and GNU development tools*. O'Reilly Media Inc.

Baršauskas, P., Šarapovas, T., & Cvilikas, A. (2008). The evaluation of e-commerce impact on business efficiency. *Baltic Journal of Management, 3*(1), 71–91. doi:10.1108/17465260810844275

Barth, R. J., & Kinder, B. N. (1988). A theoretical analysis of sex differences in same-sex friendships. *Sex Roles, 19*(5–6), 349–363. doi:10.1007/BF00289842

Basbaum, J. P. (2010). Sentencing for possession of child pornography: A failure to distinguish voyeurs from pederasts. *The Hastings Law Journal, 61*, 1–24.

Bauman, S., Toomey, R. B., & Walker, J. L. (2013). Associations among bullying, cyberbullying, and suicide in high school students. *Journal of Adolescence, 36*(2), 341–350. doi:10.1016/j.adolescence.2012.12.001 PMID:23332116

Bauman, S., Underwood, M. K., & Card, N. A. (2013). Definitions: Another perspective and a proposal for beginning with cyberaggression. In S. Bauman, D. Cross, & J. Walker (Eds.), *Principles of cyberbullying research: Definitions, measures, methodology* (pp. 26–40). New York, NY: Routledge.

Bayar, Y., & Ucanok, Z. (2012). School social climate and generalized peer perception in traditional and cyberbullying status. *Educational Sciences: Theory and Practice, 12*, 2352–2358.

Beck, A. T., Steer, R. T., & Brown, G. K. (1996). *Manual for the Beck Depression Inventory-II*. San Antonio, TX: Psychological Corporation.

Beckman, L., Hagquist, C., & Hellstrom, L. (2012). Does the association with psychosomatic health problems differ between cyberbullying and traditional bullying? *Emotional & Behavioural Difficulties, 17*(3-4), 421–434. doi:10.1080/13632752.2012.704228

Benet-Martínez, V., & Haritatos, J. (2005). Bicultural identity integration (BII): Components and psychological antecedents. *Journal of Personality, 73*(4), 1015–1050. doi:10.1111/j.1467-6494.2005.00337.x PMID:15958143

Benet-Martínez, V., Lee, F., & Leu, J. (2006). Biculturalism and cognitive complexity: Expertise in cultural representations. *Journal of Cross-Cultural Psychology, 37*(4), 386–407. doi:10.1177/0022022106288476

Benet-Martínez, V., Leu, J., Lee, F., & Morris, M. (2002). Negotiating biculturalism: Cultural frame-switching in biculturals with oppositional vs. compatible cultural identities. *Journal of Cross-Cultural Psychology, 33*(5), 492–516. doi:10.1177/0022022102033005005

Bennett, G. G., & Glasgow, R. E. (2009). The delivery of public health interventions via the Internet: Actualizing their potential. *Annual Review of Public Health, 30*(1), 273–292. doi:10.1146/annurev.publhealth.031308.100235 PMID:19296777

Beran, T., & Li, Q. (2007). The relationship between cyberbullying and school bullying. *Journal of Student Well-being, 1*(2), 15–33.

Berenbaum, H. (1992). Posed facial expressions of emotion in schizophrenia and depression. *Psychological Medicine, 22*(4), 929–937. doi:10.1017/S0033291700038502 PMID:1362618

Berger, H. (1929). Über das elektrenkephalogramm des menschen. *European Archives of Psychiatry and Clinical Neuroscience, 87*(1), 527–570.

Beyens, I., Vandenbosch, L., & Eggermont, S. (2015). Early adolescent boys' exposure to internet pornography Relationships to pubertal timing, sensation seeking, and academic performance. *The Journal of Early Adolescence, 35*(8), 1045–1068. doi:10.1177/0272431614548069

Billieux, J., Van der Linden, M., & Rochat, L. (2008). The role of impulsivity in actual and problematic use of mobile phone. *Applied Cognitive Psychology, 22*(9), 1195–1210. doi:10.1002/acp.1429

Bimba, A. T., Idris, N., Al-Hunaiyyan, A., Mahmud, R. B., & Shuib, N. L. B. M. (2017). Adaptive feedback in computer-based learning environments: A review. *Adaptive Behavior, 25*(5), 217–234. doi:10.1177/1059712317727590

Birbaumer, N., Gallegos-Ayala, G., Wildgruber, M., Silvoni, S., & Soekadar, S. R. (2014). Direct brain control and communication in paralysis. *Brain Topography, 27*(1), 4–11. doi:10.100710548-013-0282-1 PMID:23536247

Birbaumer, N., Ghanayim, N., Hinterberger, T., Iversen, I., Kotchoubey, B., Kubler, A., ... Flor, H. (1999). A spelling device for the paralysed. *Nature, 398*(6725), 297–298. doi:10.1038/18581 PMID:10192330

Birbaumer, N., Kubler, A., Ghanayim, N., Hinterberger, T., Perelmouter, J., Kaiser, J., ... Flor, H. (2000). The thought translation device (TTD) for completely paralyzed patients. *IEEE Transactions on Rehabilitation Engineering, 8*(2), 190–193. doi:10.1109/86.847812 PMID:10896183

Blankertz, B., Muller, K.-R., Curio, G., Vaughan, T. M., Schalk, G., Wolpaw, J. R., ... Hinterberger, T. (2004). The BCI competition 2003: Progress and perspectives in detection and discrimination of EEG single trials. *Biomedical Engineering. IEEE Transactions on, 51*(6), 1044–1051. PMID:15188876

Bloom, Z. D., & Hagedorn, W. B. (2015). Male adolescents and contemporary pornography: Implications for marriage and family counselors. *The Family Journal (Alexandria, Va.)*, *23*(1), 82–89. doi:10.1177/1066480714555672

Bogaert, A. F. (2001). Personality, individual differences, and preferences for the sexual media. *Archives of Sexual Behavior*, *30*(1), 29–53. doi:10.1023/A:1026416723291 PMID:11286004

Bogale, A., & Seme, A. (2014). Premarital sexual practices and its predictors among in-school youths of Shendi town, West Gojjam zone, north western Ethiopia. *Reproductive Health*, *11*(1), 49. doi:10.1186/1742-4755-11-49 PMID:24961239

Bogost, I. (2011). *How to Do Things with Videogames (Electronic Mediations)*. University of Minnesota Press. doi:10.5749/minnesota/9780816676460.001.0001

Bonanno, R. A., & Hymel, S. (2013). Cyber bullying and internalizing difficulties: Above and beyond the impact of traditional forms of bullying. *Journal of Youth and Adolescence*, *42*(5), 685–697. doi:10.100710964-013-9937-1 PMID:23512485

Bond, L., & Nolan, T. (2011). Making sense of perceptions of risk of diseases and vaccinations: A qualitative study combining models of health beliefs, decision-making and risk perception. *BMC Public Health*, *11*(1), 1471–2458. doi:10.1186/1471-2458-11-943 PMID:22182354

Boneva, B., Kraut, R., & Frohlich, D. (2001). Using e-mail for personal relationships: The difference gender makes. *The American Behavioral Scientist*, *45*(3), 530–549. doi:10.1177/00027640121957204

Bonnet, L., Lotte, F., & Lécuyer, A. (2013). Two brains, one game: Design and evaluation of a multi-user BCI video game based on motor imagery. *IEEE Transactions on Computational Intelligence and AI in Games*, *5*(2), 185–198. doi:10.1109/TCIAIG.2012.2237173

Bonnin, G., Segard, O., & Vialle, P. (2005). Relationship marketing and innovation: The case of the launch of wireless local loop telecommunication services in France. *Journal of Services Research*, 149–171.

Bos, D.-O., Reuderink, B., van de Laar, B., Gurkok, H., Muhl, C., Poel, M., . . . Nijholt, A. (2010). *Human-computer interaction for BCI games: Usability and user experience*. Paper presented at the Cyberworlds (CW), 2010 International Conference on. 10.1109/CW.2010.22

Botrel, L., Holz, E., & Kübler, A. (2015). Brain Painting V2: Evaluation of P300-based brain-computer interface for creative expression by an end-user following the user-centered design. *Brain-Computer Interfaces*, *2*(2-3), 135–149. doi:10.1080/2326263X.2015.1100038

Boulton, M., Lloyd, J., Down, J., & Marx, H. (2012). Predicting undergraduates' self-reported engagement in traditional and cyberbullying from attitudes. *Cyberpsychology, Behavior, and Social Networking*, *15*(3), 141–147. doi:10.1089/cyber.2011.0369 PMID:22304402

Boyce, M. W., Duma, K. M., Hettinger, L. J., Malone, T. B., Wilson, D. P., & Lockett-Reynolds, J. (2011). *Human performance in cybersecurity: A research agenda*. Paper presented at the the Human Factors and Ergonomics Society Annual Meeting, Santa Monica, CA. 10.1177/1071181311551233

Boyd, J. R. (1986). *Patterns of conflict.* Retrieved from http://www.dnipogo.org/boyd/patterns_ppt. pdf

Bransford, J. D., Brown, A. L., & Cocking, R. R. (Eds.). (1999). *How people learn: Brain, mind, experience and school.* Washington, DC: National Academy Press.

Braun-Courville, D. K., & Rojas, M. (2009). Exposure to sexually explicit web sites and adolescent sexual attitudes and behaviors. *The Journal of Adolescent Health, 45*(2), 156–162. doi:10.1016/j. jadohealth.2008.12.004 PMID:19628142

Bravo-Lillo, C., Cranor, L. F., Downs, J. S., & Komanduri, S. (2011). Bridging the Gap in Computer Security Warnings: A Mental Model Approach. *IEEE Security and Privacy, 9*(2), 18–26. doi:10.1109/MSP.2010.198

Brehmer, B. (2005). *The dynamic OODA loop: Amalgamating Boyd's OODA loop and the cybernetic approach to command and control.* Paper presented at the the the 10th International Command and Control Research and Technology Symposium: The Future of C2, McLean, VA.

Brighi, A., Guarini, A., Melotti, G., Galli, S., & Genta, M. L. (2012). Predictors of victimisation across direct bullying, indirect bullying and cyberbullying. *Emotional & Behavioural Difficulties, 17*(3-4), 375–388. doi:10.1080/13632752.2012.704684

Brown, J. D., & L'Engle, K. L. (2009). X-Rated: Sexual attitudes and behaviors associated with US. Early adolescents' exposure to sexually explicit media. *Communication Research, 36*(1), 129–151. doi:10.1177/0093650208326465

Brumley, L., Kopp, C., & Korb, K. (2006). *The Orientation Step of the OODA Loop and Information Warfare.* Paper presented at the 7th Australian Information Warfare & Security Conference 2006 Proceedings, Clayton School of Information Technology, Monash University, Perth, Australia.

Brunborg, G. S., Mentzoni, R. A., Molde, H., Myrseth, H., Skouverøe, K. J., Bjorvatn, B., & Pallesen, S. (2011). The relationship between media use in the bedroom, sleep habits and symptoms of insomnia. *Journal of Sleep Research, 20*(4), 569–575. doi:10.1111/j.1365-2869.2011.00913.x PMID:21324013

Bruner, J. S. (1960). *The Process of education.* Cambridge, MA: Harvard University Press.

Bruner, J. S. (1973). *The relevance of education.* New York: Norton.

Bryan, A. (2017). *Ellwood THompasson's falls for phishing scam; data compromised.* Retrieved from http://wtvr.com/2017/02/23/ellwood-thompsons-falls-for-phishing-scam-1/

Builder, C. H., Bankes, S. C., & Nordin, R. (1999). *Command concepts: A Theory Derived from the Practice of Command and Control.* Santa Monica, CA: RAND Corporation.

Bukowski, W. M., Newcomb, A. F., & Hartup, W. (Eds.). (1996). *The company they keep.* Cambridge, UK: Cambridge University Press.

Bulduc, J. L., Caron, S. L., & Logue, M. E. (2007). The effects of parental divorce on college students. *Journal of Divorce & Remarriage*, *46*(3-4), 83–104. doi:10.1300/J087v46n03_06

Bulgurcu, B., Cavusoglu, H., & Benbasat, I. (2010). Information Security Policy Compliance: An Empirical Study of Rationality-Based Beliefs and Information Security Awareness. *Management Information Systems Quarterly*, *34*(3), 523–A527. doi:10.2307/25750690

Bullying Statistics. (2012). *Cyberbullying statistics*. Retrieved from http://www.bullyingstatistics. org/content/cyber-bullying-statistics.html

Burger, J. M. (2008). *Personality* (7th ed.). Belmont: Thomson Higher Education.

Burton, K. A., Florell, D., & Wygant, D. B. (2013). The role of peer attachment and normative beliefs about aggression on traditional bullying and cyberbullying. *Psychology in the Schools*, *50*(2), 103–114. doi:10.1002/pits.21663

Cabanac, M. (2002). What is emotion? *Behavioural Processes*, *60*(2), 69–83. doi:10.1016/S0376-6357(02)00078-5 PMID:12426062

Caetano, A. P., Amado, J., Martins, M. J. D., Veiga-Simão, A. M., Freire, I., & Pessoa, M. T. (2017). Cyberbullying: motivos da agressão na perspectiva de jovens portugueses [Cyberbullying: aggression motives in the perspective of young Portuguese]. *Education and Society*, *38*(141), 1017–1034. doi:10.1590/es0101-73302017139852

Caetano, A. P., Freire, I., Veiga-Simão, A. M., Martins, M. J. D., & Pessoa, M. T. (2016). Emoções no Cyberbullying: um estudo com adolescentes portugueses [Emotions in Cyberbullying: a study with Portuguese adolescents]. *Education and Research*, *42*(1), 199–212.

Cain, N., & Gradisar, M. (2010). Electronic media use and sleep in school-aged children and adolescents: A review. *Sleep Medicine*, *11*(8), 735–742. doi:10.1016/j.sleep.2010.02.006 PMID:20673649

Calamaro, C. J., Mason, T. B. A., & Ratcliffe, S. J. (2009). Adolescents living the 24/7 lifestyle; effects of caffeine and technology on sleep duration and daytime functioning. [National Sleep Foundation]. *Pediatrics*, *123*(6), e1005–e1010. doi:10.1542/peds.2008-3641 PMID:19482732

Calvete, E., Orue, I., Estévez, A., Villardón, L., & Padilla, P. (2010). Cyberbullying in adolescents: Modalities and aggressors' profile. *Computers in Human Behavior*, *26*(5), 1128–1135. doi:10.1016/j.chb.2010.03.017

Canadian Centre for Child Protection. (2016, January). *Child sexual abuse images on the internet: A cybertip.ca analysis*. Retrieved December 18, 2018 from https://www.cybertip.ca/pdfs/CTIP_CSAResearchReport_2016_en.pdf

Capgemini. (2013). *Evolving E-Commerce Market Dynamics: Changing Merchant Payment Needs and the Impact on Banks*. Retrieved on September 8, 2017, from http://www.capgemini.com/cards

Cappadocia, M. C., Craig, W. M., & Pepler, D. (2013). Cyberbullying: Prevalence, stability and risk factors during adolescence. *Canadian Journal of School Psychology, 28*(2), 171–192. doi:10.1177/0829573513491212

Carney, C. E., Edinger, J. D., Meyer, B., Lindman, L., & Istre, T. (2006). Daily activities and sleep quality in college students. *Chronobiology International, 23*(3), 623–637. doi:10.1080/07420520600650695 PMID:16753946

Case, T., Burns, O. M., & Dick, G. N. (2001). Drivers of Online Purchases among U.S. Students. *Proceedings of 7ᵗʰ American conference on Information Systems*, 900-907.

Cassidy, W., Brown, K., & Jackson, M. (2012a). "Making kind cool": Parents' suggestions for preventing cyber bullying and fostering cyber kindness. *Journal of Educational Computing Research, 46*(4), 415–436. doi:10.2190/EC.46.4.f

Cassidy, W., Brown, K., & Jackson, M. (2012b). "Under the radar": Educators and cyberbullying in schools. *School Psychology International, 33*(5), 520–532. doi:10.1177/0143034312445245

CBSNews. (2012, September 30). Tyler Clementi suicide sparks outrage, remorse. *CBSNews.* Retrieved from http://www.cbsnews.com/news/tyler-clementi-suicide-sparks-outrage-remorse/

Center for Disease Control and Prevention. (2014). *Youth risk behavior surveillance — United States 2013.* Washington, DC: U.S. Department of Health and Human Services. Retrieved from http://www.cdc.gov/mmwr/pdf/ss/ss6304.pdf

Center for Imagineering Leadership and Renewal. (2011). *What is Imagineering?* Retrieved from http://www.bernardfranklinphd.com/2011/04/what-is-imagineering.html

Center for Strategic and International Studies. (2013). *The Economic Impact of Cybercrime and Cyber Espionage.* Retrieved from https://www.mcafee.com/us/resources/reports/rp-economic-impact-cybercrime.pdf

Centers for Disease Control and Prevention. (2012). *Youth suicide.* Retrieved from http://www.cdc.gov/violenceprevention/pub/youth_suicide.html

Chan, K., Mikami, K., & Kondo, K. (2010). *Measuring interest in linear single player FPS games.* Paper presented at the ACM Siggraph Asia 2010 Sketches. 10.1145/1899950.1899953

Chang, L., & Krosnick, J. A. (2009). Winter. National surveys via RDD telephone interviewing versus the internet: Comparing sample representativeness and response quality. *Public Opinion Quarterly, 73*(4), 641–678. doi:10.1093/poq/nfp075

Chapin, J. (2000). Third-person perception and optimistic bias among urban minority at-risk youth. *Communication Research, 27*(1), 51–81. doi:10.1177/009365000027001003

Chapin, J. (2011). Optimistic bias about intimate partner violence among medical personnel. *Family Medicine, 43*(6), 429–432. PMID:21656399

Chard, K., Caton, S., Rana, O., & Bubendorfer, K. (2010). Social Cloud: Cloud Computing in Social Networks. *2010 IEEE 3rd International Conference on Cloud Computing*, 99–106. 10.1109/CLOUD.2010.28

Chard, K., Bubendorfer, K., Caton, S., & Rana, O. F. (2012). Social cloud computing: A vision for socially motivated resource sharing. *IEEE Transactions on Services Computing*, 5(4), 551–563. doi:10.1109/TSC.2011.39

Charlton, J. P., & Danforth, I. D. (2010). Validating the distinction between computer addiction and engagement: Online game playing and personality. *Behaviour & Information Technology*, 29(6), 601–613. doi:10.1080/01449290903401978

Chaturvedi, S., & Gupta, S. (2014). Effect of Social Media on Online Shopping Behaviour of Apparels in Jaipur City- An Analytical Review. *Journal of Business Management, Commerce & Research*, 2(7), 1–8.

Chen, L., Gong, T., Kosinski, M., Stillwell, D., & Davidson, R. L. (2017). Building a profile of subjective well-being for social media users. *PLoS One*, 12(11), e0187278. doi:10.1371/journal.pone.0187278 PMID:29135991

Chen, N., Ko, H., Kinshuk, & Lin, T. (2006). A model for synchronous learning using the Internet. *Innovations in Education and Teaching International*, 42(2), 181–194. doi:10.1080/14703290500062599

Cheung, A. C. K., & Slavin, R. E. (2013). The effectiveness of educational technology applications for enhancing mathematics achievement in K–12 classrooms: A meta-analysis. *Educational Research Review*, 9, 88–113. doi:10.1016/j.edurev.2013.01.001

Choi, H. S., Lee, H. K., & Ha, J. (2012). The influence of smartphone addiction on mental health, campus life and personal relations—Focusing on K university students. *Journal of Korean Data & Information Science Society*, 235(5), 1005–1015. doi:10.7465/jkdi.2012.23.5.1005

Christodoulides, G., & Michaelidou, N. (2011). Shopping motives as antecedents of e-satisfaction and e-loyalty. *Journal of Marketing Management*, 27(1-2), 181–197. doi:10.1080/0267257X.2010.489815

Chung, S., & Moon, S. (2016). Is the third-person effect real? A critical examination of the rationales, testing methods, and previous findings of the third-person effect on censorship attitudes. *Human Communication Research*, 42(2), 312–337. doi:10.1111/hcre.12078

Churchman, C. W. (1967). Wicked problems. *Management Science*, 14(4), 141–142.

Clark, R. A., Pua, Y. H., Fortin, K., Ritchie, C., Webster, K. E., Denehy, L., & Bryant, A. L. (2012). Validity of the microsoft kinect for assessment of postural control. *Gait & Posture*, 36(3), 372–377. doi:10.1016/j.gaitpost.2012.03.033 PMID:22633015

Collins, L. (2017, February 27). Europe's Child-Refugee Crisis. *The New Yorker*.

Connolly, M., & Giouroukakis, V. (2012). Cyberbullying: Taking control through research-based letter writing. *English Journal, 101*(6), 70–74.

Connor, P. (2016, August 2). *Number of Refugees to Europe Surges to Record 1.3 Million in 2015.* Pew Research Center.

Cooper, C. R. (2003). Bridging multiple worlds: Immigrant youth identity and pathways to college. *International Society for the Study of Behavioral Development Newsletter, 38*, 1–4.

Corcoran, L., Connolly, I., & O'Moore, M. (2012). Cyberbullying in Irish schools: An investigation of personality and self-concept. *The Irish Journal of Psychology, 33*(4), 153–165. doi:10.1080 /03033910.2012.677995

Correa, T., Hinsley, A. W., & De Zuniga, H. G. (2010). Who interacts on the Web?: The intersection of users' personality and social media use. *Computers in Human Behavior, 26*(2), 247–253. doi:10.1016/j.chb.2009.09.003

Costa, P. T., & MacCrae, R. R. (1992). *Revised NEO personality inventory (NEO PI-R) and NEO five-factor inventory (NEO-FFI): Professional manual.* Psychological Assessment Resources, Incorporated.

Cox. (2014). *Cox 2014 Internet Safety Survey (conducted by The Futures Company).* Retrieved from http://docplayer.net/16377341-2014-teen-internet-safety-survey-conducted-by-the-futures-company.html

Crane, E., & Gross, M. (2007). *Motion Capture and Emotion: Affect Detection in Whole Body Movement.* In *Affective Computing and Intelligent Interaction.* Springer Berlin Heidelberg.

Cranor, L. F. (2008). A framework for reasoning about the human in the loop. *Proceedings of the 1st Conference on Usability, Psychology, and Security.*

Crowley, K., Sliney, A., Pitt, I., & Murphy, D. (2010). *Evaluating a Brain-Computer Interface to Categorise Human Emotional Response.* Paper presented at the Advanced Learning Technologies (ICALT), 2010 IEEE 10th International Conference on.

Crowley, S. J., Tarokh, L., & Carskadon, M. A. (2014). Sleep during adolescence. In S. H. Sheldon & ... (Eds.), *Principles and practice of pediatric sleep medicine* (2nd ed.; pp. 45–52). London: Elsevier.

Cui, L., Li, S., & Zhu, T. (2016). Emotion Detection from Natural Walking. In *International Conference on Human Centered Computing* (pp.23-33). Springer International Publishing. 10.1007/978-3-319-31854-7_3

Curelaru, M., Iacob, I., & Abalasei, B. (2009). *School bullying: Definition, characteristics, and intervention strategies.* Lumean Publishing House.

Cyberbullying Research Center. (2015). *2015 Cyberbullying Data.* Retrieved from https://cyberbullying.org/2015-cyberbullying-data

Cyberbullying Research Center. (2016). *2016 Cyberbullying Data*. Retrieved from https://cyberbullying.org/2016-cyberbullying-data

D'Andrade, R. G. (1984). Cultural meaning systems. In R. A. Shweder & R. A. LeVine (Eds.), *Cultural theory: Essays on mind, self, and emotion* (pp. 88–119). Cambridge, UK: Cambridge University Press.

D'Arcy, J., Hovav, A., & Galletta, D. (2009). User Awareness of Security Countermeasures and Its Impact on Information Systems Misuse: A Deterrence Approach. *Information Systems Research, 20*(1), 79–98. doi:10.1287/isre.1070.0160

Dai, H., Luo, X., Liao, Q., & Cao, M. (2015). Explaining consumer satisfaction of services: The role of innovativeness and emotion in an electronic mediated environment. *Decision Support Systems, 70*, 97–106. doi:10.1016/j.dss.2014.12.003

Daiute, C. (2013). Educational uses of the digital world for human development. *Learning Landscapes, 6*(2), 63–83.

Daiute, C. (2014). *Narrative inquiry: A dynamic approach*. Thousand Oaks, CA: Sage.

Daiute, C., & Griffin, T. M. (1993). The social construction of narrative. In C. Daiute (Ed.), *The development of literacy through social interaction*. San Francisco, CA: Jossey Bass.

Daiute, C., & Lucić, L. (2010). Situated cultural development among youth separated by war. *International Journal of Intercultural Relations, 34*(6), 615–628. doi:10.1016/j.ijintrel.2010.07.006

Daiute, C., & Lucić, L. (2011). *The Skill of Relational Complexity for Global Children and Youth in the United States*. Unpublished NSF Grant Proposal.

Daly, J. J., & Wolpaw, J. R. (2008). Brain–computer interfaces in neurological rehabilitation. *Lancet Neurology, 7*(11), 1032–1043. doi:10.1016/S1474-4422(08)70223-0 PMID:18835541

Das, A., Bonneau, J., Caesar, M., Borisov, N., & Wang, X. (2014). The Tangled Web of Password Reuse. *Symposium on Network and Distributed System Security (NDSS)*. Retrieved from https://www.cs.cmu.edu/~anupamd/paper/NDSS2014.pdf

Davies, H. T. O., Crombie, I. K., & Tavakoli, M. (1998). When can odds ratios mislead? *British Medical Journal, 316*(7136), 989–991. doi:10.1136/bmj.316.7136.989 PMID:9550961

De Bruyn, A., & Lilien, G. L. (2008). A multi-stage model of word-of-mouth influence through viral marketing. *International Journal of Research in Marketing, 25*(3), 151–163. doi:10.1016/j.ijresmar.2008.03.004

de Meijer, M. (1989). The contribution of general features of body movement to the attribution of emotions. *Journal of Nonverbal Behavior, 13*(4), 247–268. doi:10.1007/BF00990296

Dehue, F., Bolman, C., & Vollink, T. (2008). Cyberbullying: Youngsters' experiences and parental perception. *CyberPscyhology & Behavior, 11*(2), 217–223. doi:10.1089/cpb.2007.0008 PMID:18422417

Dehue, F., Bolman, C., Vollink, T., & Pouwelse, M. (2012). Cyberbullying and traditional bullying in relation to adolescents' perceptions of parenting. *Journal of Cyber Therapy and Rehabilitation*, *5*, 25–34.

Delafrooz, N., Paim, L. H., Haron, S. A., Sidin, S. M., & Khatibi, A. (2009). Factors affecting students' attitude toward online shopping. *African Journal of Business Management*, *3*(5), 200–209.

deLara, E. W. (2012). Why adolescents don't disclose incidents of bullying and harassment. *Journal of School Violence*, *11*(4), 288–305. doi:10.1080/15388220.2012.705931

Demirci, K., Akgönül, M., & Akpinar, A. (2015). Relationships of smartphone use severity with sleep quality, depression, and anxiety in university students. *Journal of Behavioral Addictions*, *4*(2), 85–92. doi:10.1556/2006.4.2015.010 PMID:26132913

Demirci, K., Orhan, H., Demirdas, A., Akpinar, A., & Sert, H. (2014). Validity and reliability of the Turkish Version of the Smartphone Addiction Scale in a younger population. *Bulletin of Clinical Psychopharmacology*, *24*(3), 226–234. doi:10.5455/bcp.20140710040824

Denney, A. S., & Tewksbury, R. (2017). ICTs and Sexuality. In M. R. P. McGuire & T. J. Holt (Eds.), *Handbook of Technology, Crime, and Justice* (pp. 113–133). New York, NY: Routledge.

Deshpande, G., Rangaprakash, D., Oeding, L., Cichocki, A., & Hu, X. P. (2017). A new generation of brain-computer interfaces driven by discovery of latent EEG-fMRI linkages using tensor decomposition. *Frontiers in Neuroscience*, *11*, 246. doi:10.3389/fnins.2017.00246 PMID:28638316

Di Milia, L., Adan, A., Natale, V., & Randler, C. (2013). Reviewing the psychometric properties of contemporary circadian typology measures. *Chronobiology International*, *30*(10), 1261–1271. doi:10.3109/07420528.2013.817415 PMID:24001393

Diamanduros, T., & Downs, E. (2011). Creating a safe school environment: How to prevent cyberbullying at your school. *Library Media Connection*, *30*(2), 36–38.

Dictionarist. (2011). *Imagineering*. Retrieved from http://www.dictionarist.com/Imagineering

Didden, R., Scholte, R. H. J., Korzilius, H., de Moor, J. M. H., Vermeulen, A., O'Reilly, M., ... Lancioni, G. E. (2009). Cyberbullying among students with intellectual and developmental disability in special education settings. *Developmental Neurorehabilitation*, *12*(3), 146–151. doi:10.1080/17518420902971356 PMID:19466622

Dietterich, T. G., & Horvitz, E. J. (2015). Rise of concerns about AI: Reflections and directions. *Communications of the ACM*, *58*(10), 38–40. doi:10.1145/2770869

Dodou, D., & de Winter, J. C. F. (2014, July). Social desirability is the same in offline, online, and paper surveys: A meta-analysis. *Computers in Human Behavior*, *36*, 487–495. doi:10.1016/j.chb.2014.04.005

Dombeck, M. (2007, July 24). *The long-term effects of bullying*. Retrieved from https://www.mentalhelp.net/articles/the-long-term-effects-of-bullying/

Dombrowski, S. C., Gischlar, K. L., & Durst, T. (2007). Safeguarding young people from cyber pornography and cyber sexual predation: A major dilemma of the Internet. *Child Abuse Review*, *16*(3), 153–170. doi:10.1002/car.939

Donchin, E., & Smith, D. (1970). The contingent negative variation and the late positive wave of the average evoked potential. *Electroencephalography and Clinical Neurophysiology*, *29*(2), 201–203. doi:10.1016/0013-4694(70)90124-0 PMID:4194603

Donchin, E., Spencer, K. M., & Wijesinghe, R. (2000). The mental prosthesis: Assessing the speed of a P300-based brain-computer interface. *IEEE Transactions on Rehabilitation Engineering*, *8*(2), 174–179. doi:10.1109/86.847808 PMID:10896179

Donegan, R. (2012). Bullying and cyberbullying: History, statistics, law, prevention and analysis. *The Elon Journal of Undergraduate Research in Communications*, *3*(1), 33–42.

Donevan, M., & Mattebo, M. (2017). The relationship between frequent pornography consumption, behaviors, and sexual preoccupancy among male adolescents in Sweden. *Sexual & Reproductive Healthcare: Official Journal of the Swedish Association of Midwives*, *12*, 82–87. doi:10.1016/j.srhc.2017.03.002 PMID:28477937

Doornwaard, S. M., Bickham, D. S., Rich, M., ter Bogt, T. F. M., & van den Eijnden, R. J. J. M. (2015). Adolescents' use of sexually explicit Internet material and their sexual attitudes and behavior: Parallel development and directional effects. *Developmental Psychology*, *51*(10), 1476–1488. doi:10.1037/dev0000040 PMID:26376287

Döring, N. M. (2009). The internet's impact on sexuality: A critical review of 15 years of research. *Computers in Human Behavior*, *25*(5), 1089–1101. doi:10.1016/j.chb.2009.04.003

Dörnyei, Z., & Ushioda, E. (2009). *Motivation, language identity and the L2 self* (Vol. 36). Multilingual Matters Ltd.

Drennan, M. D., Klauber, M. R., Kripke, D. F., & Goyette, L. M. (1991). The effects of depression and age on the Horne-Ostberg morningness-eveningness score. *Journal of Affective Disorders*, *23*(2), 93–98. doi:10.1016/0165-0327(91)90096-B PMID:1753041

Duolingo. (2018). Retrieved from https://www.duolingo.com/

Dutt, V., Ahn, Y.-S., & Gonzalez, C. (2013). Cyber Situation Awareness: Modeling Detection of Cyber Attacks with Instance-based Learning Theory. *Human Factors*, *55*(3), 605–618. doi:10.1177/0018720812464045 PMID:23829034

Eaton, J., & Miranda, E. (2013). *Real-time notation using brainwave control*. Paper presented at the Sound and Music Computing Conference.

Eden, S., Heiman, T., & Olenik-Shemesh, D. (2013). Teachers' perceptions, beliefs and concerns about cyberbullying. *British Journal of Educational Technology*, *44*(6), 1036–1052. doi:10.1111/j.1467-8535.2012.01363.x

Eftekhar, A., Fullwood, C., & Morris, N. (2014). Capturing personality from Facebook photos and photo-related activities: How much exposure do you need? *Computers in Human Behavior*, *37*, 162–170. doi:10.1016/j.chb.2014.04.048

Egelman, S., & Peer, E. (2015). The Myth of the Average User: Improving Privacy and Security Systems through Individualization. *Proceedings of the 2015 New Security Paradigms Workshop*. 10.1145/2841113.2841115

Ekman, P., & Friesen, W. V. (1967). Head and body cues in the judgment of emotion: A reformulation. *Perceptual and Motor Skills*, *24*(3), 711–724. doi:10.2466/pms.1967.24.3.711 PMID:5622764

Ekman, P., & Rosenberg, E. L. (1997). *What the Face Reveals: Basic and Applied Studies of Spontaneous Expression Using the Facial Action Coding System (FACS)*. Oxford University Press.

Elias, N., & Zeltser-Shorer, M. (2006). Immigrants of the world unite? A virtual community of Russian-speaking immigrants on the Web. *Journal of International Communication*, *12*(2), 70–90. doi:10.1080/13216597.2006.9752014

Elledge, L. C., Williford, A., Boulton, A. J., DePaolis, K. J., Little, T. D., & Salmivalli, C. (2013). Individual and contextual predictors of cyberbullying: The influence of children's provictim attitudes and teachers' ability to intervene. *Journal of Youth and Adolescence*, *42*(5), 698–710. doi:10.100710964-013-9920-x PMID:23371005

Emily, S., & Paul, A. (2009). Creating and inhabiting virtual places: Indian immigrants in cyberspace. *National Identities*, *11*(2), 127–147. doi:10.1080/14608940902891161

Endrass, J., Urbaniok, F., Hammermeister, L. C., Benz, C., Elbert, T., Laubacher, A., & Rossegger, A. (2009). The consumption of internet child pornography and violent and sex offending. *BMC Psychiatry*, *9*(1), 43. doi:10.1186/1471-244X-9-43 PMID:19602221

Enough.org. (2017, November 10). *Cyberbullying Statistics*. Retried from http://enough.org/stats_cyberbullying

Erdur-Baker, O. (2010). Cyberbullying and its correlation to traditional bullying, gender and frequent and risky usage of internet-mediated communication tools. *New Media & Society*, *12*(1), 109–125. doi:10.1177/1461444809341260

Ezoe, S., Iida, T., Inoue, K., & Toda, M. (2016). Development of Japanese version of Smartphone Dependence Scale. *Open Journal of Preventive Medicine*, *6*(07), 179–185. doi:10.4236/ojpm.2016.67017

Falconier, M. K., Nussbeck, F., Bodenmann, G., Schneider, H., & Bradbury, T. (2015). Stress from daily hassles in couples: Its effects on intradyadic stress, relationship satisfaction, and physical and psychological well-being. *Journal of Marital and Family Therapy*, *41*(2), 221–235. doi:10.1111/jmft.12073 PMID:24807831

Fanti, K. A., Demetriou, A. G., & Hawa, V. V. (2012). A longitudinal study of cyberbullying: Examining risk and protective factors. *European Journal of Developmental Psychology*, *8*(2), 168–181. doi:10.1080/17405629.2011.643169

Farwell, L. A., & Donchin, E. (1988). Talking off the top of your head: Toward a mental prosthesis utilizing event-related brain potentials. *Electroencephalography and Clinical Neurophysiology*, *70*(6), 510–523. doi:10.1016/0013-4694(88)90149-6 PMID:2461285

Fazel-Rezai, R., Allison, B. Z., Guger, C., Sellers, E. W., Kleih, S. C., & Kübler, A. (2012). P300 brain computer interface: Current challenges and emerging trends. *Frontiers in Neuroengineering*, 5. PMID:22822397

Ferrante, A., & Gellerman, D. (2015). Diurnal preference predicts phase differences in expression of human peripheral circadian clock genes. *Journal of Circadian Rhythms*, *13*(4), 1–7. PMID:27103930

Ferreira, P., Veiga Simão, A. M., Ferreira, A., Souza, S., & Francisco, S. (2016). Student bystander behavior and cultural issues in cyberbullying: When actions speak louder than words. *Computers in Human Behavior*, *60*, 301–311. doi:10.1016/j.chb.2016.02.059

Festl, R. (2016). Perpetrors on the internet. Analysing individual and structural explanation factors of cyberbullying in school context. *Computers in Human Behavior*, *59*, 237–248. doi:10.1016/j. chb.2016.02.017

Festl, R., Schwarkow, M., & Quandt, T. (2013). Peer influence, internet use and cyberbullying: A comparison of different context effects among German adolescents. *Journal of Children and Media*, *7*(4), 446–462. doi:10.1080/17482798.2013.781514

Finke, A., Lenhardt, A., & Ritter, H. (2009). The MindGame: A P300-based brain–computer interface game. *Neural Networks*, *22*(9), 1329–1333. doi:10.1016/j.neunet.2009.07.003 PMID:19635654

Fishbein, M., & Ajzen, I. (1975). *Belief, attitude, intention and behavior: An introduction to theory and research*. Reading, MA: Addison-Wesley.

Fisher, W. A., & Barak, A. (2001). Internet pornography: A social psychological perspective on internet sexuality. *Journal of Sex Research*, *38*(4), 312–323. doi:10.1080/00224490109552102

Fish, J., Brimson, J., & Lynch, S. (2016). Mindfulness interventions delivered by technology without facilitator involvement: What research exists and what are the clinical outcomes? *Mindfulness*, *7*(5), 1011–1023. doi:10.100712671-016-0548-2 PMID:27642370

Fitbit. (2018). Retrieved from https://www.fitbit.com/home

Flannery, D., Todres, J., Bradshaw, C., Amar, A., Graham, S., Hatzenbuehler, M., ... Rivara, F. (2016). Bullying prevention: A summary of the report of the National Academies of Sciences, Engineering, and Medicine. *Prevention Science*, *17*(8), 1044–1053. doi:10.100711121-016-0722-8 PMID:27722816

Flood, M., & Hamilton, C. (2003, February). *Youth and pornography in Australia: Evidence on the extent of exposure and likely effects*. The Australian Institute.

Flood, M. (2009). The harms of pornography exposure among children and young people. *Child Abuse Review*, *18*(6), 384–400. doi:10.1002/car.1092

Forgas, J. P. (1995). Mood and judgment: The affect infusion model (AIM). *Psychological Bulletin, 117*(1), 39–66. doi:10.1037/0033-2909.117.1.39 PMID:7870863

Foster, D., Linehan, C., Kirman, B., Lawson, S., & James, G. (2010). Motivating physical activity at work: Using persuasive social media for competitive step counting. *14th International Academic MindTrek Conference: Envisioning Future Media Environments*, 111–116.

Francisco, S., Veiga Simão, A. M., Ferreira, P. C., & Martins, M. J. D. (2015). Cyberbullying: The hidden side of college students. *Computers in Human Behavior, 43*, 167–182. doi:10.1016/j.chb.2014.10.045

Frank, J., Mannor, S., & Precup, D. (2011). *Activity Recognition with Mobile Phones*. In *Machine Learning and Knowledge Discovery in Databases*. Springer Berlin Heidelberg. doi:10.1007/978-3-642-23808-6_44

Freeman, G. H., & Halton, J. H. (1951). Note on exact treatment of contingency, goodness of fit and other problems of significance. *Biometrika, 38*(1-2), 141–149. doi:10.1093/biomet/38.1-2.141 PMID:14848119

Freire, I., Alves, M. M., Breia, A. P., Conceição, D., & Fragoso, L. (2013). Cyberbullying e Ambiente Escolar: Um Estudo Exploratório e Colaborativo entre a Escola e a Universidade [Cyberbullyingand school climate: An exploratory and collaborative study between school and university]. *Revista Portuguesa de Pedagogia, 47*(1), 43–64. doi:10.14195/1647-8614_47-2_3

Friedman, E. (2010, September 29). Victim of secret dorm sex tape posts Facebook goodbye, jumps to his death. *ABC News*. Retrieved from http://abcnews.go.com/US/victim-secret-dorm-sex-tape-commits-suicide/story?id=11758716

Fritz, S., & Lusardi, M. (2009). White paper: "walking speed: the sixth vital sign. *Journal of Geriatric Physical Therapy, 32*(2), 46. doi:10.1519/00139143-200932020-00002 PMID:20039582

Frontex Risk Analysis Unit. (2017). *The Western Balkans Annual Risk Analysis 2017*. European Border and Coast Guard Agency. Accessed 11/11/17 from http://frontex.europa.eu/assets/Publications/Risk_Analysis/WB_ARA_2017.pdf

Gao, M., Zhao, X., & McJunkin, M. (2016). Adolescents' experiences of cyberbullying: Gender, age, and reasons for not reporting to adults. *International Journal of Cyber Behavior, Psychology and Learning, 6*(4), 13–27. doi:10.4018/IJCBPL.2016100102

Gao, Y. (Ed.). (2005). *Web systems design and online consumer behavior*. IGI Global. doi:10.4018/978-1-59140-327-2

Garcia, G. (2008). *High frequency SSVEPs for BCI applications*. Paper presented at the Computer-Human Interaction.

Gartner. (2017). *Report "The Nexus of Forces: Social, Mobile, Cloud and Information"*. Retrieved from http://www.gartner.com/DisplayDocument?doc_cd=234840

Geertz, C. (1973). *The interpretation of cultures*. New York: Basic Books.

Giannotti, F., Cortesi, F., Sebastiani, T., & Ottaviano, S. (2002). Circadian preference, sleep and daytime behaviour in adolescence. *Journal of Sleep Research, 11*(3), 191–199. doi:10.1046/j.1365-2869.2002.00302.x PMID:12220314

Gibson, J. J. (1977). The Theory of Affordances. In R. Shaw & J. Bransford (Eds.), *Perceiving, Acting, and Knowing: Toward an Ecological Psychology* (pp. 67–82). Hillsdale, NJ: Lawrence Erlbaum.

Gillespie, M., Ampofo, L., Cheesman, M., Faith, B., Iliadou, E., Issa, A., Osseiran, S., & Skleparis, D. (2016). *Mapping Refugee Media Journeys: Smartphones and Social Media Networks*. Project Report. The Open University / France Médias Monde.

Goebert, D., Else, I., Matsu, C., Chung-Do, J., & Chang, J. Y. (2011). The impact of cyberbullying on substance use and mental health in a multiethnic sample. *Maternal and Child Health Journal, 15*(8), 1282–1286. doi:10.100710995-010-0672-x PMID:20824318

Görzig, A. (2016). Adolescents' viewing of suicide-related web content and psychological problems: Differentiating the roles of cyberbullying involvement. *Cyberpsychology, Behavior, and Social Networking, 19*(8), 502–509. doi:10.1089/cyber.2015.0419 PMID:27448043

Gosling, S. D., Augustine, A. A., Vazire, S., Holtzman, N., & Gaddis, S. (2011). Manifestations of personality in online social networks: Self-reported Facebook-related behaviors and observable profile information. *Cyberpsychology, Behavior, and Social Networking, 14*(9), 483–488. doi:10.1089/cyber.2010.0087 PMID:21254929

Gosling, S. D., Rentfrow, P. J., & Swann, W. B. Jr. (2003). A very brief measure of the Big-Five personality domains. *Journal of Research in Personality, 37*(6), 504–528. doi:10.1016/S0092-6566(03)00046-1

Gosling, S. D., Vazire, S., Srivastava, S., & John, O. P. (2004). February/March. Should we trust web-based studies? A comparative analysis of six preconceptions about internet questionnaires. *The American Psychologist, 59*(2), 93–104. doi:10.1037/0003-066X.59.2.93 PMID:14992636

Goswami, A., Baruah, P., & Borah, S. (2013). Customer Satisfaction towards Online Shopping with Special Reference to Teenage Group of Jorhat Town. *PARIPEX - Indian Journal of Research, 3*(4), 239-241.

Gradinger, P., Strohmeier, D., & Spiel, C. (2009). Traditional bullying and cyberbullying. *The Journal of Psychology, 217*, 205–213.

Grazioli, S. (2004). Where Did They Go Wrong? An Analysis of the Failure of Knowledgeable Internet Consumers to Detect Deception Over the Internet. *Group Decision and Negotiation, 13*(2), 149–172. doi:10.1023/B:GRUP.0000021839.04093.5d

Grigg, D. W. (2012). Definitional constructs of cyberbullying and cyber aggression from a triangulatory overview: A preliminary study into elements. *Journal of Aggression, Conflict and Peace Research, 4*(4), 202–215. doi:10.1108/17596591211270699

Grigonis, H. (2017, July 20). *Cyberbullying happens more often on Instagram*. Retrieved from https://www.digitaltrends.com/social-media/cyberbullying-statistics-2017-ditch-the-label/

GSMA. (2017). *The Importance of Mobile for Refugees: A Landscape of New Services and Approaches*. Accessed 11/11/17 from https://www.gsma.com/mobilefordevelopment/wp-content/uploads/2017/02/The-Importance-of-mobile-for-refugees_a-landscape-of-new-services-and-approaches.pdf

Guger, C., Allison, B. Z., & Müller-Putz, G. R. (2015). *Brain-Computer Interface Research: A State-of-the-Art Summary 4. In Brain-Computer Interface Research* (pp. 1–8). Springer. doi:10.1007/978-3-319-25190-5

Guger, C., Allison, B., & Ushiba, J. (2017). *Recent Advances in Brain-Computer Interface Research—A Summary of the BCI Award 2015 and BCI Research Trends. In Brain-Computer Interface Research* (pp. 131–136). Springer.

Guo, K. H., Yuan, Y., Archer, N. P., & Connelly, C. E. (2011). Understanding Nonmalicious Security Violations in the Workplace: A Composite Behavior Model. *Journal of Management Information Systems, 28*(2), 203–236. doi:10.2753/MIS0742-1222280208

Guo, X., Ling, K. C., & Liu, M. (2012). Evaluating factors influencing customer satisfaction towards online shopping in China. *Asian Social Science, 8*(13), 40–50. doi:10.5539/ass.v8n13p40

Gupta, D. K., & Khincha, P. K. (2015). Factors Influencing Online Shopping Behavior of Customers: An Empirical Study. *Common Wealth Journal of Commerce & Management Research, 2*(7), 39–50.

Gürkök, H. (2012). *Mind the sheep! User experience evaluation & brain-computer interface games*. University of Twente.

Haas, C., Caton, S., Chard, K., & Weinhardt, C. (2013). Co-operative infrastructures: An economic model for providing infrastructures for social cloud computing. In *System Sciences (HICSS), 2013 46th Hawaii International Conference on*. IEEE. 10.1109/HICSS.2013.147

Haber, J. D., & Daley, L. A. (2011). A cyberbullying protection plan. *Camping Magazine, 84*(2), 32–37.

Häggström-Nordin, E., Hanson, U., & Tydén, T. (2005). Association between pornography consumption and sexual practices among adolescents in Sweden. *International Journal of STD & AIDS, 16*(2), 102–107. doi:10.1258/0956462053057512 PMID:15807936

Hald, G. M., Kuyper, L., Adam, P. C. G., & de Wit, J. B. F. (2013). Does viewing explain doing? Assessing the association between sexually explicit materials use and sexual behaviors in a large sample of Dutch adolescents and young adults. *Journal of Sexual Medicine, 10*(12), 2986–2995. doi:10.1111/jsm.12157 PMID:23621804

Hald, G. M., & Štulhofer, A. (2016). What types of pornography do people use and do they cluster? Assessing types and categories of pornography consumption in a large-scale online sample. *Journal of Sex Research, 53*(7), 849–859. doi:10.1080/00224499.2015.1065953 PMID:26445007

Hall, J. A., Park, N., Song, H., & Cody, M. J. (2010). Strategic misrepresentation in online dating: The effects of gender, self-monitoring, and personality traits. *Journal of Social and Personal Relationships*, *27*(1), 117–135. doi:10.1177/0265407509349633

Hamburger, Y. A., & Ben-Artzi, E. (2000). The relationship between extraversion and neuroticism and the different uses of the Internet. *Computers in Human Behavior*, *16*(4), 441–449. doi:10.1016/S0747-5632(00)00017-0

Hango, D. (2016). *Insights on Canadian Society: Cyberbullying and cyberstalking among Internet users aged 15 to 29 in Canada.* Retrieved from https://www.statcan.gc.ca/pub/75-006-x/2016001/article/14693-eng.htm

Hann, D. M., Denniston, M. M., & Baker, F. (2000). Measurement of fatigue in cancer patients: Further validation of the fatigue symptom inventory. *Quality of Life Research: An International Journal of Quality of Life Aspects of Treatment, Care and Rehabilitation*, *9*(7), 847–854. doi:10.1023/A:1008900413113 PMID:11297027

Hao, B., Li, L., Gao, R., Li, A., & Zhu, T. (2014, August). Sensing subjective well-being from social media. In *International Conference on Active Media Technology* (pp. 324-335). Springer.

Harada, T., Morikuni, M., & ... . (2002). Usage of mobile phone in the evening or at night makes Japanese students evening-typed and night sleep uncomfortable. *Sleep and Hypnosis*, *4*, 149–153.

Hardcastle, S. J., Hancox, J., Hattar, A., Maxwell-Smith, C., Thøgersen-Ntoumani, C., & Hagger, M. S. (2015). Motivating the unmotivated: How can health behavior be changed in those unwilling to change? *Frontiers in Psychology*, *6*, 835. doi:10.3389/fpsyg.2015.00835 PMID:26136716

Haritatos, J., & Benet-Martínez, V. (2002). Bicultural identities: The interface of cultural, personality, and socio- cognitive processes. *Journal of Research in Personality*, *36*(6), 598–606. doi:10.1016/S0092-6566(02)00510-X

Harper, C., & Hodgins, D. C. (2016). Examining correlates of problematic internet pornography use among university students. *Journal of Behavioral Addictions*, *5*(20), 179–191. doi:10.1556/2006.5.2016.022 PMID:27156383

Harris, J. (2001). Structuring internetenriched learning spaces for understanding and action. *Learning and Leading with Technology*, *28*(4), 50–55.

Hasslinger, A., Hodzic, S., & Obazo, C. (2007). *Consumer behaviour in online shopping* (Master's Thesis). Department of Business Studies, Kristianstaad University.

Haythornthwaite, C. (2006). Facilitating collaboration in online learning. *Journal of Asynchronous Learning Networks, 10*(1), 7 – 24. Retrieved November 20, 2006 from http://www.sloanc.org/publications/jaln/v10n1/pdf/v10n1_2haythornthwaite.pdf

Heller, P. (2012). *Forensic Oceanography Report on the "Left-To-Die Boat."* Situ Studio.

Henri, F. (1992). Computer conferencing and content analysis. In A. R. Kaye (Ed.), *Collaborative learning through computer conferencing: The Najaden Papers* (pp. 117–136). Berlin: Springer Verlag. doi:10.1007/978-3-642-77684-7_8

He, Q., Glas, C. A., Kosinski, M., Stillwell, D. J., & Veldkamp, B. P. (2014). Predicting self-monitoring skills using textual posts on Facebook. *Computers in Human Behavior, 33*, 69–78. doi:10.1016/j.chb.2013.12.026

Herrero, J., Urueña, A., Torres, A., & Hidalgo, A. (2017). My computer is infected: The role of users' sensation seeking and domain-specific risk perceptions and risk attitudes on computer harm. *Journal of Risk Research, 20*(11), 1466–1479. doi:10.1080/13669877.2016.1153504

Herrmann, C. S. (2001). Human EEG responses to 1–100 Hz flicker: Resonance phenomena in visual cortex and their potential correlation to cognitive phenomena. *Experimental Brain Research, 137*(3-4), 346–353. doi:10.1007002210100682 PMID:11355381

Higuchi, S., Motohashi, Y., Liu, Y., & Maeda, A. (2005). Effects of playing a computer game using a bright display on presleep physiological variables, sleep latency, slow wave sleep and REM sleep. *Journal of Sleep Research, 14*(3), 267–273. doi:10.1111/j.1365-2869.2005.00463.x PMID:16120101

Hinduja, S., & Patchin, J. (2010). Bullying, cyberbullying, and suicide. *Archives of Suicide Research, 14*(3), 206–221. doi:10.1080/13811118.2010.494133 PMID:20658375

Hinduja, S., & Patchin, J. W. (2007). Offline consequences of online victimization. *Journal of School Violence, 6*(3), 89–112. doi:10.1300/J202v06n03_06

Hinduja, S., & Patchin, J. W. (2012). Cyberbullying: Neither and epidemic nor a rarity. *European Journal of Developmental Psychology, 9*(5), 539–543. doi:10.1080/17405629.2012.706448

Hinduja, S., & Patchin, J. W. (2013). Social influences on cyberbullying behaviors among middle and high school students. *Journal of Youth and Adolescence, 42*(5), 711–722. doi:10.100710964-012-9902-4 PMID:23296318

Hinterberger, T., Widman, G., Lal, T. N., Hill, J., Tangermann, M., Rosenstiel, W., ... Birbaumer, N. (2008). Voluntary brain regulation and communication with electrocorticogram signals. *Epilepsy & Behavior, 13*(2), 300–306. doi:10.1016/j.yebeh.2008.03.014 PMID:18495541

Hirata, F. C., Lima, M. C., de Bruin, V. M., Nóbrega, P. R., Wenceslau, G. P., & de Bruin, P. F. (2007). Depression in medical school: The influence of morningness-eveningness. *Chronobiology International, 24*(5), 939–946. doi:10.1080/07420520701657730 PMID:17994347

Hochberg, L. R., Serruya, M. D., Friehs, G. M., Mukand, J. A., Saleh, M., Caplan, A. H., ... Donoghue, J. P. (2006). Neuronal ensemble control of prosthetic devices by a human with tetraplegia. *Nature, 442*(7099), 164–171. doi:10.1038/nature04970 PMID:16838014

Hoff, D. L., & Mitchell, S. N. (2009). Cyberbullying: Causes, effects, and remedies. *Journal of Educational Administration, 47*(2), 652–665. doi:10.1108/09578230910981107

Hollinger, R. C. (1988). Computer hackers follow a guttman-like progression. *Sociology and Social Research, 72*(3), 199–200.

Holt, T. J., Bossler, A. M., & May, D. C. (2012). Low self-control, deviant peer associations, and juvenile cyberdeviance. *American Journal of Criminal Justice, 37*(3), 378–395. doi:10.100712103-011-9117-3

Holz, E. M., Botrel, L., Kaufmann, T., & Kübler, A. (2015). Long-term independent brain-computer interface home use improves quality of life of a patient in the locked-in state: A case study. *Archives of Physical Medicine and Rehabilitation, 96*(3), S16–S26. doi:10.1016/j.apmr.2014.03.035 PMID:25721543

Holz, E. M., Botrel, L., & Kübler, A. (2015). Independent home use of Brain Painting improves quality of life of two artists in the locked-in state diagnosed with amyotrophic lateral sclerosis. *Brain-Computer Interfaces, 2*(2-3), 117–134. doi:10.1080/2326263X.2015.1100048

Hong, Y. Y., Chiu, C. Y., & Kung, T. (1997). Bringing culture out in front: Effects of cultural meaning system activation on social cognition. In K. Leung, Y. Kashima, U. Kim, & S. Yamaguchi (Eds.), *Progress in Asian social psychology* (Vol. 1, pp. 135–146). Singapore: Wiley.

Hong, Y. Y., Morris, M., Chiu, C. Y., & Benet-Martínez, V. (2000). Multicultural minds: A dynamic constructivist approach to culture and cognition. *The American Psychologist, 55*(7), 709–720. doi:10.1037/0003-066X.55.7.709 PMID:10916861

Horne, J. A., & Östberg, O. (1976). A self-assessment questionnaire to determine morningness–eveningness in human circadian rhythms. *International Journal of Chronobiology, 4*(2), 97–110. PMID:1027738

Horzum, M. B., Randler, C., Masal, E., Beşoluk, Ş., Önder, İ., & Vollmer, C. (2015). Morningness-eveningness and the environment hypothesis – A cross-cultural comparison of Turkish and German adolescents. *Chronobiology International, 32*(6), 814–821. doi:10.3109/07420528.2015.1041598 PMID:26061589

Huang, J. H., & Yang, Y. C. (2010). The relationship between personality traits and online shopping motivations. *Social Behavior and Personality, 38*(5), 673–679. doi:10.2224bp.2010.38.5.673

Huang, Y., & Chou, C. (2010). An analysis of multiple factors of cyberbullying among junior high school students in Taiwan. *Computers in Human Behavior, 26*(6), 1581–1590. doi:10.1016/j.chb.2010.06.005

Huggins, J. E., Guger, C., Ziat, M., Zander, T. O., Taylor, D., Tangermann, M., . . . Rupp, R. (2017). Workshops of the Sixth International Brain–Computer Interface Meeting: brain–computer interfaces past, present, and future. *Brain-Computer Interfaces*, 1-34.

Human Factors and Ergonomics Society (HFES). (2018). *What is Human Factors/Ergonomics?* Retrieved from https://www.hfes.org/Security/ContentPages/?Id=40

Humphrey, N., & Symes, W. (2010). Responses to bullying and use of social support among pupils with autism spectrum disorders (ASDs) in mainstream schools: A qualitative study. *Journal of Research in Special Educational Needs, 10*(2), 82–90. doi:10.1111/j.1471-3802.2010.01146.x

Hwang, H.-J., Kim, S., Choi, S., & Im, C.-H. (2013). EEG-based brain-computer interfaces: A thorough literature survey. *International Journal of Human-Computer Interaction, 29*(12), 814–826. doi:10.1080/10447318.2013.780869

Ignacio, N. (2000). "Ain't I a Filipino (woman)": An analysis of authorship and authority through the construction of "Filipina" on the net. *The Sociological Quarterly, 41*(4), 551–572. doi:10.1111/j.1533-8525.2000.tb00073.x

International Centre for Missing and Exploited Children. (2016). *Child pornography: Model legislation and global review* (8th ed.). Author. Retrieved from www.icmec.com

Internet Crime Complaint Center. (2017). *2016 Internet Crime Report.* Retrieved from https://pdf.ic3.gov/2016_IC3Report.pdf

Internet Watch Foundation. (2017, April 3). *IWF Annual Report 2016.* Retrieved December 18, 2017 from iwf.org.uk

Internet World Statistics. (2018). *Usage and population statistics.* Retrieved from https://www.internetworldstats.com/stats.htm

Intille, S. S. (2004). *Ubiquitous computing technology for just-in-time motivation of behavior change.* Retrieved March 15, 2018 from http://citeseerx.ist.psu.edu/viewdoc/download?doi=10.1.1.5.7011&rep=rep1&type=pdf

Jacobsen, D. M. (2001). *Building different bridges: Technology integration, engaged student learning, and new approaches to professional development.* Paper presented at AERA 2001: What We Know and How We Know It, the 82nd Annual Meeting of the American Educational Research Association, Seattle, WA. Retrieved November 20, 2006, from http://www.ucalgary.ca/~dmjacobs/aera/building_bridges.html

Jäger, T. (Ed.). (2010). *Taking action against cyberbullying – Training Manual.* Landau: Verlag Empirische Padagogik. Retrieved from http://www.cybertraining-project.org/book/

Jäger, T., Stelter, C., Amado, J., Matos, A., & Pessoa, T. (Eds.). (2012). *Cyberbullying - Um manual de formação de pais* [Cyberbullying: a Parents' training manual]. Retrieved from http://ct4p.zepf.eu/CT4P_Training_manual_PT.pdf

James, W. (1884). What Is an Emotion? *Mind, 9*(34), 188–205. doi:10.1093/mind/os-IX.34.188

Jang, H., Song, J., & Kim, R. (2014). Does the offline bully-victimization influence cyberbullying behavior among youths? Application of general strain theory. *Computers in Human Behavior, 31,* 85–93. doi:10.1016/j.chb.2013.10.007

Jansen, L., Applebaum, P., Klein, W., Weinstein, N., Cook, J., & Sulmasy, D. (2011). Unrealistic optimism in early-phase oncology trials. *Ethics and Human Research, 33*(1), 1–8. PMID:21314034

Janssen, D., Schöllhorn, W. I., Lubienetzki, J., Fölling, K., Kokenge, H., & Davids, K. (2008). Recognition of emotions in gait patterns by means of artificial neural nets. *Journal of Nonverbal Behavior, 32*(2), 79–92. doi:10.100710919-007-0045-3

Jarosiewicz, B., Sarma, A. A., Bacher, D., Masse, N. Y., Simeral, J. D., Sorice, B., . . . Gilja, V. (2015). Virtual typing by people with tetraplegia using a self-calibrating intracortical brain-computer interface. *Science Translational Medicine, 7*(313).

Johnson, D. W., & Johnson, R. (1994). *Joining together: Group theory and group skills* (5th ed.). Boston: Allyn & Bacon.

Johnson, P. E., Grazioli, S., Jamal, K., & Berryman, G. (2001). Detecting deception: Adversarial problem solving in a low base rate world. *Cognitive Science, 25*(3), 355–392. doi:10.120715516709cog2503_2

Joinson, A. (1999, August). Social desirability, anonymity, and internet-based questionnaires. *Behavior Research Methods, Instruments, & Computers: A Journal of the Psychonomic Society, 31*(3), 433-438.

Jones, S. E., Manstead, A. S. R., & Livingstone, A. G. (2011). Ganging up or sticking together? Group processes and children's responses to text-message bullying. *British Journal of Psychology, 102*(1), 71–96. PMID:21241286

Jordan, T., Raubal, M., Gartrell, B., & Egenhofer, M. (1998). An affordance-based model of place in GIS. *Eight International Symposium on Spatial Data Handling*, 98–109.

Juniper Research. (2015). *Cybercrime will Cost Businesses Over $2 Trillion by 2019*. Retrieved from https://www.juniperresearch.com/press/press-releases/cybercrime-cost-businesses-over-2trillion

Jusoh, Z. M., & Ling, G. H. (2012). Factors Influencing Consumers' Attitude Towards E-Commerce Purchases Through Online Shopping. *International Journal of Humanities and Social Science, 2*(4), 223–230.

Kahneman, D. (2011). *Thinking, fast and slow*. New York, NY: Farrar, Straus and Giroux.

Kaiser Family Foundation. (2017, July). *The U.S. government and global non-communicable disease efforts*. Retrieved from https://www.kff.org/global-health-policy/fact-sheet/the-u-s-government-and-global-non-communicable-diseases/

Kale, A., Sundaresan, A., Rajagopalan, A. N., Cuntoor, N. P., Roy-Chowdhury, A. K., & Krüger, V. (2004). Identification of humans using gait. *IEEE Transactions on Image Processing, 13*(9), 1163-1173.

Kanoun, O. (2016). *Chair for Measurement and Sensor Technology Embedded Systems*. Retrieved from https://www.tu-chemnitz.de/studium/studiengaenge/flyer/ embedded_ systems_eng.pdf

Kaplan, A., Zhigulskaya, D., & Kirjanov, D. (2016). Studying the ability to control human phantom fingers in P300 brain-computer interface. *Вестник Российского государственного медицинского университета*(2 (eng)).

Karg, M., Jenke, R., Kühnlenz, K., & Buss, M. (2009). A Two-fold PCA-Approach for Inter-Individual Recognition of Emotions in Natural Walking. In *Machine Learning and Data Mining in Pattern Recognition, International Conference, Mldm 2009, Leipzig, Germany, July 2009, Poster Proceedings* (pp. 51-61). DBLP.

Karg, M., Kühnlenz, K., & Buss, M. (2010). Recognition of affect based on gait patterns. *IEEE Transactions on Systems Man & Cybernetics Part B Cybernetics, 40*(4), 1050-61.

Karim, A. A., Hinterberger, T., Richter, J., Mellinger, J., Neumann, N., Flor, H., ... Birbaumer, N. (2006). Neural internet: Web surfing with brain potentials for the completely paralyzed. *Neurorehabilitation and Neural Repair, 20*(4), 508–515. doi:10.1177/1545968306290661 PMID:17082507

Kashima, Y. (2000). Conceptions of culture and person for psychology. *Journal of Cross-Cultural Psychology, 31*(1), 14–32. doi:10.1177/0022022100031001003

Kastbom, A. A., Sydsjö, G., Bladh, M., Priebe, G., & Svedin, C.-G. (2015). Sexual debut before the age of 14 leads to poorer psychosocial health and risky behaviour in later life. *Acta Paediatrica (Oslo, Norway), 104*(1), 91–100. doi:10.1111/apa.12803 PMID:25213099

Katta, R. M. R., & Patro, C. S. (2016). Online Shopping Behavior: A Study of Factors Influencing Consumer Satisfaction on Online viz-a-viz Conventional Store Shopping. *International Journal of Sociotechnology and Knowledge Development, 8*(4), 21–36. doi:10.4018/IJSKD.2016100102

Katta, R. M. R., & Patro, C. S. (2017). Influence of Web Attributes on Consumer Purchase Intentions. *International Journal of Sociotechnology and Knowledge Development, 9*(2), 1–16. doi:10.4018/IJSKD.2017040101

Kauderer, S., & Randler, C. (2013). Differences in time use among chronotypes in adolescents. *Biological Rhythm Research, 44*(4), 601–608. doi:10.1080/09291016.2012.721687

Keisidou, E., Sarigiannidis, L., & Maditinos, D. (2011). Consumer characteristics and their effect on accepting online shopping in the context of different product types. *International Journal of Business Science and Applied Management, 6*(2), 31–51.

Kelava, M. (2013, October 23). *Budi dobar susjed, podjeli internet vezu! H-alter*. Retrieved November 2, 2017, from http://h-alter.org/vijesti/budi-dobar-susjed-podijeli-internet-vezu

Kelley, P. G., Cranor, L. F., & Sadeh, N. (2013). Privacy as Part of the App Decision-making Process. *Proceedings of the 2013 ACM Annual Conference on Human Factors in Computing Systems*. 10.1145/2470654.2466466

Kennedy, H. (2010, March 29). Phoebe Prince, South Hadley High School's 'new girl,' driven to suicide by teenage cyber bullies. *New York Daily News*. Retrieved from http://www.nydailynews.com/news/national/phoebe-prince-south-hadley-high-school-new-girl-driven-suicide-teenage-cyber-bullies-article-1.165911

Kennedy, C. M., Powell, J., Payne, T. H., Ainsworth, J., Boyd, A., & Buchan, I. (2012). Active Assistance Technology for Health-Related Behavior Change: An Interdisciplinary Review. *Journal of Medical Internet Research*, *14*(3), e80. doi:10.2196/jmir.1893 PMID:22698679

Kettleborough, D. G., & Merdian, H. L. (2017). Gateway to offending behaviour: Permission-giving thoughts of online users of child sexual exploitation material. *Journal of Sexual Aggression*, *23*(1), 19–32. doi:10.1080/13552600.2016.1231852

Khristianto, W., Kertahadi, I., & Suyadi, I. (2012). The influence of information, system and service on customer satisfaction and loyalty in online shopping. *International Journal of Academic Research*, *4*(2), 28–32.

Kim, D. I., & Lee, Y. H. (2012). New patterns in media addiction: Is smartphone a substitute or a complement to the Internet? *Korean Journal of Youth Counseling*, *201*, 71–88.

Kim, D. I., Lee, Y. H., Lee, J., Nam, J. E. K., & Chung, Y. (2014). Development of Korean smartphone addiction proneness scale for youth. *PLoS One*, *9*(5), e97920. doi:10.1371/journal.pone.0097920 PMID:24848006

Kim, H. (2016). The role of emotions and culture in the third-person effect process of news coverage of election poll results. *Communication Research*, *43*(1), 109–130. doi:10.1177/0093650214558252

Kim, N. S., & Lee, K. E. (2012). Effects of self-control and life stress on smartphone addiction of university students. *Journal of the Korean Society of Health Informatics and Statistics*, *372*, 72–83.

Kim, S., & Stoel, L. (2004). Apparel retailers: Website quality dimensions and satisfaction. *Journal of Retailing and Consumer Services*, *11*(2), 109–117. doi:10.1016/S0969-6989(03)00010-9

Kim, Y.-H. (2001). Korean adolescents' health risk behaviors and their relationships with the selected psychological constructs. *The Journal of Adolescent Health*, *29*(4), 298–306. doi:10.1016/S1054-139X(01)00218-X PMID:11587914

Kim, Y.-H. (2011). Adolescents' health behaviours and its associations with psychological variables. *Central European Journal of Public Health*, *19*(4), 205–209. PMID:22432395

King, A. V. (2010). Constituency of cyberbullying laws: Keeping the online playground safe for both teens and free speech. *Vanderbilt Law Review*, *63*(3), 845–884.

Ko, C., & Takahashi, J. S. (2006). Molecular components of the mammalian circadian clock. *Human Molecular Genetics*, *15*(suppl_2), 271–277. doi:10.1093/hmg/ddl207 PMID:16987893

Kochenderfer-Ladd, B., & Pelletier, M. (2008). Teachers' views and beliefs about bullying: Influences on classroom management strategies and students' coping with peer victimization. *Journal of School Psychology*, *46*(4), 431–453. doi:10.1016/j.jsp.2007.07.005 PMID:19083367

König, A., Golwitzer, M., & Steffegen, G. (2010). Cyberbullying as an act of revenge? *Journal of Australian of Guidance and Counselling*, *20*(2), 210–224. doi:10.1375/ajgc.20.2.210

Koolhaas, J. M., Bartolomucci, A., Buwalda, B. D., De Boer, S. F., Flügge, G., Korte, S. M., ... Richter-Levin, G. (2011). Stress revisited: a critical evaluation of the stress concept. *Neuroscience & Biobehavioral Reviews, 35*(5), 1291-1301.

Ko, S.-G., Lee, T.-H., Yoon, H.-Y., Kwon, J.-H., & Mather, M. (2010). How does context affect assessments of facial emotion? The role of culture and age. *Psychology and Aging.*

Kosinski, M., Stillwell, D., Kohli, P., Bachrach, Y., & Graepel, T. (2012). Personality and website choice. *Age, 15*(51.10), 21-24.

Kosinski, M., Stillwell, D., & Graepel, T. (2013). Private traits and attributes are predictable from digital records of human behavior. *Proceedings of the National Academy of Sciences of the United States of America, 110*(15), 5802–5805. doi:10.1073/pnas.1218772110 PMID:23479631

Koskenvuo, M., Hublin, C., Partinen, M., Heikkilä, K., & Kaprio, J. (2007). Heritability if diurnal type: A nation-wide study of 8753 adult twin pairs. *Journal of Sleep Research, 16*(2), 156–162. doi:10.1111/j.1365-2869.2007.00580.x PMID:17542945

Kowalski, R. M., & Limber, S. P. (2007). Electronic bullying among middle school students. *The Journal of Adolescent Health, 41*(6), 22–30. doi:10.1016/j.jadohealth.2007.08.017 PMID:18047942

Kowalski, R., Giummetti, G., Schroeder, A., & Lattanner, M. (2014). Bullying in the digital age: A critical review and meta-analysis of cyberbullying research among youth. *Psychological Bulletin*, 1–61. doi:10.1037/a0035618 PMID:24512111

Kowalski, R., Limber, S., & Agaston, P. (2008). *Cyberbullying*. Oxford, UK: Blackwell P.

Kraepelin, E. (1921). Dementia praecox and paraphrenia. *The Journal of Nervous and Mental Disease, 54*(54), 384. doi:10.1097/00005053-192110000-00104

Kübler, A., Halder, S., Furdea, A., & Hösle, A. (2008). Brain painting – BCI meets art. *Proceedings of the 4th International Brain-Computer Interface Workshop and Training Course*, 361–366.

Kübler, A., Nijboer, F., Mellinger, J., Vaughan, T. M., Pawelzik, H., Schalk, G., ... Wolpaw, J. R. (2005). Patients with ALS can use sensorimotor rhythms to operate a brain-computer interface. *Neurology, 64*(10), 1775–1777. doi:10.1212/01.WNL.0000158616.43002.6D PMID:15911809

Kucukyildiz, G., Ocak, H., Karakaya, S., & Sayli, O. (2017). Design and implementation of a multi sensor based brain computer interface for a robotic wheelchair. *Journal of Intelligent & Robotic Systems*, 1–17.

Kumar, S., & Sharma, M. (2012). BCI: Next Generation for HCI. *International Journal of Advanced Research in Computer Science and Software Engineering, 2*(3), 146–151.

Kwan, G. C. E., & Skoric, M. M. (2013). Facebook bullying: An extension of battles in school. *Computers in Human Behavior, 29*(1), 16–25. doi:10.1016/j.chb.2012.07.014

Kwon, M., Kim, D. J., Cho, H., & Yang, S. (2013). The Smartphone Addiction Scale: Development and validation of a short version for adolescents. *PLoS One, 8*(12), e83558. doi:10.1371/journal. pone.0083558 PMID:24391787

Kwon, M., Lee, J. Y., Won, W.-Y., Park, J.-W., Min, J.-A., Hahn, C., ... Kim, D.-J. (2013). Development and validation of a smartphone addiction scale (SAS). *PLoS One, 8*(2), e56936. doi:10.1371/journal.pone.0056936 PMID:23468893

Labov, W. (1997). Narrative analysis: Oral versions of personal experience. *Journal of Narrative and Life History, 1997, 7*.

Labov, W., & Waletzky, J. (1967). Narrative analysis: Oral versions of personal experience. In J. Helm (Ed.), *Essays on the verbal and visual arts* (pp. 12–44). Seattle, WA: University of Washington Press.

Laftman, S. B., Modin, B., & Ostberg, V. (2013). Cyberbullying and subjective health: A large-scale study of students in Stockholm, Sweden. *Children and Youth Services Review, 35*(1), 112–119. doi:10.1016/j.childyouth.2012.10.020

Lakoff, G. (1987). *Women, Fire, and Dangerous Things*. Chicago, IL: University of Chicago Press. doi:10.7208/chicago/9780226471013.001.0001

Lang, P. J., Bradley, M. M., & Cuthbert, B. N. (1998). Emotion, motivation, and anxiety: Brain mechanisms and psychophysiology. *Biological Psychiatry, 44*(12), 1248–1263. doi:10.1016/S0006-3223(98)00275-3 PMID:9861468

Laursen, D. (2005). Please reply! The replying norm in adolescent SMS communication. In R. Harper, L. Palen, & A. Taylor (Eds.), *The Inside Text: Social, Cultural and Design Perspectives on SMS* (pp. 53–73). Dordrecht, The Netherlands: Springer. doi:10.1007/1-4020-3060-6_4

Lave, J., & Wenger, E. (1991). *Situated Learning: Legitimate peripheral participation*. New York: Cambridge University Press. doi:10.1017/CBO9780511815355

Lazuras, L., Barkoukis, V., Ourda, D., & Tsorbatzoudis, H. (2013). A process model of cyberbullying in adolescence. *Computers in Human Behavior, 29*(3), 881–887. doi:10.1016/j.chb.2012.12.015

Leeb, R., Lancelle, M., Kaiser, V., Fellner, D. W., & Pfurtscheller, G. (2013). Thinking penguin: Multimodal brain–computer interface control of a vr game. *IEEE Transactions on Computational Intelligence and AI in Games, 5*(2), 117–128. doi:10.1109/TCIAIG.2013.2242072

Lee, E., Ahn, J., & Kim, Y. J. (2014). Personality traits and self-presentation at Facebook. *Personality and Individual Differences, 69*, 162–167. doi:10.1016/j.paid.2014.05.020

Lee, Y. K., Chang, C. T., Lin, Y., & Cheng, Z. H. (2014). The dark side of smartphone usage: Psychological traits, compulsive behavior and technostress. *Computers in Human Behavior, 31*, 373–383. doi:10.1016/j.chb.2013.10.047

Lemke, M. R., Wendorff, T., Mieth, B., Buhl, K., & Linnemann, M. (2000). Spatiotemporal gait patterns during over ground locomotion in major depression compared with healthy controls. *Journal of Psychiatric Research*, *34*(4–5), 277–283. doi:10.1016/S0022-3956(00)00017-0 PMID:11104839

Lemola, S., Perkinson-Gloor, N., Brand, S., Dewald-Kaufmann, J. F., & Grob, A. (2014). Adolescents' electronic media use at night, sleep disturbance, and depressive symptoms in the smartphone age. *Journal of Youth and Adolescence*, *44*(2), 405–418. doi:10.100710964-014-0176-x PMID:25204836

Lenhart, A. (2015). *Teens, social media & technology overview 2015*. Retrieved from: http://www.pewinternet.org/2015/04/09/teens-social-media-technology-2015/

Lepeska, D. (2016). Refugees and the Technology of Exile. *The Wilson Quarterly*. Accessed 11/11/17 from https://wilsonquarterly.com/quarterly/looking-back-moving-forward/refugees-and-the-technology-of-exile/

Lepp, A., Barkley, L. E., & Karpinski, A. C. (2014). The relationship between cell phone use, academic performance, anxiety, and satisfaction with life in college students. *Computers in Human Behavior*, *31*, 343–350. doi:10.1016/j.chb.2013.10.049

Leuthardt, E. C., Schalk, G., Wolpaw, J. R., Ojemann, J. G., & Moran, D. W. (2004). A brain–computer interface using electrocorticographic signals in humans. *Journal of Neural Engineering*, *1*(2), 63–71. doi:10.1088/1741-2560/1/2/001 PMID:15876624

Lewenberg, Y., Bachrach, Y., & Volkova, S. (2015, October). Using emotions to predict user interest areas in online social networks. In *Data Science and Advanced Analytics (DSAA), 2015. 36678 2015. IEEE International Conference on* (pp. 1-10). IEEE. 10.1109/DSAA.2015.7344887

Li, N., & Zhang, P. (2002). Consumer Online Shopping Attitudes and Behavior: An Assessment of Research. *Proceedings of Eight American Conference on Information Systems*, 508-517.

Lian, J., & Lin, T. (2008). Effects of consumer characteristics on their acceptance of online shopping: Comparisons among different product types. *Computers in Human Behavior*, *24*(1), 48–65. doi:10.1016/j.chb.2007.01.002

Liao, L.-D., Chen, C.-Y., Wang, I.-J., Chen, S.-F., Li, S.-Y., Chen, B.-W., ... Lin, C.-T. (2012). Gaming control using a wearable and wireless EEG-based brain-computer interface device with novel dry foam-based sensors. *Journal of Neuroengineering and Rehabilitation*, *9*(1), 5. doi:10.1186/1743-0003-9-5 PMID:22284235

Li, L., Li, A., Hao, B., Guan, Z., & Zhu, T. (2014). Predicting active users' personality based on micro-blogging behaviors. *PLoS One*, *9*(1), e84997. doi:10.1371/journal.pone.0084997 PMID:24465462

Lim, M. S. C., Agius, P. A., Carrotte, E. R., Vella, A. M., & Hellard, M. E. (2017). Young Australians' use of pornography and associations with sexual risk behaviours. *Australian and New Zealand Journal of Public Health*, *41*(4), 438–443. doi:10.1111/1753-6405.12678 PMID:28664609

Linnell, J. (2016, January 13) Border controls: Refugee fences fragment wildlife. *Nature*.

Lin, Y. H., & Gau, S. S. F. (2013). Association between morningness-eveningness and the severity of compulseive Internet use: The moderating role of gender and parenting style. *Sleep Medicine*, *14*(12), 1398–1404. doi:10.1016/j.sleep.2013.06.015 PMID:24157101

Li, Q. (2007). Bullying in the new playground: Research into cyberbullying and cybervictimization. *Australian Journal of Educational Technology*, *23*, 435–454.

Li, Q. (2007). New bottle but old wine: A research of cyberbullying in schools. *Computers in Human Behavior*, *23*(4), 1777–1791. doi:10.1016/j.chb.2005.10.005

Li, Q. (2008). A cross-cultural comparison of adolescents' experience related to cyberbullying. *Educational Research*, *50*(3), 223–234. doi:10.1080/00131880802309333

Li, Q. (2008). Cyberbullying in schools: An examination of preservice teacher's perception. *Canadian Journal of Learning and Technology*, *34*(2). Retrieved from http://www.cjlt.ca/index. php/cjlt/article/view/494/225

Li, Q. (2010). Cyberbullying in high schools: A study of students' behavior and beliefs about this phenomenon. *Journal of Aggression, Maltreatment & Trauma*, *19*(4), 372–392. doi:10.1080/10926771003788979

Liu, L., Preotiuc-Pietro, D., Samani, Z. R., Moghaddam, M. E., & Ungar, L. H. (2016, May). *Analyzing Personality through Social Media Profile Picture Choice* (pp. 211–220). ICWSM.

Liu, M., Xue, J., Zhao, N., Wang, X., Jiao, D., & Zhu, T. (2018, February). Using Social Media to Explore the Consequences of Domestic Violence on Mental Health. *Journal of Interpersonal Violence*. doi:10.1177/0886260518757756 PMID:29441804

Liu, X., He, M., Gao, F., & Xie, P. (2008). An empirical study of online shopping customer satisfaction in China: A holistic perspective. *International Journal of Retail & Distribution Management*, *36*(11), 919–940. doi:10.1108/09590550810911683

Liu, X., & Zhu, T. (2016). Deep learning for constructing microblog behavior representation to identify social media user's personality. *PeerJ Computer Science*, *2*, e81. doi:10.7717/peerj-cs.81

Liu, Y., Wang, J., & Jiang, Y. (2016). PT-LDA: A latent variable model to predict personality traits of social network users. *Neurocomputing*, *210*, 155–163. doi:10.1016/j.neucom.2015.10.144

Livingstone, S., Haddon, L., Gorzig, A., & Olafsson, K. (2011). *Risks and safety on the Internet: the perspective of European children. Full findings*. Retrieved from www.eukidsonline.net

Li, X. (2008). Third-person effect, optimistic bias, and sufficiency resource in Internet use. *Journal of Communication*, *58*(3), 568–587. doi:10.1111/j.1460-2466.2008.00400.x

Lopes, P. N., Salovey, P., Côté, S., Beers, M., & Petty, R. E. (2005). Emotion regulation abilities and the quality of social interaction. *Emotion (Washington, D.C.)*, *5*(1), 113–118. doi:10.1037/1528-3542.5.1.113 PMID:15755224

Lotte, F., Congedo, M., Lécuyer, A., Lamarche, F., & Arnaldi, B. (2007). A review of classification algorithms for EEG-based brain–computer interfaces. *Journal of Neural Engineering*, *4*(2), R1–R13. doi:10.1088/1741-2560/4/2/R01 PMID:17409472

Loughran, S. P., Wood, A. W., Barton, J. M., Croft, R. J., Thompson, B., & Stough, C. (2005). The effects of electromagnetic fields emitted by mobile phones on human sleep. *Neuroreport*, *16*(17), 1973–1976. doi:10.1097/01.wnr.0000186593.79705.3c PMID:16272890

Lo, V., Neilan, E., Sun, M., & Chiang, S. (1999). Exposure of Taiwanese adolescents to pornographic media and its impact on sexual attitudes and behaviour. *Asian Journal of Communication*, *9*(1), 50–71. doi:10.1080/01292989909359614

Lo, V., & Wei, R. (2005). Exposure to Internet pornography and Taiwanese adolescents' sexual attitudes and behavior. *Journal of Broadcasting & Electronic Media*, *49*(2), 221–237. doi:10.120715506878jobem4902_5

Lowrey, P., & Takahashi, J. S. (2004). Mammalian circadian biology: Elucidating genome-wide levels of temporal organization. *Annual Review of Genomics and Human Genetics*, *5*(1), 407–441. doi:10.1146/annurev.genom.5.061903.175925 PMID:15485355

Lucić, L. (2017, April). *"Not everyone wants to go to Western Europe": Exploring the decision of Syrian Refugees to permanently settle in Turkey*. Presented at: Mapping the Discursive Landscape, Center for the Humanities, The Graduate Center of The City University of New York.

Lucić, L. (2013). Use of evaluative devices by youth for sense-making of culturally diverse interactions. *International Journal of Intercultural Relations*, *37*(4), 434–449. doi:10.1016/j.ijintrel.2013.04.003

Lucić, L. (2016a). Changing landscapes, changing narratives: Socio-cultural approach for teaching global migrants. *Pedagogy, Culture & Society*, *24*(2), 221–237. doi:10.1080/1468136 6.2016.1149504

Lucić, L. (2016b). Narrative approaches to conflict resolution across technologically mediated landscapes. *International Journal of Cyber Behavior, Psychology and Learning*, *6*(1), 42–59. doi:10.4018/IJCBPL.2016010103

Lucić, L. (2016c). Developmental affordances of war-torn landscapes: Growing up in Sarajevo under siege. *Human Development*, *59*(2-3), 81–106. doi:10.1159/000448228

Luder, M.-T., Pittet, I., Berchtold, A., Akré, C., Michaud, P.-A., & Surís, J.-C. (2011). Associations between online pornography and sexual behavior among adolescents: Myth or Reality? *Archives of Sexual Behavior*, *40*(5), 1027–1035. doi:10.100710508-010-9714-0 PMID:21290259

Lvovich, N. (1997). *The multilingual self: An inquiry into language learning*. Hillsdale, NJ: Lawrence Erlbaum.

Lyons, G. (2012). *Facebook to hit a billion users in the summer. Analytics and Insights*. Retrieved from http://connect.icrossing.co.uk/facebook-hit-billion-users-summer_7709

Lyons, E. J., Lewis, Z. H., Mayrsohn, B. G., & Rowland, J. L. (2014). Behavior change techniques implemented in electronic lifestyle activity monitors: A systematic content analysis. *Journal of Medical Internet Research*, *16*(8), e192. doi:10.2196/jmir.3469 PMID:25131661

Maag, C. (2007, November 28). A hoax turned fatal draws anger but no charges. *The New York Times*. Retrieved from http://www.nytimes.com/2007/11/28/us/28hoax.html?_r=0

Machackova, H., Dedkova, L., & Mezulanikova, K. (2015). Brief report: The bystander effect in cyberbullying incidents. *Journal of Adolescence*, *43*, 96–99. doi:10.1016/j.adolescence.2015.05.010 PMID:26070168

Machackova, H., Dedkova, L., Sevcikova, A., & Cerna, A. (2013). Bystanders' support of cyberbullied schoolmates. *Journal of Community & Applied Social Psychology*, *23*(1), 25–36. doi:10.1002/casp.2135

Maher, C. A., Lewis, L. K., Ferrar, K., Marshall, S., De Bourdeaudhuij, I., & Vandelanotte, C. (2014). Are health behavior change interventions that use online social networks effective? A systematic review. *Journal of Medical Internet Research*, *16*(2), e40. doi:10.2196/jmir.2952 PMID:24550083

Manaf, M. R. A., Tahir, M. M., Sidi, H., Midin, M., Nik Jaafar, N. R., Das, S., & Malek, A. M. A. (2014). Pre-marital sex and its predicting factors among Malaysian youths. *Comprehensive Psychiatry*, *55*(Suppl. 1), S82–S88. doi:10.1016/j.comppsych.2013.03.008 PMID:23587530

Mancuso, V. F. (2014). *Human factors in cyber warfare II: Emerging perspectives*. Paper presented at the Human Factors and Ergonomics Society 58th Annual Meeting, Santa Monica, CA. 10.1177/1541931214581085

Man, J., & Bhanu, B. (2006). Individual recognition using gait energy image. *IEEE Transactions on Pattern Analysis and Machine Intelligence*, *28*(2), 316–322. doi:10.1109/TPAMI.2006.38 PMID:16468626

Marshall, T. C., Lefringhausen, K., & Ferenczi, N. (2015). The Big Five, self-esteem, and narcissism as predictors of the topics people write about in Facebook status updates. *Personality and Individual Differences*, *85*, 35–40. doi:10.1016/j.paid.2015.04.039

Martin, R. (2016). *Ready for More: Four Key Focus Areas for Global Ecommerce in 2016*. Retrieved on August 12, 2017, from http://blogs.pb.com/ecommerce/2016/01/04/four-key-focus-areas-for-global-ecommerce-in-2016

Martins, M. J. D., Veiga Simão, A., Freire, I., Caetano, A. P., & Matos, A. (2016). Cyber-victimization and cyber-aggression among Portuguese adolescents: The relation to family support and family rules. *International Journal of Cyber Behavior, Psychology and Learning*, *6*(3), 65–78. doi:10.4018/IJCBPL.2016070105

Mason, K. (2008). Cyberbullying: A preliminary assessment for school personnel. *Psychology in the Schools*, *45*(4), 323–348. doi:10.1002/pits.20301

Mathur, A., & Chetty, M. (2017). *Impact of User Characteristics on Attitudes Towards Automatic Mobile Application Updates*. Paper presented at the Thirteenth Symposium on Usable Privacy and Security (SOUPS 2017), Santa Clara, CA.

Matos, A., Vieira, C., Amado, J., Pessoa, T., & Martins, M. J. D. (2018). Cyberbullying in Portuguese Schools: Prevalence and Characteristics. *Journal of School Violence, 17*(1), 123-137. DOI: 10.1080/15388220.2016.1263796

Mattebo, M., Tydén, T., Häggström-Nordin, E., Nilsson, K. W., & Larsson, M. (2014). Pornography and sexual experiences among high school students in Sweden. *Journal of Developmental and Behavioral Pediatrics, 35*(3), 179–188. doi:10.1097/DBP.0000000000000034 PMID:24695119

McCarthy, J. A. (2010, June). Internet sexual activity: A comparison between contact and non- contact child pornography offenders. *Journal of Sexual Aggression, 16*(2), 181–195. doi:10.1080/13552601003760006

McGukin, C., Perren, S., Corcoran, L., Cowie, H., Dehue, F., Sevciková, A., ...Volink, T. (2013). Coping with cyberbullying: How can we prevent cyberbullying and how victims can cope with it. In P. K. Smith & G. Steffengen (Eds.), Cyberbullying: through the new media. Findings from an international network (pp. 121-135). East Sussex, UK: Psychology Press.

McHugh, M. L. (2009). The odds ratio: Calculation, usage, and interpretation. *Biochemia Medica, 19*(2), 120–126. doi:10.11613/BM.2009.011

McLoughlin, C., & Luca, J. (2000). Cognitive engagement and higher order thinking through computer conferencing: We know why but do we know how? In A. Herrmann & M. M. Kulski (Eds.), *Flexible Futures in Tertiary Teaching. Proceedings of the 9th Annual Teaching Learning Forum, 24 February 2000*. Perth: Curtin University of Technology. Retrieved November 20, 2006, from http://lsn.curtin.edu.au/tlf/tlf2000/mcloughlin.html

McQuade, C. S., Colt, P. J., & Meyer, B. N. (2009). *Cyber bullying: Protecting kids and adults from online bullies*. Westport, CT: Praeger.

Mellinger, J., Hinterberger, T., Bensch, M., Schröder, M., & Birbaumer, N. (2003). Surfing the web with electrical brain signals: the brain web surfer (BWS) for the completely paralysed. *Proc. 2nd World Congr. Int. Soc. Physical and Rehabilitation Medicine*, 731-738.

Mellinger, J., Schalk, G., Braun, C., Preissl, H., Rosenstiel, W., Birbaumer, N., & Kübler, A. (2007). An MEG-based brain–computer interface (BCI). *NeuroImage, 36*(3), 581–593. doi:10.1016/j.neuroimage.2007.03.019 PMID:17475511

Mendez-Baldwin, M., Cirillo, K., Ferrigno, M., & Argento, V. (2015). Cyberbullying among teens. *Journal of Bullying and Social Aggression, 1*(1). Retrieved from http://sites.tamuc.edu/bullyingjournal/cyber-bullying-among-teens/

Mendoza-Denton, R., Shoda, Y., Ayduk, O., & Mischel, W. (1999). Applying cognitive-affective processing system theory to cultural differences in social behavior. In *Merging past, present, and future in cross-cultural psychology: Selected proceedings from the 14th International Congress of the International Association for Cross-Cultural Psychology* (pp. 205–217). Lisse, Netherlands: Swets & Zeitlinger.

Menesini, E., Smith, P., & Zukauskiene, R. (Eds.). (2010). Cyberbullying. COST IS 0801. Vilnius, Lithuania: Mylolas Romeris University Publishing Center.

Merdian, H. L., Wilson, N., Thakker, J., Curtis, C., & Boer, D. P. (2013). "So why did you do it?": Explanations provided by child pornography users. *Sexual Offender Treatment*, *8*(1). Retrieved from http://www.sexualoffender-treatment.org/117.html

Mesch, G. S. (2009). Parental mediation, online activities, and cyberbullying. *Cyberpsychology & Behavior*, *12*(4), 387–393. doi:10.1089/cpb.2009.0068 PMID:19630583

Mesch, G. S., & Maman, T. L. (2009). Intentional online pornographic exposure among adolescents: Is the Internet to blame? *Verhaltenstherapie & Verhaltensmedizin*, *30*(3), 352–367.

Messer, D., Horan, J. J., Turner, W., & Weber, W. (2015). The effects of internet-delivered mindfulness training on stress, coping, and mindfulness in university students. *AERA Open*, *2*(1). doi: 2332858415625188

Michalak, J., Troje, N. F., Fischer, J., Vollmar, P., Heidenreich, T., & Schulte, D. (2009). Embodiment of sadness and depression--gait patterns associated with dysphoric mood. *Psychosomatic Medicine*, *71*(5), 580–587. doi:10.1097/PSY.0b013e3181a2515c PMID:19414617

Michie, S., Thomas, J., Johnston, M., Aonghusa, P., Shawe-Taylor, J., Kelly, M. P., ... West, R. (2017a). The human behaviour-change project: Harnessing the power of artificial intelligence and machine learning for evidence synthesis and interpretation. *Implementation Science; IS*, *12*(121). doi:10.118613012-017-0641-5 PMID:29047393

Michie, S., Yardley, L., West, R., Patrick, K., & Greaves, F. (2017b). Developing and evaluating digital interventions to promote behavior change in health and health care: Recommendations resulting from an international workshop. *Journal of Medical Internet Research*, *19*(6), 27–39. doi:10.2196/jmir.7126 PMID:28663162

Mikal, J. P., & Woodfield, B. (2015). Refugees, post-migration stress, and internet use: A Qualitative analysis of intercultural adjustment and internet use among Iraqi and Sudanese refugees to the United States. *Qualitative Health Research*, *25*(10), 1319–1333. doi:10.1177/1049732315601089 PMID:26290542

Ming, Z., Pietikainen, S., & Hannien, O. (2006). Excessive texting in pathophysiology of first carpometacarpal joint arthritis. *Pathophysiology*, *13*(4), 269–270. doi:10.1016/j.pathophys.2006.09.001 PMID:17049823

Ministry of Internal Affairs and Communications. (2016). *Communications usage trend survey*. Retrieved from http://www.soumu.go.jp/johotsusintokei/whitepaper/ja/h28/html/nc252110.html

Miranda, E. R., Durrant, S., & Anders, T. (2008). *Towards brain-computer music interfaces: progress and challenges*. Paper presented at the Applied Sciences on Biomedical and Communication Technologies, 2008. ISABEL'08. First International Symposium on. 10.1109/ISABEL.2008.4712626

Miranda, E. R. (2010). Plymouth brain-computer music interfacing project: From EEG audio mixers to composition informed by cognitive neuroscience. *International Journal of Arts and Technology*, *3*(2-3), 154–176. doi:10.1504/IJART.2010.032562

Mischel, W., Shoda, Y., & Ayduk, O. (2007). *Introduction to personality: Toward an integrative science of the person*. John Wiley & Sons.

Mistry, J., & Wu, J. (2010). Navigating cultural worlds and negotiating identities: A conceptual model. *Human Development*, *53*(1), 5–25. doi:10.1159/000268136

Mitchell, K. J., Ybarra, M., & Finkelhor, D. (2007). The relative importance of online victimization in understanding depression, delinquency, and substance use. *Child Maltreatment*, *12*(4), 314–324. doi:10.1177/1077559507305996 PMID:17954938

Mittu, R., & Lawless, W. I. (2015). *Human factors in cybersecurity and the role for AI*. Paper presented at the Foundations of Autonomy and Its (Cyber) Threats: From Individual to Interdependence, AAAI Spring Symposium Series.

Moghimi, S., Kushki, A., Marie Guerguerian, A., & Chau, T. (2013). A review of EEG-based brain-computer interfaces as access pathways for individuals with severe disabilities. *Assistive Technology*, *25*(2), 99–110. doi:10.1080/10400435.2012.723298 PMID:23923692

Mok, J. Y., & Choi, S. W. (2014). Latent class analysis on internet and smartphone addiction in college students. *Neuropsychiatric Disease and Treatment*, *10*, 817–828. PMID:24899806

Montepare, J. M., Goldstein, S. B., & Clausen, A. (1987). The identification of emotions from gait information. *Journal of Nonverbal Behavior*, *11*(1), 33–42. doi:10.1007/BF00999605

Montepare, J., Koff, E., Zaitchik, D., & Albert, M. (1999). The use of body movements and gestures as cues to emotions in younger and older adults. *Journal of Nonverbal Behavior*, *23*(2), 133–152. doi:10.1023/A:1021435526134

Morahan-Martin, J., & Schumacher, P. (2000). Incidence and correlates of pathological Internet use among college students. *Computers in Human Behavior*, *16*(1), 13–29. doi:10.1016/S0747-5632(99)00049-7

Mueller, J., Jacobsen, D., & Schwarzer, R. (2000). What are computing experiences good for?: A case study in online research. In M. H. Birnbaum (Ed.), *Psychological experiments on the internet* (pp. 195–216). New York, NY: Academic Press. doi:10.1016/B978-012099980-4/50009-5

Muglerab, E., Benschc, M., Haldera, S., Rosenstielc, W., Bogdancd, M., Birbaumerae, N., & Kübleraf, A. (2008). Control of an internet browser using the P300 event-related potential. *International Journal of Bioelectromagnetism*, *10*(1), 56–63.

Mugler, E. M., Ruf, C. A., Halder, S., Bensch, M., & Kubler, A. (2010). Design and implementation of a P300-based brain-computer interface for controlling an internet browser. *IEEE Transactions on Neural Systems and Rehabilitation Engineering*, *18*(6), 599–609. doi:10.1109/TNSRE.2010.2068059 PMID:20805058

Mühl, C., Gürkök, H., Bos, D. P.-O., Thurlings, M. E., Scherffig, L., Duvinage, M., ... Heylen, D. (2010). Bacteria hunt. *Journal on Multimodal User Interfaces*, *4*(1), 11–25. doi:10.100712193-010-0046-0

Mullins-Sweatt, S. N., Jamerson, J. E., Samuel, D. B., Olson, D. R., & Widiger, T. A. (2006). Psychometric properties of an abbreviated instrument of the five-factor model. *Assessment*, *13*(2), 119–137. doi:10.1177/1073191106286748 PMID:16672728

Munezawa, T., Kaneita, Y., Osaki, Y., Kanda, H., Minowa, M., Suzuki, K., ... Ohida, T. (2011). The association between use of mobile phones after lights out and sleep disturbances among Japanese adolescents: A nationwide cross-sectional survey. *Sleep*, *34*(8), 1013–1020. doi:10.5665/SLEEP.1152 PMID:21804663

Münßinger, J. I., Halder, S., Kleih, S. C., Furdea, A., Raco, V., Hösle, A., & Kübler, A. (2010). Brain painting: First evaluation of a new brain–computer interface application with ALS-patients and healthy volunteers. *Frontiers in Neuroscience*, *4*. PMID:21151375

Mustacchi, J. (2009). R U Safe? *Educational Leadership*, *66*(6), 78–82.

Naseer, N., & Hong, K.-S. (2015). fNIRS-based brain-computer interfaces: A review. *Frontiers in Human Neuroscience*, *9*.

Natale, V., & Cicogna, P. (2002). Morningness-eveningness dimension: Is it really a continuum? *Personality and Individual Differences*, *32*(5), 809–816. doi:10.1016/S0191-8869(01)00085-X

National Center for Education Statistics. (2013). *Student reports of bullying and cyberbullying: Results from the 2011 school crime supplement to the National Crime Victimization Survey*. Washington, DC: U.S. Department of Education. Retrieved from https://nces.ed.gov/pubs2013/2013329.pdf

National Crime Prevention Council. (2007). *Teens and cyberbullying: Executive summary of a report on research*. Retrieved from http://www.ncpc.org/resources/files/pdf/bullying/Teens%20and%20Cyberbullying%20Research%20Study.pdf

National Crime Prevention Council. (2012). *Cyber bullying law and legal definition*. Retrieved from http://definitions.uslegal.com/c/cyber-bullying/

National Sleep Foundation. (2006). *2006 Sleep in America Poll*. Washington, DC: National Sleep Foundation.

Nayak, P. K., & Debashish, S. S. (2017). Young consumers' online shopping decision influencers: A study on university students of Odisha. *Effulgence*, *15*(1), 45–50.

Nelson, K. (1985). *Making sense: The acquisition of shared meaning*. New York: Academic Press.

Nelson, K. (1996). *Language in cognitive development: The emergence of the mediated mind.* Cambridge University Press. doi:10.1017/CBO9781139174619

Networking and Information Technology Research and Development Program. (2014). *Federal cybersecurity game—change R&D: Science of security.* Retrieved from https://www.nitrd.gov/cybersecurity/

Newman, L. H. (2017, September 14). Equifax Officially Has No Excuse. *Wired.* Retrieved from https://www.wired.com/story/equifax-breach-no-excuse/

Newmann, F. M., & Wehlage, G. G. (1993). Five standards of authentic instruction. *Educational Leadership, 50*(7), 812.

Nguyên, T. T., & Mark, L. (2014). Cyberbullying, sexting, and on-line sharing a comparison of parent and school faculty perspectives. *Journal of Cyber Behavior, Psychology and Learning, 4*(1), 76-86.

Niedermeyer, E., & da Silva, F. H. L. (2005). *Electroencephalography: basic principles, clinical applications, and related fields.* Wolters Kluwer Health.

Nijholt, A. (2009). *BCI for games: A 'state of the art' survey. In Entertainment Computing-ICEC 2008* (pp. 225–228). Springer.

Nijholt, A., Bos, D. P.-O., & Reuderink, B. (2009). Turning shortcomings into challenges: Brain–computer interfaces for games. *Entertainment Computing, 1*(2), 85–94. doi:10.1016/j.entcom.2009.09.007

Nijholt, A., & Tan, D. (2007). Playing with your brain: brain-computer interfaces and games. *Proceedings of the international conference on Advances in computer entertainment technology.* 10.1145/1255047.1255140

Nimrod, G. (2015). Early birds and night owls: Difference in media preferences, usages, and environments. *International Journal of Communication, 9,* 21.

Norman, G. J., Zabinski, M. F., Adams, M. A., Rosenberg, D. E., Yaroch, A. L., & Atienza, A. A. (2007). A review of eHealth interventions for physical activity and dietary behavior change. *American Journal of Preventive Medicine, 33*(4), 336-345. doi: 10.1016/j.amepre.2007.05.007

Notar, C. E., Padgett, S., & Roden, J. (2013). Cyberbullying: A review of the literature. *Universal Journal of Educational Research, 1*(1), 1–9. doi:10.12189/ujer.2013.010101

Nuseir, M. T., Arora, N., Al-Masri, M. M., & Gharaibeh, M. (2010). Evidence of Online Shopping: A Consumer Perspective. *International Review of Business Research Papers, 6*(5), 90–106.

O'Mara, E., McNulty, J., & Karney, B. (2011). Positively biased appraisals in everyday life: When do they benefit mental health and when do they harm it? *Journal of Personality and Social Psychology, 101*(3), 415–432. doi:10.1037/a0023332 PMID:21500926

Odom, J. V., Bach, M., Barber, C., Brigell, M., Marmor, M. F., Tormene, A. P., & Holder, G. E. (2004). Visual evoked potentials standard. *Documenta ophthalmologica, 108*(2), 115-123.

Oka, Y., Suzuki, S., & Inoue, Y. (2008). Bedtime activities, sleep environment, and sleep/wake patterns of Japanese elementary school children. *Behavioral Sleep Medicine, 6*(4), 220–233. doi:10.1080/15402000802371338 PMID:18853306

Olenik-Shemesh, D., Heiman, T., & Segal, E. (2015). Bystander's behavior in cyberbullying episodes: Active and passive patterns in the context of socio-emotional factors. *Journal of Interpersonal Violence*, 1–26. doi:10.1177/0886260515585531 PMID:25948644

Olweus, D. (1993). *Bullying at school: What we know and what we can do*. Cambridge, MA: Blackwell.

Olweus, D. (2012). Cyberbullying: An overrated phenomenon? *European Journal of Developmental Psychology, 9*(5), 520–538. doi:10.1080/17405629.2012.682358

Ortega, R., Elipe, P., Mora-Merchan, J., Calmaestra, J., & Vega, E. (2009). The emotional impact on victims of tradicional bullying and cyberbullying. *Journal of Psychology, 217*(4), 197-204. doi: 10.27/0044-3409.217.4.197

Ortega, R., Calmaestra, J., & Mora-Merchan, J. (2008). Cyberbullying. *International Journal of Psychology & Psychological Therapy, 8*(2), 183–192.

Ortega, R., Elipe, P., Mora-Merchán, J. A., Genta, M. L., Brighi, A., Guarini, A. K., ... Tippett, N. (2012). The Emotional impact of bullying and cyberbullying on victims: A European cross-national study. *Aggressive Behavior, 38*(5), 342–356. doi:10.1002/ab.21440 PMID:22782434

Ortiz, R. R., & Thompson, B. (2017). Content effects: Pornography and sexually explicit content. In P. Rossler (Ed.), *The International Encyclopedia of Media Effects* (pp. 246–257). Malden, MA: John Wiley & Sons. doi:10.1002/9781118783764.wbieme0122

Osman, S., Yin-Fah, B. C., & Choo, B. H. (2010). Undergraduates and online purchasing behavior. *Asian Social Science, 6*(10), 133. doi:10.5539/ass.v6n10p133

Owens, E. W., Behun, R. J., Manning, J. C., & Reid, R. C. (2012). The impact of internet pornography on adolescents: A review of the research. *Sexual Addiction & Compulsivity, 19*(1-2), 99–122. doi:10.1080/10720162.2012.660431

Öztunç, M. (2013). Analysis of problematic mobile phone use, feelings of shyness and loneliness in accordance with several variables. *Procedia: Social and Behavioral Sciences, 106*, 456–466. doi:10.1016/j.sbspro.2013.12.051

Padilla, A. (2006). Bicultural social development. *Hispanic Journal of Behavioral Sciences, 28*(4), 467–497. doi:10.1177/0739986306294255

Paladino, B., Menesini, E., Nocentini, A., Luik, P., Naruskov, K., Ucanok, Z., ... Sheithauer, H. (2017). Perceived severity of cyberbullying: Differences and similarities across four countries. *Frontiers in Psychology, 8*, 1–12. doi:10.3389/fpsyg.2017.01524 PMID:28197108

Parab, J., Shinde, S. A., Shelake, V. G., Kamat, R. K., & Naik, G. M. (2008). *Practical aspects of embedded system design using microcontrollers*. Springer Science & Business Media; doi:10.1007/978-1-4020-8393-8

Paradise, A., & Sullivan, M. (2012). (In)visible threats? The third-person effect in perceptions of the influence of Facebook. *Cyberpsychology, Behavior, and Social Networking, 15*(1), 55–60. doi:10.1089/cyber.2011.0054 PMID:21988734

Parris, L., Varjas, K., Meyers, J., & Cutts, H. (2012). High school students' perceptions of coping with cyberbullying. *Youth & Society, 44*(2), 284–306. doi:10.1177/0044118X11398881

Patchin, J. W., & Hinduja, S. (2006). Bullies move beyond the schoolyard: A preliminary look at cyberbullying. *Youth Violence and Juvenile Justice, 4*(2), 148–169. doi:10.1177/1541204006286288

Patchin, J. W., & Hinduja, S. (2010). Cyberbullying and self-esteem. *The Journal of School Health, 80*(12), 614–621. doi:10.1111/j.1746-1561.2010.00548.x PMID:21087257

Patel, M. S., Asch, D. A., & Volpp, K. G. (2015). Wearable devices as facilitators, not drivers, of health behavior change. *Journal of the American Medical Association, 313*(5), 459–460. doi:10.1001/jama.2014.14781 PMID:25569175

Patro, C. S. (2016). Attitudes of E-Shoppers and Non E-Shoppers towards E-Shopping: A Comparative Study. *International Journal of Cyber Behavior, Psychology and Learning, 6*(2), 96–108. doi:10.4018/IJCBPL.2016040106

Patro, C. S. (2017). Consumer Attitude and Loyalty in Online Shopping Environments: A Study of Facets Driving Shoppers Towards E-Stores. *International Journal of Cyber Behavior, Psychology and Learning, 7*(3), 57–72. doi:10.4018/IJCBPL.2017070105

Paul, B. (2009). Predicting internet pornography use and arousal: The role of individual difference variables. *Journal of Sex Research, 46*(4), 344–357. doi:10.1080/00224490902754152 PMID:19219657

Paul, S., Smith, P., & Blumberg, H. (2012). Revisiting cyberbullyingin schools using the quality circle approach. *School Psychology International, 33*(5), 492–504. doi:10.1177/0143034312445243

Pea, R. D. (2002). Learning science through collaborative visualization over the Internet. In N. Ringertz (Ed.), *Nobel Symposium: Virtual museums and public understanding of science and culture*. Stockholm, Sweden: Nobel Academy Press.

Pea, R. D. (2004). The social and technological dimensions of "scaffolding" and related theoretical concepts for learning, education and human activity. *Journal of the Learning Sciences, 13*(3), 423–451. doi:10.120715327809jls1303_6

Pegg, S. (2016, January 15). Could your taste for 'teen' porn land you in legal trouble? *The Conversation*. Retrieved December 18, 2017 from theconversation.com

Peham, D., Bock, A., Schiestl, C., Huber, E., Zimmermann, J., Kratzer, D., ... Benecke, C. (2015). Facial Affective Behavior in Mental Disorder. *Journal of Nonverbal Behavior*, *39*(4), 371–396. doi:10.100710919-015-0216-6

Peluchette, J. V., Karl, K., Wood, C., & Williams, J. (2015). Cyberbullying victimization: Do victims' personality and risky social network contribute to the problem? *Computers in Human Behavior*, *52*, 424–435. doi:10.1016/j.chb.2015.06.028

Pennebaker, J. W., Boyd, R. L., Jordan, K., & Blackburn, K. (2015). *The development and psychometric properties of LIWC2015*. Academic Press.

Perdue, A., & Lockwood, R. (2014). *Animal cruelty and freedom of speech: When worlds collide*. West Lafayette, IN: Purdue University Press.

Peren, S., & Gutzwiller-Heltenfinger, E. (2012). Cyberbullying and traditional bullying in adolescence: Differential roles of moral disengagement, moral emotions and moral values. *European Journal of Developmental Psychology*, *9*(2), 195–209. doi:10.1080/17405629.2011.643168

Perren, S., Dooley, J., Shaw, T., & Cross, D. (2010). Bullying in school and cyberspace: Associations with depressive symptoms in Swiss and Australian adolescents. *Child and Adolescent Psychiatry and Mental Health*, *4*(1), 1–10. doi:10.1186/1753-2000-4-28 PMID:21092266

Pessoa, T., Matos, A., Amado, J., Freire, I., & Caetano, A. P. (2017). Cyberbullying entre adolescentes y jóvenes portugueses. Contribución para una definición de los perfiles de víctimas y de agresores [Cyberbullying among Portuguese adolescents and youth. Contributions for a description of victims and aggressors profiles]. *Communication Education*, *297/298*, 11–19.

Peter, C., & Beale, R. (2008). *Affect and Emotion in Human-Computer Interaction*. Springer Berlin Heidelberg. doi:10.1007/978-3-540-85099-1

Peter, J., & Valkenburg, P. M. (2006a). Adolescents' exposure to sexually explicit material on the internet. *Communication Research*, *533*(2), 178–204. doi:10.1177/0093650205285369

Peter, J., & Valkenburg, P. M. (2006b). Adolescents' exposure to sexually explicit online material and recreational attitudes toward sex. *Journal of Communication*, *56*(4), 639–660. doi:10.1111/j.1460-2466.2006.00313.x

Peter, J., & Valkenburg, P. M. (2008). Adolescents' exposure to sexually explicit Internet material, sexual uncertainty, and attitudes toward uncommitted sexual exploration: Is there a link? *Communication Research*, *35*(5), 579–601. doi:10.1177/0093650208321754

Peter, J., & Valkenburg, P. M. (2010). Processes underlying the effects of adolescents' use of sexually explicit Internet material: The role of perceived realism. *Communication Research*, *37*(3), 375–399. doi:10.1177/0093650210362464

Peter, J., & Valkenburg, P. M. (2011). The use of sexually explicit internet material and its antecedents: A longitudinal comparison of adolescents and adults. *Archives of Sexual Behavior*, *40*(5), 1015–1025. doi:10.100710508-010-9644-x PMID:20623250

Peter, J., & Valkenburg, P. M. (2016). Adolescents and pornography: A review of 20 years of research. *Journal of Sex Research*, *53*(4-5), 509–531. doi:10.1080/00224499.2016.1143441 PMID:27105446

Pfurtscheller, G., Müller, G. R., Pfurtscheller, J., Gerner, H. J., & Rupp, R. (2003). 'Thought'–control of functional electrical stimulation to restore hand grasp in a patient with tetraplegia. *Neuroscience Letters*, *351*(1), 33–36. doi:10.1016/S0304-3940(03)00947-9 PMID:14550907

Pfurtscheller, G., Neuper, C., Flotzinger, D., & Pregenzer, M. (1997). EEG-based discrimination between imagination of right and left hand movement. *Electroencephalography and Clinical Neurophysiology*, *103*(6), 642–651. doi:10.1016/S0013-4694(97)00080-1 PMID:9546492

Pfurtscheller, G., Stancak, A. Jr, & Neuper, C. (1996). Event-related synchronization (ERS) in the alpha band—an electrophysiological correlate of cortical idling: A review. *International Journal of Psychophysiology*, *24*(1), 39–46. doi:10.1016/S0167-8760(96)00066-9 PMID:8978434

Pichiorri, F., Morone, G., Petti, M., Toppi, J., Pisotta, I., Molinari, M., ... Cincotti, F. (2015). Brain–computer interface boosts motor imagery practice during stroke recovery. *Annals of Neurology*, *77*(5), 851–865. doi:10.1002/ana.24390 PMID:25712802

Piwek, L., Ellis, D. A., Andrews, S., & Joinson, A. (2016). The rise of consumer health wearables: Promises and barriers. *PLoS Medicine*, *13*(2), e1001953. doi:10.1371/journal.pmed.1001953 PMID:26836780

Pornari, C. D., & Wood, J. (2010). Peer and cyber aggression in secondary school students: The role of moral disengagement, hostile attribution bias, and outcome expectancies. *Aggressive Behavior*, *36*(2), 81–94. doi:10.1002/ab.20336 PMID:20035548

PornHub. (2017). *Pornhub's 2016 year in review*. Retrieved December 18, 2017 from pornhub.com.

Poulin, F., & Boivin, M. (2000). Reactive and proactive aggression: Evidence of a two factor model. *Psychological Assessment*, *12*(2), 115–122. doi:10.1037/1040-3590.12.2.115 PMID:10887757

Prensky, M. (2001). Digital natives, digital immigrants. *On the Horizon, 9*(5). Retrieved from: http://www.marcprensky.com/writing/Prensky%20-%20Digital%20Natives,%20Digital%20Immigrants%20-%20Part1.pdf

Proctor, R. W., & Chen, J. (2015). The Role of Human Factors/Ergonomics in the Science of Security: Decision Making and Action Selection in Cyberspace. *Human Factors*, *57*(5), 721–727. doi:10.1177/0018720815585906 PMID:25994927

Quayle, E., & Taylor, M. (2002). Child pornography and the internet: Perpetuating a cycle of abuse. *Deviant Behavior: An Interdisciplinary Journal*, *23*(4), 331–361. doi:10.1080/01639620290086413

Quayle, E., & Taylor, M. (2003). Model of problematic internet use in people with a sexual interest in children. *Cyberpsychology & Behavior*, *6*(1), 93–106. doi:10.1089/109493103321168009 PMID:12650567

Randler, C. (2008). Psychometric properties of the German version of the Composite Scale of Morningness. *Biological Rhythm Research*, *39*(2), 151–161. doi:10.1080/09291010701424796

Randler, C., Horzum, M. B., & Vollmer, C. (2013). Internet addiction and its relationship to chronotype and personality in a Turkish University student sample. *Social Science Computer Review*, *32*(4), 484–495. doi:10.1177/0894439313511055

Randler, C., & Wolfgang, L. (2016). Smartphone addiction proneness in relation to sleep and morningness-eveningness in German adolescents. *Journal of Behavioral Addictions 5* (3), 465-473. *Journal of Biological Rhythms*, *19*(3), 193–195.

Rao, K. R. M., & Patro, C. S. (2016). Online Marketing-The Powerful Astra in the Strategic Armory of Marketers. *Mizoram University Journal of Humanities and Social Sciences*, *2*(2), 1–17.

Rao, K. R. M., & Patro, C. S. (2017). Shopper's Stance towards Web Shopping: An Analysis of Students Opinion of India. *International Journal of Online Marketing*, *7*(3), 42–54. doi:10.4018/IJOM.2017070104

Raskauskas, J., & Stoltz, A. D. (2007). Involvement in traditional and electronic bullying among adolescents. *Developmental Psychology*, *43*(3), 564–575. doi:10.1037/0012-1649.43.3.564 PMID:17484571

Rebsamen, B., Guan, C., Zhang, H., Wang, C., Teo, C., Ang, M. H., & Burdet, E. (2010). A brain controlled wheelchair to navigate in familiar environments. *Neural Systems and Rehabilitation Engineering. IEEE Transactions on*, *18*(6), 590–598.

Renneberg, B., Heyn, K., Gebhard, R., & Bachmann, S. (2005). Facial expression of emotions in borderline personality disorder and depression. *Journal of Behavior Therapy and Experimental Psychiatry*, *36*(3), 183–196. doi:10.1016/j.jbtep.2005.05.002 PMID:15950175

Reportlinker. (2017, June). *For America's youth, standing up to the cyberbully is now a life skill*. Retrieved from https://www.reportlinker.com/insight/americas-youth-cyberbully-life-skill.html

Reppert, S. M., & Weaver, D. R. (2002). Coordination of circadian timing in mammals. *Nature*, *418*(6901), 935–941. doi:10.1038/nature00965 PMID:12198538

Ribbink, D., van Riel, A. C. R., Liljander, V., & Streukens, S. (2004). Comfort your online customer: Quality, trust and loyalty on the internet. *Managing Service Quality*, *14*(6), 446–456. doi:10.1108/09604520410569784

Richa, D. (2012). Impact of demographic factors of consumers on online shopping behaviour: A study of consumers in India. *International Journal of Engineering and Management Sciences*, *3*(1), 43–52.

Rideout, V. J., Roberts, D. F., & Foehr, U. G. (2005). *Generation M: Media in the lives of 8-18-year-olds: Executive summary*. Menlo Park, CA: Henry J. Kaiser Family Foundation.

Rittel, H. W. J., & Webber, M. M. (1973). Dilemmas in a General Theory of Planning. *Policy Sciences*, *4*(2), 155–169. doi:10.1007/BF01405730

Roberts, M., Gibbons, F., Gerrard, M., & Alert, M. (2011). Optimism and adolescent perception of skin cancer risk. *Health Psychology, 30*(6), 810–813. doi:10.1037/a0024380 PMID:21688914

Roenneberg, T. (2004). *The decline in human seasonality*. Academic Press.

Roenneberg, T., Kuehnle, T., Pramstaller, P. P., Ricken, J., Havel, M., Guth, A., & Merrow, M. (2004). A marker for the end of adolescence. *Current Biology, 14*(24), R1038–R1039. doi:10.1016/j.cub.2004.11.039 PMID:15620633

Rogers, M., Smoak, N. D., & Liu, J. (2006). Self-reported computer criminal behavior: A big-5, moral choice and manipulative exploitive behavior analysis. *Deviant Behavior, 27*(3), 1–24. doi:10.1080/01639620600605333

Roschelle, J., Pea, R., Hoadley, C., Gordin, D., & Means, B. (2001). Changing how and what children learn in school with collaborative cognitive technologies. The Future of Children, 10(2), 76-101.

Rosen, L. D. (2007). *Me, Myspace, and I: Parenting the Net Generation*. New York: Palgrave Macmillan.

Ruby, K. (2016). E-tailing in India- Growth, Challenges and Opportunities. *Journal of Marketing and HR, 2*(1), 102–112.

Ruiz, S., Buyukturkoglu, K., Rana, M., Birbaumer, N., & Sitaram, R. (2014). Real-time fMRI brain computer interfaces: Self-regulation of single brain regions to networks. *Biological Psychology, 95*, 4–20. doi:10.1016/j.biopsycho.2013.04.010 PMID:23643926

Sabina, C., Wolak, J., & Finkelhor, D. (2008). The nature and dynamics of internet pornography exposure for youth. *Cyberpsychology & Behavior, 11*(6), 1–3. doi:10.1089/cpb.2007.0179 PMID:18771400

Sahin, M. (2010). Teachers' perceptions of bullying in high schools: A Turkish study. *Social Behavior and Personality, 38*(1), 127–142. doi:10.2224bp.2010.38.1.127

Şahin, M. (2012). The relationship between the cyberbullying/cybervictmization and loneliness among adolescents. *Children and Youth Services Review, 34*(4), 834–837. doi:10.1016/j.childyouth.2012.01.010

Salmivalli, C., & Niemenen, E. (2002). Proactive and reactive aggression among school bullies, victims, and bully-victims. *Aggressive Behavior, 28*(1), 30–44. doi:10.1002/ab.90004

Sanders, J. B., Bremmer, M. A., Deeg, D. J. H., & Beekman, A. T. F. (2012). Do Depressive Symptoms and Gait Speed Impairment Predict Each Other's Incidence? A 16-Year Prospective Study in the Community. *Journal of the American Geriatrics Society, 60*(9), 1673–1680. doi:10.1111/j.1532-5415.2012.04114.x PMID:22905679

Sands, S. F., & Sands, J. A. (2012). Recording brain waves at the supermarket: What can we learn from a shopper's brain? *IEEE Pulse, 3*(3), 34–37. doi:10.1109/MPUL.2012.2189170 PMID:22678838

Saprikis, V., Chouliara, A., & Vlachopoulou, M. (2010, December). Perceptions towards online shopping: Analyzing the Greek University students' attitude. *Communications of the IBIMA*, 1-13.

Şar, A. H., Ayas, T., & Horzum, M. B. (2015). Developing the smart phone addiction scale and its validity and reliability study. *Online Journal of Technology Addiction & Cyberbullying*, *2*(3), 1–17.

Saravanan, R., Yoganandan, G., & Ruby, N. (2013). A Study on Online Shopping Behaviour of Teachers Working in Self-Financing Colleges in Namakkal District With Special Reference to K.S.R College of Arts And Science, Tiruchengode, Namakkal District. *International Journal of Research in Commerce, IT & Management*, *3*(6), 31–37.

Sardi, L., Idri, A., & Fernández-Alemán, J. L. (2017). A systematic review of gamification in e-health. *Journal of Biomedical Informatics*, *71*, 31–48. doi:10.1016/j.jbi.2017.05.011 PMID:28536062

Sardon, J. P. (2001). Demographic Change in the Balkans since the End of the 1980s. *Population. English Selection*, *13*(2), 49–70.

Sasson, H., & Mesch, G. (2017). The role of parental mediation and peer norms on likelihood of cyberbullying. *The Journal of Genetic Psychology*, *178*(1), 15–27. doi:10.1080/00221325.2 016.1195330 PMID:27391950

Sasson, H., & Mesch, G. S. (2014). Parental mediation, peer norms and risky online behaviors among adolescents. *Computers in Human Behavior*, *33*, 32–38. doi:10.1016/j.chb.2013.12.025

Saulynas, S., Lechner, C., & Kuber, R. (2017). Towards the use of brain–computer interface and gestural technologies as a potential alternative to PIN authentication. *International Journal of Human-Computer Interaction*, 1–12.

Scardamalia, M., & Bereiter, C. (2003). Knowledge building. In G. W. Guthrie (Ed.), *Encyclopedia of Education* (2nd ed.; pp. 1370–1373). New York: Macmillan Reference.

Schalk, G. (2008). Brain–computer symbiosis. *Journal of Neural Engineering*, *5*(1), 1. doi:10.1088/1741-2560/5/1/P01 PMID:18310804

Schnabel, M. A., & Ham, J. J. (2014). The Social Network Learning Cloud: Architectural Education for the 21st Century. *International Journal of Architectural Computing*, *12*(3), 225–241. doi:10.1260/1478-0771.12.3.225

Schneier, B. (2015). *Secrets and Lies: Digital Security in a Networked World* (1st ed.). John Wiley and Sons. doi:10.1002/9781119183631

Schrijvers, D., Hulstijn, W., & Sabbe, B. G. C. (2008). Psychomotor symptoms in depression: A diagnostic, pathophysiological and therapeutic tool. *Journal of Affective Disorders*, *109*(1–2), 1–20. doi:10.1016/j.jad.2007.10.019 PMID:18082896

Schroeder, S. (2015). Refugees in Croatia can't get to the Internet, so the Internet comes to them. *Mashable*. September 15. Accessed 10/17/17 from http://mashable.com/2015/09/21/mobile-free-internet-refugees/#eM04iz5nHgqL

Schwartz, D. L. (1999). Rethinking transfer: A simple proposal with interesting implications. In *Review of research in education, 24*. Washington, DC: American Educational Research Association.

Schwartz, H. A., Eichstaedt, J. C., Kern, M. L., Dziurzynski, L., Ramones, S. M., Agrawal, M., ... Ungar, L. H. (2013). Personality, gender, and age in the language of social media: The open-vocabulary approach. *PLoS One, 8*(9), e73791. doi:10.1371/journal.pone.0073791 PMID:24086296

Seigfried, K. (2007). *Self-reported online child pornography behavior: A psychological analysis* (Unpublished master's thesis). John Jay College of Criminal Justice, New York, NY.

Seigfried, K. C., Lovely, R. W., & Rogers, M. K. (2008). Self-reported consumers of internet child pornography: A psychological analysis. *International Journal of Cyber Criminology, 2*(1), 286–297.

Seigfried-Spellar, K. C. (2011). *The role of individual differences in predicting the type of images collected by internet child pornography consumers* (Unpublished Dissertation). Purdue University, West Lafayette, IN.

Seigfried-Spellar, K. C. (2016). Deviant pornography use: The role of early-onset adult pornography use and individual differences. *International Journal of Cyber Behavior, Psychology and Learning, 6*(3), 34–47. doi:10.4018/IJCBPL.2016070103

Seigfried-Spellar, K. C., Lovely, R. W., & Rogers, M. K. (2011). Self-reported internet child pornography consumers: A personality assessment using Bandura's theory of reciprocal determinism. In K. Jaishankar (Ed.), *Cyber Criminology: Exploring Internet Crimes and Criminal Behavior* (pp. 65–77). Boca Raton, FL: Taylor and Francis. doi:10.1201/b10718-8

Seigfried-Spellar, K. C., & Rogers, M. K. (2013). Does deviant pornography use follow a guttman- like progression? *Computers in Human Behavior, 29*(5), 1997–2003. doi:10.1016/j.chb.2013.04.018

Seo, Y. J., Matsumoto, K., Park, Y., Shinkoda, H., & Noh, T. (2000). The relationship between sleep and shift system, age, and chronotype in shift workers. *Biological Rhythm Research, 31*(5), 559–579. doi:10.1076/brhm.31.5.559.5655

Sephton, S. E., & Spiegel, D. (2003). Circadian disruption in cancer: A neuroendocrine-immune pathway from stress to disease? *Brain, Behavior, and Immunity, 17*(5), 321–328. doi:10.1016/S0889-1591(03)00078-3 PMID:12946654

Sevcikova, A., Machackova, H., Wright, M. F., Dedkova, L., & Cerna, A. (2015). Social support seeking in relation to parental attachment and peer relationships among victims of cyberbullying. *Australian Journal of Guidance & Counselling, 15*, 1–13. doi:10.1017/jgc.2015.1

Shanholtz, C. E., Messer, D., Davidson, R. D., Randall, A. K., & Horan, J. J. (2017). A randomized clinical trial of online stress inoculation for adult children of divorce. *Journal of Divorce & Remarriage, 58*(8), 599–613. doi:10.1080/10502556.2017.1354278

Shapka, J. D., & Law, D. M. (2013). Does one size fit all? Ethnic differences in parenting behaviors and motivations for adolescent engagement in cyberbullying. *Journal of Youth and Adolescence, 42*(5), 723–738. doi:10.100710964-013-9928-2 PMID:23479327

Shariff, S., & Hoff, D. L. (2007). Cyber bullying: Clarifying legal boundaries for school supervision in cyberspace. *International Journal of Cyber Criminology, 1*, 76–118.

Sharpe, D. (2015). Your chi-square test is statistically significant: Now what? *Practical Assessment, Research & Evaluation, 20*(8). Retrieved from http://pareonline.net/getvn.asp?v=20&n=8

Sheng, S., Holbrook, M., Kumaraguru, P., Cranor, L. F., & Downs, J. (2010). Who falls for phish?: a demographic analysis of phishing susceptibility and effectiveness of interventions. *Proceedings of the SIGCHI Conference on Human Factors in Computing Systems,* 373-382. 10.1145/1753326.1753383

Shenjie, S., Thomas, K. P., & Vinod, A. (2014). *Two player EEG-based neurofeedback ball game for attention enhancement.* Paper presented at the Systems, Man and Cybernetics (SMC), 2014 IEEE International Conference on. 10.1109/SMC.2014.6974412

Sheppard, B. H., Hartwick, J., & Warshaw, P. (1988). The theory of reasoned action: A meta-analysis of past research with recommendations for modifications and future research. *The Journal of Consumer Research, 15*(3), 325–343. doi:10.1086/209170

Shergill, G. S., & Chen, Z. (2005). Web-Based Shopping: Consumers' attitudes Towards Online Shopping in New Zealand. *Journal of Electronic Commerce Research, 6*(2), 78.

Shim, J. W., Lee, S., & Paul, B. (2007). Who responds to unsolicited sexually explicit materials on the Internet?: The role of individual differences. *Cyberpsychology & Behavior, 10*(1), 71–79. doi:10.1089/cpb.2006.9990 PMID:17305451

Short, M. B., Black, L., Smith, A. H., Wetterneck, C. T., & Wells, D. E. (2012). A review of internet pornography use research: Methodology and content from the past 10 years. *Cyberpsychology, Behavior, and Social Networking, 15*(1), 13–23. doi:10.1089/cyber.2010.0477 PMID:22032795

Sijtsema, J. J., Ashwin, R. J., Simona, C. S., & Gina, G. (2014). Friendship selection and influence in bullying and defending. *Effects of moral disengagement. Developmental Psychology, 50*(8), 2093–2104. doi:10.1037/a0037145 PMID:24911569

Silberstein, R. B., & Nield, G. E. (2012). Measuring Emotion in Advertising Research: Prefrontal Brain Activity. *IEEE Pulse, 3*(3), 24–27. doi:10.1109/MPUL.2012.2189172 PMID:22678836

Silverstein, B. (2002). *Business to Business internet marketing.* Jim Hoskins.

Sinković, M., Štulhofer, A., & Božić, J. (2013). Revisiting the association between pornography use and risky sexual behaviors: The role of early exposure to pornography and sexual sensation seeking. *Journal of Sex Research, 50*(7), 633–641. doi:10.1080/00224499.2012.681403 PMID:22853694

SIPA. (2012). *SIPA Reports results of a survey software market and Software Services Thailand Year 2014.* Retrieved from http://www.sipa.or.th/th/news/2007

Sitaram, R., Weiskopf, N., Caria, A., Veit, R., Erb, M., & Birbaumer, N. (2008). fMRI brain-computer interfaces. *IEEE Signal Processing Magazine, 25*(1), 95–106. doi:10.1109/MSP.2008.4408446

Sivin-Kachala, J., & Bialo, E. R. (1999). *1999 research report on the effectiveness of technology in schools* (6th ed.). Washington, DC: Software and Information Industry Association.

Sjurso, I. R., Fandream, H., & Roland, E. (2016). Emotional problems in traditional and cyber victimization. *Journal of School Violence, 15*(1), 114–131. doi:10.1080/15388220.2014.996718

Skowron, M., Tkalčič, M., Ferwerda, B., & Schedl, M. (2016, April). Fusing social media cues: personality prediction from twitter and instagram. In *Proceedings of the 25th international conference companion on world wide web* (pp. 107-108). International World Wide Web Conferences Steering Committee. 10.1145/2872518.2889368

Slotte, V., & Tynjälä, P. (2005). Communication and collaborative learning at work: Views expressed on a crossCultural elearning course. *International Journal on E-Learning, 4*(2), 191–207.

Smith, C. A., & Lazarus, R. S. (1990). Emotion and adaptation. In L. A. Pervin (Ed.), *Handbook of Personality: Theory and Research* (pp. 609–636). New York: Guilford. Retrieved from http://people.ict.usc.edu/~gratch/CSCI534/Readings/Smith&Lazarus90.pdf

Smith, C. S., Reily, C., & Midkiff, K. (1989). Evaluation of three circadian rhythm questionnaires with suggestions for an improved measure of morningness. *The Journal of Applied Psychology, 74*(5), 728–738. doi:10.1037/0021-9010.74.5.728 PMID:2793773

Smith, P. (2009). Cyberbullying – Abusive relationships in cyberspace. *The Journal of Psychology, 217*(4), 180–181. doi:10.1027/0044-3409.217.4.180

Smith, P. K. (2015). The nature of cyberbullying and what we can do about it. *Journal of Research in Special Educational Needs, 15*(3), 176–184. doi:10.1111/1471-3802.12114

Smith, P. K., Del Barrio, C., & Tokunaga, R. S. (2013). Definitions of bullying and cyberbullying: How useful are the terms? In S. Bauman, D. Cross, & J. Walker (Eds.), *Principles of cyberbullying research: Definitions, measures, methodology* (pp. 26–40). New York, NY: Routledge.

Smith, P. K., Mahdavi, J., Carvalho, M., Fisher, S., Russell, S., & Tippett, N. (2008). Cyberbullying: Its nature and impact in secondary school pupils. *Journal of Child Psychology and Psychiatry, and Allied Disciplines, 49*(4), 376–385. doi:10.1111/j.1469-7610.2007.01846.x PMID:18363945

Snakenborg, J., Van Acker, R., & Gable, R. A. (n.d.). Cyberbullying: Prevention and intervention to protect our children and youth. *Preventing School Failure, 55*(2), 88-95. doi: .10.1080/1045988X.2011.539454

Snell, E. (2017). *Anthem Data Breach Reportedly Caused by Foreign Nation Attack*. Retrieved from https://healthitsecurity.com/news/anthem-data-breach-reportedly-caused-by-foreign-nation-attack

Sonawane, H., Gupta, D., & Jadhav, A. (n.d.). Social Cloud Computing Using Social Network. *IOSR Journal of Computer Engineering, 1*(16), 15.

Sorce, P., Perotti, V., & Widrick, S. (2005). Attitude and Age Differences in Online Buying. *International Journal of Retail & Distribution Management*, *33*(2), 122–132. doi:10.1108/09590550510581458

Sourander, A., Brunstein, A., Ikonen, M., Lindroos, J., Luntamo, T., Koskelainen, M., ... Helenius, H. (2010). Psychosocial risk factors associated with cyberbullying among adolescents: A population-based study. *Archives of General Psychiatry*, *67*(7), 720–728. doi:10.1001/archgenpsychiatry.2010.79 PMID:20603453

Souza, S. B., Veiga Simão, A. M., Ferreira, A. I., & Ferreira, P. C. (2017). University students' perceptions of campus climate, cyberbullying and cultural issues: Implications for theory and practice. *Studies in Higher Education*, 1–16. doi:10.1080/03075079.2017.1307818

Springate, J., & Omar, H. A. (2013). The impact of the Internet on the sexual health of adolescents: A brief review. *International Journal of Child and Adolescent Health*, *6*(4), 469–471.

Starner, T., & Rhodes, B. J. (1996). *Remembrance Agent*. Retrieved March 15th, 2018 from http://alumni.media.mit.edu/~rhodes/Papers/remembrance.html

Stevens, R., Dunaev, J., Malven, E., Bleakley, A., & Hull, S. (2016). Social media in the sexual lives of African American and Latino youth: Challenges and opportunities in the digital neighborhood. *Media and Communication*, *4*(3), 60–70. doi:10.17645/mac.v4i3.524

Stoll, L. C., & Block, R. Jr. (2015). Intersectionality and cyberbullying: A study of cybervictimization in a Midwestern high school. *Computers in Human Behavior*, *52*, 387–391. doi:10.1016/j.chb.2015.06.010

Stopbullying.gov. (n.d.). *Effects of bullying*. Retrieved from http://www.stopbullying.gov/at-risk/effects/index.html

StopCyberBullying.org. (n.d.). *What is cyberbullying, exactly?* Retrieved from http://www.stopcyberbullying.org/what_is_cyberbullying_exactly.html

Strickland, J. (2018). *10 Worst Computer Viruses of All Time*. Retrieved from https://computer.howstuffworks.com/worst-computer-viruses2.htm

Strohmeier, D., Aoyama, I., Gradinger, P., & Toda, Y. (2013). Cybervictimization and cyberaggression in Eastern and Western countries: Challenges of constructing a cross-cultural appropriate scale. In S. Bauman, D. Cross, & J. L. Walker (Eds.), *Principles of cyberbullying research: Definitions, measures, and methodology* (pp. 202–221). New York: Routledge.

Suárez-Orozco, C., Todorova, I., & Qin, B. D. (2006). The well-being of immigrant adolescents: A longitudinal perspective on risk and protective factors. In The crisis in youth mental health. Academic Press.

Suarez-Orozco, M. M. (2000). Everything you ever wanted to know about assimilation but were afraid to ask. *Daedalus*, *129*(4), 1–30.

Suen, L. K., Ellis Hon, K. L., & Tam, W. W. (2008). Association between sleep behavior and sleep-related factors among university students in Hong Kong. *Chronobiology International*, *25*(5), 760–775. doi:10.1080/07420520802397186 PMID:18780202

Suganuma, N., Kikuchi, T., Yanagi, K., Yamamura, S., Morishima, H., Adachi, H., & Takeda, M. (2007). Using electronic media before sleep can curtail sleep time and result in self-perceived insufficient sleep. *Sleep and Biological Rhythms*, *5*(3), 204–214. doi:10.1111/j.1479-8425.2007.00276.x

Suler, J. (2004). The online disinhibition effect. *Cyberpsychology & Behavior*, *7*(3), 321–326. doi:10.1089/1094931041291295 PMID:15257832

Sutter, E. E. (1992). The brain response interface: Communication through visually-induced electrical brain responses. *Journal of Microcomputer Applications*, *15*(1), 31–45. doi:10.1016/0745-7138(92)90045-7

Svedin, C. G., Ånkerman, I., & Priebe, G. (2011). Frequent users of pornography. A population based epidemiological study of Swedish male adolescents. *Journal of Adolescence*, *34*(4), 779–788. doi:10.1016/j.adolescence.2010.04.010 PMID:20888038

Swan, K. (2005). A constructivist model for thinking about learning online. In J. Bourne & J. C. Moore (Eds.), *Elements of Quality Online Education: Engaging Communities*. Needham, MA: SloanC. Retrieved November 20, 2006, from http://www.kent.edu/rcet/Publications/upload/constructivist%20theory.pdf

Tadmor, C. T., Tetlock, P. E., & Peng, K. (2009). Acculturation strategies and integrative complexity: The cognitive implications of biculturalism. *Journal of Cross-Cultural Psychology*, *40*(1), 105–139. doi:10.1177/0022022108326279

Takao, M., Takahashi, S., & Kitamura, M. (2009). Addictive personality and problematic mobile phone use. *Cyberpsychology & Behavior*, *12*(5), 501–507. doi:10.1089/cpb.2009.0022 PMID:19817562

Tam, L., Glassman, M., & Vandenwauver, M. (2010). The psychology of password management: A tradeoff between security and convenience. *Behaviour & Information Technology*, *29*(3), 233–244. doi:10.1080/01449290903121386

Tanadi, T., Samadi, B., & Gharleghi, B. (2015). The Impact of Perceived Risks and Perceived Benefits to Improve an Online Intention among Generation-Y in Malaysia. *Asian Social Science*, *11*(26), 226. doi:10.5539/ass.v11n26p226

Tandera, T., Suhartono, D., Wongso, R., & Prasetio, Y. L. (2017). Personality Prediction System from Facebook Users. *Procedia Computer Science*, *116*, 604–611. doi:10.1016/j.procs.2017.10.016

Tangen, D., & Campbell, M. (2010). Cyberbullying prevention: One primary school's approach. *Australian Journal of Guidance & Counselling*, *20*(02), 225–234. doi:10.1375/ajgc.20.2.225

Tassabehji, R. (2003). *Applying E-commerce in Business*. New Delhi, India: Sage Publications.

Thailand. (2000). *I. C. T. Policy Framework BE 2554-2563*. Ministry of Information and Communication Technology.

The Economist. (2017, February 11). Migrants with mobiles: Phones are now indispensable for refugees. *The Economist.*

Thorpe, J., van Oorschot, P. C., & Somayaji, A. (2005). Pass-thoughts: authenticating with our minds. *Proceedings of the 2005 workshop on New security paradigms.* 10.1145/1146269.1146282

Thrasher, R., Andrew, D., & Mahoney, D. (2007). The efficacy of the Theory of Reasoned Action to explain gambling behavior in college students. *College Students Affairs Journal, 27*(1), 57–75. PMID:20803059

Toda, M., Monden, K., Kubo, K., & Morimoto, K. (2004). Cellular phone dependence tendency of female university students. *Japanese Journal of Hygiene, 59*(4), 383–386. doi:10.1265/jjh.59.383 PMID:15626025

Toda, M., Monden, K., Kubo, K., & Morimoto, K. (2006). Mobile phone dependence and health-related lifestyle of university students. *Social Behavior and Personality, 34*(10), 1277–1284. doi:10.2224bp.2006.34.10.1277

Toda, M., Nishio, N., Ezoe, S., & Takeshita, T. (2015). Chronotype and smartphone use among Japanese medical students. *International Journal of Cyber Behavior, Psychology and Learning, 5*(2), 75–80. doi:10.4018/IJCBPL.2015040106

Toledano, S., Werch, B. L., & Wiens, B. A. (2015). Domain-specific self-concept in relation to traditional and cyber peer aggression. *Journal of School Violence, 14*(4), 405–423. doi:10.1080/15388220.2014.935386

To, S., Iu Kan, S., & Ngai, S. S. (2015). Interaction effects between exposure to sexually explicit online materials and individual, family, and extrafamilial factors on Hong Kong high school students' beliefs about gender role equality and body-centered sexuality. *Youth & Society, 47*(6), 747–768. doi:10.1177/0044118X13490764

To, S., Ngai, S. S., & Iu Kan, S. (2012). Direct and mediating effects of accessing sexually explicit online materials on Hong Kong adolescents' attitude, knowledge, and behavior relating to sex. *Children and Youth Services Review, 34*(11), 2156–2163. doi:10.1016/j.childyouth.2012.07.019

Trull, T. J., & Widiger, T. A. (2013). Dimensional models of personality: The five factor model and the DSM-5. *Dialogues in Clinical Neuroscience, 15*(2), 135–146. PMID:24174888

Trumbo, C., Luek, M., Marlatt, H., & Peek, L. (2011). The effect of proximity to Hurricanes Katrina and Rita on subsequent hurricane outlook and optimistic bias. *Risk Analysis, 31*(12), 1907–1918. doi:10.1111/j.1539-6924.2011.01633.x PMID:21605150

Tsitsika, A., Critselis, E., Kormas, D., Konstantoulaki, E., Constantopoulos, A., & Kafetzis, D. (2009). Adolescent pornographic internet site use: A multivariate regression analysis of the predictive factors of use and psychosocial implications. *Cyberpsychology & Behavior, 12*(5), 545–550. doi:10.1089/cpb.2008.0346 PMID:19772438

Tuckson, R. V., Edmunds, M., & Hodgkins, M. L. (2017). Telehealth. *The New England Journal of Medicine*, *377*(16), 1585–1592. doi:10.1056/NEJMsr1503323 PMID:29045204

Twyman, W., Saylor, C., Taylor, A., & Comeaux, C. (2010). Comparing children and adolescents engaged in cyberbullying to matched peers. *Cyberpsychology, Behavior, and Social Networking*, *13*(2), 195–200. doi:10.1089/cyber.2009.0137 PMID:20528278

UN High Commissioner for Refugees (UNHCR). (2011). *The 1951 Convention Relating to the Status of Refugees and its 1967 Protocol*. Available at: http://www.refworld.org/docid/4ec4a7f02.html [accessed 15 May 2018]

UNHCR. (2016). *Connecting Refugees: How internet and mobile connectivity can improve refugee well-being and transform humanitarian action*. Accessed 11/11/17 from http://www.unhcr.org/5770d43c4.pdf

UNHCR. (2016). *Global Trends: Forced Displacement in 2016*. United Nation High Commissioner for Refugees. Accessed 11/11/17 from http://www.unhcr.org/globaltrends2016/

UPRIGHT. (2018). Retrieved from https://www.uprightpose.com/

Vahid, F., & Givargis, T. (2002). *Embedded system design: a unified hardware/software introduction* (Vol. 4). New York, NY: John Wiley & Sons.

Van den Bulck, J. (2003). Text messaging as a cause of sleep interruption in adolescents, evidence from a cross-sectional study. *Journal of Sleep Research*, *12*(3), 263. doi:10.1046/j.1365-2869.2003.00362.x PMID:12941066

Veiga Simão, A. M., Ferreira, P. C., Freire, I., Caetano, A. P., Martins, M. J. D., & Vieira, C. (2017). Adolescent cybervictimization – Who they turn to and their perceived school climate. *Journal of Adolescence*, *58*, 12–23. doi:10.1016/j.adolescence.2017.04.009 PMID:28475930

Venture, G., Kadone, H., Zhang, T., Grèzes, J., Berthoz, A., & Hicheur, H. (2014). Recognizing emotions conveyed by human gait. *International Journal of Social Robotics*, *6*(4), 621–632. doi:10.100712369-014-0243-1

Verhoeks, C., Teunissen, D., van der Stelt-Steenbergen, A., & Lagro-Janssen, A. (2017, August). Women's expectations and experiences regarding e-health treatment: A systematic review. *Health Informatics Journal*, 1–17. doi:10.1177/1460458217720394 PMID:28764600

Vieira, C. C., Matos, A., Amado, J., Freire, I., & Veiga-Simão, A. M. (2016). Boys' and girls' cyberbullying behaviours in Portugal: exploring sex differences in adolescence using gender lenses. *Ex aequo*, *34*, 143-159. Retrieved from: http://www.scielo.mec.pt/scielo.php?script=sci_arttext&pid=S0874-55602016000200011&lng=pt&nrm=iso&tlng=en

Vollmer, C., Michel, U., & Randler, C. (2012). Outdoor light at night (LAN) is correlated with eveningness in adolescents. *Chronobiology International*, *29*(4), 502–508. doi:10.3109/07420528.2011.635232 PMID:22214237

Vollmer, C., Randler, C., Horzum, M. B., & Ayas, T. (2014). Computer game addiction in adolescents and its relationship to chronotype and personality. *SAGE Open*, *4*(1), 1–9. doi:10.1177/2158244013518054

Vu, K.-P. L., Chambers, V., Creekmur, B., Cho, D., & Proctor, R. W. (2010). Influence of the Privacy Bird® user agent on user trust of different web sites. *Computers in Industry*, *61*(4), 311–317. doi:10.1016/j.compind.2009.12.001

Vygotsky, L. S. (1978). *Mind in society*. Harvard University Press.

Wade, A., & Beran, T. (2011). Cyberbullying: The new era of bullying. *Canadian Journal of School Psychology*, *26*(1), 44–61. doi:10.1177/0829573510396318

Wadeson, A., Nijholt, A., & Nam, C. S. (2015). Artistic brain-computer interfaces: State-of-the-art control mechanisms. *Brain-Computer Interfaces*, *2*(2-3), 70–75. doi:10.1080/2326263X.2015.1103155

Walker, C., Sockman, B., & Koehn, S. (2011). An exploratory study of cyberbullying with undergraduate university students. *TechTrends*, *55*(2), 31–38. doi:10.100711528-011-0481-0

Wallbott, H. G. (1998). Bodily expression of emotion. *European Journal of Social Psychology*, *28*(6), 879–896. doi:10.1002/(SICI)1099-0992(1998110)28:6<879::AID-EJSP901>3.0.CO;2-W

Walsh, S. P., White, K. M., Cox, S., & Young, R. M. (2011). Keeping in constant touch: The predictors of young Australians' mobile phone involvement. *Computers in Human Behavior*, *27*(1), 333–342. doi:10.1016/j.chb.2010.08.011

Wang, N., Liu, D., & Cheng, J. (2008). Study on the influencing factors of online shopping. In *Proceedings of the 11ᵗʰ Joint Conference on Information Sciences*. Atlantis Press.

Wantland, D. J., Portillo, C. J., Holzemer, W. L., Slaughter, R., & McGhee, E. M. (2004). The effectiveness of Web-based vs. non-Web-based interventions: A meta-analysis of behavioral change outcomes. *Journal of Medical Internet Research*, *6*(4), e40. doi:10.2196/jmir.6.4.e40 PMID:15631964

Wash, R., & Rader, E. (2015). *Too Much Knowledge? Security Beliefs and Protective Behaviors Among United States Internet Users*. Paper presented at the Eleventh Symposium On Usable Privacy and Security (SOUPS 2015), Ottawa, Canada.

Watthananon, J. (2015). A Comparison of the Effectiveness of STEM Learning and Imagineering Learning by Undergraduate Student in Computer Science. *International Journal of the Computer, the Internet and Management, 23*(1), 45-52.

Weber, M., Quiring, O., & Daschmann, G. (2012). Peers, parents, and pornography: Exploring adolescents' exposure to sexually explicit material and its developmental correlates. *Sexuality & Culture*, *16*(4), 408–427. doi:10.100712119-012-9132-7

Webster, L., Li, J., Zhu, Y., Luchsinger, A., Wan, A., & Tatge, M. (2016). Third-person effect, religiosity and support for censorship of satirical religious cartoons. *Journal of Media and Religion*, *15*(4), 186–195. doi:10.1080/15348423.2016.1248183

Wegge, D., Vendebosch, V., Eggermont, S., & Pabian, S. (2016). Popularity through on-line harm: The longitudinal associations between cyberbullying and sociometric status in early adolescence. *The Journal of Early Adolescence*, *36*(1), 86–107. doi:10.1177/0272431614556351

Weinstein, N. (1980). Unrealistic optimism about future life events. *Journal of Personality and Social Psychology*, *39*(5), 806–460. doi:10.1037/0022-3514.39.5.806

Wei, R., & Lo, V. (2007). The third-person effects of political attack ads in the 2004 U.S. presidential election. *Media Psychology*, *9*(2), 367–388. doi:10.1080/15213260701291338

Wei, R., & Lo, V. (2013). Examining sexting's effects among adolescent mobile phone users. *International Journal of Mobile Communications*, *11*(2), 176–193. doi:10.1504/IJMC.2013.052640

Weisskirch, R., & Murphy, L. (2004, Summer). Friends, porn, and punk: Sensation seeking in personal relationships, internet activities, and music preference among college students. *Adolescence*, *39*(154), 189–201. PMID:15563033

Wenli, C., & Wenting, X. (2012). *Cyber Behavior of Immigrants. The Encyclopedia of Cyber Behavior*. IGI Global.

West, R., & Michie, S. (2016). *A guide to development and evaluation of digital behaviour change interventions in healthcare*. London: Silverback Publishing.

Whitty, M., Doodson, J., Creese, S., & Hodges, D. (2015). Individual Differences in Cyber Security Behaviors: An Examination of Who Is Sharing Passwords. *Cyberpsychology, Behavior, and Social Networking*, *18*(1), 3–7. doi:10.1089/cyber.2014.0179 PMID:25517697

Wickens, C. D. (2014). Effort in Human Factors Performance and Decision Making. *Human Factors*, *56*(8), 1329–1336. doi:10.1177/0018720814558419 PMID:25509817

Widiger, T. (2004). *Five Factor Model Rating Form (FFMRF)*. Retrieved October 13, 2010 from www.uky.edu/~widiger/ffmrf.rtf

Widiger, T. A., & Lowe, J. R. (2007). Five-factor model assessment of personality disorder. *Journal of Personality Assessment*, *89*(1), 16–29. doi:10.1080/00223890701356953 PMID:17604531

Wiedemann, H. R. (1994). Hans Berger. *European Journal of Pediatrics*, *153*(10), 705–705. doi:10.1007/BF01954482 PMID:7813523

Wiederhold, B. K. (2014). The Role of Psychology in Enhancing Cybersecurity. *Cyberpsychology, Behavior, and Social Networking*, *17*(3), 131–132. doi:10.1089/cyber.2014.1502 PMID:24592869

Willard, N. (2004). *Educator's guide to cyberbullying: Addressing the harm caused by online social cruelty*. Retrieved from http://cyberbully.org

WillardN. (2005). *Educator' guide to cyberbullying and cyberthreats*. Retrieved from http://www.accem.org/pdf/cbcteducator.pdf

Williams, K., Howell, T., Cooper, B., Yuille, J., & Paulhus, D. (2004, May). *Deviant sexual thoughts and behaviors: The roles of personality and pornography use*. Poster Sessions presented at the 16th Annual American Psychology Society, Chicago, IL.

Williams, D., & Skoric, M. (2005). Internet fantasy violence: A test of aggression in an online game. *Communication Monographs*, *72*(2), 217–233. doi:10.1080/03637750500111781

Williams, K., Cooper, B., Howell, T., Yuille, J., & Paulhus, D. (2009). Inferring sexually deviant behavior from corresponding fantasies: The role of personality and pornography consumption. *International Journal of Criminal Justice and Behavior*, *36*(2), 198–222. doi:10.1177/0093854808327277

Wittgenstein, L. (1953). *Philosophical Investigations*. Oxford, UK: Blackwell Publishing.

Wogalter, M. S. (2006). Communication-Human Information Processing (C-HIP) Model. In M. S. Wogalter (Ed.), *Handbook of Warnings* (pp. 51–61). Mahwah, NJ: CRC Press.

Wolak, J., Mitchell, K., & Finkelhor, D. (2007). Unwanted and wanted exposure to online pornography in a national sample of youth internet users. *Pediatrics*, *119*(2), 247–257. doi:10.1542/peds.2006-1891 PMID:17272613

Wolchik, S. A., Sandler, I. N., Millsap, R. E., Plummer, B. A., Greene, S. M., Anderson, E. R., ... Haine, R. A. (2002). Six-year follow-up of preventive interventions for children of divorce: A randomized controlled trial. *Journal of the American Medical Association*, *288*(15), 1874–1881. doi:10.1001/jama.288.15.1874 PMID:12377086

Wolever, R. Q., Bobinet, K. J., McCabe, K., Mackenzie, E. R., Fekete, E., Kusnick, C. A., & Baime, M. (2012). Effective and viable mind-body stress reduction in the workplace: A randomized controlled trial. *Journal of Occupational Health Psychology*, *17*(2), 246–258. doi:10.1037/a0027278 PMID:22352291

Wolfers, M., de Zwart, O., & Kok, G. (2011). Adolescents in the Netherlands underestimate risk for sexually transmitted infections and deny the need for sexually transmitted infection testing. *AIDS Patient Care and STDs*, *25*(5), 311–319. doi:10.1089/apc.2010.0186 PMID:21542726

Wolpaw, J. R., Birbaumer, N., McFarland, D. J., Pfurtscheller, G., & Vaughan, T. M. (2002). Brain–computer interfaces for communication and control. *Clinical Neurophysiology*, *113*(6), 767–791. doi:10.1016/S1388-2457(02)00057-3 PMID:12048038

Wolpaw, J. R., & McFarland, D. J. (2004). Control of a two-dimensional movement signal by a noninvasive brain-computer interface in humans. *Proceedings of the National Academy of Sciences of the United States of America*, *101*(51), 17849–17854. doi:10.1073/pnas.0403504101 PMID:15585584

Wolpaw, J. R., McFarland, D. J., & Vaughan, T. M. (2000). Brain-computer interface research at the Wadsworth Center. *IEEE Transactions on Rehabilitation Engineering*, *8*(2), 222–226. doi:10.1109/86.847823 PMID:10896194

Wong, D. S., Chan, H. C. O., & Cheng, C. H. (2014). Cyberbullying perpetration and victimization among adolescents in Hong Kong. *Children and Youth Services Review*, *36*, 133–140. doi:10.1016/j.childyouth.2013.11.006

Wood, A. W., Loughran, S. P., & Stough, C. (2006). Does evening exposure to mobile phone radiation affect subsequent metatonin production? *International Journal of Radiation Biology*, *82*(2), 69–76. doi:10.1080/09553000600599775 PMID:16546905

Wood, D. J., Bruner, J. S., & Ross, G. (1976). The role of tutoring in problem solving. *Journal of Child Psychiatry and Psychology*, *17*(2), 89–100. doi:10.1111/j.1469-7610.1976.tb00381.x PMID:932126

Woolley, D., & Eining, M. (2006). Software piracy among accounting students: A longitudinal comparison of changes and sensitivity. *Journal of Information Systems*, *20*(1), 49–63. doi:10.2308/jis.2006.20.1.49

World Health Organization. (2017, June). *Noncommunicable diseases: Fact sheet*. Retrieved from http://www.who.int/mediacentre/factsheets/fs355/en/

Wright, A. (2008). *The Imagineering Field Guide to Disneyland: An Imagineer's-eye Tour*. Disney.

Wright, M. F. (2013). The relationship between young adults' beliefs about anonymity and subsequent cyber aggression. *Cyberpsychology, Behavior, and Social Networking*, *16*(12), 858–862. doi:10.1089/cyber.2013.0009 PMID:23849002

Wright, M. F. (2014a). Cyber victimization and perceived stress: Linkages to late adolescents' cyber aggression and psychological functioning. *Youth & Society*.

Wright, M. F. (2014b). Predictors of anonymous cyber aggression: The role of adolescents' beliefs about anonymity, aggression, and the permanency of digital content. *Cyberpsychology, Behavior, and Social Networking*, *17*(7), 431–438. doi:10.1089/cyber.2013.0457 PMID:24724731

Wright, M. F. (2014c). Longitudinal investigation of the associations between adolescents' popularity and cyber social behaviors. *Journal of School Violence*, *13*(3), 291–314. doi:10.1080/15388220.2013.849201

Wright, M. F. (2015). Cyber victimization and adjustment difficulties: The mediation of Chinese and American adolescents' digital technology usage. *Cyberpsychology (Brno)*, *1*(1), 1. Retrieved from http://cyberpsychology.eu/view.php?cisloclanku=2015051102&article=1

Wright, M. F. (in press). Adolescents' cyber aggression perpetration and cyber victimization: The longitudinal associations with school functioning. *Social Psychology of Education*.

Wright, M. F., Kamble, S., Lei, K., Li, Z., Aoyama, I., & Shruti, S. (2015). Peer attachment and cyberbullying involvement among Chinese, Indian, and Japanese adolescents. *Societies (Basel, Switzerland)*, *5*(2), 339–353. doi:10.3390oc5020339

Wright, M. F., & Li, Y. (2012). Kicking the digital dog: A longitudinal investigation of young adults' victimization and cyber-displaced aggression. *Cyberpsychology, Behavior, and Social Networking*, *15*(9), 448–454. doi:10.1089/cyber.2012.0061 PMID:22974350

Wright, M. F., & Li, Y. (2013a). Normative beliefs about aggression and cyber aggression among young adults: A longitudinal investigation. *Aggressive Behavior*, *39*(3), 161–170. doi:10.1002/ab.21470 PMID:23440595

Wright, M. F., & Li, Y. (2013b). The association between cyber victimization and subsequent cyber aggression: The moderating effect of peer rejection. *Journal of Youth and Adolescence*, *42*(5), 662–674. doi:10.100710964-012-9903-3 PMID:23299177

Wu, C.-H., Liu, C. J., & Tzeng, Y.-L. (2011). *Brain Wave Analysis in Optimal Color Allocation for Children's Electronic Book Design*. Paper presented at the TANET 2011.

Wu, D., Li, C., & Yao, D. (2013). Scale-free brain quartet: Artistic filtering of multi-channel brainwave music. *PLoS One*, *8*(5), e64046. doi:10.1371/journal.pone.0064046 PMID:23717527

Wyckoff, S. N., Sherlin, L. H., Ford, N. L., & Dalke, D. (2015). Validation of a wireless dry electrode system for electroencephalography. *Journal of Neuroengineering and Rehabilitation*, *12*(1), 95. doi:10.118612984-015-0089-2 PMID:26520574

Xie, G. (2016). Deceptive advertising and third-person perception: The interplay of generalized and specific suspicion. *Journal of Marketing Communications*, *22*(5), 494–512. doi:10.1080/13527266.2014.918051

Yampolskiy, R. V. (2017). AI Is the Future of Cybersecurity, for Better and for Worse. *Harvard Business Review*. Retrieved from https://hbr.org/2017/05/ai-is-the-future-of-cybersecurity-for-better-and-for-worse

Yan, Z., & Greenfield, P. (Eds.). (2006). Children, adolescents, and the Internet (Special Section). *Developmental Psychology*, *42*, 391–458. PMID:16756431

Yarkoni, T., & Westfall, J. (2017). Choosing prediction over explanation in psychology: Lessons from machine learning. *Perspectives on Psychological Science*, *12*(6), 1100–1122. doi:10.1177/1745691617693393 PMID:28841086

Ybarra, M. L., Diener-West, M., & Leaf, P. (2007). Examining the overlap in internet harassment and school bullying: Implications for school intervention. *The Journal of Adolescent Health*, *1*(6), 42–50. doi:10.1016/j.jadohealth.2007.09.004 PMID:18047944

Ybarra, M. L., & Mitchell, K. J. (2004). Online aggressor/targets, aggressors, and targets: A comparison of associated youth characteristics. *Journal of Child Psychology and Psychiatry, and Allied Disciplines*, *45*(7), 1308–1316. doi:10.1111/j.1469-7610.2004.00328.x PMID:15335350

Yellowlees, P., Marks, S., Hilty, D., & Shore, J. H. (2008). Using e-Health to Enable Culturally Appropriate Mental Healthcare in Rural Areas. *Telemedicine Journal and e-Health*, *14*(5), 486–492. doi:10.1089/tmj.2007.0070 PMID:18578685

Yörük, D., Dündar, S., Moga, L.M., & Neculita, M. (2011). Drivers and Attitudes towards Online Shopping: Comparison of Turkey with Romania. *Communications of the IBIMA*, 1-13. DOI: 10.5171/2011.575361

Yoshida, K., Sakamoto, Y., Satou, Y., Miyaji, I., Yamada, K., & Fujii, S. (2011). *Trial of a distance learning system using a brain wave sensor. In Knowledge-Based and Intelligent Information and Engineering Systems* (pp. 86–95). Springer.

Young, K. S. (1998). *Caught in the Net*. New York: John Wiley & Sons.

Young, K. S. (1998). Internet addiction: The emergence of a new clinical disorder. *Cyberpsychology & Behavior*, *1*(3), 237–244. doi:10.1089/cpb.1998.1.237

Young, K. S. (2001). *Tangled in the Web: Understanding Cybersex from Fantasy to Addiction*. Bloomington, IN: AuthorHouse.

Yousef, W. S. M., & Bellamy, A. (2015). The impact of cyberbullying on the self-esteem and academic functioning of Arab American middle and high school students. *Electronic Journal of Research in Educational Psychology*, *23*(3), 463–482.

Youyou, W., Kosinski, M., & Stillwell, D. (2015). Computer-based personality judgments are more accurate than those made by humans. *Proceedings of the National Academy of Sciences of the United States of America*, *112*(4), 1036–1040. doi:10.1073/pnas.1418680112 PMID:25583507

Yu, T., Li, Y., Long, J., & Gu, Z. (2012). Surfing the internet with a BCI mouse. *Journal of Neural Engineering*, *9*(3), 036012. doi:10.1088/1741-2560/9/3/036012 PMID:22626911

Zander, T. O., Kothe, C., Jatzev, S., & Gaertner, M. (2010). *Enhancing human-computer interaction with input from active and passive brain-computer interfaces. In Brain-Computer Interfaces* (pp. 181–199). Springer.

Zander, T. O., Lehne, M., Ihme, K., Jatzev, S., Correia, J., Kothe, C., ... Nijboer, F. (2011). A dry EEG-system for scientific research and brain–computer interfaces. *Frontiers in Neuroscience*, 5. PMID:21647345

Zeiter, J. M., & Dijk, D.-J. (2000). Sensitivity of the Human Circadian Pacemaker to Nocturnal Light: Melatonin Phase Resetting and Suppression. *The Journal of Physiology*, *526*(3), 695–702. doi:10.1111/j.1469-7793.2000.00695.x PMID:10922269

Zeng, M., & Reinartz, W. (2003). Beyond online search: The road to profitability. *California Management Review*, *45*(2), 107–130. doi:10.2307/41166168

Zhang, R., Li, Y., Yan, Y., Zhang, H., Wu, S., Yu, T., & Gu, Z. (2016). Control of a Wheelchair in an Indoor Environment Based on a Brain–Computer Interface and Automated Navigation. *IEEE Transactions on Neural Systems and Rehabilitation Engineering*, *24*(1), 128–139. doi:10.1109/TNSRE.2015.2439298 PMID:26054072

Zhou, E., Fan, H., Cao, Z., Jiang, Y., & Yin, Q. (2013, December). Extensive facial landmark localization with coarse-to-fine convolutional network cascade. In *Computer Vision Workshops (ICCVW), 2013 IEEE International Conference on* (pp. 386-391). IEEE. 10.1109/ICCVW.2013.58

Zhou, Z., Tang, H., Tian, Y., Wei, H., Zhang, F., & Morrison, C. M. (2013). Cyberbullying and its risk factors among Chinese high school students. *School Psychology International*, *34*(6), 630–647. doi:10.1177/0143034313479692

Index

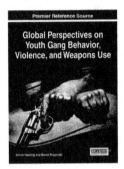
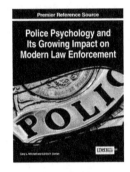
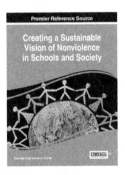
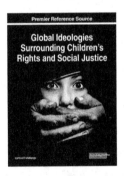
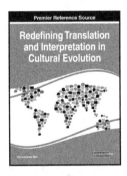

Ensure Quality Research is Introduced to the Academic Community

Become an IGI Global Reviewer for Authored Book Projects

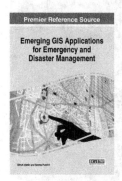
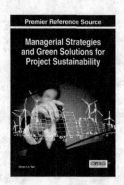

The overall success of an authored book project is dependent on quality and timely reviews.

In this competitive age of scholarly publishing, constructive and timely feedback significantly expedites the turnaround time of manuscripts from submission to acceptance, allowing the publication and discovery of forward-thinking research at a much more expeditious rate. Several IGI Global authored book projects are currently seeking highly qualified experts in the field to fill vacancies on their respective editorial review boards:

Applications may be sent to:
development@igi-global.com

Applicants must have a doctorate (or an equivalent degree) as well as publishing and reviewing experience. Reviewers are asked to write reviews in a timely, collegial, and constructive manner. All reviewers will begin their role on an ad-hoc basis for a period of one year, and upon successful completion of this term can be considered for full editorial review board status, with the potential for a subsequent promotion to Associate Editor.

If you have a colleague that may be interested in this opportunity, we encourage you to share this information with them.